The Fen Management Handbook

Edited by Andrew McBride,
Iain Diack, Nick Droy,
Bobbie Hamill, Peter Jones,
Johan Schutten, Ann Skinner
and Margaret Street

D1438374

Scottish Natural Heritage
Dualchas Nàdair na h-Alba
All of nature for all of Scotland
Nàdar air fad airson Alba air fad

Northern Ireland
Environment
Agency

ENVIRONMENT
AGENCY

Cyngor Cefn Gwlad Cymru
Countryside Council for Wales

RSPB

SEPA
Scottish Environment
Protection Agency

NATURAL
ENGLAND

The Scottish
Government

Acknowledgements

Production of the Fen Management Handbook has been co-ordinated by an editorial steering group comprising (in alphabetical order) Iain Diack, Senior Wetland Specialist at Natural England (NE); Nick Droy, Wetlands Adviser for Royal Society for Protection of Birds (RSPB); Bobbie Hamill, Northern Ireland Environment Agency (NIEA); Pete Jones, Peatland Ecologist for the Countryside Council for Wales (CCW); Hans Schutten, Senior Wetlands Adviser for Scottish Environment Protection Agency (SEPA); Ann Skinner, National Conservation Policy Adviser for the Environment Agency (EA) and Margaret Street, Wetland Specialist for NE. Andrew McBride, Wetland Ecologist for Scottish Natural Heritage (SNH) chaired the steering group. Vyv Wood-Gee, freelance Countryside Management Consultant, was contracted to edit the draft text.

The Editorial Group and Vyv Wood-Gee have produced the text from that provided by the following lead authors who we gratefully acknowledge for their contribution; Roger Meade, Rob Low, Alistair Headley, Richard Robinson and Sarah Ross.

The Editorial Board would also like to acknowledge the help given in Peer review by Dr Sue Shaw, Dr Brian Wheeler, Andrew Panter, Nick Haycock, Craig MacAdam, Alistair Headley and Alan Stubbs. Special thanks to Andrea Kelly and her team at the Broads Authority (particularly Sue Stephenson) for their comments and guidance on the handbook.

In addition, we would like to acknowledge the contribution from the following people;
Becky Barrett, Matt Fasham, Max Wade, Rob Pitcher, Robin Ward, Roger Buisson, Simon Jones, Edwin Lomas, Sam Bosanquet, Gerard Hawley, Matt Sutton, Jacky Carrol, Andrew Excell and Jim Jeffrey.

Sections 6, 7 and 9 Fen Vegetation, Water Management and Fen Creation – the assistance of Sandie Tolhurst and the Broads Authority in making the text of their publications freely available is gratefully acknowledged. Thanks are also due to Simon Weymouth of the Forestry Commission (FC) who has provided text from the New Forest Management guidelines, and Rick Southwood of Natural England for the benefit of his experience in managing Woodbastwick National Nature Reserve, and Tim Coleshaw of Natural England for the Wybunbury Moss case study.

Section 11 Fens and People – Sarah Eno, Chris Soans, Tim Strudwick, Andrea Kelly, Matt Bradbury, George Taylor, John Blackburn, Steve Hughes, Tom Hill, Mike Page, Jane Stevens, Helen Smith and Stuart Warrington very generously provided information or images and commented on drafts of this section.

Diagrams were drawn by Craig Ellery of Ellery Design, Edinburgh.

Design and typeset by River Design, Edinburgh

Citation
For bibliographic purposes this book should be referred to as *The Fen Management Handbook*, (2011), Editors A. McBride, I. Diack, N Droy, B. Hamill, P.Jones, J. Schutten, A. Skinner, and M. Street. Scottish Natural Heritage, Perth.

Contents

1. Introduction and Basic Principles

Fens are magical places; they are an essential part of our cherished landscape. They support a rich variety of wildlife, and are often a repository of evidence of many generations of past economic use and management. With so much in their favour, it is perhaps surprising that fens are one of the least well recognised habitats, and a part of our countryside which most people understand little about.

This handbook has been produced to improve understanding of fens and how they function, to explain why fens need management and to provide best practice guidance. Case studies are included at the end of most sections as practical examples of the principles and techniques outlined in the text. The handbook is aimed at anyone interested in fens, or who might become involved in fen management, creation or restoration from a practical, policy or planning perspective.

Key points and good practice are highlighted in green boxes. Cautions about activities which might be legislatively controlled or which might potentially damage the interest of fens are highlighted in red boxes. Snapshot case studies in the text to illustrate specific points are highlighted in yellow.

1.1 What are fens?

> The word 'fen' is derived from the old English word 'fenn' meaning marsh, dirt or mud.

A fen is a wetland that receives water and nutrients from surface and/or groundwater, as well as from rainfall.

> **Differentiating between fens and bogs**
>
> **Fens** receive most of their water via rock and soil which contain dissolved minerals creating growing conditions that allow more lush vegetation than bogs.
>
> **Bogs** receive water exclusively from rainfall which is acidic and contains very few minerals; consequently rain-fed acid bogs support a less diverse range of vegetation than fens.

Fens are found from sea level up into the hills, across the whole of the British Isles. They range in size from tiny flushes of only a few square metres, to extensive floodplain fens covering hundreds of hectares, forming important features in the wider landscape and river catchments.

Map showing an indicative
distribution of lowland
fens in the UK (JNCC)

1.2   What's so special about fens?

Fens were prized by our ancestors for the range of products they yield: reeds and
sedge for thatching, willow for basketry, hay and lush aftermath grazing for cattle.
It is the past management and human interaction with fens for such purposes that
has created the extremely diverse and ever-changing habitat which attracts and
supports a rich variety of plants, insects, mammals and birds, and which explains
why fens are described as semi-natural rather than natural habitats. **Section 2:
Fen Flora and Fauna** explains more about the flora and fauna which make fens so
special from a wildlife perspective.

The UK contains a large proportion of fen types found in Europe, the surviving
fragments of previously much more extensive wetlands. In his book *The Illustrated
History of the Countryside*, Oliver Rackham suggested that "about a quarter of the
British Isles is, or has been some kind of wetland." As in other parts of Europe, the
quality and extent of wetlands including fens has declined dramatically as a result
of drainage, development and neglect. Some of our best agricultural soils have
been provided by fens, following drainage and decades of tillage. However, the
organic component of the soil that makes it so suitable for root and other crops has
gradually broken down releasing carbon and lowering the land level, making the
land more difficult to drain.

It is estimated that of 3400 km^2 of fen present in England in 1637, only 10 km^2
remains today. In intensively farmed lowland areas of England, fens now occur less
frequently, are smaller in size and are more isolated than in other parts of the UK.
Despite these losses, the UK still boasts some large fens such as the 300 ha Insh
Marshes in the floodplain of the River Spey in Scotland, the calcareous rich-fen and
swamp of Broadland covering 3,000 ha in Norfolk and Suffolk, and the Lough Erne
system in Northern Ireland with extensive areas of fen and swamp. In some lowland
areas, such as the Scottish Borders and southern parts of Northern Ireland, there
are large numbers of fens which although small (many less than 3 ha in size), are
still of European importance for the rich wildlife they support.

Estimates of the original coverage of fen are based on the extent of deep peat soils that consist of plant remains, formed under the fen. Surviving peat deposits show how the type of fen found at a particular location can change over time. Fens can also yield valuable palaeo-ecological evidence, such as pollen, artefacts such as tools, weapons and implements, or even human bodies. Some of the best preserved pre-historic archaeological remains have been recovered from fen sites such as Flag Fen in Cambridgeshire, Star Carr in Yorkshire and the Sweet Track at Shapwick Heath in Somerset. Such finds can help reconstruct aspects of the history of fens, and our ancestors. Further information on archaeology is found in Section 11.

1.3   Understanding fens

Deciding how best to manage and create fens depends on understanding how fens work, how fens relate to the wider landscape, and how past management has influenced fens and the wildlife they support.

Topography, hydrology and geology all play important roles in determining how a fen develops and is maintained. It is not only the geographical location of a fen which matters but also the type of rock and the way land is managed elsewhere in the catchment through which water feeding the fen has passed. The different types of fen are manifest in terms of the mix of plant species and how these interact with each other, to provide structural niches in which other wildlife such as dragonflies and birds can flourish.

Fens can be classified in a variety of ways, including the height and/or type of dominant plant species, for example short sedge fens and tall reed fens, but the type and stature of vegetation is intrinsically linked to other environmental factors. Fens are therefore most commonly defined by their association with particular landscape features, and according to the source of water which feeds the fen. **Section 3: Understanding Fen Hydrology** explains more about fen hydrology and different types of fen. **Section 4: Understanding Fen Nutrients** explains about the different types and sources of nutrient critical to fens and how the nutrient status of individual fens can be assessed.

Floodplain landscape of the Biebrza River in north-east Poland. The naturally occurring diversity of wetland habitats including fens, wet grassland, reed-bed and scrub reflect constantly changing natural processes such as fluctuating water-levels (M. Street).

1.4 Fen management and restoration

Wetland habitats, including fens, change with time. Without intervention, first reeds and then trees such as willow establish around the edge of open water. Silt carried by water flowing into the fen is trapped by the reeds, scrub and trees, and speeds up the transition to drier habitat. In the place of open water, open fen forms, which in turn becomes wet woodland. Fens may also transform into other habitats such as raised bog or dry woodland. These processes are referred to by ecologists as succession, or sometimes as hydroseral succession, to link the process specifically to the sequence of changes from open water. In addition once fen vegetation is established the dead and decaying plant material can form peat; this process known as paludification.

In the past, harvesting and use of reeds and other fen products helped keep fens open but as traditional crafts and management practices have ceased, trees have gradually taken over many open fens, producing a different landscape with less diverse wildlife habitats.

Guiding principles for fen management, restoration and creation

– Maintain or create 'the right fen in the right place'. This means the most appropriate type for the geo-hydrological setting.

– Aim for diversity, not uniformity. Resist the temptation to create the same type of fen everywhere just because it is easy to do so.

– Take account of the surroundings and neighbouring habitats, such as lowland bog, wet grassland and wet woodland, in order to complete eco-hydrological units.

– Consider the site within the context of the wider landscape. Many of today's small fen sites and other wetlands are remnants of what were once much more extensive wetland systems.

Section 5: Fen Management and Restoration outlines some of the common problems associated with managing fens and provides a framework for deciding when intervention may be necessary to maintain wildlife interest. Section 5 also offers guidance on setting objectives, identifying which type of fen to aim for and appropriate management options. **Section 6: Fen Vegetation Management, Section 7: Fen Water Management** and **Section 8: Managing Fen Nutrient Enrichment** explore in more detail the many different techniques for fen management.

When planning any project involving fens and other wetland habitats, it is essential to be aware of the legal and regulatory context and requirements. These are summarised in **Appendix V**. It is strongly recommended that anyone considering a fen or wetland related project should contact the relevant authorities at an early stage; they are there to help, advise and facilitate, and have access to a wealth of experience.

1.5   Fen creation

Prompted by the dramatic reduction in the number, extent and wildlife interest of many fens, various projects are under way to create new fen habitat. In East Anglia, for example, The Great Fen Project aims to create 3,000 ha of fen in Cambridgeshire, where 138,000 ha of the county was once a complex of wetland habitats, including fen. **Section 9: Creating Fen Habitat** considers opportunities for fen creation and the practicalities involved.

1.6   Monitoring

Monitoring is essential to demonstrate change, to gauge the effectiveness of management and to inform what changes might be necessary to meet agreed objectives. **Section 10: Monitoring to Inform Fen Management** explains the range of techniques applicable to different aspects of fens, including water quality and quantity, flora and fauna and different methods of data analysis.

Botanical survey of
a fen on Orkney
(E. Pawley)

1.7 Fens and people

The fens of today are a product of past centuries of human intervention and management. Harvesting and use of fen products is no longer such an important part of the rural economy as it once was but there is still an important symbiosis between fens and people. **Section 11: Fens and People** reveals more about the long relationship we have had with fens and explores various aspects of involving people in fen management, as well as encouraging and allowing public access to fens.

1.8 Multi-function fens

In the current economic and political climate, conservation action must increasingly deliver, and be recognized as delivering, a variety of benefits beyond the purely ecological. Fens have a long tradition of fulfilling many functions and as the case studies within this handbook demonstrate, fens present many opportunities capable of delivering multiple benefits.

To quote but one example, providing a large area of land over which flood waters can spread/be stored without significant damage to property can reduce flood risk in towns downstream. It also provides opportunities for fen creation. Similarly, blocking appropriate drainage systems in upland peat can restore active bog with carbon storage and play an important part in attenuating floods in the lower catchment. At the other end of the scale, the small size and enclosure of many basin fens can led to a loss of resilience or ability to withstand natural and human change. Muck and fertiliser spreading, cultivation and stock husbandry on other land in the catchment add to the nutrient load of water feeding the fen, to the detriment of the wildlife interest. More targeted fertiliser application can save money for farmers and reduce undesirable nutrient enrichment of the fen.

Section 12: Fens from an Economic Perspective considers the various economic issues and opportunities relating to fen management, including commercial outputs and sources of funding.

1.9 References and further reading

There is a vast array of information directly and indirectly relevant to fens, as well as that which is specific to fens. Key references for each of the main aspects of fen management are included at the end of the relevant section. **Appendix IX** suggests further reading for those interested in exploring fens further.

2. Fen Flora and Fauna

Fens support an incredibly rich and diverse range of plants and animals. Plants vary from species characteristic of highly acidic low-nutrient situations to those tolerant of nutrient-rich highly alkaline environments, and from species adapted to seasonally wet conditions through to those that thrive in permanent standing water. An indication of the enormous diversity of fen vegetation is demonstrated by the 45 different plant communities recognised in the National Vegetation Classification (NVC) that are encompassed within the wider definition of 'fen' (see Appendix IV). This rich variety of vegetation communities is reflected in the extensive range of fauna, especially invertebrates, associated with fens.

This section offers an introduction to the variety of different plants and animals associated with fens, with emphasis on those that live and/or breed within fens, and/or which have been identified as priorities for conservation in the UK. This diversity of species, as well as vegetation communities, underpins the significance of fens in nature conservation terms. At the end of this section is a brief introduction to conservation designations in relation to fens. Section 5: Site Assessment for Fen Management and Restoration goes into more detail about prioritisation of different species and communities when deciding on appropriate management options.

Aerial view of Bemersyde
Moss in the Scottish
Borders
an oasis for wildlife in
an intensively managed
agricultural landscape
(P& A MacDonald/SNH).

2.1   Diversity and conservation significance

Two of the major factors which determine the botanical composition of fens are
fertility and base-richness/pH (see **Section 4: Understanding Fen Nutrients** and
Wheeler and Proctor, 2000). To some extent these directly affect fauna as well,
particularly invertebrates, but their major effect is indirect in that faunal composition
of fens is determined largely by vegetation structure and water levels.

In general, the wider the range of habitats, the higher the diversity of associated
vertebrate and invertebrate species, although less diverse fens can also be very
important for uncommon vegetation communities and specialised plants and
animals. Reedbeds, which are a type of fen, are a good example of this. They can
be botanically poor, but are one of our most important bird habitats, supporting
highly specialised species such as bittern (*Botaurus stellaris*) and marsh harrier
(*Circus aeruginosus*).

Elsewhere, specific and often very restricted areas of a particular fen type may
support other specialised species such as the Irish damselfly (*Coenagrion
lunulatum*), a native of northern Europe, rarely found outside northern Finland. The
Irish population is thought to be one of the largest in western Europe, highlighting
the fact that even fens which are not particularly diverse in terms of the range of
species they support, can be of very high conservation importance.

Irish damselfly is
restricted to open pools
and small lakes within
acid fens frequently
associated with cutover
bog (G. Campbell).

Corbally Fen

Corbally Fen in County Down Northern Ireland, which is part of the Lecale Fens SAC (P. Corbett). From a distance, or to the untrained eye, this small inter-drumlin fen may not look particularly exciting, but closer inspection reveals the profusion of flora fens such as this support, including colourful carpets of ragged robin (*Lychnis flos-cuculi*) as pictured below (B.Hamill).

Some birds, amphibians and many fish species do not depend specifically on fens for breeding or foraging, but are found in some of the habitats which tend to be associated with fens, such as wet woodland, ditches and ponds.

2.2 Fen flora

Perhaps the most widely-recognised fen vegetation type is that associated with floodplain fens such as the Norfolk and Suffolk Broads and Wicken Fen where tall, flower-rich vegetation is characterised by common reed (*Phragmites australis*), tall sedges (*Carex* spp.), purple and yellow loosestrife (*Lythrum salicaria* and *Lysimachia vulgaris*), and yellow iris (*Iris pseudacorus*). Distinctive and rare species such as marsh pea (*Lathyrus palustris*) and milk-parsley (*Peucedanum palustre*), the food-plant of the swallowtail butterfly (*Papilio machaon*), are found in this type of fen, intermingled with blunt-flowered rush (*Juncus subnodulosus*), hemp agrimony (*Eupatorium cannabinum*), fen bedstraw (*Galium uliginosum*) and angelica (*Angelica sylvestris*).

Often the most species-rich tall-herb fens are mown on a rotational basis or lightly grazed; this management maintains ideal conditions for the typical orchids of fens such as the rare fen orchid (*Liparis loeslii*), early marsh-orchid (*Dactylorhiza incarnata*), fragrant orchid (*Gymnadenia conopsea ssp. densiflora*) and marsh helleborine (*Epipactis palustris*).

Part of Cropple How
Mire in Cumbria, a
northern tall-herb fen
with common angelica,
water horsetail, purple
loosestrife and yellow
iris. This section of
the site lies in a basin,
downslope of a spring-
fed, nutrient-poor acidic
fen, and occasionally
receives floodwater from
the River Esk, providing
the nutrients necessary
to support taller
vegetation.

Marsh helleborine (P.
Corbett) – found in
open areas of tall fen
at Strumpshaw Fen,
Norfolk.

The diversity of species-rich tall-herb fens varies across the country with floodplains in the northwest of the UK dominated by tall sedges, where bottle sedge (*Carex rostrata*) is more prominent and uncommon species such as cowbane (*Cicuta virosa*), greater water-parsnip (*Sium latifolium*) and marsh stitchwort (*Stellaria palustris*) occur. Upper Lough Erne in Northern Ireland and Insh Marshes in Scotland provide good examples of these northern floodplain fens.

Seepages and springs on calcareous bedrock provide suitable conditions for a very different but equally diverse fen flora, characterised by much shorter vegetation and a greater diversity of low-growing plants, particularly sedges and mosses. In lowland valley fens fed by low nutrient calcareous groundwater (often from chalk), black bog-rush (*Schoenus nigricans*) is often abundant. In the south and east of the UK this species is restricted to highly calcareous situations, but it also occurs widely in more acidic conditions in oceanic parts of the country, particularly on blanket bog in the west of Scotland and Ireland. In amongst the black bog-rush tussocks a very diverse mix of plants thrive, including small sedges, bog pimpernel (*Anagallis tenella*), marsh lousewort (*Pedicularis palustris*), fen pondweed (*Potamogeton coloratus*) and the rare narrow-leaved marsh orchid (*Dactylorhiza traunsteineroides*). Many of the remaining sites with this rare fen type are found in East Anglia, particularly in Norfolk; other important sites are found at Cothill Fen in Oxfordshire and on Anglesey and the Lleyn peninsula in north Wales.

■	1987-1999 Native
■	1970-1986 Native
	Pre-1970 Native
■	1987-1999 Alien
■	1970-1986 Alien

Tussocks of black bog-rush, with brown mosses in the runnel. The map alongside shows the UK and Ireland distribution of black bog-rush. (I. Diack)

Black bog-rush map is from the Preston, C.D., Pearman, D.A. & Dines, T.D. (2002) New Atlas of the British Flora. Oxford University Press.

The northern and upland equivalent of this fen type is usually found around springs and flushes on carboniferous limestone, and also supports a very distinctive flora, dominated by small sedges including dioecious sedge (*Carex dioica*) and flat sedge (*Blysmus compressus*). Other characteristic plants include the carnivorous common butterwort (*Pinguicula vulgaris*), marsh valerian (*Valeriana dioica*), and scarcer species such as bird's-eye primrose (*Primula farinosa*) and lesser clubmoss (*Selaginella selaginoides*). These generally small fens are particularly characteristic of the north and west, for example the Craven limestone of Yorkshire and Creag nam garmin, near Tomintoul, and flushes associated with the basalt rocks of the Garron Plateau in Northern Ireland.

Insectivorous common butterwort in a low-nutrient base-rich flush (I. Diack).

Marsh saxifrage, restricted to small, base rich fens in the uplands (M. Wright)

'Brown' mosses – *Scorpidium scorpioides* and *Campylium stellatum* in a base-rich flush at Glenuig, Argyll (I. Diack).

The moss flora of base-rich springs is very distinctive, with carpets and hummocks of vivid greens, yellows and deep browns comprising species such as *Palustriella commutata, Campylium stellatum* and *Scorpidium scorpioides.*

Overall, mosses and liverworts (collectively known as bryophytes) are a critical part of fen vegetation. They help define the character of fen vegetation and may also inform its conservation significance. Some species-groups, such as the bog-mosses (*Sphagna*) of more acidic fens, also play a key role in determining successional development and may dictate the range of niches available to other wetland plants and animals. Despite this ecological significance, the mosses and liverworts of most British fens are generally under recorded.

The fens of Britain and Ireland support many vulnerable and declining bryophytes, such as fen notchwort *Leiocolea rutheana* and marsh flapwort *Jamesoniella undulifolia.* Relatively few of these species are considered of European significance because of the relative abundance of wetlands in northern Europe, but as a result of habitat loss and widespread nutrient enrichment in temperate Europe, fen mosses and liverworts are threatened in many countries.

An intimate mix of acid-loving plants (e.g. *Sphagnum* mosses and sundews) on the rain-fed hummocks, and base-loving plants (e.g. Grass-of-Parnassus *Parnassia palustris* and long-stalked yellow-sedge *Carex lepidocarpa*) growing close to the base-rich stream water. Claife Heights, Cumbria (I. Diack).

Fens transitional between the strongly alkaline and strongly acidic (see **Section 4: Understanding Fen Nutrients**) can be very species-rich, supporting elements of both types. Typically sedge-dominated, bottle sedge (*Carex rostrata*) is often prominent, but the slender sedge (*C. lasiocarpa*), lesser tussock-sedge (*C. diandra*), common sedge (*C. nigra*) and carnation sedge (*C. panicea*) are also characteristic. Other plants particularly characteristic of these fens include bog bean (*Menyanthes trifoliata*), water horsetail (*Equisetum fluviatile*), marsh cinquefoil (*Potentilla palustris*), meadowsweet (*Filipendula ulmaria*), devil's-bit scabious (*Succisa pratensis*), marsh bedstraw (*Galium palustre*) and common valerian (*Valeriana officinalis*). Some of the rich-fen brown mosses occur, accompanied by the more base-tolerant bog-mosses, such as *Sphagnum contortum, S. teres* and *S. warnstorfii.*

Marsh cinquefoil, a characteristic plant of mesotrophic fen and 'transition mire', here growing at Dowrog Common, Pembrokeshire (I. Diack).

Bog bean growing in a transitional fen on Orkney (A. McBride).

Brown mosses are absent from fens receiving water with little or no base-enrichment, and bog-moss species dominate, particularly *Sphagnum fallax, S. squarrosum*, and *S. palustre*, commonly accompanied by bottle sedge (*Carex rostrata*), common sedge (*C. nigra*) and common cotton-grass (*Eriophorum angustifolium*). These fens can be very wet, with a quaking surface. In some situations, usually in confined basins, a floating raft of *Sphagnum* and sedges, sometimes known as a 'schwingmoor', develops over water and sloppy peat. At Wybunbury Moss in Cheshire (see case study at the end of Section 6), the raft floats over a basin 14 m deep. In some fens, this floating mat grows above the influence of the groundwater and surface water, and develops vegetation more characteristic of raised bogs, with species such as round-leaved sundew (*Drosera rotundifolia*), cranberry (*Vaccinium oxycoccus*), and ombrotrophic bog mosses such as *Sphagnum papillosum* and *S. capillifolium*.

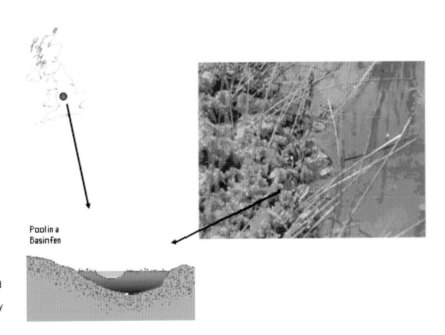

Pool in a Basin fen

Round-leaved sundew and Sphagnum fallax on the edge of a pool, Wybunbury Moss, Cheshire (I. Diack).

Single-species dominated swamps tend to occur in permanent standing water, ranging from those in base-poor conditions dominated by bottle sedge (*Carex rostrata*) or bladder sedge (*C. vesicaria*), to those characteristic of more nutrient- or base-enriched conditions dominated by great fen-sedge (*Cladium mariscus*), large sedges including tufted-sedge (*Carex elata*), greater tussock-sedge (*C. paniculata*), greater and lesser pond sedges (*C. riparia* and *C. acutiformis*), common reed (*Phragmites australis*), bulrush and lesser bulrush (*Typha latifolia* and *T. angustifolia*).

Cullentra Lough in County Tyrone, in Northern Ireland shows a well developed transition from open water fringed by single species swamp/fen, through to more diverse drier fen and wet woodland (B. Hamill).

Transition from open water through swamp to wet woodland on the shores of Upper Lough Erne in Northern Ireland (B. Hamill).

Lesser pond-sedge dominated fen in a moderately nutrient-enriched site, Bagmere, Cheshire (I. Diack.)

Mesotrophic open-water transition fen at Berrington Pool, Shropshire with bottle sedge, slender sedge, yellow loosestrife and white water lily (*Nymphaea alba*) (I. Diack).

Water horsetail, which can form single species stands in standing water up to and around 1m deep. St. David's Airfield, Pembrokeshire (I. Diack).

Brimstone on alder buckthorn, Shomere Pool, Shropshire (I. Diack)

Wooded areas of fen, also known as fen-carr, are dominated by willows (*Salix spp.*), alder (*Alnus glutinosa*) and birch (*Betula spp.*). Scarcer woody species associated with fens include buckthorn (*Rhamnus catharticus*) and alder buckthorn (*Frangula alnus*), both food plants of the brimstone butterfly (*Gonepteryx rhamni*). The understorey of shade-tolerant fen plants can include uncommon species such as marsh fern (*Thelypteris palustris*) and elongated sedge (*Carex elongata*). These wet fen woodlands give the impression of a primeval swampy wilderness, with huge up-standing tussocks of greater tussock sedge emerging from peat-stained water amongst gnarly alders, over which large mosquitoes and dragonflies hawk and hover.

Pools within fens and fen-carr provide additional habitat for many specialist plant and animal species. Here the uncommon least bur-reed (*Sparganium natans*) is growing in a fen woodland pool at Cliburn Moss, Cumbria (I. Diack).

Tall herb fen with willow scrub, an important habitat for many invertebrates and birds, at Wybunbury Moss, Cheshire (I. Diack).

Alder – greater tussock-sedge fen woodland, a late successional stage, typically occurs in very wet conditions, as here at Wybunbury Moss in Cheshire (I. Diack).

2.3 Mammals

Although there are no mammal species exclusive to fens in the UK, many different animals take advantage of fens for food and shelter (see Appendix III, Table 1), particularly where the fen is associated with open water and other semi-natural habitats.

Water voles (*Arvicola terrestris*) burrow in the earth banks of all kinds of slow-moving rivers, streams and ditches frequently associated with fen, swamp and wet grassland. Although not present in Ireland, they are found throughout England, Wales and Scotland. However, their distribution and population is decreasing rapidly due to loss of suitable habitat, especially in England and they are now vulnerable to extinction. Water voles depend on clean, fresh water and un-shaded riparian vegetation, feeding on grasses and other plant material.

Water shrews (*Neomys fodiens*), also present in England Wales and Scotland, but not Ireland and harvest mice (*Micromys minuta*), restricted to southern England and parts of Wales, are also found along the banks of watercourses and open water, and in reedbeds, marsh and other fen habitats. As with so many wetland specialists, the populations and distribution of all three of these species is patchy having suffered significantly because of habitat loss and fragmentation, pollution and disturbance.

Drier areas of ungrazed grassland and purple moor-grass (*Molinia caerulea*) dominated fen with plenty of dense cover support populations of field vole (*Microtus agrestis*), another species widespread in Britain which is absent from Ireland.

Otters (*Lutra lutra*) were once widespread throughout the UK, but declined rapidly in the late 20th century, becoming increasingly restricted to the north and west of the country at that time. The decline of otters across southern England and Wales was primarily due to the build-up of persistent organo-chlorine pesticides which affected their ability to breed. This decline has now largely been halted since these chemicals were banned and otters are once more becoming widespread throughout the UK. Otters are mainly found in still and running freshwater systems and along the coast, especially in Scotland, but associated habitats including fens and swamps are important for breeding, feeding and resting as the tall vegetation provides cover.

Otters are often found in fens and swamps (Lorne Gill).

Bat species associated with wetland habitats include pipistrelle bats (*Pipistrellus spp.*) noctule bats (*Nyctalus noctula*), brown long-eared bat (*Plecotus auritus*) and Daubenton's bat (*Motis daubentonii*). Although the latter are particularly associated with aquatic habitats and some of the other species noted may be more generic in their habitat requirements, they all occur in fens and reflect the mosaic of habitats within the wetland and its surroundings.

2.4 Birds

Many species of birds, often in large concentrations, feed, roost and/or breed in fens because of their wide range of vegetation communities and associated habitats (see Appendix III Table 2). For example over 200 bird species have been listed at Wicken Fen (see link Wicken Fen: History).

> In Scotland, the RSPB reserve at Loch of Strathbeg attracts 20,000 wintering wildfowl including whooper swans (*Cygnus cygnus*), pink-footed geese (*Anser brachyrhynchus*), teal (*Anas crecca*) and other wetland wildlife. This reserve comprises Scotland's largest dune loch plus its surrounding wetlands, grassland and woodland. It is managed by means of grazing and water level controls to maintain a mosaic of wetland habitats.
>
> Source: http://www.rspb.org.uk/reserves/guide/l/lochofstrathbeg/work.asp

The diagram below helps to depict the range of vegetation structures associated with fens and their utilisation by different bird species.

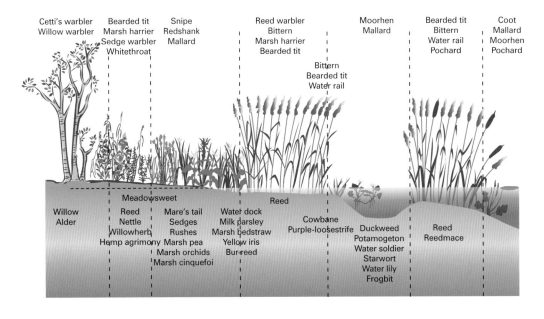

The wide variety of bird species found on fens are typically associated with different types and structure of vegetation, and different water levels. (After Hawke & Jose)

Bird species commonly associated with fens are generally classified into four categories, based on habitat features most likely to be used by different groups of birds, notably the presence or absence of water and vegetation structure.

- Vegetated margins of open water bodies
- Reedbeds and mixed fen swamp
- Grazed or cut fen in floodplain
- High marsh and carr

2.4.1 Vegetated margins of open water bodies

Species frequently associated with water margins include mute swans (*Cygnus olor*), moorhen (*Gallinula chloropus*) and ducks including mallard (*Anas platyrhynchos*) and teal (*A. crecca*). These birds prefer shallow open waters and reedbeds where they nest and forage for floating and emergent vegetation.

A family of mute swans nesting in swamp vegetation at the edge of open water (RSPB).

Grey Heron feeding on a frog in shallow water at the edge of a fen (RSPB).

Grey heron (*Ardea cinerea*) and little egret (*Egretta garzetta*) are amongst the birds which hunt for fish and amphibians amongst the open water margins of fens.

Sedge warblers are
amongst the passerines
that favour dense fen
vegetation for breeding
(RSPB).

2.4.2 Reedbeds and mixed fen swamp

Some of the species associated with mixed fen swamp are also typically associated
with reedbeds, including water rail (*Rallus aquaticus*), which feeds in open mud
between stands of tall aquatic vegetation, and bittern which hunts for fish in shallow
water. Migrants such as reed warbler (*Acrocephalus scirpaceus*) and the rare
Savi's warbler (*Locustella luscinioides*) also breed in large stands of reeds. Other
passerines that favour lower, dense fen vegetation and wet grassland for breeding
include sedge warbler (*Acrocephalus schoenobaenus*) and grasshopper warbler
(*Locustella naevia*). The rare spotted crake (*Porzana porzana*) also occurs in
extensive wetlands with low growing fen vegetation.

In southern England, marsh harriers (*Circus aeruginosus*) breed
and feed over fen, marsh and reedbeds throughout the year.
Outside the breeding season, hen harriers (*Circus cyaneus*)
forage over fens during the day and have been recorded roosting
communally in trees and woods associated with extensive
wetlands.

Adult marsh harrier
hunting over reedbeds
and mixed fen swamp
in the Norfolk Broads
(RSPB).

2.4.3 Grazed or cut fen in floodplain

Lapwing (*Vanellus vanellus*), redshank (*Tringa totanus*), curlew (*Numenius arguata*) and common snipe (*Gallinago gallinago*) are amongst the wading birds which breed in fens and wet grasslands where grazing and cutting result in a short sward in early spring. Other birds which also frequent open floodplain fens include short-eared owl (*Asio flammeus*) and yellow wagtail (*Motacilla flava*).

Redshank is one of the wading birds which commonly breed in short, wet grassland/fen in early spring (RSPB).

2.4.4 High marsh (tall herb) and carr

The range of birds associated with scrub, wet woodland and carr includes long-eared owl (*Asio otus*), willow tit (*Poecile montanus*), reed bunting (*Emberiza schoeniclus*) and the rare Cetti's warbler (*Cettia cetti*).

Reed bunting with food for young (RSPB) pictured alongside high marsh and carr, ideal habitat for breeding reed bunting (B. Hamill).

A study at Attenborough, in Nottinghamshire has shown that managed stands of reed and green osier support the highest concentration of nesting reed warblers, feeding sedge warblers and reed buntings of all English habitats.

2.5 Reptiles

Grass snakes (*Natrix natrix*), the largest of the UK's six native reptile species, are rare in Scotland but can be found hunting for amphibians and other prey, on fens throughout lowland England and Wales. However, within wetlands, they require plenty of hiding places and access to sunshine as well as egg-laying sites and hibernacula which are not susceptible to flooding. Ireland has no resident snakes.

As their name suggests, grass snakes are most commonly found in grasslands, but may favour fens and open water where they hunt for amphibians (RSPB).

Adders (*Vipera berus*) are found throughout mainland Britain, sometimes moving seasonally between generally drier habitats during autumn and spring, and wetter habitats such as ponds, lakes and fens in summer where they feed on amphibians. Slow-worm (*Anguis fragilis*) and common lizard (*Zootoca vivipara*) are both occasionally found in the drier parts of fens or adjacent habitat. Common lizard is the only reptile found in Northern Ireland.

Common lizards are often found on the drier margins of fens and wetter areas dominated by heather (A. McBride).

2.6   Amphibians

Amphibians are dependent on open water for breeding and frequently forage in associated wetlands. All of the widespread native amphibians can be found on fens: common frog (*Rana temporaria*), common toad (*Bufo bufo*), smooth newt (*Lissotriton vulgaris*), palmate newt (*L. helveticus*) and great crested newt (*Triturus cristatus*). Only common frog and smooth newt are found in Northern Ireland. Other rarer amphibians such as the natterjack toad (*Bufo calamita*) and the reintroduced population of pool frog (*Pelophylax lessonae*) in Norfolk do not occur in fen habitats.   Amphibians do not depend on fen sites per se, but frequently forage in fen vegetation, which provides suitable foraging and hibernation sites (see Appendix III, Table 3).

Female great crested newt basking on a log in fen vegetation (RSPB).

A mass of frog spawn is not uncommon on fens. Amphibians often thrive in ditches and isolated pools where there is a reduced presence of fish predators during the breeding season. (A. McBride).

Amphibians which are relatively widespread, such as common frog, may not be considered as conservation priorities in their own right, but their importance as a food source for a wide range of predators such as bittern or grass snake, may be influential in determining appropriate management.

2.7   Fish

Fish found in open water associated with fens (see Appendix III Table 4) are also important food sources for a number of species of conservation concern including otter and bittern, which may justify targeting of management action for the benefit of fish.

Native fish species likely to occur in association with fens include roach (*Rutilus rutilus*), pike (*Esox lucius*), common bream (*Abramis brama*) and the three-spined stickleback (*Gasterosteus aculeatus*). These species are typical of lowland rivers, drains, slow flowing and still open water with low oxygen concentrations.

2.8   Invertebrates

In summer, wetland habitats support a wide variety of flying insects which can be readily seen on a good day. However, this is just the tip of the iceberg, with the ecological diversity of fens supporting huge numbers of other invertebrates which require wet conditions for some of their life cycle, but are seldom seen (see Appendix III Table 5). As wetland habitats, it is hardly surprising that fens attract one of the most diverse ranges of aquatic invertebrates and also support a significant range of host-specific phytophagous invertebrates (i.e. which feed on herbaceous and woody plants), are regularly found in, but not confined to, fens.

The lunar hornet moth (*Sesia bembeciformis*) is a widely distributed species of fen woodland. The larvae of this species spend two winters feeding exclusively on the roots and trunks of old willows (D. Allen).

Damselfly eating a stone fly. The large range and numbers of invertebrates in fens attracts other predator invertebrates (A. McBride).

As with vertebrates, it is the structure of fen vegetation that is of most significance in determining the distribution of invertebrates, although water chemistry and quality (see **Section 4: Understanding Fen Nutrients**) are also important the existence of aquatic invertebrates. Recent work in the Norfolk Broads has revealed the importance of hydrology and water levels in determining the diversity and quality of some invertebrate assemblages, particularly those associated with rich fens. www.broads-authority.gov.uk

The ground beetle *Pterostichus aterrimus*, a UK priority species restricted to high quality fen habitats. Although now thought to be extinct in Britain, it is widespread in the interdrumlin fens of Counties Down and Armagh in Northern Ireland, where this photograph was taken (Dr. Roy Anderson).

As invertebrates are generally so much smaller than vertebrates, their specific habitat niches are also much smaller. Some invertebrates, such as soldier flies and craneflies, are completely reliant on mossy seepages of restricted distribution and size. In contrast, exposed sediments and muds are crucial for the existence of some water beetles. The mud snail *Omphiscola glabra* is a red data book species restricted to nutrient poor waters associated with small fen areas prone to drying out in summer. Few other aquatic plants and animals are able to survive in this very restricted habitat type.

The mud snail
Omphiscola glabra
(12–20mm in length),
is restricted to very
specific, and often small
habitat niches. (Dr. Roy
Anderson).

The great diving beetle
(*Dytiscus marginalis*) is one
of many large predatory
water beetlews commonly
found in fens and is easily
observed in pools. They
predate in both their larval
and adult form on smaller
aquatic invertebrates,
tadpoles and small fish
(Dr. Roy Anderson).

The taxonomic range of interest amongst fenland invertebrates is so large that
the list of associated groups is little more than a checklist of major invertebrate
groups. For example Wicken Fen, in Cambridgeshire, has recorded over 1000
species in each of three groups of insects, the flies (1,893 species), the beetles
(1,527 species) and the moths (1,083 species). In general, emphasis is on those
invertebrate groups with the largest number of species, for example water beetles
and moths as well as highly visible groups, such as butterflies and dragonflies.

The black darter
(*Sympetrum danae*), a
dragonfly of acidic pools
particularly associated
with poor fen vegetation
and cutover bogs (Dr.
Roy Anderson).

A similar approach to that applied to birds can be adopted when considering the
invertebrate fauna and interest associated with different vegetation structures
and fen habitats. The table below provides a structural classification, albeit an
artificial one, in that it presents, as discrete categories, features and structures that
are in reality part of a continuum. This is a more useful checklist to have in mind
when considering management other than that based on taxonomy, but it must
be emphasised that this mosaic of fen communities is frequently associated with
other semi-natural habitats such as open water and woodland carr, which are often
essential for many invertebrate groups found in fens.

Further guidance on habitat characteristics and features beneficial
to invertebrates can be found in Kirby (1992) and Fry and Lonsdale
(1991). Further information on the groups of invertebrates associated
with fens is also available from www.buglife.org.uk, but bear in mind that
not all groups are included, and there is implied variation in the definition
of fen in the accounts of different groups in this multi-authored work.

Feature	Key/representative groups and species	Important habitat characteristics
Permanent and near-permanent water, including emergent and aquatic vegetation	A range of predominantly aquatic and semi-aquatic species: water beetles, water bugs, molluscs, caddisflies and dragonflies are obvious key groups, but there are important species in other groups, such as fen raft-spider (*Dolomedes plantarius*). Flies, including snail-killing flies on emergent vegetation.	The richest faunas are in unshaded water bodies with dense aquatic vegetation, but late successional pools are also important (and liable to become increasingly temporary) and shaded pools support species not found in the open. Whereas small open pools are especially important for predatory water beetles and water bugs, vegetation of particular structure, such as saturated mosses or grasses in the shallows, also provide distinct and important niches for invertebrates.
Mossy fens	Small predatory and phytophagus water beetles	
Tall monocotyledon-dominated water margins and swamp	Many species over a broad taxonomic range, notably including phytophagus moths, beetles and bugs, and an important range of spiders; also many species living, or at least developing, in the shallow water, mud, or plant litter amongst the stems; especially beetles (ground beetles, rove beetles, and members of smaller families) and flies (many families, including long-footed flies (*Dolichopodidae*) and crane-flies).	Assemblage varies according to species of plants, the duration and extent of flooding, and the amount of litter build-up.
Tall continuous herbaceous vegetation on damp soil	A wide range of phytophagous species, especially amongst moths, beetles, bugs, sawflies; also a range of flies.	The greater the range of plant species present, the greater the potential range of species supported, but good populations of individual plant species are critical.
Short and open-structured vegetation over wet ground with little litter, including bare ground	Ground beetles, rove beetles, flies, spiders, molluscs, including narrow-mouthed whorl snail (*Vertigo angustior*). Low vegetation and little litter make for warm conditions at ground level and easy mobility for ground-active species.	Permanently wet, or long-duration wetness, in the surface layers may be critical: developing larvae are often confined to the surface layers. Easy access to bare wet ground may be important for flies laying eggs in damp ground. Often best as a mosaic with taller vegetation.
Tussocks and mosaics of tall and short fen/wet grassland	Individual species of a number of groups, including beetles, bugs and flies; some tussock-forming plants, such as tufted hair-grass (*Deschampsia cespitosa*), have a specialised fauna; structural variation may be important for some species, such as marsh fritillary (*Eurodryas aurinia*).	A mosaic structure of tussocky or patchy tall vegetation with shorter vegetation and bare ground may increase the interest of both.
Scattered trees and scrub	A wide range of phytophagous species, especially beetles, bugs and moths, and their associated predators and parasites; shrubs may provide foraging, swarming and resting sites for species, especially various species of flies, breeding in open wetland. Assembly points for soldierflies. Sallow catkins important for nectar and pollen by day for flies and bees, and night for moths. Sloe and hawthorn also of value.	Different ages and species of scrub and trees support different species. Some species are dependent on young or invasive scrub, for example, others may require profusely flowering mature trees/shrubs.

Old trees and dead wood	Saproxylic beetles of a range of families; also saproxylic flies, including hoverflies, craneflies, *Tipuloidea*, and a range of other groups; solitary bees and wasps nesting in dead wood, especially old beetle holes; and a good range of phytophagous species, with the varied structure of older trees providing a range of hibernation sites.	Standing living trees with dead wood provide the best resource, but dead standing trees and fallen wood may be valuable. Fallen wood on shaded seepages has a particular fauna.
Continuous and near-continuous scrub/woodland with shaded wet conditions	*Diptera*, especially craneflies, but also a range of other families; species associated with foliage and timber will be similar to those of more scattered trees and shrubs; they will be generally less diverse, but will include specialist species not found in more open conditions.	Permanently or near-permanently wet conditions are critical for high interest, because many larvae develop in the surface layers. All conditions from sheltered but sunny areas amongst scrub to densely shaded wet leaf litter support interesting species.
Fen-edge transitions	A wide scatter of species in varied groups, with phytophagous beetles, bugs and moths key amongst them. Fen-edge grassland shares some species with calcareous grassland; the marsh moth (*Athetis pallustris*) and the marsh fritillary (*Eurodryas aurinia*) are both found in relatively dry grassland.	Transitional habitats may be anything from open grassland to woodland. Open grassland and grass/scrub mosaics are generally the richest in uncommon and characteristic species.
Seasonally exposed marginal sediments	Surface-active beetles, especially ground beetles and rove beetles; many flies with larvae which develop in the sediments or stranded snails.	Bare sediments in a mosaic with or well-structured transition to wetland vegetation are usually richest.
Temporary pools and areas of seasonal flooding	There are temporary pool specialists in a number of groups, especially including a number of uncommon water beetles; a wider range of species tolerant of seasonality may benefit from the absence of fish and the oxidation of organic sediments in temporary waters.	The richest specialist faunas are in unshaded pools, but those amongst taller vegetation or beneath shade of woody vegetation have uncommon species of their own.
Seepages and surface flow	Various groups of flies, especially soldier-flies at unshaded seepages and craneflies at shaded seepages.	Continuous seepages over a substantial area are best; seepages are long-lasting but often isolated and of limited area, so historical continuity of conditions may be critical to their interest.

2.9 Fen conservation

Widespread loss and damage to fens through drainage, nutrient-enrichment and abandonment which has occurred throughout the 20th century has resulted in many fen types, and their constituent species, becoming much less common than they were even 40 or 50 years ago.

Many of the best fen sites are now legally protected under domestic legislation as Sites of Special Scientific Interest (SSSI) or Areas of Special Scientific Interest (ASSI) in Northern Ireland. Some of these fens are also protected under international legislation. Annex 1 of the European Habitats Directive requires member states to conserve habitats identified as being of European conservation importance, through notification of a proportion of sites supporting these habitats as Special Areas of Conservation (SACs) and to maintain the entire habitat resource in 'Favourable Conservation Status'. A list of SAC fens can be found on www.jncc.gov.uk/page-1461.

Fen habitats listed under Annex 1 of the European Habitats Directive because of their significant conservation importance:

H6410 Molinia meadows on calcareous, peaty or clayey-silt-laden soils (*Molinion caeruleae*)
H7140 Transition mires and quaking bogs
H7150 Depressions on peat substrates of the *Rhynchosporion*
H7120 Calcareous fens with *Cladium mariscus* and species of the *Caricion davallianae*
H7220 Petrifying springs with tufa formation (Cratoneurion)
H7230 Alkaline fens
H7240 Alpine pioneer formations of *Caricion bicoloris-atrofuscae*

Named after the city in Iran where it was adopted in 1971, the Ramsar Convention on Wetlands of International Importance is an international treaty for the conservation and sustainable utilisation of wetlands. Many fens across the globe are identified under the Convention. In the UK, 168 fen sites are protected under the Ramsar Convention. Further details of Ramsar listed fens can be found on www.jncc.gov.uk/page-2392.

Species that have experienced the greatest declines in lowland Britain are those of low nutrient or oligotrophic situations. Plants such as bog sedge (*Carex limosa*), great sundew (*Drosera anglica*) and Grass-of-Parnassus are now entirely restricted to a few protected sites. As a result of these species declines, the fen plants listed below are now included on the UK BAP Priority Species list, which includes some of the rarest or most rapidly declining species.

Vascular plants

Flat-sedge	*Blysmus compressus*
Narrow small-reed	*Calamagrostis stricta*
Early marsh-orchid	*Dactylorhiza incarnata subsp. ochroleuca*
Crested buckler-fern	*Dryopteris cristata*
Fen orchid	*Liparis loeselii*
Pale wood-rush	*Luzula pallidula*
Marsh club-moss	*Lycopodiella inundata*
Tubular water-dropwort	*Oenanthe fistulosa*
Fly orchid	*Ophrys insectifera*
Lesser butterfly-orchid	*Platanthera bifolia*
Marsh saxifrage	*Saxifraga hirculus*
Fen ragwort	*Senecio paludosus*
Greater water-parsnip	*Sium latifolium*
Marsh stitchwort	*Stellaria palustris*
Fen violet	*Viola persicifolia*

Lower plants

Waved Fork-moss	*Dicranum bergeri*
Marsh Flapwort	*Jamesoniella undulifolia*
Fen Notchwort	*Leiocolea rutheana*
Veilwort	*Pallavicinia lyellii*
Dwarf Stonewort	*Nitella tenuissima*

Fungi

Fragile Amanita	*Amanita friabilis*
Agaric	*Armillaria ectypa*
Fen Puffball	*Bovista paludosa*
Ashen Coral	*Tremellodendropsis tuberosa*

2.10 References

Fry, R. & Lonsdale, D. 1991. Habitat conservation for invertebrates – a neglected green issue. Amateur Entomologists' Society, Middlesex.

Kirby, P. 1992. Habitat Management for Invertebrates: A Practical Handbook by Peter Kirby. RSPB.

Hawke, C.J. & Jose, P.V. 1996. Reedbed Management for Commercial and Wildlife Interests. RSPB.

Wheeler, B. D. and Proctor, M. C. F. 2000. Ecological gradients, subdivisions and terminology of north-west European mires. *Journal of Ecology.* **88**, 187-203.

3.   Understanding Fen Hydrology

Quantity and quality of water are critical to fens, playing a major role in determining the type of fen, vegetation and wildlife, what products can be harvested, and further social and economic benefits provided by fens. Understanding the basics of fen hydrology is therefore essential to successful fen management.

This section provides an overview of fen hydrology and hydrological assessment. The case studies at the end of the section illustrate how the hydrological regime has been assessed for three different fens. Guidance on managing fen hydrology, including troubleshooting and finding sustainable solutions, is covered in Section 5: Fen Management and Restoration.

3.1   The basic principles of fen hydrology

Fens are terrestrial wetlands fed by surface water and/or groundwater, as well as direct input from rainfall. They are characterised by high soil water levels for all or part of the year, and are often based on peat. The landscape setting combined with the presence of ground- or surface water largely defines the hydrological functioning of a fen. The availability of water from the various sources will obviously vary throughout the year, and will differ between years. Both water inputs to the fen (the source and method of supply which feeds the fen) and water distribution through the site need to be considered.

3.2   The importance of water

Fens require:
– a reliable source throughout the year of surface water and/or groundwater in quantity and quality appropriate to the specific type of fen;

– a location with a perennial supply of water (such as a groundwater-fed spring) or which retains water (such as a dip in the landscape with impermeable soil), either or both of which can result in high levels of surface 'wetness' for all or part of the year.

The amount of water required to maintain a particular type of fen, and how this varies throughout the year, is described as the **hydrological regime**, which might include the level of groundwater or the duration and depth of a flood. The hydrological regime is important for the ecological functioning of fens because:

a. High water tables generates physical conditions that exclude some species. For example, prolonged flooding can reduce the anchoring capacity of the soil and make it more difficult for trees to establish.
b. Higher water tables deprive soil of oxygen (i.e. generate anoxia) which limits species which have not adapted to these conditions. Anoxia can also increase concentrations of phytotoxic chemicals such as sulphide and ammonia.
c. Water is the main carrier of dissolved chemicals to a fen and thus strongly influences the acidity and fertility of the site (see **Section 4: Understanding Fen Nutrients**), which in turn affects the type and growth of vegetation and fauna which it supports (see **Section 2: Fen Flora and Fauna**).

3.3 Different types of fen

A simple classification system based on the pathway water takes, either through soil or rock, or via overland flooding, provides a framework for characterising and understanding fen hydrology.

Topogenous fens: water movement is predominantly vertical and overland, resulting in water ponding in depressions such as valleys, basins and floodplains.

Soligenous fens: water movement is predominantly lateral through the soil or discharging from the rock, such as spring fens or flushes

Some fens combine both of these types, such as valley fens.

TAKE CARE: Fen classification according to landscape setting can provide clues as to the likely key water supply and transfer mechanisms, which is a good starting point for the development of a more detailed understanding of the hydrological functioning of a site. However, wetlands in identical settings can receive water from completely different sources and from a variety of different sources simultaneously. A fen may have different water transfer mechanisms operating in different areas of the site, which may vary during the year. For example groundwater seepage might be important in spring when the groundwater tables are high, whilst the same fen might predominantly receive input from surface water via ditches in the summer.

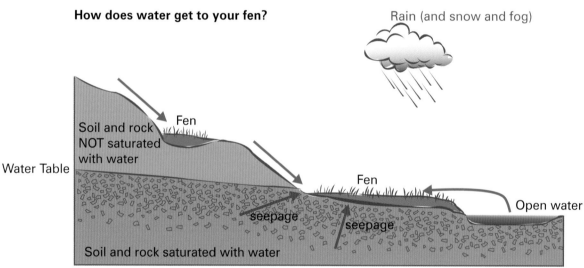

How does water get to your fen?

Fen (green)

Soligenous (purple) = discharge from saturated soil or deeper rock layers.

Topogenous (red) = overland flow and flood water from lake or river.

3.4 Water source(s) feeding the fen

All sources of water entering and leaving a fen need to be taken into account.

Rainwater – all fens are fed by rainwater (i.e. direct precipitation), the level and significance of which varies through the season but is typically more focused in the winter months, especially under the predicted climate change scenarios.

Surface water in the form of run-off or over-bank flooding often has a short-term or episodic influence, occurring in direct response to (and therefore fluctuating with) rainfall within the catchment, usually concentrated during the wetter and colder months of the year.

Groundwater discharge to fens is usually a more constant feature, but may be higher during winter and spring, occurring when the underlying or surrounding soil and geological layers are saturated with water. If the surface soil and shallow drift deposits within the fen are permeable, then groundwater is likely to discharge by diffuse upwards seepage. Alternatively, if the surface and shallow deposits are not very permeable, groundwater is likely to discharge at the margins of the soil or drift deposits through discrete springs or seepages. In practice, groundwater usually discharges to a site through some combination of these two mechanisms.

A pre-requisite for groundwater discharge to a fen, or fen discharge to groundwater, is an underlying (and/or adjacent) water-bearing formation (aquifer), such as the chalk of south-east England or the Permo-Triassic sandstones of the Midlands and north-west England. The high capacity of these aquifers for groundwater storage means that groundwater discharge is more likely to be maintained over the summer and autumn periods.

Low permeability rocks or superficial drift such as glacially-derived sands and gravels can also be important water sources for fens. Groundwater flow in these formations is usually within the immediate surface water catchment and the resulting low capacity for groundwater storage often means that groundwater discharge can be significantly reduced or even interrupted during the summer and autumn periods.

3.4.1 Fen types and associated water transfer mechanisms

The following diagrams and text provide more detail on the types of fen found in each landscape setting and their associated water transfer mechanisms.

3.4.1.1 Fens on slopes

Sites occur on gently sloping land and include many valley-head fens that form the source or headwaters of streams. Water retention is often within low permeability peat or alluvial deposits. Run-off from surrounding slopes is often an important water source, but many examples also receive a contribution from groundwater discharge. Recognised classic examples include Morrone Birkwood (Cairngorm SAC) and Mynydd Preseli (Pembrokeshire).

Morrone Birkwood SSSI in Scotland is a good example of an alkaline spring-fed fen on a slope.

3.4.1.2

Fens in topographic depressions (or basins) occur in hollows in the landscape, for example those associated with glacial or peri-glacial processes such as kettle holes, or in solution hollows on limestone. Surface run-off from surrounding slopes can be an important source of water, depending on the surrounding topography. These sites may have no surface water flow outlet. Recognised classic examples include Vicarage Moss and Salbri (Wales), Wybunbury Moss (England) and Whitlaw Mosses (Scotland).

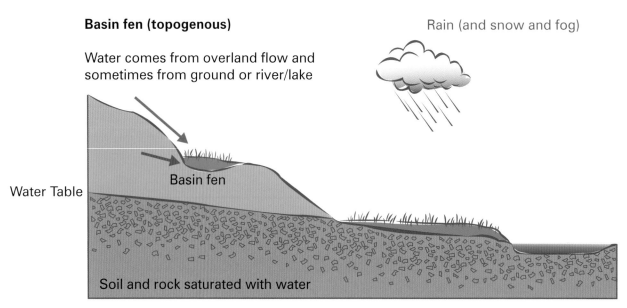

Basin fen (topogenous)

Water comes from overland flow and sometimes from ground or river/lake

Rain (and snow and fog)

Basin fen

Water Table

Soil and rock saturated with water

Soligenous (purple) = discharge from saturated soil or deeper rock layers.

Topogenous (red) = overland flow and flood water from lake or river.

3.4.1.3

Open water transition fen (topogenous)

Fen on edge of open water (lake or river)
Water comers from open water throughout the year

Rain (and snow and fog)

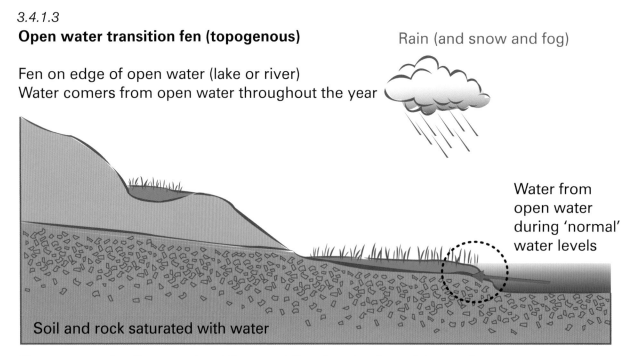

Water from open water during 'normal' water levels

Soil and rock saturated with water

Topogenous (red) = overland flow and flood water from lake or river.

3.4.1.4

Spring fed fen (Soligenous)

Water comes out of the saturated soil
or rock at one spot (spring) or
discrete zone (seepage)

Rain (and snow and fog)

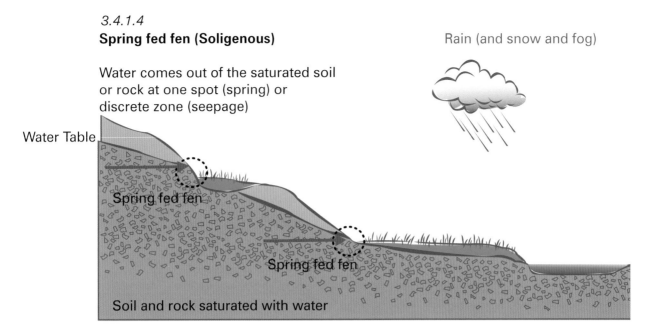

Soligenous (purple) = discharge from saturated soil or deeper rock layers.

– **Valley bottom fens.** Sites are normally located on floodplains associated with permanent or ephemeral watercourses. In the lower reaches of a catchment they may include estuaries or coastal plains. Over-bank flow from a river, in the form of 'flash' flood events in the upper/middle reaches of a catchment, or longer-term floodplain inundation in the lower reaches, is normally an important water supply mechanism.

3.4.1.5

Valley fen with soakway fen (Soligenous)

Separate fen habitat that occurs along a water tracks
WITHIN a larger fen (like a valley fen) or within a larger peatland.
Water comes from the soil.

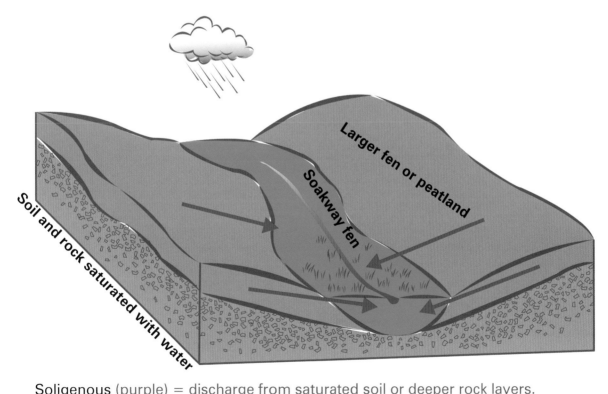

Soligenous (purple) = discharge from saturated soil or deeper rock layers.

3.4.1.6

Floodplain wetlands in addition to large rivers this includes sites on flat valley-bottoms where the watercourse is small and does not provide significant amounts of water through overbank flooding. Groundwater discharge can also be an important water supply mechanism where the wetland is underlain by an aquifer and not separated by impermeable strata. Classic examples include Insh Marshes, near Kingussie in the Scottish Highlands and Cors Erddreiniog on Anglesey in North Wales.

> **The New Forest valley mires form a complex mosaic of habitats around streams with small catchments, the water arising from springs and groundwater seepages from sand and gravel strata ranging from acidic to basic. A typical example has a central stream with a limited floodplain on which birch, willow and alder scrub have developed. Peat has usually accumulated on the more or less flat floodplain, and this merges laterally into the sand and gravel slopes from which springs and seepages arise.**

A more detailed classification characterising the relationship between fen habitats, plant communities and of wetland water supply mechanisms (termed 'WETMECs') has been developed by Bryan Wheeler and Sue Shaw (Wheeler, Shaw and Tanner, 2009) at Sheffield University. This classification describes the hydrology of many fen sites in England and Wales (further information at WETMECS). The ability to use WETMEC information depends on the expertise and information available to the site manager. A non-specialist can usefully explore some of the aspects of WETMECs to provide a predictive outlook for the site, even though the fine detail may require more information than would normally be available.

Assessing the vegetation is an important first step in understanding the hydrological functioning of a fen, as with this example of a surface water flooded fen at Loch Lubnaig, Scotland (J. Schutten).

3.5 Factors determining fen type

3.5.1 Water Movement

In common with bogs, most fens accumulate peat as plants die back but do not fully decay. Peat accumulation is greatest where the ground is permanently waterlogged and with little water movement.

3.5.2 Acidity

Some of the wide variation in the vegetation of different types of fen is associated with acidity or alkalinity, which is measured by pH (the concentration of hydrogen ions) and the presence of bicarbonate and particular metallic ions such as calcium and magnesium.

– 'Poor fens' occur mainly in the uplands or associated with lowland heaths, where the water is derived from base-poor rock such as sandstones and granites. They are characterised by short vegetation with a high proportion of bog (*Sphagnum*) mosses and acid water (pH of 5.5 or less).

– 'Base-rich fens' are fed by mineral-enriched calcareous waters (pH 5.5 or more) and tend to support a wider diversity of plant and animal communities than those fed by base-poor water. These fens are mainly confined to the lowlands or upland areas with localised occurrences of base-rich rocks such as limestone. They can be extremely species-rich, providing a habitat for around a third of our native flora, more than half the UK's species of dragonflies and several thousand other insect species, as well as being an important habitat for a range of aquatic beetles.

3.5.3 Mineral content

Fens are distinct from bogs in that the water which feeds fens has passed over or through soil and rock, in the process becoming charged with mineral salts dissolved from the rock and soil. This contact with rocks is known as 'residency time'. The concentration of minerals dissolved, which in turn determines the type of plants that will grow in the fen, can be affected by the quantity of water passing through.

A fascinating feature of some calcareous fens is the development of tufa, which is associated with springs where groundwater rich in calcium bicarbonate comes to the surface. On contact with the air, carbon dioxide is lost from the water and a hard deposit of calcium carbonate is formed as stony grey tufa.

Tufa forming on *Scorpidium cossonii*, Bryum pseudotriquetrum and sedge litter in a spring-fed calcareous fen, Trefonen Marshes, Shropshire (I. Diack).

3.5.4 Water storage and release

The type, extent and distribution of fens are also determined by the physical properties of rock and soil. Water passes quickly through coarse sediments, but only slowly, if at all, through fine ones, such as clay. Hydrologists refer to three distinct types of geology in relation to:

- **aquifers** which hold a large capacity and through which water can pass freely;

- **aquitards** through which water can pass very slowly;

- **aquicludes** which act as a seal against water movement.

3.5.5 Nutrients

The plant nutrients nitrogen, phosphorus and potassium are another factor determining the type of fen vegetation. The nutrient status gives rise to another series of descriptors – oligotrophic, mesotrophic and eutrophic – for low, medium and high nutrient situations respectively. Some eutrophic fens are entirely natural, such as in the lower catchments of rivers where water is naturally enriched compared to the upper reaches. Others are enriched by sewage and nutrient run-off where the natural situation would be oligotrophic or mesotrophic. **Section 4 Understanding Fen Nutrients** explains fen nutrient enrichment in more detail.

3.5.6 Land management

Grazing and/or cutting vegetation strongly influences species composition and structure of fens. If carried out regularly, grazing or cutting can counteract the unwanted effects of nutrient enrichment by preventing rank species from overgrowing and replacing those less able to compete. **Section 6: Fen Vegetation Management** discusses grazing and other fen vegetation management techniques.

3.6   Assessing current hydrological regime

At the simplest level, current hydrological regime can be assessed by observations made during site visits. For example, recording the wetness of the ground underfoot, using a spade or hand-auger to establish the depth of the water table below ground surface, recording the number of days a floodplain site is under water, or recording the number of over-bank flooding events and their effects on the site.

More detailed or higher level assessment of the hydrological regime requires more technical monitoring of key hydrological parameters using specialist instruments. This subject is covered in detail in **Section 10: Monitoring to Inform Fen Management**.

The most important hydrological characteristics for fens are:

- **Soil water level (in relation to ground surface)**. Most often defined as maximum and minimum elevations, which vary through the year, or over longer time periods. Optimal soil water level conditions for the establishment and growth of seedlings (and other life-cycle stages) vary between species. Tolerance of above ground water level or complete inundation also varies. For example, protracted and/or deep winter flooding is not favourable for alkaline fen habitats.

- **Flooding – frequency and magnitude**. Some habitats, such as wet woodland, are dependent on surface water flooding over a range of frequencies and magnitudes. Lower frequency – higher magnitude events are important for creating regeneration niches, whilst higher frequency - lower magnitude events are important for replenishment of sediment deposits.

- **Flooding – timing/seasonality**. Many species are vulnerable to flooding during the establishment stage of their life cycle.

- **Water quality**. Rich-fens (pH >5.5) and poor-fens (pH <5.5) are differentiated by the pH of incoming waters. The rate of seepage or flow through a site can also be a determinant of *in situ* water quality, with higher flows generally leading to more aerobic conditions.

Recording of appropriate information is essential to compare target with current hydrological regime. Conditions should be monitored during critical periods within the year, for example:

- the summer period of lowest water levels and spring flows;

- the winter period of over-bank flooding, or

- during specific rainfall events to observe surface water run-off processes or flooding events.

Hydrological measurements for a single year in isolation can be very misleading and prone to fluctuation due to weather. To take account of year-to-year variability, hydrological conditions should be monitored over a number of years (ideally 10 or more) to develop an appreciation of the longer-term hydrological regime of the site, including both extreme wet or dry years and those which are more typical in hydrological terms.

For projects particularly constrained by resources, a simple checklist can help in establishing a base-level understanding of the eco-hydrology. The following table sets out how to deduce likely important water sources by looking at the topography, the geology and the vegetation type and height. The table should be used to sketch a few possible eco-hydrological models and then look at the position of structures such as ditches, drains (including under-drainage), embankments and sources of plant nutrients to interpret what is happening. For example, does a ditch cut across a groundwater flow path, cutting off its influence from vegetation that used to depend on it? Do indicators of enrichment such as greater reedmace (*Typha latifolia*) or stinging nettles (*Urtica dioica*) form a pattern around or at the downstream end of a ditch line?

Checklist for hydrological attributes

Factor	Observation	Implication
Land form	raised	Rain-fed (bog) or groundwater pressure forming tufa mound.
	flat	Fed by rainwater, surface water, and perhaps some groundwater.
	a hollow	Rainfall and surface water collects and stagnates.
	Slope	Flowing surface water, and/or seepage. Springs.
Plant type	*Sphagnum* mosses	Raised bog, wet heath or poor fen. Low nutrients, low pH, low bicarbonate, high water table.
	short	Probably low nutrients, though could be base-rich or base poor, high to low pH. High probability of seepage. Fluctuating water table. Beware shortness of vegetation could also relate to heavy grazing.
	knee-high	Probably low to moderate nutrient, though could be base-rich or base poor, high to low pH. Surface water and groundwater. Fluctuating water table.
	chest-high	High nutrient, base-moderate, high or medium pH. Usually high water table, but may fall in summer.
	above head	Very high nutrients, base moderate, high or medium pH. Usually high water table, but may fall in summer.
	NVC community	Refer to NVC volumes and Appendix 4.
Rock/soil type	sand & gravel	Usually base-poor but exceptionally may be base-rich. Rapid water movement, inclined to dry out easily. Forms aquifers. There can be compacted layers acting as aquitards.
	clay	Can vary from base-poor to base-rich, Prevents rapid upwards or downwards water movement. Forms aquitards and aquicludes. Look for bands of clay within sands.
	chalk, limestone, basic igneous or metamorphic	Gives rise to base-rich water, depends on residence time and intimacy of contact. The degree to which they act as aquifers depends on fracturing and pore space.
	sandstones, gritstones, acid igneous or metamorphic	Can be base-rich, but usually base-poor. Porous sandstones form aquifers and others do when fractured. Shale bands can often be base-rich within otherwise base-poor strata.
	peat	Very variable, can act as aquifer or aquitard, depending on structure of each stratum. Properties change as it dries and oxidises.

Glossary: Rainfall/water refers to any atmospheric water. Surface water is water standing or flowing at the surface, and may contain rainwater, river water and groundwater. Groundwater is known to have had residence time in the ground and emerged at the point of observation.

Installing hydrological monitoring equipment in a floodplain fen at Insh Marshes, Scotland (J. Schutten).

3.7 Further information and advice

Fen hydrology is a complex subject: this handbook can only provide a basic overview. Further information and specialist advice is available from government conservation bodies, environmental protection agencies, non-governmental conservation organisations such as The Wildlife Trusts, or consultants.

3.8 References

Wheeler BD Shaw, SC. and Tanner, K. 2009. A Wetland Framework for Impact Assessment at Statutory Sites in England and Wales. Department of Animal and Plant Sciences, University of Sheffield. Environment Agency Science Report SC030232.

EA 2003. A Guide to Monitoring Water Levels and Flows at Wetlands Sites. Environment Agency National groundwater and contaminated land centre.

Podmore Pool

Hurcott & Podmore Pools SSSI is located on the north-eastern edge of Kidderminster (Worcestershire) in the English Midlands. It is recognised as an important fen wetland complex covering an area of 23.5ha. The SSSI notification (1986) refers to pools, rich riparian zones with beds of different reed and sedge species, and to stands of alder woodland (NVC communities W5 Alnus glutinosa – Carex paniculata woodland and W6 Alnus glutinosa – Urtica dioica woodland) with a diversity of ground flora with locally uncommon species, including greater tussock sedge and alternate-leaved golden saxifrage.

The site is confined to the narrow floodplain of the Blakedown Brook, a stream which rises in the Clent Hills to the north-east and flows into the River Stour shortly downstream of the site. Its landscape setting is a valley bottom fen, and this generic model, with its associated water transfer mechanisms, was used to inform the investigation and interpretation of the hydrological functioning of the site.

Historically, the Blakedown Brook has been used extensively to provide power through the development of water mills, and a direct legacy of this is the pools formed behind dams within the site. Long-term siltation upstream of these dams has resulted in (or contributed to) the presence of low permeability valley infill sediments (silt and clay, with some sand and peat) which form the quasi-flat surface of the narrow floodplain, and also form the substrate on which the wetland habitats are developed. The brook now flows in shallow braided channels through the areas of wet woodland and swamp communities. Hydrological investigation and

characterisation of the site, on behalf of the Environment Agency, was prompted by concern over areas of alder carr which were in very poor condition because of persistently low soil water levels. The investigation consisted of a detailed desk study, small-scale field investigations (including a hand-auger survey of substrate sediments) and monitoring of soil water levels in a network of shallow dipwells.

The water transfer mechanisms identified for the site are illustrated schematically below in terms of a water balance calculation. The site was confirmed to be complex and interesting in hydrological terms, for example:

Alder carr, Hurcott Wood

Groundwater inflow. Groundwater levels in the underlying Sherwood Sandstone have been lowered significantly by groundwater abstraction. Local sandstone groundwater levels were 1-4 m below ground surface over most of the site, indicating that there was no groundwater discharge to the site. However, there is anecdotal evidence of groundwater discharge to the site via peripheral springs within living memory.

Groundwater outflow. There was a downwards hydraulic gradient through the low permeability floodplain sediments into the Sherwood Sandstone, and therefore the potential for loss of water from the site through downwards percolation. The amount of water lost in this way was difficult to quantify.

Surface water inflows. These represented the only significant source of water for the site. Because of lowered groundwater levels in the Sherwood Sandstone, there is negligible groundwater-fed baseflow discharge in the Blakedown Brook. Flows were maintained almost exclusively by a constant 3.4 million litres per day discharge of treated sewage effluent upstream of the site.

Knowledge of the water transfer mechanisms for the site was used as a basis for development of a detailed hydrological conceptual model. This model was then used as a basis for the initial design of a range of remedial measures, the feasibility and cost-effectiveness of which were being explored at the time of writing (autumn 2008).

Water Transfer mechanisms for Hurcott Wood

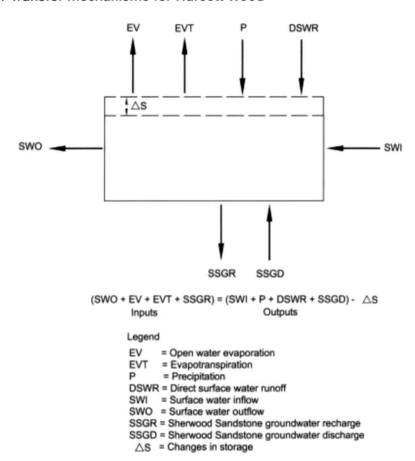

$$(SWO + EV + EVT + SSGR) = (SWI + P + DSWR + SSGD) - \triangle S$$

Inputs   Outputs

Legend

EV = Open water evaporation
EVT = Evapotranspiration
P = Precipitation
DSWR = Direct surface water runoff
SWI = Surface water inflow
SWO = Surface water outflow
SSGR = Sherwood Sandstone groundwater recharge
SSGD = Sherwood Sandstone groundwater discharge
$\triangle S$ = Changes in storage

Acknowledgements: Sarah Gaskill and Mike Averill (Environment Agency), Paul Allen (Wyre Forest District Council), Anthony Muller (Natural England), Paul Inman (WMC), and others too numerous to mention.

Case Study 3.2
Hydrological characterisation, hydrological impact assessment, and proposals for hydrological remediation, Llangloffan Fen SSSI, Pembrokeshire

The wetland complex of Llangloffan Fen SSSI extends for some 2.7 km along the valley of the upper Western Cleddau, 7.5 km south-west of Fishguard, Pembrokeshire. The site is designated as a SSSI, a National Nature Reserve (NNR), and it is a constituent part of the Afonydd Cleddau SAC. It is of conservation interest for its range of wetland vegetation types including wet woodland, fen and swamp, for its assemblages of epiphytic lichens and peatland invertebrates, and for its populations of otter, bullhead *Cottus gobio*, river lamprey *Lampetra fluviatilis*, and brook lamprey *Lampetra planeri*, all of which are reliant on the Western Cleddau River which flows through the site.

A network of shallow dipwells, arranged in six transect lines across the site, was established through successive phases of installation during the 1980s and early-1990s. Soil water levels have been measured manually at a frequency varying from weekly to monthly and continuously in three of the dipwells by either analogue chart recorder or pressure transducer and data logger. Four piezometers (with depths ranging from 5.3 to 10 m) were installed during 2007 in order to characterise the hydrogeological conditions in the formations from which groundwater discharges to the site. The groundwater level and quality measurements from these installations have been used to inform the hydro-ecological conceptual understanding of the site.

Greater tussock sedge, Llangloffan Fen

In summary, the hydrology of the site is as follows:

- The Western Cleddau flows through the site from west to east. The stream was extensively deepened and straightened between 1841 and 1946, and it is assumed that the water level in the stream was lowered through these works. Regular dredging and weed clearance will maintain these lowered stream water levels.

- The eastern part of the site is underlain by peat, silt and clay to a depth of at least 10 m; these deposits have relatively low permeability.

Analogue chart water level recorder

Sand and gravel deposits crop out on the hillsides bordering the site and possibly extend beneath the site, although this has never been proved. These deposits are water-bearing; groundwater discharges from them along the southern edge of the low permeability deposits, which is coincident with the southern boundary of the site. This water flows across the site towards the stream, through the low permeability deposits as shallow groundwater flow, maintaining soil water levels which are close to ground surface for most of the year. It also flows across the site in shallow ditches, some of which have been dammed using small-scale plastic sheet-piling.

It is likely that groundwater discharge from the sand and gravels reduces significantly during the drier summer months of each year, although this has not been proved by observation or measurement.

Groundwater also discharges vertically upwards into the site, probably in a diffuse fashion that depends on the permeability and extent of the silt and clay. It is difficult to comment on the volumetric significance of these flows with any certainty.

The figure below shows soil water levels along a transect at 90 degrees to the stream for March and August 1991. During the spring, soil water levels were universally between 0.3 and 0.5 mbgl, along the transects. During the summer however, soil water levels fall by a larger amount close to the river; at distance (50 m and more) from the stream the soil water levels fell by 0.1 to 0.3 m, whereas in the dipwells closer to the stream (0 – 50 m) the levels fell by up to 1.1 m. This behaviour is assumed to be caused by lowered in-stream water levels resulting from the straightening, deepening and regular clearance of the channel.

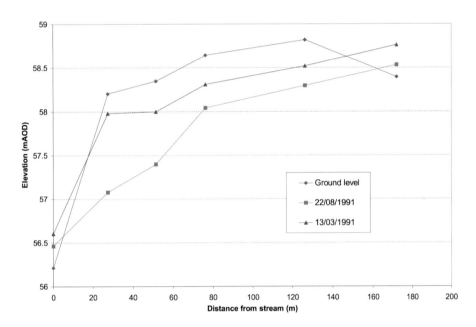

Soil water levels (March & August 1991) and ground surface transects

Since the soil water level regime has been established to be unfavourable for the fen habitats within the site, options for hydrological remediation have been explored during the development of a Water Level Management Plan for the site. The following options have been identified:

– **Do nothing**: current site management practices would be continued.

– **Complete restoration of the river channel**: the aim would be to restore the natural hydrological functioning of the site, with the assumption that higher channel water levels would support soil water levels during summer periods in the vicinity of the river channel, thus restoring a more favourable hydrological regime to the site.

– **Construct a parallel channel to maintain site soil water levels**: Gilman (1990) suggested diverting part of the riverflow from immediately below the road bridge in the centre of the site, into a shallow, higher level channel parallel to the main channel. The higher water levels maintained in this parallel channel would support soil water levels in adjacent areas during dry periods.

– **Level control structures in the Western Cleddau channel**: water levels within the main river channel would be raised by installation of level control structures with the raised water levels supporting soil water levels in the adjacent fen.

- **Level control structures within ditches running across the site**: some small-scale plastic sheet-pile dams have already been installed in some of the shallow ditches which channel water across the site. The success of these dams in raising soil water levels should be reviewed and, if and where appropriate, more dams should be added.

- **Grout curtain/impermeable membrane**: the basis of this option would be installation of an impermeable vertical curtain adjacent and parallel to the Western Cleddau. This curtain would reduce significantly subsurface discharge to the main channel, thus raising water levels within the fen to a point where they would overspill the impermeable curtain and flow into the main channel.

At the time of writing, further work was being carried out to confirm the technical viability, feasibility and cost of these potential solutions.

Acknowledgements:
Bob Haycock (CCW) initiated and carried out most of the hydrological and other monitoring at the site, assisted by others too numerous to mention. The Environment Agency (Wales) funded and installed 4 groundwater monitoring boreholes at the site.

Cleddon Bog SSSI is a valley-head mire approximately 15ha in extent, located around 9 km south of Monmouth, in south-east Wales. Lowland mire habitat forms the primary interest feature, and the surviving open mire habitat is now confined to approximately one-third of its original presumed area and comprises a range of bog and poor fen plant communities, mostly dominated by purple moor-grass *Molinia caerulea*.

Central area of Cleddon Bog, purple moor-grass dominated groundwater seepage slope in the foreground, running into topogenous mire in the middle-ground

There is a comprehensive body of evidence which shows that the condition of the mire feature at the site is deteriorating. Over the past few decades an expansion of purple moor-grass and scrub at the expense of key mire species was noted. A project was commissioned by CCW to identify the causes of the deteriorating condition, and to suggest actions for remediation.

A hydrological conceptual understanding of the site was developed through a desk study and a hydrological feature and hydrochemical survey of the site. A long-term (1972–2004) hard-copy water level record for six shallow dipwells within the site was digitised and analysed (see figure below).

The following influences on site wetness were identified and assessed in detail during the study:

Quantity of water entering the site. Detailed calculations, using historical rainfall and evapotranspiration records, were carried out to model the fate of rainfall within the catchment to Cleddon Bog, and thus to assess the hydrological impacts of changes in catchment vegetation cover. The calculations showed that if conifer plantation or broadleaf woodland was replaced by open heathland, hydrologically effective rainfall (surface water runoff and groundwater flows) would be increased by 77% or 55% respectively. The recent clear-felling of the Broad Meend hillside, which overlooks and supplies water to the most important area of open mire habitat within the site, was estimated to have increased its contribution of hydrologically effective rainfall by around 77%.

Diversion of surface water inputs to site by a long peripheral track

Distribution of water inputs. The site is bounded on all sides by either minor (metalled) roads or forestry tracks which have drainage gullies along their sides opposite to the site (i.e. the upslope side). It was decided that the drainage gully along the forestry track to the north of the western arm of the site was redirecting surface water runoff over an extensive reach to discharge at one point into the site, rather than diffusely along the boundary, and therefore that the western arm of the site was losing a significant amount of water input.

Hydraulic resistance and water retention of vegetation within the site. Open mire vegetation, such as bog mosses, will retain more water within the site than the purple moor-grass which has replaced them, firstly because its specific water retention is greater, and secondly because the resistance which it offers to lateral water flow within the site, en masse, is greater. It is therefore very likely that the change in vegetation within the site has resulted in a reduction in water storage, and therefore contributed to the reduction in site wetness.

Presence of historical drains. It is known that open channel drains and concrete pipe drains were installed in the site, but no evidence of their presence could be found during the site visits. It is considered possible that one or both of these drainage installations are still partially active in lowering water levels within the site.

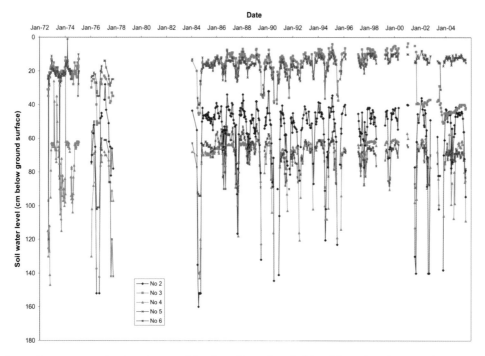

Long-term soil water level record for five dipwells, digitised from hard-copy charts

Based on the conceptual understanding of the site and the identified negative influences on its hydrological functioning, a series of measures for hydrological restoration were recommended, including: targeted remediation of the hydrological effects of trackside gullies, reduction in the dominance of purple moor-grass, to the benefit of open mire vegetation and further investigation of the existence and possible hydrological effects of historical drains.

Continued hydrological monitoring, to allow assessment of the hydrological effects of the clear-felling of the Broad Meend hillside and a targeted review of the hydrology and ecology of the site within three to five years, was also recommended.

Acknowledgements:
Liz Laurie and Peter Jones (CCW), Laura Bellis (WMC)

4. Understanding Fen Nutrients

Nutrient levels have a significant effect on fen vegetation, biodiversity and nature conservation value. Understanding how and why nutrient regimes are subject to change, and the problems which can arise as a result, is therefore critical to fen management.

This section explains the basic principles of nutrient enrichment in relation to fens and considers key factors which affect fen nutrient regimes. It also outlines methods of identifying and monitoring nutrient enrichment. Guidance on nutrient management is summarised in Section 8: Managing Fen Nutrient Enrichment.

Key terminology used in relation to nutrients – glossary:

Nutrients	The chemical building blocks of plants, the most significant of which are the macronutrients N (nitrogen), P (phosphorus) and K (potassium).
Nutrient status	The amount of nutrients found in the fen.
Nutrient enrichment	When there are more nutrients than might be considered desirable for particular fen habitats or features, also referred to as 'eutrophication'. This is often caused by an increase in nutrient input over a short period of time into the system. 'Cultural eutrophication' is the term used to describe enrichment caused by human land management activities, typically intensive agriculture.
Nutrient regime	Describes the way nutrients enter, are used within, and leave a fen. As water is the key carrier for nutrients entering or leaving fens, the nutrient regime is closely linked to the hydrological regime, and is influenced by catchment geology, shape and land use, all of which affect the chemistry of water entering the fen.
Nutrient availability	The amount of nutrients available to plants is governed by a range of microbial and redox (reduction-oxidation) mediated processes in the soil. This means that the 'plant-available' pool of nutrients may be different to (often much smaller than) the total pool in the soil, which will include organically-bound forms less immediately available for plant uptake.
Nutrient cycling	Fen plants take up nutrients during their life, which are then (partly) released when the plant, or part of it, dies. The resulting nutrients are re-cycled by the soil microflora and re-used or re-cycled by other plants.
Minerotrophic	Wetlands receiving mineral inputs from groundwater, and/or surface runoff and/or over-bank flooding, as well as rainfall.
Ombrotrophic	Wetlands fed mainly by rainwater inputs (literally, fed by cloud inputs).
Oligotrophic	Soils and fen waters which are infertile – i.e. with small pools of available macronutrients.
Mesotrophic	Moderate fertility status.
Eutrophic	High fertility status. Some fens can be naturally high in nutrients, but often this term suggests some artificial enrichment.

4.1   Key nutrients

Nitrogen (N), phosphorus (P) and potassium (K), collectively referred to as 'plant macronutrients', are the most significant agents of enrichment as they are the major plant nutrients that typically limit plant growth in a fen. Other chemical elements are also important, most notably oxygen (O), carbon (C), calcium (Ca) and a range of elements including those collectively termed micronutrients (e.g. magnesium, copper, iron, selenium).

4.1.1 Nitrogen

Nitrogen (N) is an important nutrient which can limit plant growth in many ecosystems. In peatlands, the majority of the soil's nitrogen occurs as organic N but this can be converted to ammonia and nitrate by micro-organisms via a process known as mineralisation. Dry and wet atmospheric deposition of nitrate (NO_3-) and ammonia (NH_3) add nitrogen to the soil. Ammonia can also be converted to nitrate via nitrification, a process that occurs mainly at neutral pH under aerobic conditions; both ammonia and nitrate are then available for uptake by micro-organisms and plants and excess amounts can move freely in solution. In addition, plants like alder are able to fix atmospheric nitrogen.

4.1.2 Phosphorus

Phosphorus (P) is another major plant nutrient. Bio-available phosphorus is largely in the soluble orthophosphate form, which can be taken up directly by plants.

In fens, dissolved phosphorus interacts with and becomes strongly bound to sediments, and therefore unavailable to plants. This phosphorus adsorption process, or chemical binding, can be modified by some situations, in particular when the redox potential falls to a very low level. In these conditions, chemically bound phosphorus can be released and become plant available, leading to a 'flush' of phosphorus into the fen by internal nutrient cycling, or released from the fen to adjacent habitats. In addition, some plants are able to use root surface enzymes (phosphatases) to release phosphate from organic stores.

Phosphorus availability is also strongly pH dependent. For example, under acidic conditions (below pH 6.5) iron and aluminium oxides will adsorb plant available orthophosphate, but the process is reversed when the acidity is reduced and pH rises above 6.5. This releases phosphorus, aluminium and iron back into the system and in some instances results in a potentially toxic 'flush' of aluminium and iron, some of which might be exported from the fen. Conversely, at pH values above 7, high calcium levels can result in the formation of insoluble calcium phosphates which increasingly immobilize phosphorus.

4.1.3 Other chemical ions that can influence nutrient status

Potassium is an important plant nutrient, but as it is generally available in soluble ionic form (K^+), it is rarely a limiting nutrient or a factor in enrichment.

Calcium (Ca^{2+}) is an important ion, because of its status as a nutrient, and also because of its ameliorating effect on the acidity of a wetland habitat via calcium carbonate and bicarbonate ions, which in turn affects the bioavailability of other nutrients. For example, at high concentrations, calcium can react with soluble orthophosphates to form insoluble calcium phosphates, thus helping remove bio-available phosphorus from the system. Calcium concentrations are largely determined by the local geology and groundwater inputs.

Magnesium (Mg^{2+}) and sodium (Na^+) have similar effects as calcium, such as ameliorating acidic conditions via their associated carbonate and bicarbonate ions, but they are less commonly observed in high concentrations in fen systems. Exceptions include fen systems close to the coast, where aerial precipitation of salts from the sea, and brackish influences on groundwater can increase sodium concentrations in fen systems. Fens that occur in areas of dolorite-rich geology (e.g. Magnesian Limestone that is found in parts of Nottinghamshire, South and West Yorkshire and County Durham) can have elevated magnesium concentrations.

Chloride (Cl^-) can be found in elevated concentrations in some fen habitats that are close to the sea, where concentrations of sodium are similarly increased. However, increased Cl^- can also indicate pollution inputs via ground or surface water. Aluminium (Al^{3+}) and iron (Fe) concentrations are also important in fen habitats, but this is due to their potential toxicity rather than their role as nutrients. Both aluminium and iron are soluble under acidic conditions and in base-poor fen systems these ions might therefore become bio-available in concentrations that limit productivity or are directly toxic to plants.

Key processes relating to nutrients

Mineralisation	Conversion of nutrients to inorganic and often plant-available forms – for example organic nitrogen to nitrate or organic phosphorus to phosphate, undertaken by microorganisms..
Ammonification	Conversion of organic nitrogen to ammonia by microorganisms.
Nitrification	Conversion of ammonia to nitrites and nitrate by microorganisms.
Denitrification	Conversion of nitrate to gaseous nitrogen by microorganisms.
Nitrogen fixation	Conversion of gaseous nitrogen to ammonia and then to organic nitrogen, requires specialist microorganisms often in a symbiotic relationship with plants (e.g. nitrogen-fixing bacteria and legumes).
Nitrate reduction	Conversion of nitrate to ammonium under highly anaerobic conditions.
Absorption	The process whereby atoms or molecules enter the bulk volume of a gas, liquid or solid.
Adsorption	The mechanism by which nutrients are chemically bound to soil particles. This can be an important mechanism of P immobilisation.

4.2 Sources of nutrient input

Figure 4.1 External sources of nutrients

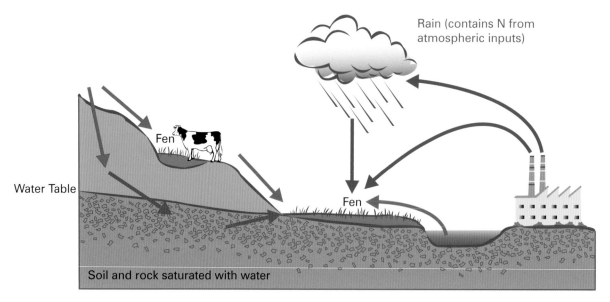

Groundwater (purple)

Surface water (red) = overland flow and flood water from lake or river.

Atmospheric (blue)

Sources of fen nutrient enrichment – key points

Groundwater inputs	Groundwater is an important source of nutrient enrichment in fens. It is linked to catchment land use and also affected by catchment geology. Nitrates (i.e. nitrogen in solution) entering a fen are a significant issue as N is one of the main nutrients which affects plant growth and therefore affects fen vegetation and habitat.
Surface water inputs	Surface water which might enter fens via streams or other surface flow often carries nitrates and/or phosphorus. Soil erosion often leads to surface water transportation of phosphorus-rich sediments into a fen.
Atmospheric inputs	Nitrous oxides and ammonia deposition are key pollutants of fens. Nitrous oxides are typically derived from fossil fuel burning (e.g. electricity generation, transport) while ammonia is associated with highly intensive agricultural systems (e.g. poultry farming, pig farming).
Point sources	Point sources of pollution or eutrophication are those where the nutrients can be traced back to a specific source, which might be a sewage works, a pollution incident, or discharge from a farm or industrial plant. Power stations and airports can be point-sources of air-borne nutrient pollutants.
Diffuse sources	Aerial and water borne nutrient enrichment attributable to more widespread or diffuse sources includes activities within the fen catchment (e.g. intensive agriculture) or further away (e.g. aerial pollution).
Internal nutrient enrichment	Nutrient cycling in fens typically involves relatively small amounts of plant-available inorganic nutrients, the availability of which are strongly affected by waterlogging. Changes to the fen habitat, especially drainage, can result in a peak of nutrients and also the conversion through oxidation of organically bound nutrients not normally available to most plants.
Nutrient limitation	When the availability of one plant nutrient prevents or limits the growth response of the vegetation to other nutrients, thus often keeping the effects of nutrient enrichment in check.

4.2.1 Groundwater and surface water

Ground and surface water are generally the most important carriers of nutrients to and from fens. Surface water can contain high levels of nitrate in solution, and phosphates, usually attached to silt particles. During high rainfall or floods, large quantities of soil particles containing adsorbed nutrients enter the fen, resulting in nutrient enrichment.

Land management practices on adjacent land and in the wider catchment can have a major impact on the nutrient status of a fen. Farming in the UK often imports more nutrients into the farming system as fertilisers and animal foodstuffs than are exported in the form of agricultural produce. Nitrogen not utilised for plant/crop growth remains in the soil and can leach out, resulting in an autumn or winter 'flush' of N into fens. Catchments affected by soil erosion can release substantial amounts of sediment-bound phosphorus that can enter a fen.

Cultivation and resultant exposure of soil in the immediate catchment of a poor fen basin mire on Anglesey, North West Wales. This practice can lead to sediment inwash and subsequent enrichment (P.Jones).

Depending on the nature of the soil and rock, the process of groundwater transmission can act as a filter mechanism to reduce nitrogen and phosphorus availability. Chalk and clay particles, for example, can bind ions such as nitrates or phosphates and therefore have a natural buffering effect which can protect wetland systems, whereas other rock types, such as sandstone, are much less effective in this respect.

Physical entrapment and retention of some nutrients (notably soil-bound P) from surface water flow is possible where the water flows through vegetated buffer strips, or where the P-laden sediment accumulates in lakes. Waterlogged conditions in fen soils can reduce nitrogen availability through denitrification.

4.2.2 Atmospheric inputs

Atmospheric inputs of nutrients can also be highly significant to fen ecosystems, particularly for very nutrient-poor systems, such as base-poor fens. The burning of fossil fuels (electricity generation and transport) is the main contributor to atmospheric nitrogen enrichment of fens, although intensive farming practices like poultry and pig farms can also emit aerial pollution.

Atmospheric emissions of nitrogen compounds have increased approximately five-fold over the last 50 years. Gases can enter fens either as dry deposition of nitrogen dioxide (NO^2) and ammonia (NH^3), usually close to the source of emission, or dissolved in rain or fog as ammonium (NH^{4+}) and nitrate (NO^{3-}) ions. The deposition of these compounds is also associated with acidification because other components of the nitrogenous bearing gases result in sulphuric acid. This acidification is a particular problem on soils that do not contain calcium or magnesium carbonate, which would otherwise neutralise the acids.

The term 'critical load' is used to identify the maximum deposition rate of nitrogen (or other air-borne pollutants) to a habitat, above which adverse effects are likely to occur. It is expressed as kilograms of nitrogen per hectare per year (kg N ha^{-1} yr^{-1}). Critical loads for fen ecosystems are shown below.

Critical loads for poor and rich fens, as defined by Bobbink et al. (2002)

Ecosystem Type	Critical Load kg N ha^{-1} yr^{-1}	Signs that critical load has been exceeded i.e. observable impact in the fen
Base-poor fens	5 – 10	Increased sedges and other vascular plants. Negative effects on peat mosses
Base-rich fens	15 – 35	Increased tall graminoids (grasses, sedges) Decreased species diversity

Fens demonstrate increased sensitivity to atmospheric nitrogen loading where:

- groundwater nutrient inputs are low;
- the system is N rather than P limited;
- there is no removal of N and P in biomass via management; and,
- the vegetation is oligotrophic.

Estimates of atmospheric nitrogen inputs (and other air-borne pollutants) to individual sites in the UK can be obtained from the Air Pollution Information System at www.apis.ac.uk, which provides modelled loads on a 5 km square basis in response to user-supplied NGR's. Where inputs approach or exceed the critical loads given, then atmospheric inputs of nitrogen represent a significant risk of enrichment to that habitat.

4.2.3 Point and diffuse sources of nutrients

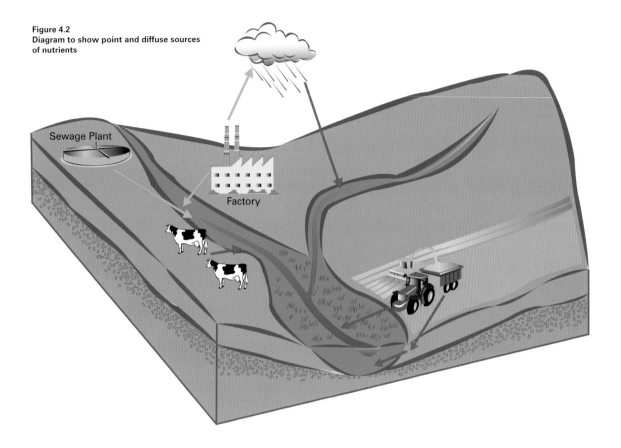

Figure 4.2
Diagram to show point and diffuse sources of nutrients

Sewage Plant

Factory

Source: Diffuse (purple), point source (orange)

Nutrient enrichment from water and aerial sources can be described as being from either a 'diffuse' or 'point' source. Point source enrichment is related to a single or focussed discharge e.g. the release of effluent from a sewage treatment plant (N and P), emissions from a motorway (NO_x) or intensive pig and poultry farming (NH_3).

Diffuse enrichment caused by land-based activities, both rural and urban, can be dispersed across a catchment. Agriculture is not the only cause but is the single biggest threat of diffuse enrichment to water and wetlands, contributing about 60% of nitrates, 25% of phosphorus and 70% of sediments entering water bodies (DEFRA, 2008).

Cors Bodeilio NNR,
Anglesey, a rich-fen
system surrounded
by relatively intensive
agriculture (P.Jones).

Point source nutrient enrichment has reduced over recent years, but there has been an increase in diffuse nutrient enrichment largely caused by agricultural intensification and the increased use of chemical fertilisers and animal manures. One result of this has been the steady increase in groundwater concentrations of nitrates where catchments have been in receipt of chemical fertilisers. In catchments where livestock farming is important, farmyard manure (FYM) is a common source of diffuse phosphorus enrichment (as soluble reactive phosphorus). Farm-yard effluent can also reach inflowing streams and seepages and result in acute localised enrichment.

Area of acute nutrient
enrichment on a north-
west Wales (Lleyn) fen
resulting from focussing
of farm-yard runoff
(P.Jones).

4.2.4 Sources within the fen – internal nutrient enrichment

Fens are generally considered to be relatively nutrient-poor habitats as the majority of nutrients are retained within the developing peat layers. However, changes in the fen environment can lead to release of nutrients from these stores, especially in the later successional phases of fen development when the drier conditions and lower soil water levels can result in the release of the nutrients which have accumulated within the soil.

The release of additional nutrients via processes within a fen is often termed 'internal nutrient enrichment'. Factors driving these changes might include increased nitrogen and phosphorus input from atmospheric inputs, and falling or fluctuating water levels due to drainage, abstraction or changes in precipitation.

4.3   Factors influencing the nutrient regime of fen habitats

The nutrient regime of a fen is affected by its relationship with the wider landscape. Influential factors include:

- **Geology** – bedrock and drift type fundamentally affects substrate and water nutrient content, and therefore affects the type of fen habitat that develops.

- **Geomorphology** – the topography will affect the rate and direction of water flow and thus to an extent its chemistry on entering a fen.

- **Catchment hydrology** – this will dictate the source of the water, its chemistry on entering the fen, along with the supply of nutrients via the volume and timing of water inputs. This includes both atmospheric (rain, fog and other precipitation) and terrestrial (ground, surface and sub-surface water) inputs.

– **Catchment land use** – modification of the catchment (e.g. through agricultural intensification) can change nutrient concentrations in soils and in sub-surface and surface water entering a fen. Atmospheric inputs can be altered by changes in land use that occur in nearby catchments or in the wider area, as airborne pollutants like ammonia are able to travel long distances before being deposited.

4.3.1 Limiting nutrients

Plant growth depends on availability of the required nutrients; low concentrations or limited availability of essential nutrients restrict plant growth. The utilisation of some nutrients may be limited by the availability of others. For example, low nitrogen concentrations would restrict utilisation of a relative surplus of phosphate, in which case nitrogen would be the limiting nutrient, but an increase in nitrogen without a change to the amount of phosphate could quickly result in enrichment.

Shortage of the nutrient that is 'limiting' is often the key to maintaining species-rich fen vegetation, as the growth of the more nutrient-responsive and often aggressive plants is kept in check. Any extra input of the limiting nutrient can release this 'brake' on plant growth and enable plants to exploit more of the available nutrients, resulting in increased growth of some plants and the loss of others less able to respond to the new source of nutrient. Fens can therefore be very vulnerable to even relatively small increases in concentration of the limiting nutrient.

Studies carried out on poor fens indicate these habitats are strongly nitrogen-limited and therefore at risk of enrichment from even marginal increases in nitrogen. Experiments in northern Sweden have shown considerable accumulation of nitrogen being associated with increasing sedge cover. In a study comparing rich-fen nutrient cycling in areas with very low and high nitrogen deposition, nitrogen mineralisation was shown to be much higher in fens receiving high nitrogen inputs, despite the fact that these fens were managed by mowing (Nohara et al., 2002).

Phosphorus limitation is particularly typical of late succession habitats. In addition, where nitrogen inputs are high, and especially where there is regular biomass removal, phosphorus will usually become the limiting nutrient over time.

In a nutrient limited system, excess of the non-limiting nutrient may not result in any signs of enrichment in the vegetation, as the plants are unable to make use of one nutrient without sufficient amounts of the other. This does not mean the site is not enriched, but that enrichment is not manifested in changes in the vegetation. It is likely to be detectable in soil/peat and water samples.

Localised processes can have a very important bearing on the nature and significance of nutrient limitation, and the role of calcium and iron in 'locking-up' P in certain situations has already been mentioned.

Despite the concept and nature of nutrient limitation, most researchers and practitioners agree that high nitrogen inputs to a phosphorus limited system would still be highly undesirable, not least because nutrient limitation varies between species, and only very small increases in the availability of a key limiting nutrient may be needed to result in a significant effect. Nitrogen enrichment even where not accompanied by phosphorus could also be a contributory factor in the loss of dissolved organic carbon (DOC) loss from fens.

4.4   Classifying water chemistry using solute and oxygen concentrations

In chemical terms, a 'base' is a substance whose molecule or ion can combine with a proton. A greater concentration of base ions is associated with increasing alkalinity. The most common bases are calcium (Ca^{2+}) and magnesium (Mg^{2+}) ions. Conversely, lower concentrations of base ions are associated with increasing acidity.

4.4.1 The acidity of solutions (pH)

The measurement of pH is a commonly used method of assessing acidity and alkalinity. A solution with a pH value of greater than 7.0 is considered alkaline, and less than 7.0 acidic. A solution at pH 7.0 is considered neutral, i.e. neither alkaline nor acidic. In practice, pH values of around 5.5. can be regarded as dividing acid fens from more base-rich fens. Rainwater contains very few bases and is slightly acidic, as it tends to absorb a small amount of carbon dioxide (CO_2) from the atmosphere, resulting in weak carbonic acid (H_2CO_3). Groundwater tends to be more alkaline, particularly when it has come into contact with calcareous rocks such as limestone from which it has picked up base ions such as Ca^{2+} and Mg^{2+} and their associated bicarbonate ions (HCO_3^-).

4.4.2 The electrical conductivity of solutions

Fen water and soil chemistry can be described in terms of electrical conductivity (EC), which estimates the concentration of dissolved chemical ions. It is measured using a probe that passes an electric current between two detectors, and is expressed as Siemens/m (S m-1). For example, the EC of drinking water is 0.005 S/m, compared to seawater that is about 5.0 S/m. Conductivity provides a useful guide to base enrichment but not macronutrient concentrations.

4.4.3 The reduction – oxidation ('redox') potential

Redox potential can provide an estimate of whether soils are aerobic or anaerobic. Aerobic soils have redox potentials of about 0.6V and anaerobic soils have redox potentials between 0.4 and -0.2V. Redox potential measurements are made using redox electrodes (usually made of platinum) and are measured in volts (V), millivolts (mV) or Eh (where 1 Eh = 1mV).

4.4.4 Ion exchange

Ion exchange is the chemical process by which mineral ions are either lost to soil solution (i.e. are available for uptake) or held on the surfaces of the soil particles (i.e. are unavailable for uptake). Peat soils generally have a greater ion exchange capacity because of their high organic content.

Water chemistry – key terms

Base-poor	Having few base ions (Ca, Mg) and generally more acidic (pH <5.5). Water source typically dominated by rainfall, either directly and/or from rainfall runoff; nutrient status typically oligotrophic
Base-rich	Having more base ions (Ca, Mg) and generally more alkaline (pH >5.5). Water source typically minerotrophic and nutrient status typically ogliotrophic or mesotrophic.
Electrical conductivity (EC)	A measure of the total concentration of chemical ions in solution, easily measured by a meter in Siemens/m ($S\ m^{-1}$) or micro-Siemens/cm ($\mu S\ cm^{-1}$). Higher values indicate higher concentrations of ions.
Redox potential	The potential for a reduction-oxidation chemical reaction occurring, gives an indication as to whether the environment is oxygenating or reducing. Measured in volts (V), millivolts (mV) or Eh (where 1 Eh = 1mV) by an electrode. More positive values indicate oxygenating environments, negative values indicate reducing environments.
Ion exchange	Process by which chemical ions move between the soil/plant surface and solution. This process leads to the acidification of bogs and fens by the release of hydrogen ions (H^+) from the peat.
pH	Measure of the acidity of a solution.

4.5 Assessing fen nutrient regimes

An assessment of a fen's nutrient regime would evaluate:

- the nutrient inputs and outputs;
- the total concentration of different nutrients within the system;
- the availability of these nutrients for biological uptake;
- the cycling of these nutrients within the fen system.

Assessing all of these aspects is costly and in a conservation context generally unrealistic. A small number of indirect measures of nutrients can usually supply enough information for effective management decisions and/or to decide whether further investigation is required. However, in order to understand how to interpret these measures and how this can guide fen management, it is important to understand what factors influence nutrient status in fen habitats, and the range of nutrient regimes that might be considered 'typical' across the UK.

Identifying the symptoms and cause(s) of enrichment is both difficult and expensive, but useful information can be gleaned using simple walk-over surveys, especially where coupled with relevant survey or monitoring information. In all cases, managers should start with the following stage 1 assessment. More detailed guidance on measuring and monitoring nutrient enrichment is provided in **Section 10: Monitoring to Inform Fen Management**.

4.6   Identifying nutrient enrichment – initial (stage 1) assessment

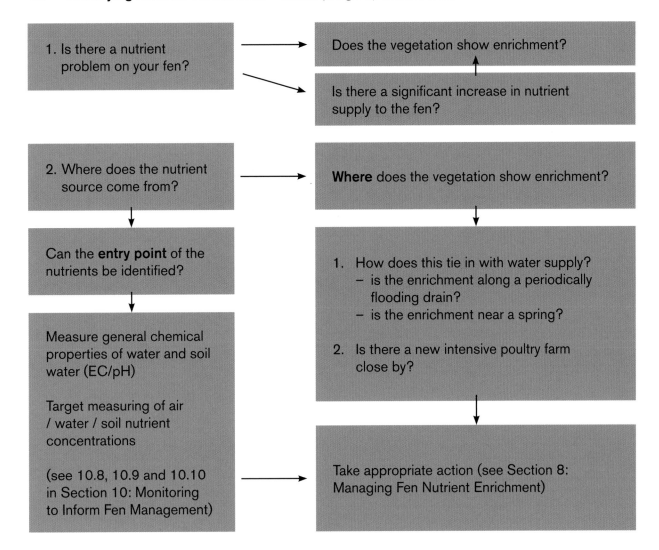

4.6.1 Deciding if your fen is at risk of nutrient enrichment

Although the varied character of fens complicates and in some cases precludes definition of generic nutrient regimes, good habitat quality is usually associated with low fertility substrata and key water inputs. This means that many fens within the UK are at some risk of enrichment due to eutrophication – including from atmospheric nitrogen deposition. In many cases this risk is significant, particularly for fens in intensively farmed landscapes, such as basin fens, or sites close to sources of enrichment such as busy roads, airports or power stations. The exceptions (i.e. fens at lesser risk of nutrient enrichment) are upland springs and flushes that are dependent on rainfall and/or fed by less enriched groundwater sources. However, even these remote fens are likely to be affected by nitrogen inputs via rainfall which may carry nutrients taken up some distance from where the rain actually falls.

Deciding if your fen is at risk of nutrient enrichment

-   Identify in broad terms the target nutrient regime for the fen.

-   Identify if the fen is moving toward a more nutrient enriched status (i.e. it is being degraded by nutrient enrichment and needs additional restoration and/or protection measures) or if the habitat is satisfactory and is being maintained by the existing management regime. Such an assessment has to be done at the individual site level but, for the purposes of an initial assessment, can be undertaken at a fairly broad scale across the site.

The Common Standards Monitoring (CSM) Guidance for Lowland Wetland Habitats (JNCC, 2004) is a useful aid to broad scale assessment of fens. The guidance provides descriptions of the different hydrological and topographical situations associated with different fen types, allowing the main fen type(s) on a site to be identified. Knowing the main fen type and the key hydrological inputs of a site along with some general information on catchment land use allows an evaluation as to whether a fen feature is likely to be associated with high or low nutrient regimes and therefore whether it may be at risk of enrichment.

Summary of the broad fen types and their likely risk of enrichment

Fen type	Susceptibility/ Risk of enrichment	Key sources of enrichment	Additional comments
Floodplain fen	Medium / High	Floodwaters and groundwater especially in intensively farmed landscapes.	May have naturally eutrophic vegetation types due to regular sediment inputs into system from river flooding.
Basin fen	High / High	Groundwater and run-off especially in intensively farmed landscapes.	Small size and situation in the landscape makes them particularly vulnerable.
Open water transition fen	Medium / Medium	Vulnerable to enrichment if associated lake/open water also enriched.	Often associated with naturally eutrophic vegetation (swamps and tall herb fen).
Valley fen	High / Medium	Groundwater and run-off, especially in intensively farmed landscapes.	Can have elements of naturally eutrophic habitat types, such as fen woodland.
Springs, flushes	High / Medium	Variable depending on situation in the landscape.	Often found within another fen/bog type.
Fen woodland	Low / Medium	Usually tolerant to higher nutrients therefore less at risk of enrichment.	Increasing woody cover might suggest the fen is drying out and undergoing internal enrichment.
Fen meadow	High / Medium	Close proximity to improved fields places fen meadow at risk to enrichment. Management can reduce build up of nutrients.	Maintain management to remove nutrients.

4.6.2 What can the vegetation tell you about nutrient enrichment?

Once the broad fen type, in terms of its hydrological and topographical status, is identified then the variation in vegetation on that fen can offer further clues to nutrient status. Plant species have different nutrient requirements and the presence of particular plants or group of plants can indicate nutrient enrichment might be occurring, especially if they are nutrient- demanding species. Such plants are often termed 'negative indicators. Clues as to the origin of enrichment are indicated by gradients in height/vigour of some of these indicators.

Negative indicator species for different fen community types (adapted from JNCC, 2004)

Species	Fen community (NVC) in which species can be considered a likely indicator of enrichment
Common reed (Phragmites australis)	M4, M5, M6, M9, M10, M13, M14, M21, M22, M25, M29, S9, S10, S19, S20, S12
Reed canary-grass (Phalaris arundinacea)	M4, M5, M6, M9, M14, M21, M22, M25, M29, S9, S10, S19, S20, S12, S27
Reed sweet-grass (Glyceria maxima)	M4, M5, M6, M9, M14, M21, M22, M25, S9, S10, S19, S20, S12, S27
Bulrush/reedmace (Typha latifolia)	M4, M5, M6, M29, S9, S10, S19, S20
Great willowherb (Epilobium hirsutum)	M4, M5, M6, M9, M14, M21, M22, M25, S27
Common nettle (Urtica dioica)	M4, M5, M6, M9, M14, M21, M22, M25, M29, S4, S24, S25, S27
Rushes (Juncus species)	M4, M5
Flote-grass (Glyceria spp.)	Any of the core oligo/meso-trophic fen communities.
Algal mats/blooms or duckweed cover	All community types where standing open water occurs

Note: Algal mats are filamentous algae on the water surface, algal blooms are planktonic algae within the water column

Nutrient inputs at Whitecross Fen (Scotland) are visible in the vegetation as zones along the farmland (in red) and directly under the factory outflow (blue arrow).

Detailed information on the nutrient (and water) requirements for different plant species or vegetation communities can also be useful in understanding a fen's nutrient regime and enrichment status. The box below summarises some of the key references in this respect. Using such information requires a more detailed vegetation survey of the site, as the information requires the correct identification of community types and/or plant species.

Sources of information on plant nutrient requirements

Plant Species Ecological Flora of the British Isles	A web site prepared by the University of York, providing summary information about ecological attributes of British plant species, including nutrient requirements. Includes information from the Biological Flora of the British Isles published papers and 'PlantAtt' information from CEH, plus links to the NBN Gateway for species distribution maps. See www.ecoflora.co.uk.
C-S-R classification	A classification system where a plant species is assigned a dominant functional type, from three main types: competitor (C), stress-tolerator (S) or ruderal (R). The three types broadly relate to the plant's nutrient requirements. Grime, J.P., Hodgson, J.G. & Hunt, R. 2007. Comparative Plant Ecology: A Functional Approach to Common British Species. 2nd ed. Dalbeattie: Castle Point Press/BSBI.
Water quality and wildlife	Report presenting a summary of published data on the range of water quality parameters that species/groups of species can tolerate, including animals and plants. Covers water quality indicators such as BOD and heavy metals along with values for nutrients and pH. Jeffries, M. 1988. Water Quality and Wildlife. A Review of Published Data. Unpublished report to the Nature Conservancy Council, Contract HF 3 03 370.
Plant Communities	
NVC	Each fen community type has a habitat description summarising general information about typical nutrient status and hydrological range. Rodwell, J.S. 1995. British Plant Communities. Volume 2 Mires and Heaths and Volume 4. Aquatic Communities, Swamps and Tall Herb Fens. Cambridge: Cambridge University Press.
Ecohydrological Guidelines for Lowland Wetland Plant Communities	Report presenting the hydrological and nutrient regimes of selected fen and bog community types (M4, M5, M9, M10,M13, M14, M18, M21, M22, M24, M29, S1, S2, S24 and S27). Wheeler et al. 2004 – see also 2010 update.

Periodic assessments of vegetation through monitoring relocatable plots and/ or by assessing changes in the abundance of key nutrient-responsive species can provide information on how plant communities are responding to enrichment. Further guidance on vegetation monitoring is given in **Section 10: Monitoring to Inform Fen Management**.

Some responses can be quite subtle and require an understanding of the differences in plant species within fen communities, and their water and nutrient requirements, rather than more easily observable changes such as the invasion or expansion of negative indicator species. For example, increased nitrogen availability can lead to an increase in the dominance of tall herbs and grass-like species and the loss of smaller and more characteristic plants, such as Sphagnum species and the brown moss assemblages of rich-fens. This might only be detected by detailed quadrat data collection that enables increased cover of herbs, grasses and/or sedges to be identified. A general 'eye-balling' of the fen habitat would not be likely to detect these changes, as many fen habitat types are dominated by a range of herbs, grasses and sedges.

Assigning the nutrient value of Ellenberg's indicator values for British Plants (which provide a measure of the ecological optimum for various environmental variables for individual plant species) to plant species survey data can give an indication of whether the site or stands of vegetation within it are enriched. A summary of how this technique can be applied is provided by Environment Agency (2009).

Many of the floristic changes which are most likely to be associated with enrichment can also result from other factors, particularly grazing at lower stocking levels or for shorter periods than would be required to maintain the vegetation without significant change in structure or species composition. Disentangling such effects can be extremely difficult but important clues can be provided by observing where change is occurring, particularly with respect to locations adjacent to key water inputs or boundaries with intensively managed farmland.

4.6.3
What can the soil, water and catchment land use tell you about nutrient enrichment?

Detailed soil and water chemical testing can be very useful for more in-depth monitoring of a fen's nutrient status; use of phytometric techniques (where the fertility of the soil is bio-assayed by measuring the growth of a test species, generally either great hairy willowherb (*Epilobium hirsutum*) or reed canary-grass (*Phalaris arundinacea*) should be considered in preference to soil testing in wet fen soils – see Wheeler et al, (1992). However, very basic but nonetheless valuable assessments can be made from observation which can provide a basis from which to develop more detailed monitoring programmes (see **Section 10: Monitoring to Inform Fen Management**).

Peat soils that dry out on a regular basis undergo a greater degree of mineralisation, which releases stored nutrients into the fen system. Even if the drying affects only part of a site, the signs of enrichment may be seen across the entire site as nutrients are 'flushed' across the fen as it rewets. A constant wetting and drying cycle is considered highly detrimental as it continually releases and flushes nutrients into the fen. In addition, peat that has a 'gritty' feel has mineral soil sediments washed onto it and these sediments may hold phosphorus stores that could be released into the system. Soil erosion may also be noticeable in the catchment and is a likely sediment and nutrient source.

The water source is likely to be the most important factor to consider in an initial assessment of nutrient enrichment on a site.

- Groundwater, sub-surface and surface flow from an intensively farmed catchment is more likely to be enriched with inorganic nitrogen.

- Fens that fall within Nitrate Vulnerable Zones are at risk of enrichment from high nitrate concentrations.

- Fens in the vicinity of aerial pollution sources such as major roads, airports and intensive animal and poultry rearing units, or fed by water from enriched rivers/lakes/canals, are also at risk of enrichment.

- Look out for obvious sources of nutrient inputs such as field drains entering a fen or regular fertiliser application or waste spreading on adjacent fields, particularly where this does not comply with good practice guidelines or statutory requirements.

Simple pH and EC monitoring of water (including inputs such as streams, water within the fen and water outputs) with relatively inexpensive field meters can provide some insight into the fen's chemistry and nutrient status. Redox can provide an indication of whether soils are chemically reducing, and thus broadly suitable for a wide range of obligate wetland plants.

An initial assessment of nutrient status – key questions

The greater number of 'yes' answers to the following questions indicates an increasing likelihood of nutrient enrichment occurring on a fen:

Vegetation	Are there any 'competitive' plants present on the site, which are not typically associated with that habitat, or not usually abundant? Are any nutrient-demanding fen species like reed or reedmace expanding over the fen? Are there any obvious variations in vegetation height and/or stem density proximal to potential enrichment sources? Are any algal mats/blooms present? Is woodland/scrub increasing on the site? Does the distribution of vegetation with an enriched appearance point to likely sources of nutrient e.g. marginal field drains, rural soakaways etc.
Air, water and soils	Is the fen close to a source of potential aerial nutrient pollution such as a busy road, airport, intensive poultry or pig rearing? Is the site bordered directly by improved grassland or arable cultivation? Is the fen likely to be receiving nutrient-rich water from nearby intensive agriculture, farmyards or polluted waterbodies? Is there evidence of catchment soil erosion with sediments entering the fen? Is the peat substrate regularly drying out or are water levels strongly fluctuating? Does reference to the Air Pollution Information Service (www.apis.ac.uk) indicate likely Critical Load Exceedance for atmospheric N deposition?
EC and pH of water	Are there any 'hot spots' of relatively high EC that might indicate high amounts of solutes entering a fen? Is there any evidence of very high pH (alkaline) water that might protect the fen from high phosphorus levels?

4.7   References

Bobbink, R., Ashmore, M., Braun, S., Fluckiger, W. & Van den Wyngaert, I.J.J. 2002. Empirical nitrogen critical loads for natural and semi-natural ecosystems: 2002 update. *In: Proceedings of the Expert Workshop on Empirical Critical Loads for Nitrogen on (semi-natural Ecosystems – Berne Switzerland, November 2002).* Unpublished report prepared by UNECE Convention on Long-range Transboundary Air Pollution.

DEFRA. 2008. Catchment Sensitive Farming. Information on the On-going Review of the Catchment Sensitive Farming Programme. Unpublished report by Defra.

EA (2009). Guidance on Monitoring and Investigation at Groundwater Dependent Terrestrial Ecosystems (GWDTE). EA Technical Note.

JNCC. 2004. Common Standards Monitoring Guidance for Lowland Wetland Habitats. Version August 2004. Peterborough: JNCC.

Nohara, S., Verhoeven J.T.A. & Whigham D.F. 2002. *Nitrogen and Phosphorus Cycling in Peatlands in Japan.* Unpublished abstract from the SWS Conference: Wetland Restoration Addressing Asian Issues through International Collaboration. Wheeler, B.D., Shaw, SC & Cook RED (1992). Phytometric assessment of the fertility of undrained rich-fen soils. *Journal of Applied Ecology*, 29, 466-475.

This 12 ha wetland site near Wigton in north Cumbria (grid reference NY258537) has some attributes of basin mire but also has an axial stream and is best classified as a floodplain fen. It lies within a shallow river valley on a bed of drift. Boulder clay, alluvium and sand & gravel act as aquitards and aquifers respectively, so that in the past, soligenous fen has developed on groundwater seepages along the edge, topogenous fen has developed on the floodplain of the beck and small areas composed of ombrotrophic peat have developed over a deep basin and where the fen has been isolated from the main water flow. Records from the 1950s show that the groundwater-fed fen supported species associated with base-rich conditions such as the moss *Scorpidium scorpioides*, and with the ombrotrophic mires, these were the main interests of the site.

In more recent times, the groundwater-fed fen vegetation has been lost. The floodplain fen has taken over in all but the ombrotrophic areas, which are thought to float and remain just a little higher than the flood waters. The beck catchment is now largely arable; it carries discharge from a sewage works and much silt. The consequence from flooding several times a year has been a build-up of nutrient-enriched silt and the spread of enriched surface water over most of the site. This is thought to be responsible for the massive expansion of S28 *Phalaris arundinacea* tall herb fen.

The fact that change has occurred is supported by the stratigraphic studies of Wheeler and Wells (1989). In their description of one of the bores taken on the western edge "The uppermost horizons were largely obscured by a thick alluvial deposit (and associated *Phalaris* rhizomes) but immediately below this (40 cm depth) the peat contained rather little wood and was apparently deposited in rather wet circumstances with rafts of *Scorpidium* and some rather more base-tolerant *Sphagna*. This may indicate a 'flooding' horizon upon more solid, woody peat."

Biglands Bog illustrates how vulnerable some types of fen can be to land-use changes and that any prospect of reversal involves fundamental changes in catchment and surface water management.

M4	*Carex rostrata-Sphagnum recurvum* mire
M9	*Carex rostrata-Calliergon cuspidatum/ giganteum* mire
M18	*Erica tetralix-Sphagnum papillosum* raised & blanket mire
M27a	M27 *Filipendula ulmaria-Angelica sylvestris* mire, *Valeriana officianalis-Rumex acetosa* sub-community
M27b	M27 *Filipendula ulmaria-Angelica sylvestris* mire, *Urtica dioica-Vicia cracca* sub-community
S27a	*Carex rostrata-Potentilla palustris* tall fen, *Carex rostrata-Equisetum fluviatile* sub-community
S28	*Phalaris arundinacea* tall-herb fen
W3	*Salix pentandra-Carex rostrata* woodland.
W4	*Betula pubescens-Molinia caerulea* woodland

5. Site Assessment for Fen Management and Restoration

The Introduction to this handbook (Section 1) set the scene for fen management and restoration in describing the significant loss of fen habitat since the 18th century, through drainage and subsequent intensive management for agriculture and latterly abandonment. Conserving and restoring the fens which are left is therefore all the more critical, but as a result of changes in the cultural and economic landscape, today's fen manager has many issues to grapple with.

This section explains why fens need management, offers some guidance on setting objectives and a step-by-step guide to site assessment, and then provides a framework for deciding what kind of fen, or what stage in succession, management should aim for. More detailed guidance on the practicalities of management is provided in Section 6: Fen Vegetation Management, Section 7: Fen Water Management, and Section 8: Managing Fen Nutrient Enrichment.

Fen management for mosses and liverworts, and for specific types of insect, bird, reptile or mammal, are fascinating but specialist subjects. Detailed requirements of these types of flora and fauna, and guidance on how best to manage fens in their favour, is included in Appendix VI Fen Management for Bryophytes, Appendix VII Fen Management for Vertebrates, and Appendix VIII Fen Management for Invertebrates.

5.1   Why do fens need management?

In ecological terms, 'fen' is not a stablised 'climax' condition, but a transitional habitat or seral stage in which pioneer plant communities are replaced by successive colonists as part of the natural process of succession from open water to mature woodland or ombrotrophic bog or dry land. This process of succession results from interactions between both different species and between species and their environment, and is highly variable both in terms of sequence and the time, in some cases taking thousands of years. A more detailed explanation is included in Conserving Bogs – The Management Handbook (Brooks and Stoneman, 1997).

Favourable condition of fens in nature conservation terms was once a consequence of economic management. Cutting fens for hay and aftermath grazing, for example, prevented the sward becoming dominated by a few vigorous plants, such as reed, reed canary grass, reed sweet grass and bulrush and was responsible for producing and maintaining many traditional fenland landscapes.

As a result of the reduction in traditional management such as reed-cutting and the production of bog hay, many fens have been abandoned. Without active management, most fens are quickly colonised by scrub and trees, a process that is accelerated by nutrient enrichment and drainage around or within the site. The fen carr or woodland that develops has wildlife interest but cannot support many of the species of open fen.

In a completely natural system, rivers meandering across their floodplains and flooding continually re-create fen habitats. This natural dynamism also enables fluctuation of fen vegetation communities between sites without overall species loss. Human activity in the form of agricultural improvement, river engineering and urbanisation has, over the centuries, fossilised many of our rivers and wetlands, particularly in lowland Britain. Many of our lowland fens are now moving towards the end-points of natural wetland succession, often hastened by land drainage, siltation and nutrient enrichment. Maintaining the conservation interest of many wetlands depends on deliberate management to interrupt the process of succession or revert the fen to earlier successional stages which support increasingly uncommon plants and animals such as fen violet, fen orchid and swallowtail butterfly.

Management and restoration of fens for conservation usually aims to maintain the species composition of a fen community at a specified stage along the natural transitional process from open water to mature woodland or bog, which can only be achieved by intervention, in the form of management. Management aims should include the maintenance of the habitat mosaic for birds and invertebrates, as well as for the plant communities. The following section describes all the factors to be considered when drawing up objectives for fen management.

Lens of ombrotrophic peat development within the transition mire

Kebble Fen

Kebble Fen on Rathlin Island just off the north coast of Northern Ireland is a transitional basin fen. The coloured lines show how part of the fen vegetation has risen above the level of ground water influence where specialised bog plant species are colonising the ombrotrophic peats that are fed by rain water alone. (B. Hamill)

An example of the consequences of unmanaged fen succession

Aughnadarragh Lough in County Down, Northern Ireland, has been designated as an ASSI for its fen vegetation communities and its marsh fritillary butterfly population. The diagram below shows the degree of successional change from 1953 to 1996. Even in this relatively short period of time, the area of open water has significantly decreased, the fen communities around the open water have changed in extent and distribution and the amount of scrub within the ASSI boundary has increased from 32% to 47%. If left unmanaged, the entire area will eventually become wet woodland and the important fen communities that support the rare marsh fritillary butterfly will be lost.

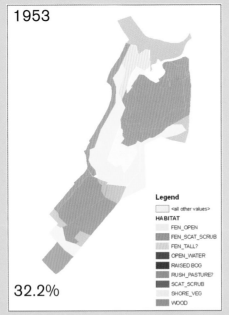

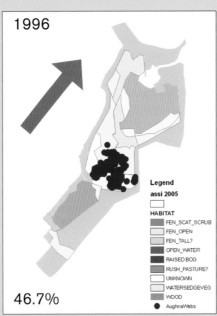

Diagrammatic maps of habitat change at Aughnadarragh Lough, Co. Down

5.2   Checklist of key stages in deciding on appropriate management for a fen

Stage	What you need to do
Look at the broader context	Information gathering/research into: Cultural history Past management Changes in extent of fen Wider catchment – land use, drainage, pollution, soils and geology. Proximity to other fens/wetlands - is the fen part of a series of wetland sites? for example Norfolk Valley Fens, Midlands Meres and Mosses
Site survey to establish what is there now	Species and habitat survey and mapping Soil and geological survey
Hydrological assessment	See Section 3: Understanding Fen Hydrology Work out sources of water inflow and outflow. Identify variations in water quality and quantity – seasonally and across the site, over life of fen – and causes.
Nutrient assessment	See Section 4: Understanding Fen Nutrients Assess the nutrient status of the fen
Identifying past and future changes	Identify past changes in flora and fauna Identify past changes in hydrological regime and nutrient status Identify factors influencing species, habitat, hydrology, nutrient regime Assess how these factors might influence flora, fauna, hydrology and nutrients in future
Identify restraints on management	Identify any restraints imposed by or associated with: Designations (site, local, regional) Archaeological evidence which may be buried in the fen Services (power, telecommunications) Public access/rights of way Land ownership or tenancy agreement
Decide what you are trying to achieve	Establish objectives (maintain or encourage key species? maintain status quo? more open water? control scrub invasion? raise water table?) Identify target habitat(s) and species Identify target hydrological regime
Compare existing and target regimes and identify issues/ problems	Establish how target species/habitat(s) differ from the current species/habitats present Establish how target hydrological/management regimes differ from current regimes Loss of or change in species/habitat Changes in hydrology or nutrient status Causes of changes in species/habitat/hydrology/nutrient status
Identify necessary changes	Establish what you need to do to achieve target regime/habitat or address problems
Identify suitable techniques to achieve changes	Consider appropriate vegetation, water and nutrient management techniques – see Section 6: Fen Vegetation Management, Section 7: Fen Water Management and Section 8: Managing Fen Nutrient Enrichment, Appendix VI Management for Bryophytes and Appendix VII Management for Vertebrates and Invertebrates Research/draw on experience elsewhere (see case studies included within this handbook)
Evaluate suitability of techniques	Consider how restraints identified above may limit choice of management options Assess what control you have over factors influencing changes, problems or issues Assess the costs of proposed management Assess whether the required management is realistically achievable Assess whether fen restoration is practical and sustainable

Develop and implement action strategy to achieve objectives	Identify funding sources (see Section 12: Fens from an Economic Perspective)
Monitor outcomes	See Section 10: Monitoring to Inform Fen Management
Review and revise strategy	Assess whether management is achieving desired objectives If so, maintain current management, if not, restart the process by revisiting the hydrological assessment

5.3   Looking at the broader context

5.3.1 Historical context

Many fens in lowland UK are likely to be a small part of a wetland which was previously more extensive and had some economic use e.g. turf cutting, reed cutting or hay crop. Much speculation and uncertainty about the reasons for present-day conditions could be by-passed by asking the right people the right questions. Was wet woodland once managed as an osier bed, or the tall single species dominated fen once used for a hay crop and grazing? Agricultural records are often a good source of relevant historical information.

One of the less species-rich parts of Cors Erddreiniog on Ynys Môn (Anglesey) was allegedly used to grow carrots during the Second World War, and this may well be the reason for its unfavourable condition and the current difficulty in restoring its rich fen potential.

- Research the historical and wider context of the fen.

- Ask local people about past history of the site.

- Look in the local library or museum for books or other documents which may record past management history.

- Check citations accompanying listings or designations to see if they can reveal more about past vegetation history. Stratigraphy may also provide valuable information.

5.3.2 Consider the site in the context of the wider catchment

All fens are inextricably linked to the surrounding catchment, which affects both quantity and quality of water and nutrients, the flora and fauna which a fen can support and the form it takes in the landscape. The links are not always immediately obvious: wetlands that appear isolated on the ground may be linked permanently or intermittently with other wetlands via underground regional aquifers. Considering the land use, type and intensity of management (both past and present) of adjacent land, and the wider catchment, is therefore critical to developing a proper understanding of fen hydrology, nutrient status, and effective fen management.

Fen conservation requires an understanding of underlying physical processes such as geomorphological, geological and hydrological, as well as biological processes. Connectivity between these processes within the landscape is important, particularly with regard to water supply and nutrient levels.

5.3.3 Scale

Although fens are linked hydrologically with the surrounding landscape, from a wildlife perspective many of the critical links between wetlands which are so crucial to the viability of individual species and population dynamics have been lost through isolation and fragmentation of individual fens. Future management must take into account other wetlands in the area, which may provide a refuge of species which could be reintroduced or encouraged to colonise the fen or form the basis for development of a linked habitat chain.

Fens are often found in association with other semi-natural habitat types, which may in turn contribute to their ecological function or conservation. Fen conservation also therefore needs to be considered in the context of broader conservation programmes, existing and proposed, which embrace other semi-natural habitats as well as fens. Equally, where other habitats or species are the primary objective for management, opportunities for fen conservation may also be possible and desirable. Integrated management of aquatic and terrestrial habitats helps maintain and re-establish the ecological and hydrological links between them. Working at a landscape scale provides an opportunity to enable dynamic plant communities to develop as part of a more natural mosaic.

Management of fens at a landscape scale, rather than individual site level, can help optimise resource use and make all the difference in the viability and sustainability of management. For example, while it may be difficult to find a suitable grazier for a single small fen, grazing a number of sites in the same area on rotation may be more cost effective than cutting.

The scale of projects will vary in different parts of the country. Projects such as the Great Fen Project and Wicken Fen are both exciting large-scale projects within intensively farmed landscapes. A major issue is going to be managing the landscape between the fens so that it is also favourable for wildlife. In the UK, removing large areas of land from intensive agricultural production to manage for nature conservation has rarely been an option. The conservation of fens at wider landscape level therefore presents a real challenge, not only in terms of habitat restoration and re-creation but also finding ways to encourage more sympathetic management of land outside protected areas. The involvement of key partners, stakeholders, and often neighbours, is critical to the success of any project.

The Lough Beg project In Northern Ireland is a good example of a large scale project. The RSPB Futurescapes programme, in partnership with NIEA and Department of Agriculture & Rural Development in Northern Ireland (DARD) is restoring wetland habitats at a landscape scale within the Lough Neagh and Lough Erne Basins.

Biffaward – This awards grants (donated by Biffa Waste Services) to community and environmental projects across the UK – enabled RSPB to employ a Restoration Officer for 12 months to write a 5 year management plan for Lough Beg. The implementation of the management plan will secure the restoration of 500ha of wetland habitat. Lough Beg, which lies just north of Lough Neagh, is an ASSI and an SPA but it is currently in unfavourable condition. The management plan, prepared in partnership with local landowners, NIEA, DARD and Rivers Agency, has identified and prescribed remedies to restore the ASSI to favourable condition.

Lough Beg (B. Hamill).

Lough Beg once held about 200 pairs of breeding waders but recently only 70 pairs have been recorded at the site. Some species have disappeared completely. The project aims to restore the wetlands, primarily grasslands and fen, to their former glory. The target is to restore breeding wader numbers to their original levels.

RSPB expertise and existing government resources have been strategically targeted to deliver the restoration plan which also restores priority habitats: fens; purple moor-grass, rush pastures and floodplain grazing marsh. The restoration plan is being implemented on privately-owned land, where solutions to the restoration and management of wetlands are being developed and carried forward to manage other wetland sites facing similar issues within the wider landscape.

Cattle grazing fen and wet grassland at Lough Beg to provide suitable condition for breeding waders (B. Hamill)

Some fen projects, such as those on basin fens, may not need to be 'big' in terms of area to achieve significant results or to function at optimal levels. This is particularly true for small wetland SSSIs which have survived as oases in a desert of intensively managed agricultural land.

West Midlands Meres and Mosses Landscape Revival Project is a good example of a successful project working across a large number of small basin fens, pools and raised bogs set within the wider landscape.

5.4   Site survey to establish what is there now

5.4.1 Ecological survey

Having established the historical and wider context for the fen, the next stage is to determine what is there now on the site in the way of wildlife. This requires an up-to-date survey. The aim is to identify and map:

- Presence, location, distribution and population of species, habitats and features of conservation interest within and around the site.

- Rare and protected species and habitats.

- Presence, location and distribution of invasive and non-native species.

- NVC plant communities within each wetland type and ways in which any differ from published descriptions.

Clearly record the limits of accuracy for any mapping.

Designated sites such as SSSIs, ASSIs, SACs and sites of county importance normally have written descriptions and recorded reasons for selection which provide an important baseline measure of what the site contained at the time of its listing or designation. There may be a statutory requirement to restore any lost features for which the site was originally chosen. Citations do not necessarily contain detailed habitat information so it may be necessary to infer the habitat type from the species listed. For example, a plant list including the moss *Scorpidium cossonii* and common butterwort (*Pinguicula vulgaris*) is likely to indicate nutrient-poor base-rich groundwater-fed fen. The loss of these plants, and replacement by tall species like great willowherb (*Epilobium hirsutum*) will require the reinstatement of suitable conditions.

For both designated and non-designated sites, recent and historical species records should be available from local biological record centres, which are usually maintained by the county or unitary authority. Vice-county recorders (or their equivalents in Scotland and Northern Ireland), and local wildlife groups (including specialist local ornithological, herpetological, bat, moth or mammal groups) may also be able to provide useful information. The county or local wildlife trust may hold species records and be able to provide useful contacts.

Species locations should then be plotted on a site map which will help to pinpoint areas of particular interest for further survey. Presence of a species or group of species should be linked with the fundamental habitat characteristics. As outlined in **Section 2: Fen Flora and Fauna**, classification of habitats for birds or invertebrates may differ from those provided by plant ecologists. For example, the breakdown of niches for invertebrates found in acid bogs is far less detailed, and reflects the structure provided by a combination of substrate and vegetation. Absence of data for a particular species is not necessarily evidence that a species is absent.

Summary of ecological survey requirements

- Map wetland types and relate to the hydrological regime of the fen;

- Survey and map NVC plant communities;

- Record limits on the validity of mapping the NVC communities;

- Compare on-site NVC examples with generic descriptions;

- Note presence, quantity and location of important plant species (including invasive nonnative species);

- Survey, map and describe fen fauna (birds, invertebrates, mammals) as well as flora;

- Similarly map and describe features important for non-plant species.

More detailed guidance on NVC and other ecological survey techniques is included in **Section 10: Monitoring to Inform Fen Management**.

The hydrological situations commonly recurring in fens are described in The Wetland Framework (Wheeler, Shaw and Tanner, 2009). The Wetland Framework presents water supply as a series of different mechanisms (WETMECs), considers how these are linked to particular fen NVC plant communities and how they might be affected by various management actions or other interventions.

5.4.2 Geological and soil survey

Information about the geology (deeper rock and soil layers) and surface (drift) layers is essential to understanding the hydro-geological functioning of a fen. Good geological maps (solid and drift) are available from the British Geological Society (BGS). The surface layers (or drift) might be available as soil maps (contact BGS).

Information about the original wetland lies within its layers of peat and silt. Specialists or informed amateurs can identify the plants in the sediments from fragments (macrofossils) and from spores and pollen (microfossils). The succession from one type of fen to another is evident from the sequence of the plant remains in these deposits. For example, it is possible to see if the site once supported rich fen (a highly valued type of fen because of its ecological diversity) even though it is currently covered by reed canary grass (often a less valued type of fen).

Section 9: Creating Fen Habitat goes into more detail about soil and geological assessment.

5.5   Hydrological and nutrient assessment

Section 3: Understanding Fen Hydrology and **Section 4: Understanding Fen Nutrients** described how the quantity and quality of water reaching the fen is of fundamental importance in determining fen type and features. Detailed hydrological studies can become very complicated but they may be essential when assessing the potential impact of plans and projects such as abstractions and discharges. However, a simplified approach may provide sufficient understanding to inform decisions on management objectives, for example whether the fens or their sub-units are fed by rainwater, groundwater or surface water. The next step is to work out the current hydrological regime i.e. sources of water inflow and outflow, their variability and how these relate to areas supporting particular features or habitats of interest. An informed walk-over survey (preferably with hydrologist and ecologist) is the best starting point.

Make sure you understand how the fen works hydrologically (i.e. how water enters, moves through and leaves a fen and its chemistry and quality), how it has changed in the past, or might change in future. Don't forget man-made structures such as ditches and work out how they affect the fen. The next step is to consider the eco-hydrology, i.e. how the hydrology interacts with the fen flora and fauna.

Newbald Becksies is a spring-fed fen on the edge of the chalk of the Yorkshire Wolds. It once supported plants typical of rich fen, such as butterwort, Grass of Parnassus and mosses such as *Scorpidium cossonii*. Investigations are underway to find out whether abstractions from the chalk aquifer have starved the rich fen of lime-rich water, or whether it is 'simply' that quantities of agricultural fertiliser have entered the aquifer which has encouraged stronger plants around the spring-heads. A more detailed case study of this site is included at the end of this section (5.1)

5.6 Identify past and future changes

Past changes in presence and population of key species, extent and condition of habitat, hydrological and nutrient regime should all be identified. Changes in hydrology or nutrients and how these might have affected fen flora and fauna, or how they might affect it in future, should be considered. Interest features may be in very poor condition, or even absent from a site, because of historical changes in the hydrological regime or other factors. Under these circumstances, other forms of evidence, including field observations (e.g. landscape situation, presence and type of peat or recent alluvial sediments), historical maps or aerial photographs, anecdotal evidence or old photographs can be used to identify the fen's potential.

Predictions for climate change are for drier, hotter summers and wetter, warmer winters which would have implications for the sustainability of wetlands, should be taken into account in setting management objectives. However, unlike rain-fed bogs, fens are dependent on the behaviour of water after it has run over the soil, infiltrated it and emerged again as groundwater. The effect on fens of seasonal changes in precipitation patterns may be even more difficult to predict.

Biglands Bog, Cumbria

This 12 ha mixed valley and basin fen historically supported a small raised bog, base-rich seepage and floodplain fen. More recently the flow characteristics of the input stream have changed, depositing much silt and spreading nutrients into all but the raised bog, which probably floats. Management must address factors upstream of the fen, such as changes in agriculture and nutrient-rich discharges. For more about this site see Case Study 4.1.

5.7   Identify restraints on management

5.7.1 Statutory designations

Internationally or nationally important sites such as SACs or SSSIs (see Section 2.9 Fen conservation) have 'Reasons for Notification' which take precedence over other management considerations. Failure to maintain an SAC feature in favourable condition – or to restore it if damaged – may result in infraction procedures against the UK Government in the European Court. Advice from statutory agency specialists should be obtained if there are conflicts between internationally important features.

The choice of SAC examples is based on knowledge of the distribution and extent of the type, but Annex 1 features, i.e. habitats of European importance, occur beyond designated SACs. Site managers should ensure that if Annex 1 features are identified, their needs are addressed as a priority.

5.7.2 Archaeological interest

Many fens are rich repositories of archaeological evidence. Pollen grains in the peat profile or particles generated from burning can reveal fascinating information about a site's history, vegetation changes and man's past activities.

There is no UK wide inventory of wetland sites of archaeological importance, but a map of wetlands of archaeological importance has been produced as part of the Wetland Vision for England (see below 5.8.1) Priority Areas for the historic environment, and for Scotland SWAD: Scottish Wetlands Archaeological Database.

Any removal of peat or disturbance has the potential to uncover or destroy irreplaceable archaeological remains. Prior consultation with the relevant planning authority archaeologist is essential to determine the likelihood of encountering archaeological remains before undertaking any work which might affect water levels on fen sites. The use of nutrient-enriched water may accelerate decomposition of organic archaeological remains.

5.8   Decide what you are trying to achieve

Deciding what to do usually boils down to a series of choices: maintaining the status quo or encouraging or discouraging certain species or habitat types. The key is deciding which species, habitats, stage of succession, hydrological and nutrient regime to aim for.

Where the fen habitats themselves, rather than any rare or specialised species that they support, have intrinsic conservation interest, direct management at maintaining specific vegetation communities. For example in calcareous fen NVC M10 *Carex dioica–Pinguicula vulgaris* mire, manage the vegetation community as a whole entity.

- The fauna which inhabit the fen can be as significant, if not more so, than fen flora in deciding on appropriate management.

- The potential adverse effect of fen management on sensitive species should always be considered.

- Vertebrates or invertebrates listed as selection features for a designated site must be given consideration when determining the management objective for the area.

A few species may require small-scale micro-management to maintain features necessary for their continued survival on a site. An example is the fen violet (*Viola persicifolia*), now restricted to a handful of sites in England, which requires some degree of disturbance to maintain its population.

The uncommon argent and sable moth (*Rheumaptera hastata*) which in the southern part of its range is primarily a woodland species largely associated with birch, is also found on fen and raised bog with young birch re-growth. A healthy population of the moth is found at Chartley Moss in Staffordshire, which is designated as an SAC for transition mire and quaking bog. Appropriate management of the open fen surface allows more birch to regrow than would be the case if the site were being managed solely for the benefit of fen vegetation.

5.8.1 Individual fens in the context of the Wetland Vision

The Wetland Vision for England (www.wetlandvision.org.uk) which was launched in 2008 sets out a 50-year vision for England's freshwater wetlands. The Vision was based on looking at what was there historically, what's there now and the wetland potential of specific geographical areas. Maps show where new wetlands could be created and current wetlands restored. The implementation of the Vision aims to ensure that wetlands, including fens, remain a valuable component of the landscape and contribute to both a sustainable society and landscape. The project is run as a partnership – English Heritage, the Environment Agency, Natural England, the RSPB, Wildfowl and Wetland Trust and the Wildlife Trusts. The Wetland Vision can help provide context and suggest possibilities and habitat priorities in a general area, including for different types of fen but local visions are likely to be of more relevance at site level. A database of local visions is included on the Wetland Vision website.

The North West England wetland vision is an example of a more detailed local vision (Penny Anderson Associates, 2004, 2006, 2007). It developed decision-rules based on the principles described above, such as geology, soils, hydrology and topography, but also based on the location of existing sites that can be made more secure by creating new wetland, perhaps of a different type, around its edge. A map was then produced to show where wetlands could be created in the lowlands of the region, in particular highlighting opportunities to expand and buffer existing sites.

5.8.2 WETMECs

WETMEC descriptions (see 5.4.1 above) may also help identify how a particular site should relate to particular hydrological circumstances and what might be required to restore the relationship. It may not be possible to restore a particular type of fen for example where connections with an essential supply of groundwater have been severed, but every opportunity should be explored to retain hydrologically sustainable fens, or return them to desirable condition.

5.8.3 Designated sites

Benchmarks for setting conservation objectives on statutory sites are provided by the JNCC (http://www.jncc.gov.uk/default.aspx?page=2235). They provide guidance on quality criteria for all wetland types, using NVC communities and the plants that occur most frequently within them. The actual species used as indicators of favourable condition can be made site-specific, and this is where accurate and recent site survey information is important.

Statutory nature conservation bodies carry out condition assessments on SSSI/ASSIs every few years, based on habitats and species known to be present. Depending on the type and level of detail of survey undertaken, this may help provide some pointers on fen management.

In general, the more diverse range of habitats present on a site, the greater the diversity of associated vertebrate and invertebrate species. Management should therefore aim to maximise the diversity of habitats present, appropriate to the locality and without compromising delivery of habitat conditions and area for those habitats, features and species that take priority (e.g. features for which a site is designated). The size of the site is of key importance, as trying to maintain a large number of habitat types on a small site may result in patch size being too small to support the full range of species.

5.8.4 Establishing priorities for fen management and restoration

Nationally and internationally, wetland conservation aims to maintain examples of all fen types. However, management to enhance one type of habitat may be to the detriment of another. For example, scrub clearance will result in loss of wet woodland, but it will be replaced with a type of open fen.

The UK Biodiversity Action Plan (UKBAP) identifies a number of Habitat Action Plans (HAPs) and Species Action Plans (SAPs) which can help with management decisions. The two most relevant priority habitats are Lowland Fens and Upland Fens, Flushes and Swamps, for which a series of actions and targets to improve the conservation status of habitats has been written (www.ukbap.org.uk).

Guidance supporting the Lowland Fens HAP aims to ensure that the full range of fens is considered when embarking on fen restoration or creation. In addition it is important to ensure that rare hydro-geological situations with potential to support equally rare types of fen are not 'wasted' creating habitat easily created in a wide range of situations.

- Prioritise objectives to achieve Habitat and Species Action Plan targets.

- Consult national, regional and local visions for habitats including wetlands, for example the England 50 year Wetland Vision.

- Generally the rarest habitats are those which take precedence in terms of conservation management.

- Balance the site owner's wishes with statutory obligations and nature conservation objectives.

- Intra-nationally agreed guidelines for setting conservation objectives, such as the JNCC's Common Standards for Monitoring (CSM) contain much helpful information.

Fens which are characteristic of low-nutrient situations are generally regarded as conservation priorities, particularly in the UK lowlands, because of the significant loss of this type of habitat over the past 200 years. Base-rich groundwater-fed fens are amongst the rarest type of fen because of the very limited existence of conditions matching their requirement for a permanent supply of low-nutrient, high base status water. Priority should therefore be given to nurturing and expanding this type of habitat where opportunities arise rather than creation of other less restricted habitats such as reedbed or wet grassland in a situation where a base-rich groundwater-fed fen could be restored.

A coarse prioritisation of wetland restoration effort, based on habitat rarity and 'difficulty to restore or recreate' has been attempted in several reports and visions (e.g. Penny Anderson Associates, 2004 and England Wetland Vision (Hume, 2008)). The main purpose of the ranking is to ensure that the very limited opportunities available to restore or create the rarer habitats are not missed but clearly each of these habitats has its own value and should not be considered 'second rate'. In some parts of the country it may only be feasible to recreate less rare habitats. The suggested order is:

    Lowland raised bog
    Base-rich groundwater-fed fen
    Transition mire and quaking bog
    Floodplain fen
    Fen meadow/Molinia meadows
    Low-diversity wet grassland
    Reedbed
    Wet woodland

As always, there are exceptions where maintaining the status quo, rather than management intervention is in the best interests of nature conservation.

Within the Montiaghs Moss ASSI in Northern Ireland there are areas where fen has developed on a degraded bog and is now of value in its own right. Given that raised bog is widespread in Northern Ireland, it would not be appropriate to loose the valuable fen communities, which support a rare and diverse invertebrate fauna by recreating raised bog. However, natural succession means that the fen will eventually develop into wet woodland and/or bog over a longer period of time unless it is deliberately managed to maintain fen communities. Further details of Montiagh's Moss are included in the case study at the end of **Section 7: Fen Water Management.**

Management objectives for a wetland site can rarely be set in isolation from the surrounding land. It is possible, for example, that wetting up a fen may cause wetting up in adjacent non-fen land, especially if this land was originally part of the same wetland. The consequences of proposed management, particularly installation or removal of structures which may influence water level, should be carefully considered and neighbouring land owners/managers consulted at the earliest opportunity. **See Section 11: Fens and People**.

5.8.5 Defining a target hydrological regime

Defining an ideal or target hydrological regime for a particular fen can be considered at various levels depending on available resources, level of understanding or available information and the level of detail required.

- **At the most basic level**, for example for fen management undertaken through agri-environment schemes, defining a target hydrological regime involves determining which areas of a site (linked to the ecology) should be 'wet' i.e. with soil water levels within 10 cm of the ground surface during the summer months, and which should not fall more than 30 cm below ground surface for any significant period of time (say one month). This could be based upon local knowledge or on published guidance, such as the eco-hydrological guidelines described below.

- **At a more complex level**, it may be necessary to identify the key water transfer mechanisms for the site and some simple spatial (i.e. site or location specific) and/or temporal (seasonal or time specific) criteria for the operation of these. For example, perennial flow might be required from a set of springs within a sloping fen, or complete inundation by overbank flooding might be required annually for a tall-herb fen on a floodplain.

- **At the highest level**, for example more ambitious fen management schemes or those which might affect a public water supply, a lot more detail will be required, but identification of the precise hydrological requirements of many species and habitats is limited by lack of research or confinement of current research to a limited geographical area.

Historically, most wetland management was decided on the basis of expert judgement or reactive management. Recently, driven primarily by the obligation to conserve wetlands in a number of European Community Directives (such as 92/43/EEC: Conservation of Natural Habitats and of Wild Fauna and Flora), ecohydrological guidelines have been developed for lowland wetland plant communities (Wheeler et al, 2004), including wet grassland, fen and mire, ditch and swamp communities, and wet woodlands (Barsoum et al, 2005), covering the different types of wet woodland habitat.

Ecohydrological guidelines are based on the NVC system for plant communities (see Appendix IV). For example, for S24 (*Phragmites australis–Peucedanum palustre*) tall-herb fen, Wheeler et al (2004) include:

Optimal water levels. Summer water level is typically around 15 cm below ground level, but deeper levels may be a perfectly natural feature of some sites. The sub-community most often associated with a water level at or near the surface all year round (S24e) on average supports the greatest number of rare species. Winter inundation is a natural feature of many S24 stands.

Sub-optimal or damaging water levels. Strongly sub-surface winter and summer water tables are outside the normal range of this community; peat drying and degradation would lead to development of rank fen rapidly becoming wooded without management. Very wet sites with widespread summer inundation are less likely to be species-rich than those where the summer water level is subsurface.

These ecohydrological guidelines provide only generic indications of water (and nutrient) regime needs for wetland habitats, which vary from site to site because of factors such as soil type, geology and climate. Hydrological guidelines for species and habitats also tend to relate to 'average' conditions which are more easily researched and defined than tolerance of less frequently experienced hydrological events which may be critical to long-term maintenance of a habitat in good condition. For example, low-frequency, high-magnitude flooding events are required in certain wet woodland communities (e.g. NVC W6 *Alnus glutinosa – Urtica dioica* woodland) to provide bare ground for seedlings to develop, which may be essential to maintaining a healthy age distribution of trees.

Water supply mechanisms for a large number of wetland sites in England and Wales have been identified as part of the Wetland Framework Project (Wheeler et al 2009).

5.9   Compare existing and target regimes and identify necessary changes

Comparing the differences between existing and target fen type, hydrological and nutrient regimes is the starting point in identifying changes necessary to achieve agreed objectives. If the current regime matches the target regime, there is no immediate need for intervention, but appropriate hydrological monitoring (see **Section 10: Monitoring to Inform Fen Management**) and periodic review is essential. Active management or intervention is required wherever there is a disparity between existing and target regime(s).

5.10   Identify and assess viability of suitable techniques to achieve changes

A range of practical management techniques are outlined in **Section 6: Fen Vegetation Management, Section 7: Fen Water Management and Section 8: Managing Fen Nutrient Enrichment**. The case studies at the end of each of these sections illustrate how these techniques have worked in practice, which will help in assessing the suitability and viability of different techniques for a particular fen. Even though the focus has usually been on a specific site, most of the case studies have required some changes at a catchment scale. Some fens, such as the New Forest Valley Mires experience similar problems over a very large area, and have required landscape-scale solutions (see Case Study 7.1).

5.11   Sharing with agriculture

Groundwater-fed fens are often grouped over a single aquifer shared with agricultural land. Agriculture may rely on irrigation from groundwater, which can depress the water supply to the fen to a degree that causes habitat changes. A typical example experienced at Cors Bodeilio Common, Anglesey, is the change from the rare black-bog rush fen to the commoner blunt-flowered rush fen meadow, with consequent significant reduction in plant diversity and loss of many rarer species. One of the potential remedies could be to seek an alternative water supply for agriculture but this could be costly and involves consideration of issues beyond that of immediate fen management. Complications arise in that water-bearing rock strata are often fractured, making it hard to predict connectivity within the aquifer, and thus to demonstrate the impacts of abstraction on other sites such as wetlands within the same catchment.

5.12 Develop and implement a strategy to achieve desired objectives

All of the preceding stages should be drawn together in an effective strategy to achieve agreed objectives.

> – International legal obligations, such as Ramsar and the EU Habitats & Species Directive should take precedence.
>
> – National legal obligations, such as those applying to SSSIs and ASSIs must be observed.

Making Choices: management strategies and options (adapted from Benstead et al, 1999)

Habitat condition	Management strategy	Management options
Fen with high wildlife interest in good condition	Maintain existing management	**Water management:** Determine hydrological regime, e.g. spring-fed, topogenous, both etc. Maintain current hydrological regime Monitor water levels and quality **Vegetation management:** Identify existing regime by talking to owner/manager Continue with existing management Monitor vegetation change
Fen with moderate wildlife interest with potential for improvement (e.g. partially drained fen with some scrub encroachment, and suspected nutrient enrichment)	Improve/modify management	**Water management:** Investigate possibility/desirability of return to natural hydrological regime Block drains Consider lowering of fen surface Prevent flow of nutrient-enriched water into fen (e.g. install silt trap; create nutrient-stripping wetland upstream; bring surrounding land into sympathetic management) Monitor water levels and quality **Vegetation management:** Manage scrub and trees Restoration cut to remove standing crop and litter Controlled burn Introduce cutting regime Introduce grazing animals Monitor vegetation change
Area with potential for fen but currently drained and managed as other habitat, e.g. arable land or dry grassland	Implement creation/ restoration programme (see Section 9: Fen Creation)	**Water management:** Identify sources of water, chemistry and nutrient status Consider full re-instatement of natural hydrology Consider engineering options necessary for target fen type e.g. bunding, sluices, ditch creation, land forming Monitor water levels and quality **Vegetation management:** Assess feasibility of natural regeneration Consider soil remediation, e.g. topsoil removal Consider bringing in seed/green hay from nearby sources Introduce grazing animals Establish cutting regime Monitor vegetation development

5.13 References

Barsoum, N., Anderson, R., Broadmeadow, S., Bishop, H., and Nisbet, T. 2005. *Eco-hydrological guidelines for wet woodland – Phase I.* English Nature Research Reports No. 619.

Benstead, P.J., Jose, P.V., Joyce, C.B. and Wade, P.M. 1999. *European Wet Grassland. Guidelines for management and restoration.* RSPB, Sandy.

Brooks, S. And Stoneman, R. 1997. *Conserving Bogs – The Management Handbook.* The Stationery Office, Edinburgh.

Penny Anderson Associates (Hawley, Ross, Wheeler, Shaw, Taylor & Worrall). 2004. Nutrient enrichment of basin fens: options for remediation. Report to English Nature.

Wheeler, B.D. & Shaw, S.C., 2001. A Wetland Framework for impact assessment at statutory sites in Eastern England. Environment Agency Research & Development Technical Report W6-068/TR1.

Wheeler, B.D., Gowing, D. J. G., Shaw, S. C., Mountford, J.O. and Money, R. P. 2004. *Ecohydrological Guidelines for Lowland Wetland Plant Communities. Final Report* Environment Agency - Anglian Region. Edited by Brooks AW, José PV, and Whiteman MI.

Newbald Becksies is a designated SSSI fen on the western slopes of the Yorkshire Wolds, east of Beverley (grid reference SE918371). Water from a chalk aquifer emerges as springs and seepages, flowing downslope in narrow runnels to a larger stream in the floor of the shallow valley.

Records from the 1950s show that the butterwort *Pinguicula vulgaris* and the moss *Scorpidium revolvens*, both characteristic of rich fen, were present until the early 1990s. More recently, tall stands of great willowherb *Epilobium hirsutum* have spread along some of the runnels and occupy some of the springs and seepages.

Although not all the vegetation is tall, and much of the original rush-rich fen meadow remains, these species have been lost. The changes suggest an increase in the effects of plant nutrients, though the source of them has not been determined.

Management objectives
To re-establish the lost M10 plant community and maintain the M22 plant community.

Management rationale
This is one of very few spring- and seepage-fed fens in the Yorkshire Wolds. It is important to maintain low-nutrient base-rich conditions for which the SSSI was notified.

Techniques
Scrub invading the M22 plant community will be removed manually, and the fen meadow will be grazed or cut annually to maintain the M22 in an open condition.

The quality and quantity of water available from the chalk aquifer will be addressed as an issue under the Water Framework Directive as this site is a Groundwater Dependent Terrestrial Ecosystem (GWDTE) and should be maintained in good ecological status.

Monitoring and review of outcomes
The condition of the attributes for which the SSSI was notified will be assessed every five years, using a method based on the JNCC's Common Standards for Monitoring Lowland Wetlands.

Comments
The features dependent on low-nutrient, base-rich groundwater was lost between 1968 and 1986. This coincides with a steep increase in the use of agricultural fertilizers; the change is probably common to many such sites around the country.

Tall, rank great willowherb now covers more of the wetland than at designation

At 125 ha, Redgrave and Lopham Fens is one of the largest valley fens in England, forming the headwaters of the River Waveney and the Little Ouse River on the Norfolk-Suffolk border (grid reference TM050797). Noted for its rare wetland habitats since the beginning of the 20th century, it is a designated SSSI and National Nature Reserve part of the Waveney and Little Ouse Valley SAC, a Ramsar wetland, and a Suffolk Wildlife Trust nature reserve. The site supports several different types of fen including purple moor-grass meadows, saw-sedge beds, bluntflowered rush stands as well as wet heath communities. There is also an extremely rich invertebrate fauna including one of only three British populations of the fen raft spider *Dolomedes plantarius*, a Red Data Book Category 1 species.

Before the 1950s, the fen was fed by groundwater rising by artesian pressure through or past layers of sand, gravel, clay, peat and silt. Seepages and groundwater flushes were found across the site but were concentrated along the margins. The complex geology, and the variable chemistry of the soils and peat produced nutrient-poor waters of varying pH and base-content. The vegetation reflected the variation in water chemistry.

The historic management of the fen declined and was abandoned between 1940 and 1960. From the mid 1950s to the mid 1960s the River Waveney was deepened in association with more efficient drainage in other parts of the catchment. In the 1960s, a public supply borehole was brought into use next to the fens. This changed the water regime from one of a variety of sources to a dependence on winter storage of rain and floodwater. The lowered water levels and lack of traditional grazing and cutting was followed by scrub invasion and loss of the previous plant communities. The change was exacerbated by nutrient release from the drying and oxidising fen peat.

Management rationale

In the 1990s the Essex and Suffolk Water Company, managers of the borehole at Redgrave, commissioned a series of reports confirming that the borehole was removing the essential groundwater inputs to the fen. The deepening of the River Waveney was identified as another principal cause of change.

The Restoration Project Partnership

A restoration project steering group was established, and rehabilitation targets drawn up. The overall cost of restoration was estimated at £3.6m. The Heritage Lottery Fund provided funding for visitor facilities and land acquisition, and an ESA (now HLS) agreement was developed with the inclusion of a new Fen Tier area payment.

Objectives of restoration:

- To restore a groundwater-fed calcareous valley fen complex with associated wet and dry acid habitats, including restoration of river levels and river corridor habitat.

- Achieve better habitat protection for the fen raft spider.

- Provide a demonstration wetland site as an example to others, showing that major habitat problems can be resolved through environmental partnerships*.

- Ensure that a relocated, replacement borehole provides a secure water supply without damaging nearby wetlands.

- Promote the project to the public through education, improved access to the fen, and high-profile publicity.

*Project partners are Suffolk Wildlife Trust, Essex and Suffolk Water, Environment Agency and Natural England. The project received 50% funding from the European Union's LIFE fund, and won the Natura 2000 Eurosite Award for technical achievement in wetland restoration.

Techniques

Relocation of the water supply borehole:

- Alternative borehole locations were tested; two proved suitable. The chosen site had longevity of water supply and minimum detrimental effect on wetland hydrology in the local area.

- Land was acquired and a new borehole was constructed, being commissioned in July 1999.

- Monitoring was instigated to record the response. Ongoing water level monitoring of over 50 dipwells has built up a detailed dataset that has been used in the redevelopment of catchment groundwater models used by the Environment Agency.

Restoration of the River Waveney:

- A sluice was re-instated to set a higher water level and have far greater control on channel height throughout the year. An additional sluice was also constructed and commissioned further downriver to protect hydrology of the eastern region of the fen.

- Flood embankments were created along tributary ditches to prevent them flooding into the fen. Shallow ledges were created for water vole population recovery and expansion.

- Advice was given to improve water quality in the catchment and abatement notices issued. Recent advisory work in the immediate catchment has focused on Environmental Stewardship HLS uptake.

Restoration of the fen:
- Rotted and enriched peat has been scraped and removed over 23 hectares using specialist low-ground pressure machinery, retained as embankments and public access paths in some areas, and otherwise removed entirely from site.

- Scrub was removed over 77 hectares, with timber being sold to a number of outlets including local charcoal merchants, and woodchip sold to biofuel power stations or as a garden mulch All stumps were removed from peat soils, or otherwise ground out on mineral soils.

- Restoration sedge cutting, forage harvesting of tall-herb fen vegetation and flailing of young scrub re-growth has all been implemented to accompany the predominant management technique of extensive grazing.

- 14km of livestock fencing installed, along with handling units and piped water troughs. Breeding herd of konik ponies brought onto site from Poland in 1995 to extensively graze the fen, along with beef cattle and Hebridean sheep. Adjacent 'enriched' land was acquired and managed to reduce nutrients. This land is also being converted into a transitional, higher quality habitat between wet fen and dry surrounding margin.

Restoration work underway at Redgrave and Lopham Fen

Monitoring and review of outcomes

Groundwater recovery has been astonishing and complex in its development. The site is now predominantly wet year-round, with the mean water table lying within the target level for re-establishment of target fen vegetation types identified in the Habitats Directive.

The outcome of recent management has shown exceptional botanical species recovery, with over 300 plant species having been recorded since restoration. These were recorded through an NVC resurvey of the site and monitoring of permanent quadrats. Of particular note has been the return of insectivorous plant species formerly associated with the site (common bladderwort, common butterwort and round leaved sundew), wet heath assemblages (comprising several *Sphagnum* moss species and cross-leaved heath), brown-moss communities in spring flushes, charophyte carpets in newly-created turf ponds (seven species on site – of European significance) and the re-establishment of saw sedge-dominated swards over former ranges.

The fen raft spider population has survived and has shown small but significant population range expansion on the fen. Recent translocation of captively-bred cloned spiders intends to encourage the species to occupy its former range on the reserve, prior to water abstraction.

There are now 21 dragonfly species associated with the reserve. Otter have returned to the river, and the fen is now a key national site for water voles. Species such as water violet now grow within the river channel (an almost unimaginable sight a few decades ago).

Detailed monitoring of water quality in the catchment has been undertaken, including monitoring of peak flow events following storms or prolonged rainfall. The water quality is now excellent within the fen, with almost undetectable nutrient levels within the turf ponds.

Konik ponies grazing at
Regrave and Lopham Fen

Extensive grazing has proven to be extremely successful in creating great structure within the fen swards, while increasing biodiversity across the fen.

As part of the project a large visitor centre was built to provide facilities for interpretation and education programmes. The centre is heated by a very low energy ground source heat pump and has many recycled materials used in its construction. A number of additional pathways were constructed around the reserve and two viewing platforms were installed in order to increase visitor enjoyment and appreciation of the fen; one platform was provided specifically for viewing the fen raft spider in its natural habitat.

Plans for the future

Cyclical long term shallow peat scraping is likely to be proposed as a management technique, albeit on a much smaller scale than in the restoration phases of the project.

Comments

This is an example of water abstraction and nutrient enrichment causing dramatic changes in plant communities. The restoration work achieved through partnership working enabled the very first relocation of a public water supply to occur on environmental grounds alone.

Wybunbury Moss is a small basin fen, 18ha in extent, approximately 9km south-east of Nantwich in Cheshire (SJ697502). The fen has formed in one of the many glacial hollows found in this part of the country. At its centre is an oligotrophic, floating mire or schwingmoor, which has been formed through the solution and subsidence of underlying salt-bearing strata. The peat raft is surrounded by open fen, mixed woodland and wet grassland.

The site is notified as a SSSI for its raised mire, bog pool and fen communities, vascular plant assemblages and its invertebrate assemblage, the latter being arguably the most important in Cheshire. The Moss also forms part of the Midlands Meres and Mosses Ramsar site and the West Midlands Mosses SAC (transition mires and quaking bogs).

Flora and fauna

The central oligotrophic area contains much *Sphagnum fallax, S. capillifolium* and *S. papillosum*, upon which grow round-leaved sundew *Drosera rotundifolia*, bog rosemary *Andromeda polifolia* and white beak-sedge *Rhynchospora alba*. Radiating out from this, *Sphagnum recurvum* becomes the dominant and often, only *Sphagnum* species, generally occurring with common cotton-grass *Eriophorum angustifolium*, hare's-tail cotton-grass *E. vaginatum*, cross-leaved heath *Erica tetralix*, cranberry *Vaccinium oxycoccos*, crowberry *Empetrum nigrum* and heather *Calluna vulgaris*.

Fen woodland is characteristic of those parts of the mire where the peat is wet and unstable and the mire waters are eutrophic. The principal canopy species is alder with lesser amounts of rowan (*Sorbus aucuparia*), downy birch (*Betula pubescens*), oak (*Quercus robur* and *Q. petraea*), common sallow (*Salix cinerea*) with alder buckthorn (*Frangula alnus*) and guelder rose (*Viburnum opulus*) in the shrub layer. This community has the most diverse ground flora on the reserve with species including greater and lesser bulrush, common reed and saw sedge.

A rich invertebrate fauna includes two Red Data Book (RDB) species of spider, the increasingly rare argent and sable moth (*Rheumaptera hastata*) and the RDB2 leaf beetle (*Cryptocephalus decemmaculatus*).

Past management

Although Wybunbury has been an NNR since 1954, significant habitat management did not take place until the mid 1980s. Since then, management has concentrated on reversing the adverse effects of tree encroachment and eutrophication, whilst at the same time maintaining suitable habitats for the invertebrate assemblage.

The plant communities for which the site is notified are those which occupy the wetter, treeless parts of the Moss. However, attempts to drain parts of the Moss for peat cutting and the gradual encroachment of Scots pine (*Pinus sylvestris*) have led to a reduction in the extent of these communities. Management work since the 1980s has centred on restoring water levels and removing trees and scrub from these areas – the generic guidance for conservation objectives gives a guideline of <5% scrub in these habitats to achieve favourable condition. On the other hand, many of the scarce invertebrates on the Moss have very specific requirements for the presence of scrub – the requirements of the leaf beetle illustrate a classic conflict of management interest.

Habitat requirements of leaf beetle

This attractive beetle, which resembles a small ladybird, has currently only been identified on Wybunbury Moss and on a single site near Loch Rannoch in Scotland. Until recently its habitat requirements were poorly understood, with casual observations suggesting a preference for small sallow and downy birch saplings. At Wybunbury, the bulk of the population is concentrated on one willow bush in the centre of the Moss. Its larval stages were unknown although the British RDB (Shirt, 1987) suggests an association with ants nests.

In 2001 English Nature commissioned Leeds University to undertake research into the ecology of a number of the nationally rare *Cryptocephalus* beetles. Four years of observation revealed *C. decemmaculatus* to be a very immobile insect, loath to fly more than a few metres at a time and requiring hot, sunny days before it will take to the wing. The larvae were found to inhabit the leaf litter amongst *Sphagnum* moss at the base of the willow bushes. The population study confirmed that the majority of adult beetles were concentrated on one bush in the centre of the site (orange star on map) with a very small population along the northern edge of the Moss. As such, the status of the species was extremely threatened and it was therefore concluded desirable to provide a suitable habitat corridor to allow the beetle to shift its population to a series of new south-facing glades along the northern perimeter.

Current management

Current management of Wybunbury Moss aims to achieve favourable condition of plant communities whilst addressing the needs of the invertebrate assemblage. A programme of tree clearance has been underway since the early 1990s to restore former areas of oligotrophic mire and open fen. In general it takes the Moss a couple of years to re-wet following tree removal, a period in which treatment of scrub regrowth is necessary. It is the management of scrub regrowth that is used to provide suitable conditions for *C. decemmaculatus*.

Sphagnum lawns merging into scrub

Approximately 20% of scrub regrowth is allowed to re-grow and reach a height of 3m before being controlled, initially including all regrowth of *Salix* spp. In subsequent management, a willow bush is retained at least every 5 metres, creating a series of stepping stones (green dots on map) from the current leaf beetle population to new south-facing glades that have been created along the northern boundary. By 2007 the beetle had moved as far as the orange dot, with populations on several bushes between here and the original colony.

Future plans

Ultimately, once the beetle has spread to the new glades along the northern boundary, the levels of scrub in the centre of the site will be reduced to the 5% required to achieve favourable condition of the mire and open fen communities. A fringe of scrub will also be retained between the open mire and fen communities and the peripheral fen woodland will be managed by regular coppicing.

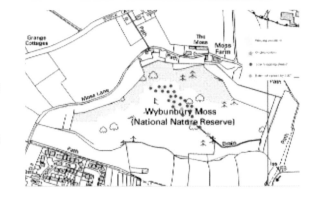

6. Fen Management and Restoration – Vegetation Management

Vegetation management is necessary on most fens to maintain or restore the conservation interest. This section considers the many different factors that influence which method of vegetation management is the most appropriate for any particular fen, and demonstrates through examples from around the UK the most commonly used vegetation management techniques which can be used to achieve agreed objectives. These objectives might be to maintain or restore a particular habitat, community or even a particularly noteworthy plant, animal or invertebrate species, or group of species.

Techniques covered in this section include grazing, mechanical cutting, mowing for hay, burning and scrub/tree control. Reedbed management techniques are included where relevant to perpetuating the conservation interest of fens. Methods of re-establishing fen vegetation, including those specific to fen meadow, are also outlined. Section 7 discusses water management in relation to fens, and Section 8 offers guidance on managing fen nutrient enrichment.

6.1 General principles of vegetation management

Section 5 explained very briefly the basic principles of succession in relation to fens, and offers guidance on setting objectives and general fen management. The purpose of most fen management is to maintain or restore open, species-rich communities of characteristic vegetation and their associated flora and fauna. In general, the aim is to decrease the spread or dominance of scrub or tall aggressive vegetation such as great willowherb (*Epilobium hirsutum*), common bulrush (*Typha latifolia*) and common reed (*Phragmites australis*), which often results from increased nutrients and/or a lack of grazing or summer mowing.

Selshion Bog in Northern Ireland was extensively cut for turf in the past, exposing fen peats below and creating small open pools used by Irish damselfly. Following cessation of cutting, birch is rapidly colonising as part of the successional process from open fen towards wet woodland (B. Hamill).

The most extensive fen management has been carried out on floodplains, and to a lesser extent valley mires, particularly in the Norfolk and Suffolk Broads. Although basin fens, water-fringe fens and spring-fed fens are usually managed, they occupy a much smaller area. Consequently there are fewer or less extensive examples of different vegetation management techniques to draw from in respect of these types of fen. Most of the techniques described below are nevertheless easily transferable to other areas.

6.2 Grazing

Controlled grazing of fens by livestock is effectively an extension of a natural process, and can be a valuable fen management conservation tool. Grazing can help:

– Maintain open species-rich fen communities by reducing plant biomass;

– Control scrub invasion to maintain or restore open habitat;

– Contribute to the diverse wetland surface in terms of structure and species composition;

– Keep the effects of nutrient enrichment in check by removing vegetation biomass and preventing the dominance of nutrient-demanding species, or reducing the development of scrub and wood on sites that are drying out (and therefore have increased mineralisation rates).

Re-establishment of grazing, especially by cattle, can reverse the successional process and also suppress (though not prevent) scrub encroachment by cropping seedlings or by taking off the re-growth from cut stumps.

Short open species-rich fen with lesser water parsnip (*Berula erecta*) maintained by light grazing (B. Hamill).

Grazing should generally be considered as the first option over any other form of management:

– where a fen has been grazed in the past but grazing has stopped for some reason;

– where there is no history of mowing/cutting and where it is possible to introduce grazing to a fen site to inhibit succession;

– where selective removal of vegetation has been identified as the most appropriate form of management.

Both the benefits and potentially less desirable consequences must be considered before introducing grazing. Animals will not graze all parts of a fen equally if they are free to roam widely. Other practices such as cutting, mowing and scrub management may also be required to complement grazing.

The Grazing Animals Project (GAP) has established and documented significant experience of grazing various different habitats, including fens, which can be found in the GAP handbooks or through the GAP website http://www.grazinganimalsproject.org.uk. Some of the key considerations in relation to grazing on fens are summarised below.

6.2.1 Which fens benefit from grazing?

Grazing should be considered wherever the desired vegetation is low, open and species-rich, but vulnerable to being taken over by tall aggressive species, many of which consolidate their dominance through the build-up of dense litter. Fen meadows dominated by purple moor-grass (*Molinia caerulea*) and rushes but with a rich diversity of associated herb and sedge species (NVC communities M22, M24 and M26), are obvious candidates for regular grazing to maintain their species diversity. Other much wetter fens, such as NVC communities S27 and M9, may be grazed on a more ad hoc basis. (See Appendix IV for further details of NCV communities found on fens.)

Open species-rich fen in the foreground maintained by extensive grazing by suckler cows. Tall reeds and herbs dominate the ungrazed fen beyond the fenceline in the middle distance, which prevents cattle from moving into the wettest part of the fen where they might drown (B. Hamill).

Drier fen meadows are ideal candidates for grazing management (B. Hamill).

Fast-growing plants that cause unwanted change may be responding to more than one factor. It could simply be the cessation of a previous grazing regime, and/ or a change in nutrient status, such as over-bank flooding from a river which has become more eutrophic. Whatever the cause, re-introduction of grazing is likely to be beneficial by removing biomass and reducing the nutrient content of the soil.

Field surveyor kneeling in short transition mire maintained by light grazing in the foreground which contrasts with unmanaged taller fen vegetation in the background (B. Hamill).

Introducing grazing on fens with a long history of mowing is likely to have a considerable impact on vegetation composition and associated invertebrates. Depending on the conservation objectives for the site, such changes may or may not be desirable.

Species-rich fen being rapidly colonised by willow and downy birch due to lack of grazing management. If left unchecked, the scrub will quickly develop into wet woodland, shading out the species-rich fen sward below (B. Hamill).

On some low productivity sites, grazing may not be necessary to maintain short open fen, for example on base-rich groundwater-fed fens where phosphorus, one of the two major plant nutrients, combines with other chemical complexes making it unavailable to plants. This emphasises the importance of assessing the hydrological functions of the fen when setting management objectives (see **Section 3: Understanding Fen Hydrology and Section 4: Understanding Fen Nutrients).**

6.2.2 Assessing whether grazing is feasible

The following factors need to be considered in deciding whether grazing is feasible for any particular fen.

Ground stability   Ground stability is a fundamental consideration in deciding whether grazing is feasible. Many fens have developed on floating mats (schwingmoor) over open water, through which animals can break through and drown. On sites where the safety of livestock would be at risk, alternative methods of management such as cutting or mowing should be introduced to reduce biomass and halt habitat succession.

Flooding   Flooding can have serious consequences for animal welfare, through potential drowning and/or deprivation of food and shelter. **Rapidity** of flooding is important to take into account as well as **frequency of flooding**. Grazing is only feasible on sites prone to rapid flooding if there are sufficient resources to check stock frequently and to move them quickly to another safe site as and when required.

Cattle forced by flooding
to the edge of the fenced
enclosure, Inishroosk,
Northern Ireland
(B. Hamill).

Availability of dry land Dry land is important to provide a refuge for livestock to lie up on, and because it influences selective grazing patterns. Generally livestock do not venture onto wetter areas (which are often those that most need grazing) until they have exhausted drier areas of grazing. Consequently if the proportion of dry land is too high, the animals may not venture into the wetter areas at all.

Dry land adjacent to areas
subject to flooding provides
safe refuge for grazing
livestock
(B. Hamill).

Shelter Most livestock need some form of shelter, such as scrub or woodland, either on the fen or on adjacent land (see GAP - Habitat/Land Management)

Fencing Fencing may be necessary to avoid risk of animals straying into the wettest areas of the fen, and/or to concentrate grazing and thereby prevent succession to wet woodland or tall reed. Intensive grazing at high densities (i.e. well above normal recommended rates) for short periods of time may be required at appropriate times of the year (see below) when the ground is sufficiently dry to support livestock. Careful monitoring is particularly vital during periods of intensive grazing to protect animal welfare. Electric fencing may be a more flexible option for short-term grazing.

Access to water All livestock should have unrestricted access to an adequate supply of fresh drinking water. Where reliable safe drinking points are not available on the fen, drinkers should be provided in sufficiently dry areas to prevent poaching.

In Montiaghs Moss in Northern Ireland (see Case Study 7.1) a large number of drinkers placed along deep drains help disperse grazing. When livestock use the drinkers, a pumping system is activated which automatically draws water from the drain to refill the drinker (B. Hamill).

Animal welfare

Meeting the welfare requirements of grazing livestock is essential. The GAP Handbook includes more information on this subject http://www.grazinganimalsproject.org.uk/. Until stock are familiar with grazing any wetland area, the frequency of checking their welfare should be high, to ensure animals adjust to the site conditions and any associated risks. Frequency of checking once animals are familiar with the site should be determined through a risk assessment process, informed by specific site conditions and the animals being used.

6.2.3 Different types of grazing livestock

Different types of livestock, and different breeds, all have different grazing habits and preferences. Some are more capable of surviving harsh environmental conditions, whilst others are best suited to grazing particular types of fen vegetation, or achieving specific objectives. The grazing habits of various types and breeds of animal in the Broads are described by Tolhurst (1997). General guidance on selecting appropriate stock can be found at GAP – The Breed Profiles Handbook: A Guide to the Selection of Livestock Breeds for Grazing Wildlife Sites). The following notes are offered as a brief overview.

Cattle are ideal for removing long, coarse grass and sedge growth. Using their tongues to pull tufts of vegetation into their mouth, they are less selective grazers than either horses or sheep which both use their front teeth to nibble the vegetation and consequently graze the sward much shorter.

Cattle happily graze the tall fen vegetation around lake margins preventing a build up of dead plant material and halting successional changes (B. Hamill).

At low/medium stocking density, cattle grazing results in a comparatively long tussocky sward of relatively uniform height which favours a rich flora and many invertebrates.

Dexter cattle grazing rank fen vegetation at Tidcombe Fen, Devon (A.Skinner).

Cattle also serve a very useful role in trampling bracken and low scrub, breaking up mats of dead litter and creating pathways through tall, dense vegetation. However, cattle spend up to 16 hours a day resting while they digest their food, congregating on dry land or shelter. Dung accumulation, turf damage and localised poaching can be a problem around these favoured rest spots or around supplementary feeding sites, particularly with heavier animals, on soft ground, or in wet weather.

Cattle trampling through colonising woodland around the margin of Upper Lough Erne maintain pockets of open fen right down to the water's edge (P. Corbett).

Water buffalo are one of the oldest breeds of cattle in the world. The combination of their hardiness and box hooves make them ideal for grazing wetlands, and they can help maintain a diverse and low height structure (down to 6 cm) within fens year-round. Initially, like most stock, water buffalo will graze the lush grasses and sedges around the edge of the fen but will move on to tougher reeds once this food supply reduces. Willow scrub, gorse, reeds and reed mace are all fodder for these beasts. In addition they use their horns to pull out brambles in their path. A habit of wallowing to keep cool creates open water beneficial to wetland invertebrates and amphibians. Water buffalo will track through the tall fen vegetation which opens up otherwise impenetrable reedbed in deeper water. If a site is set up for cattle grazing, few modifications are required except raising the height of handling pens by 30 cm, but water buffalo are intolerant of sheep. However, an added advantage over domestic cattle is that water buffalo are immune to many bovine diseases, particularly tick-borne Redwater fever.

Sheep are good pioneers for grazing some fens. Being lightweight and of small body size, they move easily around sites to areas inaccessible to larger animals, but sheep are of limited use in taller vegetation unless tracks are cut through to encourage them to move into new areas. Sheep are highly selective grazers preferring flowering heads and shorter grasses. Rushes and sedges are an important component of their diet in both summer and winter. Some sheep, particularly traditional breeds, are excellent at controlling scrub regrowth if put onto fens in spring when buds are bursting. Poaching by sheep can be a localised problem but rarely causes problems on fens unless stocked at very high densities. Intensive grazing by sheep may also result in a short even sward with little vegetation structure. This may result in a decrease in biodiversity, especially a loss in invertebrates. Sheep grazing should therefore be closely monitored to ensure the desired vegetation structure is achieved.

Hebridean sheep are one of various hardy native breeds ideally suited to extensive grazing of wet fens (A.McBride)

Horses and ponies are selective grazers. Grazed extensively (i.e. at low stocking densities or over large areas), equines – aided by their slightly forward pointing incisors - create a mosaic of shortly grazed 'lawns' interspersed with areas of taller, undisturbed vegetation used for dunging. This structural diversity benefits a range of species, including for example, invertebrates, small mammals and birds of prey. The issue of ungrazed areas becoming rank can be resolved by concentrating a larger number of horses on a smaller area, or preferably, by grazing equines in combination with other species. Sheep work particularly well with horses. On softer ground, grazing by horses and ponies is likely to create bare ground, which in moderation can be beneficial in allowing colonisation by certain species.

Welsh mountain ponies grazing black bog-rush and blunt flowered rush fen at Cors Bodeilio National Nature Reserve in Wales (P. Jones).

Goats have narrow muzzles and a flexible upper lip which allows them to be highly selective, often targeting grass seed heads before they eat the leaves. They are agile and good climbers, allowing them to access a greater range of forage than sheep, flourishing best where they have access to a wide range of plant species and structurally diverse habitat which allows them to graze or browse. Goats typically graze a sward to approximately 6 cm height (in contrast to 3 cm by sheep), but browse and graze to 2 m or more with ease. In grass, tall herb and scrub mosaics, sheep will graze only the first two types of vegetation whereas goats favour the tall herb and scrub layers but tend to ignore the grass layer. However, due to their agility, goats are very difficult to enclose.

Pigs grazed at very low densities can be beneficial in killing or removing unwanted invasive species and creating bare ground or muddy wallows suitable for colonisation by some preferred plant species and favoured by some invertebrates and reptiles. However, pigs' rooting habits can have a devastating impact, particularly on wet fens. Pigs are not therefore generally recommended on fens unless used for very specific management, and even then, only for a very short period of time.

6.2.4 Choosing the right livestock

Different types and breeds of animal consume differing amounts of scrub. For example, Konik ponies browse saplings in winter, whereas Welsh ponies rarely eat woody plants.

– **Traditional cattle breeds tend to be better suited to extensive systems.** Modern breeds have been bred for meat/milk production and are not adapted to harsh conditions. Older breeds are often found to be more suitable.

– **Individual animals with prior experience of grazing fen habitat are ideal.** Keeping the same group of animals allows them to learn the site layout and how best to use it. Youngsters can learn directly from experienced adults.

– **Match the animal to the management system.** A number of grazing projects have demonstrated great success with minimal intervention. However, the benefits of more natural or instinctive behaviour may be offset by animals becoming more difficult to handle when livestock movement or veterinary attention is required.

– **Mixed social structure.** The more natural the group composition is, the better they seem to thrive. With ponies, age, sex and position within the hierarchy has a role in the functioning of the herd.

6.2.5 Timing of grazing

Grazing at different times of year has different effects on fen wildlife, for example through its impact on seed setting. Ground conditions will dictate when stock are introduced and removed. Stock should always be removed before poaching becomes severe.

– **Autumn grazing** opens out the sward by removing summer growth and helps finer grasses and herbs to gain a foothold. It also allows the majority of wetland plants to set seed.

– **Winter grazing** removes coarse meadow grasses without affecting, for example, over-wintering buds of reed. However, it can easily lead to poaching. In general winter grazing is usually limited by the low food value of vegetation and consequent increased requirement for supplementary feeding. Due to the effect of runoff and poaching, supplementary feeding should be placed in fields adjacent to the fen and not within the fen. Where adjacent fields are not grazed as part of the unit, supplementary feeding must only be undertaken at the edge of the fen on dry ground.

- **Spring grazing** hits hardest those species which start growing early. These are often the most competitive species such as common reed (*Phragmites australis*) and reed canary-grass (*Phalaris arundinacea*). If left ungrazed, these tall fen species will swamp the lower-growing species which are less common and more highly valued. Where birch scrub and/ or purple moor-grass (*Molinia caerulea*) are a problem, graze intensively during March, April and May (0.5 to 1 head cattle/ha or 6 ewes/ha). Spring grazing can be beneficial for wetlands but, if high stocking rates are used, it can result in livestock trampling the nests of ground nesting bird species. Hence the importance of evaluating all the important features on a site prior to undertaking any management
See **Section 5: Fen Management and Restoration**.

- **Summer grazing** can prevent flowering and seeding of key plant species and may also cause trampling of birds nests.

Cattle grazing an area of fen and wet grassland extending to over 50 ha at Lough Beg, Northern Ireland. The wetter areas in the foreground are grazed later when the ground dries or when cattle have exhausted higher wet grassland and are forced into the lower, wetter areas in search of food (B. Hamill).

Cattle grazing is effective for rush management and/or managing sward structure for breeding waders. Although cattle tend not to graze rushes, they can destroy dense tussocks by trampling. In addition, if rushes are mown and removed in August, after the last wader chicks have fledged, cattle can then be introduced to graze the aftermath and will eat some of the young rush growth.

There is clear evidence that grazing can be an extremely valuable tool for maintaining and restoring conservation interest but grazing with the wrong type or number of livestock, at the wrong time, or for too long, can have disastrous consequences. Careful monitoring and adjustment of grazing regimes is therefore essential to avoid any negative impacts on fen flora and fauna or the health of grazing livestock.

6.2.6 Stocking rates and duration of grazing

Many variables influence and impact upon the 'ideal' grazing density. It is therefore difficult to offer meaningful generic guidance on precise stocking levels. The aim is to achieve the right balance between having sufficient animals to manage a range of vegetation types across the site. The best way to establish the optimum grazing regime is by trial and careful observation of ground conditions, the condition of the grazing livestock and effect of grazing on habitat structure and species composition. Extreme weather conditions, especially high rainfall must also be given due consideration at all times throughout the year.

Fens usually feature a range of different associated habitats, and the overall stocking density is determined by the relative proportions of habitats in the area to be managed. In general, it is best to graze fen habitats in conjunction with adjacent semi-improved or improved grassland which give livestock a choice of forage, helps maintain stock condition and usually means that the fen is lightly grazed. The figures below are a general guide, drawing on experience of grazing a range of different fens.

Open bog	0.02 LU/ha/yr
Fen/swamp	0.1 LU/ha/yr
Wet purple moor-grass heath	0.25 LU/ha/yr
Semi natural grassland	0.3 to 0.5 LU/ha/yr
Rush pasture	0.4 LU/ha/yr
Improved grassland	0.8 to 3.0 LU/ha/yr

One livestock unit (LU) is equivalent to one adult cow. One sheep is equivalent to 0.15 LU.

> In general, extensive grazing at low stocking rates is recommended with livestock free to roam widely across large management units.

Intensive grazing (i.e. stocking at high densities or well above normal recommended stocking rates) is generally not advisable on fens because wet soils are easily damaged by poaching. However, short periods of 2-3 weeks grazing in dry weather may be used to check scrub growth, where identified as appropriate within the fen management plan.

Always start grazing with low numbers, and adjust the stocking rates as the results of the grazing become apparent.

Careful monitoring is required to avoid overgrazing and poaching, as in the foreground of this picture, or undergrazing, as in the background (P. Corbett).

6.2.7 The benefits of extensive (low intensity) fen grazing

- **Promotes structural diversity** – extensive grazing creates good structural diversity in the sward (height and density).

- **Creates ecotones and habitat diversity** – in an extensive system grazing animals create ecotones, for example, at the transition between scrub and fen. In year-round grazing systems, animals make seasonal use of the site, move around and change grazing patterns according to the seasons, as their dietary requirements adjust to the changing environment.

- **Wet sites can be grazed** – water buffalo, Highland cattle and Hebridean sheep are able to graze schwingmoor (a floating mat of vegetation) and very wet peat, including areas flooded with significant surface water, provided dry areas are also available.

- **Animal dung provides an important habitat and food source for a wide range of invertebrates and in turn, their predators**. Many conservation organisations have now banned the use of worming drugs such as Ivermectins owing to their toxicity and long residence time in the dung, which can be detrimental to the invertebrates supported by dung.

6.2.8 The limitations of extensive fen grazing

- Localised over-grazing may be a problem in favoured areas. In contrast, some areas may be avoided by stock, allowing the vegetation to become rank and more unpalatable.

- Extensive grazing will not arrest succession, control or remove scrub but can maintain clearings open and check re-growth.

- The health and welfare of livestock can be seriously compromised if livestock are not used to harsh conditions, if the sward is of insufficient nutritional quality, or if there is a lack of dry refuge land.

Cattle grazing in a valley mire in the New Forest, preventing succession to scrub or woodland. Access to higher, drier ground allows cattle refuge from the wetter fen (I. Diack).

At Loughkeelan in Northern Ireland cattle tend to stay on adjacent higher drier ground, only grazing the periphery of the inter-drumlin fen. Although heavily poached, the grazed area of fen is much more diverse than the ungrazed tall reed-dominated area of fen. This fen would benefit from mowing the tall reeds back towards the open water to encourage cattle to graze a larger proportion of the fen, which would enhance overall diversity (P. Corbett).

6.2.9 Poaching: good or bad?

Hoof damage by livestock, commonly referred to as poaching, is almost inevitable when grazing wetlands, particularly around gateways, feeding and watering points, during wet weather, and when stock are confined to a small area. Poaching macerates the vegetative cover and causes soil compaction, which in turn makes it more prone to erosion, surface run-off of soil and manure, and colonisation by weedy species. However poaching on a limited scale creates bare ground for seed germination and provides microhabitats for other species (see **Section 9: Creating Fen Habitat**). The problem is judging when poaching is causing more harm than good.

Excessive poaching where cattle have congregated and ranged along a fence line, exacerbated by a blocked drain. Poaching like this exposing more than 80% bare soil allows colonisation by weedy species and recovery may take several years (A. McBride).

Established and dense swards are more resilient to hoof damage than swards which are open or newly established.

Localised temporary poaching photographed the day after stock were removed for the winter. This route is regularly tracked by sheep accessing different parts of the wetland. Although muddy, there is no standing water and the vegetation quickly recovers (A. McBride).

Close-up of the poached area pictured above taken the following spring, showing good recovery from poaching (A. McBride).

As a general guide, stock should be removed when 10% of bare soil is visible across the surface area of a representative sample of the vegetation of the grazed area(s).

Localised poaching caused by sheep. This is not currently affecting the main part of the fen, but is a warning of the need to start thinking about removing or reducing stock numbers on the site to allow vegetation recovery. If stock remain on the site too long, recovery will be slow and could encourage weedy species (A. McBride).

113

Tips for reducing poaching

- Wherever possible include the fen as part of a larger grazing unit, allowing livestock access to drier areas to which they will instinctively move during wet weather.

- Position gates and fences away from the edges of the fen and where possible choose places that are firm and well drained.

- Place sleeper bridges over ditches on the fen to provide crossing points, close to where stock enters the site. Slats attached to the deck of the bridge can encourage stock onto bridges and reduces slipping.

- If supplementary feeding of stock is required, use sacrificial feed areas well away from the fen, ideally on hard standing.

- Whatever the season, exclude stock from the fen during prolonged or extreme wet weather.

Sleeper bridges will reduce poaching but need to be sited in relatively dry areas as they are a focus for stock movement (A. McBride).

6.2.10 Monitoring grazing

Grazing needs careful monitoring, both from a conservation perspective to ensure that it is achieving the desired management objectives, and from an animal welfare perspective. Most grazing animals are selective, and some plants are not palatable or are only eaten when at their most tender in early growth stages. Rushes, though important components of some fen communities, may become dominant if the site is grazed by animals that find them unpalatable. **Section 10: Monitoring to Inform Fen Management** includes further guidance on monitoring techniques and analysis.

6.3   Mechanical cutting and mowing

The following notes provide a very brief introduction to mechanical cutting and mowing. Detailed advice on reedbed management is provided in "Reedbed Management for Commercial and Wildlife Interests" (Hawke and Jose, 1996).

6.3.1 Commercial cutting and mowing

Marsh hay can be commercially cut, although its production is highly weather dependent. The more common commercial cutting and mowing of fens is for high quality reed for thatching, which is an age-old tradition which has helped maintain extensive areas of wetlands which would otherwise have been drained and used for intensive agriculture. A number of birds such as bittern and reed warbler, and a wide range of invertebrates, are associated with commercially cut reedbeds. Reed grown for commercial purposes has to meet certain criteria in terms of strength, shape and height, and is typically harvested from pure beds of common reed (*Phragmites australis*). Cutting biennially on a double wale cycle is preferable to annual (single wale) cutting because the areas left uncut each year in the longer rotation provide a refuge for birds and invertebrates. Tied bundles of cut reed are removed from site, often by boat, ready for sale to local thatchers. Removal of all of the material from the site without the need for burning or piling makes it more environmentally friendly than some other management methods. As well as the cost effectiveness of cutting reed for sale, additional benefits of commercial cutting include the small size machines typically used which limit the level of disturbance, and consistency in management by one or two people which allows opportunity for them to build up a detailed knowledge of the site.

Commercially grown great fen-sedge (*Cladium mariscus*) is cut on average every three to four years, which allows time for regrowth to harvestable length, and is also ideal for most fen plant communities. If the sedge beds are left much longer than four years before cutting, they may become non-commercial and the accumulation of plant litter shades out some of the smaller associated plant species. On seasonally flooded fens, cutting is usually carried out in summer which allows the cut stems to grow above the anticipated floodwater level in winter. If the sedge is cut later in the year or grazed, the sedge beds can be destroyed by winter flooding. However, at Bure marshes NNR, winter cutting has been undertaken successfully by cutting the vegetation much higher with a scythe.

6.3.2 Small scale conservation cutting and mowing

In contrast to commercial reedbeds, mixed reed and sedge-dominated fen habitats usually yield poor quality thatching material and are consequently of low economic value, but these mixed stands are of significant value for conservation because of the diversity of flora and fauna they support. Cutting or mowing has become a widely-practised conservation management technique to maintain open fen, allowing more flexibility than grazing, and scope to adapt the method of mowing or cutting to meet individual site requirements.

Mowing an area of wet fen associated with a spillway adjacent to North Esk Reservoir on the Pentland Hills, near Edinburgh. Sheep had preferentially grazed extensive drier areas to which they had access, resulting in the fen becoming rank. A scythe attachment powered by a BCS Bankcommander tractor unit was used for mowing, and a CAEB mini-baler for baling, powered by the same tractor. The resultant bales were heavy and difficult to move, but the fresh regrowth after mowing prompted the sheep to resume grazing of the fen (A. McBride).

No outlets yet exist for material cut for conservation purposes, which is usually raked into habitat piles that benefit invertebrates or burned on site (see 6.4.3). However, trials in the Broads to turn cut reed into small pellets for use in multi-fuel burners for small-scale heat generation, are now complete. The technology for harvesting, processing and burning pellets is now well established. However, there are a number of constraints which must be met for the process to be economically viable. Further information on the development of reed pellets may be found in the final report produced by the Broad's Authority in 2010.

Cutting sites in small patches, avoiding very wet or unstable parts, ensures that some tall vegetation is left standing to provide habitat continuity for associated flora and fauna and is more desirable on fens of high conservation value than large-scale short rotation cutting.

All mowing techniques cut to a uniform height reducing variability within the vegetation, which in turn, can result in loss of associated flora and fauna. This is a particular problem for invertebrates and other animals dependent on tussocks. Mechanical cutting or mowing can also cause damage through compaction, even where specially designed machinery is used to reduce ground pressure.

6.3.3 Cutting and mowing machinery

Various types of mowing and cutting machinery are suitable for use on fens. Hand tools or small machines can be ideal for small, isolated sites, but are neither cost effective nor viable on large areas of fen. Up until recently, the major limitation on fen management was often not the cutting but the gathering and removal of cut material from sites. Mechanical developments have revolutionised fen management, enabling the Broads Authority to cut 250 ha fen each year. The main types of machinery used for cutting and mowing fens are:

Small hand-operated mowers, best suited to small basin fens such as those found in the drumlin belts of Northern Ireland or the Scottish Borders.

Pedestrian-driven mowers with reciprocating blades, as used by most modern-day reed and sedge cutters, and equally suitable for conservation mowing. They can cope with tall, thick reeds, sedges, grasses and herbs. Walk behind brush mowers are also an important tool for conservation mowing. These work like a large tractor-driven field mower, scaled down to affordable walk-behind size which is ideal for keeping tall vegetation under control, including small woody saplings.

Pedestrian mower being used to cut fen meadow (A.McBride).

'Soft track' machines, such as that used by the RSPB on their Ham Wall reserve in Somerset, are also designed for large-scale mowing and collection.

Softrac with 'cut and collect' harvester in use at Aber Bogs, Loch Lomond NNR (A.McBride)

Machines developed specifically for wet conditions include the Swedish manufactured 'Truxor' which is both amphibious and capable of tracking across dry ground. This type of machine is being used at Amwell Nature Reserve in Hertfordshire to improve the structure of reedbeds for bitterns.

Rubber tracked tractor with Ryetec contractor flail collector cutting fen on the Leckford Estate on the River Test, Hampshire. This type of machine works well on land which is too soft or steep for a wheeled tractor, and has facility for attachment of swipes, flails, rotovators and chippers (S. Duffield).

Fen harvesters have recently been developed to make annual cutting and mowing of large areas such as the Norfolk and Suffolk Broads more viable. This type of machine cuts in a single pass with double reciprocating blades, and simultaneously collects cut material using an augur. The cut vegetation is then fed via rollers into a forage harvester which chops it into strands approximately 20 mm long, which are thrown via a chute into a large 8 cubic metre bin. The harvester can then either tip and pile the material, or it is fed with air into a pipeline which either blows the cut material off-site or into a bulk trailer, thus avoiding risk of damage to the fen surface from repeated use of terrestrial vehicles.

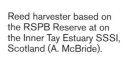
Reed harvester based on the RSPB Reserve at on the Inner Tay Estuary SSSI, Scotland (A. McBride).

Fen harvester use in the Broads

The European Union funded 'New Wetland Harvests' project which ran for three years from 1997 developed and demonstrated the use of a highly specialised mechanical harvester with very low ground pressure, designed to cope with wet, soft and uneven terrain of high environmental sensitivity.

Fen Harvester (Broads Authority)

Effects on conservation interest – species diversity has increased significantly following a harvester cut on previously abandoned sites and others classified as species-poor stands of tall reed-dominated vegetation.

Costs – machinery running costs and costs associated with removing cut material from site by blowing are high, but still lower than hand mowing if the costs of removing cut vegetation are taken into account. Revenue costs for cutting with the fen harvester are approximately £2-3,000 per hectare

Limitations – there are a number of sites in the Broads and elsewhere, which either the blower cannot access, or where the size of the site prevents the use of the pipeline. This limits the application of the harvester quite significantly. The proximity of outlets such as suitable burning facilities is also a limitation.

The design of the pipeline allows for cut fen vegetation to be blown over distances of more than 1000 m. However, in practice, blowing performance tends to decrease after 700 m owing to a reduction of air pressure leading to blockages in the pipe. When blockages or holes occur within the pipe, they have to be cleared and repaired manually before the operation can continue. Moving the machine and setting up on new sites is time consuming and expensive, which makes small sites less suitable.

6.4   Burning

Burning can rapidly remove large amounts of material, and is used in commercially managed reedbeds destined for thatching to favour dominance of reeds, to burn unwanted or poor quality reed, and to encourage shoots to grow straight, all of which helps produce a higher quality product. In the Broads, the general principle is that burning should only be used in fen restoration where the proposed habitat modification is so great that there is likely to be little continuity of the original vegetation communities and associated fauna. In some uplands, muirburn or burning on a larger scale to regenerate heather for grazing livestock and game may have benefits for spring flushes found amongst the heather by keeping them clear of encroaching dwarf shrub heath. Some farmers traditionally burned grass litter on fens to stimulate new growth and provide an 'early bite' for cattle. In North America, burning is a commonly occurring natural phenomenon and widely prescribed for fen management, but in the UK burning of fen vegetation can have seriously detrimental effects on plant communities, the viability of invertebrate populations or breeding success of birds.

Burning can be highly detrimental for many species of conservation concern if undertaken inappropriately, and is therefore generally NOT recommended for conservation management of fens.

Burning should only be considered where it has been used historically to successfully manage habitats and species, and should only be undertaken with extreme caution under strict conditions.

Burning on fens at the Leckford Estate in Hampshire has successfully rejuvenated rank fen vegetation with greater tussock sedge, but can have disastrous consequences if not carefully supervised or undertaken on inappropriate sites (Simon Duffield).

6.4.1 The risks of burning

Plant litter is an important part of many animals' environment. Species of invertebrate live or lay eggs in dead stems of reeds and other tall graminoids, grass snakes and adders seek shelter in plant litter, mammals such as water vole may pass through plant litter, and birds nest in and above it. In addition, purple moor-grass litter provides cover for field voles and its removal exposes them to predation. Therefore, burning litter is not selective and can be lethal to many vertebrates and invertebrates living or hibernating in the dead or live vegetation. For example, the rare Annex II species, Desmoulin's whorl snail (*Vertigo moulinsiana*), may over-winter in dead litter. There is no guarantee that burned areas will be re-colonised from surrounding areas.

The natural growth sequence in fens is for much of the partially rotted remains of plants growing each year to accumulate as peat, which locks up atmospheric carbon. Although burning may appear useful as a management tool in preventing peat accumulation and thus slowing hydroseral succession, burning releases carbon and nutrients that would otherwise remain bound in the peat. Another hazard of burning vegetation on peat is that the peat itself may ignite and smoulder for days or even weeks as a deep-seated fire, bursting into flames whenever fanned by the wind, and releasing large amounts of carbon dioxide into the atmosphere.

> The extract below from Wicken Fen management plan explains why on many fens managed for conservation, other more reliable methods have been favoured over burning.
>
> There is no tradition of the use of burning at Wicken Fen. Extensive fires have generally been considered a hazard on Sedge Fen, although burning has been proposed from time to time as a management tool. It has been used to assist in localised bush clearance, normally of very small areas, since the war.
>
> Major accidental fires occurred in 1929 and 1952. In April 1980, the standing litter in one compartment was burned, but the fire got out of control and spread across Cross Dyke to another compartment. Much of the northern third of this was burnt-out, many trees and bushes were killed and the sedge crop lost. In 1989 and 1991, a smouldering litter heap flared up after hours, and led to major fires in two additional compartments.
>
> The deliberate burning of standing vegetation is likely to be a rare event, and should only be considered for specific areas with careful precautions and when no other management is appropriate.
> http://www.ecoln.com/wicken_fen/m97a6000.html

6.4.2 When and how to burn

Where burning is chosen as a last resort management tool, it should preferably be undertaken in winter when peat, if present, is more likely to be waterlogged and is therefore slower to ignite. Even so, winter burning can kill hibernating animals such as grass snakes and over-wintering invertebrates. Spring is the poor second choice, but standing reed should not be burned after March 31st.

Protocol for burning standing reedbeds and other types of tall fen vegetation

- Flames can reach considerable height and fire can spread rapidly in standing reed, so adjoining landowners should be informed of intention to burn, proposed time and date.

- Create a fire-break around the plot to be burnt, which should consist of a cleared area of a minimum width of three to four times the height of the standing reed. Breaks may be cut either using a reed harvester or brush cutter to gain better control of the fire. Reed-free ditches that are more than three metres wide may also sometimes be effectively used as firebreaks.

- Burn directly into the wind for greater control and a slower, but deeper burn.

- Control fire margins with beaters/water.

- Where more control is desired, the reeds may be flattened (to reduce flame height) prior to burning.

- Avoid block-burning of sedge beds.

From: Heather & Grass Burning Code 2007. Best Practice Guide 5: Use of Fire to Manage Reedbeds and Saw-Sedge. Defra, 2007

The Broads Authority have established the following policy on sites where burning is considered acceptable:

- Sites that have been managed traditionally through burning for a long period of time to maintain them in an open condition.

- Small-scale restoration burns to restore mixed fen or to rejuvenate commercial reedbeds and sedge beds.

- Where an area has been cleared of scrub and is destined to be turf ponded.

- Mown material may be piled and burnt on recognised fire sites in all but the most sensitive areas.

6.4.3 Safe burning of cut vegetation (incineration)

Burning or incinerating heaps of cut material is generally safer than burning standing vegetation, but the above principles should still be followed to create sufficient firebreaks to prevent fire spreading to neighbouring vegetation or landholdings. The effect of nutrients released by burning (including those which find their way into local watercourses or underlying aquifer), destruction of vegetation, fauna and peat beneath the bonfire sites and the persistence of the ash, also need to be taken into account.

Unless the burning takes place in a sump or hollow (not recommended), the products of combustion should flush out over the course of time. Burning on metal sheeting will help contain ash, but the heat will still affect what lies beneath. The ideal is to burn in a trailer or skip, which is raised above the ground, contains any leachate and in which the ash can be removed. However the risk of damage caused by repeated passes to remove ash must be weighed against that from nutrient enrichment from a bonfire.

Health and safety requirements associated with ash disposal include legislative requirement for the operator to wear full safety equipment. Further information on incineration methods is provided under scrub management.

Specialised burning crates developed on the Whitlaw Mosses in the Scottish Borders to burn vegetation cut as part of conservation management - see Case Study 6.1 for more details (A. McBride).

Check with Natural England, CCW, SNH or NIEA whether burning would be consented on a legally protected site.

6.5 Scrub management

Traditionally, scrub was kept in check by grazing and mowing. Without such active management, open fen vegetation can rapidly become colonised by scrub. Changes in agricultural management practices at a national scale in recent decades have resulted in many fen communities converting to scrub and wet woodland.

Rapid colonisation of downy birch and willow scrub on Drumcrow Fen in Northern Ireland as a result of abandonment of peat cutting and removal of grazing. This is threatening the diverse range of fen habitats and important invertebrate assemblage (B. Hamill).

Tree removal may reduce water lost by evapo-transpiration and the interception of rainfall, which can be particularly important in summer, when precipitation tends to be lower and evaporation high. In one study the rates of evapo-transpiration from reedbeds were found to be around 98% of that from open water, whilst evapo-transpiration from wet woodland was between 89% and 164%. Modelling the hydrological budget of the site is the only way to be sure whether the removal of a large stand of trees is likely to increase the height of the water-table.

Long rotation scrub clearance may be the most practical or desirable management option, particularly where follow-up management of the open fen may be difficult to arrange. While this form of management does not manage the sward beneath the scrub, it is an important pre-requisite for doing so.

Key points to consider in relation to scrub management are summarised below. Scrub removal is described in detail in The Scrub Management Handbook (English Nature, 2003) and the Reedbed Management Handbook (Hawke and Jose, 1996).

> Depending on the size of trees and scale of work being carried out, a felling licence may be required, and the disposal of cut material by burning or other activities may have to be registered with the relevant statutory authority as an exemption. See Appendix V.

6.5.1 General guidelines on scrub management

- **Prioritise scrub removal** on areas which are likely to produce good quality fen following restoration, and areas of fen most recently or partially invaded to prevent further deterioration or habitat change.

- **Avoid clearing established scrub and woodland communities** which are now more valuable in conservation terms than the original fen habitat, or the type of habitat which could be restored.

- **Consider the whole site when deciding on the proportion of scrub to open fen**. In England the Environmentally Sensitive Area (ESA) scheme's Fen Tier target is for 10% of a potentially open fen area to remain as scrub. This same target figure is also used in the JNCC's Common Standards for Monitoring guidance for lowland wetlands. However other targets may be more appropriate depending on local priorities for birds or invertebrate interest. For example, in the Norfolk and Suffolk Broads, the target for scattered scrub within open fens is a maximum of 5%. This excludes small blocks of dense and continuous scrub which may be associated with the open fen and contributes to an overall target figure of 10%.

- Consider the distribution pattern of scrub as well as the overall proportion in relation to other habitat types.

- **Grind stumps or treat with appropriate herbicide after clearance** to limit re-growth and to facilitate follow-up management. Combining herbicide treatment and stump grinding should ensure that most trees are killed. (see section 6.5.3)

Take account of follow-up management requirements in choosing which method of scrub clearance is most appropriate. Pulled stumps leave holes, but high stumps may obstruct the use of machinery in the future. For further information see The Scrub Management Handbook: Guidance on the Management of Scrub on Nature Conservation, English Nature, 2003.

Scrub clearance from an area of fen at Betley Mere SSSI in Cheshire. The cut stumps have been treated with herbicide to prevent (or at least reduce) the amount of scrub regrowth (B. Hamill).

6.5.2 Methods of Scrub Clearance

The table below summarises the most common methods of scrub clearance and disposal of the cut material.

Method	Advantages/ suitable sites	Disadvantages	Examples
Hand clearance by volunteers or contractors using manual saws or chainsaws. Scrub is normally cut at the base of the trunk. The material is then either burned on site at a designated bonfire site or loaded into a chipping machine. All cut stumps should be treated with herbicide to prevent re-growth.	Small and inaccessible sites	Labour intensive Expensive	
JCB Excavator removes the entire tree including the root system by pulling/ pushing and digging around it. Some machines include facility for stump grinding. Woody material can be buried under spoil banks if the operation is combined with dyke restoration, or chipped, burned or transported off site. If chipped, the material should be removed from the site unless spreading is known to be harmless or beneficial. In some cases the chipped material can be used on site to create paths. Typically the machine weighs 8 tonnes with a ground pressure of 4.5 psi (pounds per square inch). It travels around sites on tracks using existing banks, but can also run on the fen itself if dry or on mats if the surface is too wet. The mats weigh 1ton each and reduce the ground pressure of the machine to 1.09 psi.	A single machine can restore dykes and remove scrub in the same operation, maximising efficiency and cost-effectiveness. If scrub is burned, no need for additional machinery on site. No stumps remain to produce regrowth. Large scrub can be tackled by digging around the roots and pushing the tree over.	Heavy machinery causes compaction by repeated passes when tracking directly on the fen surface. Pulling the entire tree from the ground leaves holes within the peat and destabilises the surrounding surface, which creates problems for both livestock and mowing machines and the surface may remain unstable for a number of years. There can be a huge amount of woody material for disposal.	Norfolk and Suffolk Broads

'Bird-eye' and incineration A tracked excavator working on mats is fitted with a special 'bird-eye' cutting head consisting of one spinning disc which fells trees up to 75 cm diameter and grinds stumps. Once trees are felled, they are placed within a large portable incinerator where they are reduced to ash. Initial trials suggest that 1 hectare of scrub can be cut within 4-6 days, with an incineration rate of a further 4-6 days. The excavator has a ground pressure of 1.5 psi. The incinerator itself can be moved around the site using the excavators, although a new system of locomotion is being investigated for use in the Broads using an experimental air platform, i.e. similar to a hovercraft. The incinerator has a ground pressure of 0.8 psi with floats, and 1.3 psi without floats.	Wide reach and low number of passes causes little damage to peat surface. Grinding process kills many stumps, especially if they are flooded at the time or shortly afterwards. Complete burn by the incinerator enables huge amounts of material to be reduced to manageable proportions. The cutting machine and incinerator carry large reserves of fuel and one refuelling trip per hectare is anticipated.	Some stump re-growth may need treating.	Norfolk and Suffolk Broads where bird eye cutting has been combined with a large portable incinerator to dispose of woody material.
Winches used to drag trees			
Sky line extraction which partially suspends the cut trees and scrub	Reduces damage from dragged material		Fenn's and Whixall Mosses, Clwyd
Helicopter extraction, usually of bundled tree trunks	Minimises damage from dragging	Very expensive	Roudsea Moss, Cumbria

6.5.3 Chemical control

Stumps should normally be treated immediately after cutting with an approved chemical to prevent regrowth. Stumps should be cut as low as possible to minimise the treatment area and as much herbicide as possible applied to the stump and basal bark without risk of liquid running off. The technique of 'drill and kill' before felling and physical removal has recently been used with some success on Portmore Lough in Northern Ireland (see Case Study 7.2) and has the potential advantage of reducing the amount of re-growth from tree stumps/roots left in the fen.

Formulations containing ammonium sulphamate (commonly marketed as Amcide) or glyphosate (Roundup) are the most common herbicides used for stump treatment, but recommended herbicides and their use are tightly controlled to avoid risk of pollution or other environmental damage. Details of herbicides suitable for use on nature conservation sites are listed in Natural England's Information Note 125 The Herbicide Handbook – Guidance on the use of herbicides on nature conservation sites. **If in doubt, always seek expert advice.**

6.6   Re-establishment of fen vegetation

The previous sections describe methods for influencing the direction of habitat change in fens where natural succession is causing the loss of features of interest. **Section 9: Creating Fen Habitat** offers guidance on creation of entirely new fens, often as part of larger wetlands.

Where fen is being re-created on sites that have been destroyed through past human activities, such as drainage, the ability to re-establish characteristic fen communities and the most suitable techniques to use, will depend on a number of factors including:

- the length of time the fen has been drained;
- the plant species present in any refugia within the area to be re-wetted;
- the proximity of extant fen habitat with a similar species composition.

6.6.1 Regeneration from the seed bank

The number of characteristic plant seeds surviving in the seed bank decreases as the length of time since the fen was drained increases. Only 4% of the seeds of fen species persist in the seed bank after 10 years (Maas and Schopp-Guth, 1995). Only the commoner hay meadow species persist in the seed bank where there has been agricultural improvement of former fen sites. The rarer species of hay and floodplain meadows have short-lived seed banks (Grootjans et al, 2002). The species present in the seed bank can easily be determined by spreading large soil samples out in seed trays and placing them in containers where the water level is kept permanently high.

6.6.2 Refugia

Most species of fen plants have rhizomes by which they will spread into wet areas vegetatively, as well as by seed. The speed at which fenland plants spread by rhizome varies: for reed this is usually somewhere between 10 cm and 2 m per annum. For those plants which do not readily produce viable seed, the deliberate transfer of small (30 cm x 30 cm) turfs will help accelerate the re-establishment of fen species. Care must be taken to cut turfs with sufficient depth of soil to include the rhizomes. This technique should not be used if invasive alien species such as parrot's-feather (*Myriophyllum aquaticum*) and New Zealand pygmy-weed (*Crassula helmsii*) are present on the donor site. Further guidance on planting of vegetative propagules and seeding is included in **Section 9: Creating Fen Habitat**.

6.6.3 Proximity of extant fen

Colonisation by seed from nearby fens is unlikely to occur unless there are direct channels along which vegetative fragments and seeds can float into the receptor site. Aquatic plants appear to spread more readily between wetlands than sedges and other emergent fen species. In North America (Johnson & Valppu 2003) it has been found necessary to take plugs of sedges and other plants from nearby fens to re-establish characteristic vegetation on cut-over fens. Turf removal to reduce nutrient levels in the surface layers (see **Section 8: Managing Fen Nutrient Enrichment**) removes the seed bank, making the re-establishment of species-rich meadow vegetation unlikely, unless donor plants are available.

6.7 Restoring fen meadow

Many former fen meadows across Europe have been lost through drainage and fertilisation for intensive agriculture. In their review of attempts to re-establish fen meadows on drained agricultural land, Grootjans et al. (2002) found that although grazing and cutting regimes helped to re-establish the target vegetation, results were generally poor if there had been long-term fertiliser use. It was possible to restore rich-fen vegetation where only fertiliser had been used, without drainage, by resuming mowing for hay and light grazing by livestock without the addition of fertilisers. Cropping the vegetation and rearing young animals on these sites made it possible to reduce nutrient levels in the vegetation and soils (Bakker & Olff 1995).

A fen meadow community of importance (*Cirsio-Molinietum*) has been restored on agriculturally improved mesotrophic grassland sites (*Holcus lanatus–Juncus effusus* rush-pasture) that had not received inorganic fertiliser for more than 13 years. This was achieved through a combination of treatments (straw and/or lignitic-clay) to reduce the availability of nutrients, primarily phosphate. Cropping the vegetation over a number of years or applying an organic material with very low concentrations of nitrogen and phosphorus encourages soil micro-organisms to temporarily remove these nutrients. However, the most effective measure was to strip-off some of the topsoil (15-20 cm) thereby removing the nutrient-enriched surface layers (Tallowin & Smith 2001). Where the topsoil was not removed, the vegetation became dominated by a handful of competitive species; few of the planted *Cirsio-Molinietum* species were still present after four years.

6.8 References

Bakker & Olff 1995. Nutrient dynamics during restoration of fen meadows by hay making without fertiliser application. In: *Restoration of Temperate Wetlands* (eds. Wheeler, B.D., Shaw, S.C, Fojt, W.J. & Robertson, R.A.), pp. 143-166. John Wiley, Chichester.

Broads Authority, 2004. *A supplement to the Fen Management Strategy, Incorporating the Fen Audit.* Prepared by Sue Stephenson, edited by Sandie Tolhurst.

English Nature, 2003. The Scrub Management Handbook: Guidance on the Management of Scrub on Natural Conservation Sites. IN124. English Nature, Peterborough.

Grootjans, A.P., Bakker, J.P., Jansen, A.J.M. & Kemmer, R.H. 2002. Restoration of brook valley meadows in the Netherlands. Hydrobiologia 478, 149-170.

Hawke, C.J. & José, P.V. 1996. *Reedbed Management for Commercial and Wildlife Interests.* Royal Society for the Protection of Birds, Sandy.

Johnson, K.W. & Valppu, S.H. 2003. *Fen restoration final project report.* Natural Resources Research Institute, University of Minnesota, Duluth.

Maas, D. & Schopp-Guth, A. (1995). Seed banks in fen areas and their potential use in restoration ecology. In: *Restoration of Temperate Wetlands* (eds. B.D. Wheeler, S.C. Shaw, W.J. Fojt & R.A. Robertson), pp. 189-206. John Wiley & Sons, Chichester.

Tallowin, J.R.B. & Smith, R.E.N. 2001. Restoration of a *Cirsio-Molinietum* Fen Meadow on an Agriculturally Improved Pasture. Restoration Ecology 9, 167-178.

Tolhurst, S., 1997. Investigation into the use of domestic herbivores for fen grazing management: a document for discussion. Broads Authority/English Nature/ Norfolk Wildlife Trust.

The Whitlaw Mosses National Nature Reserve (NNR) (Whitlaw Mosses) forms the core of an important series of around 200 basin mires in the central part of the Scottish Borders. The four component mosses occupy small shallow elongated basins in a corrugated landscape which formed from locally calcareous and tightly folded Silurian shales, from which base-rich groundwater arises in the form of springs and up-wellings. Each of the mosses on the composite site demonstrates at least one stage of hydroseral succession from open water/poor fen to willow carr. The mosses support a wide range of northern rarities such as holy grass, coralroot orchid and narrow small reed. In addition, the fens are home to rare mosses and several Red Data Book fly and water beetle species. Management of these small sites (2ha to 10 ha), therefore takes account of a wide range of specialised species. The overall aims of the NNR are to support those rare and specialised species by maintaining suitable conditions across the mosaic of habitats.

Overview of Murder Moss part of the Whitlaw Mosses NNR (A.McBride).

Historical Management

As a result of legal disputes, records of the historical management and use of the mosses are well detailed from the 1770s onwards. Uses and management at that time included all year grazing by sheep and lambs, cutting of bog hay and reeds, wood and brush cutting, and paring and burning of adjacent rough pasture to grow five successive arable crops before reseeding.

The two further historical operations which have created the mosses we see today are peat cutting and digging of marl, a substance found under the peat formed from the tiny shells of molluscs. Marl was used as a liming agent to improve acid land around the mosses before ground limestone was made widely available once the railways arrived. As traditional in other parts of Scotland, the turfs were replaced after peat cutting, which on Whitlaw Mosses rejuvenated the hydrosere whilst retaining some of the original surface vegetation. The digging of the marl had lowered the fen surface and also increased the pH of the water. In time, the drainage channels that allowed the removal of peat and marl fell into disrepair allowing water levels to rise.

The current management of the site replicates the historical management and tries to look at the site as a whole, rather than only the notified features, whilst recognising that much of the management is a holding operation until the effect of diffuse pollution in the catchment is resolved.

Fen cutting started in 1982. The species-rich fens are cut using a combination of pedestrian mower/baler and small tractor with cut and collect facility. The vegetation is cut in dry periods in August, dried where it is cut, collected and either burnt in mobile incinerators or used for stock bedding. The grasslands of the islands are cut in a similar manner leaving clumps of late flowering species for the benefit of butterflies and moths such as the Scotch Argus and five-spot burnet moth.

Reed management. In the late 1980s it was becoming apparent that common reed was expanding to the detriment of other fen communities, probably as result of diffuse pollution and a reduction in grazing following notification of the mosses in the 1970s. Since 1989, the reeds are cut, dried, collected and burnt in mobile incinerators at the end of August and the ash removed from the site. The timing of the cut coincides with the full extension of the reed and maximum development of the inflorescence to maximise the amount of vegetation removed. The area cut tends to be 30-40 m around the expanding edge of the reeds, which has checked expansion of the reedbeds and increased plant diversity within the cut area from three species of plant to around 25. Reeds still grow in the cut area, fed by the rhizomes of the main bed, but their height and density has been substantially reduced. In recent years to combat reed expansion in wetter areas inaccessible to machinery, a strategy of herbicide treatment with glyphosate applied with a weedwiper has been successful without negative impact on other vegetation.

Scrub and tree removal. Expanding birch scrub and trees were removed in the early 1990s and herbicide treatment continues today. A strategy of targeting the birch has paid off but in the early years the time input was high with some 30,000 birch seedlings removed from 0.1 ha alone in the summer of 1990. Regeneration has diminished dramatically since the seed source trees were removed and glyphosate treatment introduced.

Grazing. After a false start with stock being lost in deep open pools, grazing was reinstated on an annual basis in the mid 1990s. Between September and December, sheep are used to graze the regrowth following cutting. The fresh grass of the cut areas focuses grazing away from the more dangerous water holes.

Rejuvenation of the hydrosere. From 1970s aerial photographs it was apparent that the extent of open water on the sites was diminishing rapidly, to the detriment of invertebrates such as darters and damselflies, and plants like bladderwort. A programme of hand-digging small ponds was initiated in the early 1990s to partially rectify the situation. This has been a success with rapid expansion of latent colonies of bladderwort.

Catchment management. Many of the problems within the site are attributable to wider catchment management, which despite being in an upland context has had intensive arable and grassland culture. Designation as an Environmentally Sensitive Area in 1993 allowed farmers to create buffer zones and cease fertilising fields adjacent to the mosses. This has generally been a success in reducing inputs into the mosses, but many of the fields adjacent to the moss are the best on the farm for producing silage and consequently have not been included in ESA agreements.

Silt management. Silt high in phosphate is often washed into the burns and creates silt fans on the mosses, which encourage the expansion of reeds and terrestialisation. This is mainly a historical problem, partially resolved by fencing burns from stock and the installation of in-stream silt traps. However the silt fans on the mosses have encouraged the spread of reed to the more sensitive fen vegetation. Evaluation of silt removal suggests that the removal of the fans could release more silt and nutrients into the system with a further detrimental effect to those areas not affected by the silt. Therefore the site managers (SNH) rely on the vegetation management to contain the reed and conditions for a wide range of species.

Flooding of the fen
(A.McBride).

Case Study 6.2
Fen Vegetation Management
– Mid Yare

The RSPB Mid Yare Reserve in the Norfolk Broads is a good example of the effects on fen vegetation and molluscs of four years of light grazing by Highland cattle.

The aims of grazing were:

- to increase structural diversity of the fen to increase the range of microhabitats available for invertebrates

- to prevent vegetation succession,

- to increase or at least maintain the species-richness of the vegetation

Grazing management

The grazing unit was 13.6ha in extent and consisted mainly of tall-herb fen most similar to S25 reed *Phragmites australis*-hemp agrimony *Eupatorium cannabinum* tall-herb fen (see map). The fen had previously been mown on a fairly ad hoc basis, and was then heavily grazed by cattle in summer in 1996 and 1997 and left unmanaged in 1998. Highland cattle were introduced in 1999. Initially the fen was grazed year-round at densities of between 0.30-0.65 livestock units/ha, but this led to the following concerns:

- Difficulties accessing the fen for welfare checks during flood periods.

- The cattle flattened most dead reed in search of winter food, impacting on over-wintering invertebrates and breeding birds.

- There was excessive hoof growth, requiring time consuming and expensive trimming, due to the absence of hard ground

Cattle have subsequently been moved to a drier area from December to March, which allowed retention of standing reed. The stony tracks on the winter grazing area also removed the need for foot-trimming. Although the cattle have had access to green vegetation throughout the year, because of its limited availability under snow, ice or floodwater, poor quality hay has also been provided to supplement their diet between January and February.

Phasing out horned animals was suggested because of safety concerns, but observations showed that horns are important to the animals' social behaviour, and for scratching and pushing through scrub. Instead, the handling pen was redesigned, which together with careful planning and direction of handling activities, avoids the need to be in a confined space with the cattle.

The cattle have exhibited very few health problems, but they have declined in condition at 10-12 years old, at which stage older cattle have been individually culled from the herd. Establishing a mixed age structure early on was essential to ensure gradual replacement of older animals, which allows knowledge of the site to be passed on within the herd.

Monitoring and review of outcomes

It was realised at the outset that grazing had the potential to damage the mollusc fauna of the fen, which included the BAP Priority Species Desmoulin's whorl snail (*Vertigo moulinsiana*). Monitoring was therefore set up to determine the effects of

grazing on vegetation composition and structure, and on molluscs.
Measures of vegetation structure and composition were recorded in 20 quadrats in each of seven randomly located 15 x 30 m plots. One half of each plot was open to grazing, and the other half fenced off from grazing. Densities of molluscs were estimated by carrying out timed searches in eight 0.5 x 0.5 m quadrats in the grazed and ungrazed halves of each of these seven plots.

The effects of grazing

Statistical significant differences in the composition and structure of S25 tall-herb fen after four years of grazing were:

- Increased dominance of reed sweet-grass *Glyceria maxima* at the expense of reed *Phragmites australis*.

- Increased plant species-richness.

- Reduced vegetation height

- Reduced biomass of common reed and total vegetation biomass.

- Reduced inflorescence density of common reed.

Cattle were frequently observed feeding on the bark of willow scrub in winter, breaking willow branches with their horns and browsing their leaves, and so probably also reduced the growth of low scrub. No differences were detected in fine-scale (tens of centimetre) variation in habitat structure between grazed and ungrazed areas. However, the large-scale variation in grazing pressure within the fen increased large-scale (tens of metres) variation in habitat structure.

Plant species showing significant differences in frequency between grazed and ungrazed plots after four years of grazing.

Species more frequent in grazed halves of plots	Species more frequent in ungrazed halves of plots
Celery-leaved buttercup	Greater pond-sedge
Common duckweed	
Gypsywort	
Pink/blue water-speedwell	
Purple loosestrife	
Reed sweet-grass Tufted forget-me-not	

Grazing substantially decreased densities of Desmoulin's whorl snail. This species, though, remained widely distributed in areas within the grazing unit that the cattle did not graze.

Conclusions

Light grazing by Highland cattle has proved a useful method for increasing the plant species-richness and probably large-scale vegetation structure of derelict fen. It is probably also likely to slow the rate of succession to scrub.

On the negative side, grazing reduced overall densities of at least some key mollusc species. These population reductions, though, have to be set against losses which would take place if the fen was left unmanaged to succeed to scrub. They also have to be set against likely increases in abundance of other important invertebrate species which benefit from more varied habitat structure. Breeding densities and species diversity of wetland passerines increased following grazing and exceeded those in nearby mown fen.

Fen grazing is, in most cases, likely to be considerably cheaper than re-instating mowing and burning of the cut material over large areas (estimated at ca. £1,600 per ha of fen mown). The cost of the grazing project has been covered by the £150/ha annual ESA payment for fen management.

References

Ausden, M., Hall, M., Pearson, P. and Strudwick, T. (2005). The effects of cattle grazing on tall-herb fen vegetation and molluscs. *Biological Conservation*, 122, 317-326.

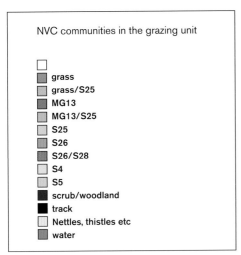

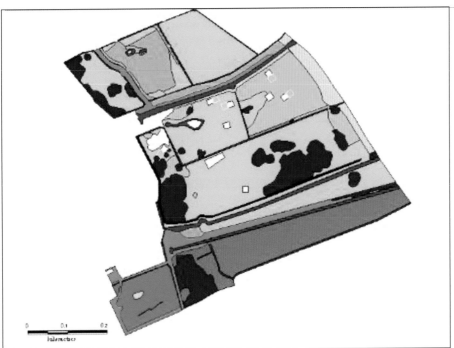

NVC Communities at the RSPB Mid Yare Reserve in the Norfolk Broads

Case Study 6.3
Fen Vegetation Management
– Bure Marshes

Bure Marshes is a 736 ha fen NNR on the Norfolk Broads (OSGR TG337166).

Past management

Prior to the second half of the 20th century, many areas of the Norfolk Broads floodplain fens which were not able to be cut for commercial reed and sedge for thatching were economically important for marsh hay. This was used as feed and bedding for cattle and horses, and was a valuable resource, due to the high productivity of the marshes. Changes in agricultural practices, notably the ability to produce high-nutrient hay from fertilised grass leys and the reduction in the agricultural labour force with increased mechanisation (not an option on these soft wet peat soils) meant that most of these areas were no longer cut.

Successional processes and the winter-wet summer-dry water regime allowed Bure Marshes to develop as a species-rich tall-fen vegetation type (NVC S24, *Peucedano-Phragmitetum australis* fen) dominated by reed with the Broads rarity milk parsley *Peucedanum palustris*, foodplant of the swallowtail butterfly. In contrast, lower areas within the floodplain remain wet for more of the year, inhibiting many plant species other than large monocots and producing species-poor reedbeds. Lack of mowing also allows the formation of tussocks, often of tussock sedge *Carex elata*, which provides habitat and refuges for plants (and animals) intolerant of prolonged flooding. These same conditions, however, also favour colonisation by woody species, particularly alder *Alnus glutinosa* and grey sallow *Salix cinerea*, which, left unchecked, can rapidly convert open fen into wet woodland.

Management rationale

While wet woodland has its virtues (and much of that found in the Broads is a feature of European importance), recently-colonised areas of fen are in the process of losing the open fen interest (swallowtail butterflies being a good example) and have not yet acquired the wet woodland interest which comes with age and a high deadwood component. Past conservation efforts have therefore concentrated on reducing the extent of wet woodland, clearing areas of recent (post Second World War) scrub and maintaining open fen interest, especially S24 NVC communities.

Techniques

Open fen maintenance initially took the form of large-scale mowing, on the reasonable grounds that this was the agricultural technique which had formerly maintained the habitat. Commercial reed and sedge cutting will not be considered here – they have their own rationale and deal successfully with well-defined communities.

Burning

While burning standing vegetation can be very effective in regenerating the plant community, its effect on invertebrates is unlikely to be beneficial across the range of species. Strip burning can reduce the problem, but requires extensive cutting of firebreaks, sometimes to the extent that burning the remainder is superfluous.

The temptation to burn large areas is considerable. Natural England does not consent fen management by burning in the Broads, except when it is considered an appropriate part of restoration to commercial cutting regimes.

Mowing
A variety of rotations have been used, from annual cutting up to about once every ten years.

Annual or biennial cutting can produce a type of species-rich fen meadow (M13, M22) where the *Phragmites* canopy is replaced by *Juncus subnodulosus*, albeit at the cost of losing the prized S24 communities. Species-rich fen meadow is now a rare vegetation type within the Broads. However, regular cutting is required to prevent the formation of a thick mat of *Juncus* litter, which can suppress many smaller species. Disadvantages include:

- Frequent cutting can destroy tussock structure; in low-lying fens, this can result in a reduction in species richness.

- Disposal of arisings – apart from the lack of demand, disposal of the material off-site is seldom possible, due to physical difficulties of moving the material over soft, wet peat soils without causing considerable structural damage, as well as the resource needs for these labour-intensive operations. On-site disposal, whether by burning in bonfires or composting, produces local nutrient enrichment and consequent vegetation changes.

- Lack of continuity and physical structure due to frequent cutting is disadvantageous to invertebrate communities.

- Operation is labour-intensive.

Despite these disadvantages, the rarity of these fen meadow communities means that this form of management is still considered worthwhile in small, more manageable patches. It is worth noting that once established by cutting, these communities can largely be maintained by low-level grazing as described below, which can allow the tussock structure to recover.

Longer-rotation cutting (5 – 10 years) maintains the S24 communities by periodically opening up the surface to allow many component species to germinate from seed, while removing woody growth and hence retarding succession to scrub and woodland.
Disadvantages include:

- Disposal of arisings: leaving cut material on the fen can produce a dense litter mat which suppresses germination and growth of many species, while on-site disposal can cause local nutrient enrichment problems. Machinery such as the Broads Authority's fen harvester can blow chopped litter some distance, but the ultimate disposal problem may just be moved to another part of the floodplain.

- Quantities of woody material from 5-10 years of scrub growth can also present disposal problems.

- Large-scale catastrophic management: because of the areas involved (typically compartments of up to 5 ha), operations involving machinery tend to be on a fairly large scale. This presents problems for many invertebrates which can be slow to recolonise, while the uniformity of habitat which results may disadvantage some species. This can be overcome by techniques such as cutting in strips.

- Labour-intensive.

Low-level grazing, using traditional breeds, seems to be an effective way of managing these areas. At Woodbastwick Marshes, part of Bure Marshes NNR, four Highland cattle have been grazing 25ha of tall-herb fen since 2000.

Mowing can be considered as mechanical grazing; it retards plant succession and opens up the surface to allow seed germination and growth, but grazing has a number of advantages over cutting:

- Lack of arisings: no bulky material to dispose of.

- Low labour requirements.

- Low maintenance: cattle cost less than machinery, do not require much in the way of fossil fuels, and traditional breeds can be very hardy.

- Continuity combined with variety of physical structure: at this level of grazing, some areas of fen are left untouched for long periods, while others are opened up. The grazed areas vary from year to year. This physically varied community would be very difficult to produce mechanically, and should be advantageous to a variety of invertebrates. Grazing at these low levels has not affected the plant community composition.

- Creation of additional microhabitats: droppings and water-filled hoofprints add valued structure at small scales.

Nothing is perfect, however. Attendant disadvantages which need to be dealt with include:

- **Site structure**: not all fen sites are suitable for grazing animals. One major requirement is for refuge areas which can be used at times of high water and flooding. At Bure Marshes there are several spoil banks which remain dry, and an adjacent field on higher ground is leased.

- **Need for infrastructure**: some capital investment is needed for handling facilities (typically a pen and race), bridges and fencing. Water-filled ditches, as at Woodbastwick, make effective wet fences.

- **Welfare considerations**: traditional breeds such as Highlands are very hardy, can cope with wet conditions without being vulnerable to foot and parasite problems and hence need little veterinary input. Less hardy commercial breeds seem unable to obtain sufficient nutrition from fen vegetation (the Woodbastwick animals have had one supplementary hay bale in eight years). However, regular checking is required.

- **Scrub**: cattle at these grazing levels do not prevent scrub growth, although they can damage it by rubbing and limited browsing. In order to prevent excessive scrub development, bushes are cut individually with brush-cutters. This allows a scattering of scrub to be maintained within the fen (typically about 5% scattered cover), necessary for a variety of fauna, including song perches for sedge warblers. Cut material is not produced in large quantities at any one time, and can be cut up and left to rapidly decompose within the fen, producing another microhabitat.

In effect, the combination of cattle and staff with brush-cutters produces a "super-grazer" and a type of "semi-natural" management for this semi-natural habitat.

Outcomes

In the eight years that the cattle have been on-site, there has been a considerable increase in the physical structure of the tall-herb fen, without changes in community composition. As well as variations in the height of the vegetation, acceptable levels of scattered scrub, good tussock structure and additional microhabitats have been maintained. Freeing-up of labour has allowed concentration on other areas requiring management. The cattle are healthy and happy (as far as it is possible to tell!), and are popular with visitors, and provide a focal point for discussion of wetland ecology and management. While it may seem common sense to assume that this should benefit fen invertebrates, there is as yet no clear evidence of this. A current three-year project, jointly funded by Natural England and the Broads Authority over a number of fen sites, will go some way to answering this.

Traditional breeds of cattle
grazing Bure Marshes.
(Broads Authority)

Swallowtail butterfly –
the result of successful
management.
(Broads Authority)

The Anglesey Fens SAC is a complex of six basin and valley-head rich-fen systems located in the Carboniferous Limestone Region of central Anglesey. The component sites range in size from a few ha to over 250 ha and support a range of plant communities referable to the Annex I types alkaline fen and calcareous fen with *Cladium mariscus* and species of the *Caricion davallianae*, as well as areas of base-enriched fen meadow referable to the Eu-Molinion (NVC community M24) and other calcareous types (notably M22). Of particular importance is the quality and range of M13 seepage communities dominated by black bog-rush (*Schoenus nigricans*); other key features include areas of open sedge- and brown-moss-rich vegetation, sometimes with great fen-sedge (*Cladium mariscus*), and less base-enriched vegetation dominated by *Cladium* with purple moor-grass (*Molinia caerulea*), blunt-flowered rush (*Juncus subnodulosus*), bog myrtle (*Myrica gale*) and a range of ericoids referable to the non-NVC *Cladio-Molinietum*.

Cors Goch, Anglesey, the most intact of the Anglesey Fens (Pete Jones).

Past management

Little detail is known about the past management of the Anglesey Fens, but it's certain that all were utilised much more extensively in the past than has been the case during the last three decades. All of the larger sites have been heavily cut-over for peat and it is likely that this has resulted in the loss of ombrogenous or near-ombrogenous surfaces on at least one site and also expanded the influence of calcareous seepage water across all sites. All sites would have been utilised for grazing, mainly in the summer, and winter/spring burns were frequent to provide a seasonal bite of vegetation. Extensive drainage was also undertaken, especially in the case of the larger sites and was sufficiently intensive to allow some conversion of habitat to agricultural grassland. After designation as SSSI, three sites were acquired by conservation bodies (CCW and the North Wales Wildlife Trust) and designated as NNR. The initial emphasis was on repairing the worst effects of drainage. Efforts to secure effective grazing proved much less successful away from the NNRs and management neglect has been a dominant feature of the site series. Together with the rich-fens of the Lleyn Peninsula, restoration work on the

Anglesey sites is now underway supported by CCW and EU LIFE+ funding, with contributions from Environment Agency Wales and Dwr Cymru/Welsh Water.

Derelict ungrazed M13 at Cors Bodeilio Common – *Schoenus nigricans* forms an overwhelmingly dominant cover (Pete Jones).

M13 at Cors Bodeilio NNR kept open by wetness and grazing (Pete Jones).

Grazing re-introduction

CCW introduced grazing by lightweight hardy Welsh Mountain Ponies in the late 1980s (Photo 4), with the largest of the fens (Cors Erddreiniog) serving as the initial focus. A year-round regime is practised, with overall site stocking rates of the order of 0.45 ponies per ha but with stock movement and enclosure being used to give temporary actual rates of up to 1.4 ponies/ha. The ponies graze a wide variety of vegetation types but are most effective in low to medium height swards of alkaline fen (M13) and fen meadow (M22, M24), tending to avoid ranker vegetation unless enclosed and provided with rides and paths to encourage access. However, even with such provisos stock tend to concentrate on the relatively few short and open areas, ignoring the taller vegetation. The provision of adjacent dry ground encourages dunging off the fen and is important for lying up and more generally during the winter and other wet periods. Husbandry requirements are relatively modest and include weekly stock counts on all sites, routine and veterinary care, daily/weekly winter supplementary feeding with pony nuts and periodic movement of stock within sites and also off-site to coastal dune systems. Foaling mares lead to excesses of stock, with young animals exported to other conservation projects in Wales and beyond. Retaining herds with stallions has been found to encourage the more adventurous movement of stock around sites and helps prevent concentrated grazing. Geldings can produce similar effects because territorial behaviour encourages some spreading of stock across sites. Handling pens at site access points have been found essential to enable loading and movement between sites. Overall, ponies play an important and cost-effective role in helping maintain rich-fen vegetation, but for best effect need to be used in conjunction with mowing, enclosure and, ideally, cattle grazing. During the summer months (April to September) grazing rates of around 1 pony/ha have been found to be most effective. Cattle are used on a very limited basis on the Welsh fens, but can be effective in helping to tackle tall rank fen vegetation.

Pony grazing at Cors
Bodeilio NNR
(Pete Jones).

Close grazed short sward of sedges including *Carex panicea*, *Carex hostiana* and *Schoenus nigricans* between *Schoenus* tussocks in M13 at Cors Bodeilio NNR (Pete Jones).

Scrub

Scrub management is widely practised, chiefly with respect to grey willow (*Salix cinerea*) and downy birch (*Betula pubescens*). The usual current technique involves cutting and removing with follow up herbicide treatment of cut stumps. Direct stem injection has also been used, allowing dead timber to fall and rot *in-situ* in areas with no direct public access. Both measures result in an acceptable kill rate. Hand-pulling of seedlings is undertaken widely but becomes almost impossible above stem heights of c. 0.75 m.

Vegetation cutting

Vegetation cutting has only been practised on a relatively small-scale basis, but will expand greatly as a result of the LIFE project. Hand strimming and raking has been used to help maintain relatively small patches of open-species rich alkaline fen and has proved effective at slowing the spread of invasive tall graminoids such as *Cladium*. Cutting to create firebreaks at Cors Goch has within 10 years resulted in the development of species-rich M9 from rank impoverished *Cladium* swamp and also aided grazing access by ponies. Trials with self-propelled mowers with interchangeable front-mounted implements including a cutter bar, rotary rake and small round baler show this method has considerable merit for locations inaccessible to heavier machinery.

Hand-strimmed area of M13 at Cors Erddreiniog NNR. Cut material is raked to the side of the stand and provides a valuable biomass pile for reptiles and amphibians (Pete Jones).

Firebreak created by mowing and raking at Cors Goch by the North Wales Wildlife Trust. These breaks provide valuable grazing and also encourage access by grazing stock to unmanaged parts of the site (Pete Jones).

Self-propelled mower purchased with EU LIFE+ funding at Cors Bodeilio NNR. Mowing with a cutter bar is followed here with the use of a power-rake to create wind-rows for subsequent baling – all using the same propulsion unit (Pete Jones).

Turf cutting

Turf cutting has been used widely and at a variety of scales to provide early successional phases of both alkaline and calcareous fen and their open water precursors. Shallow scrapes involving the removal of surface peats to a depth of c. 20 cm have been used in groundwater discharge areas to re-create open wet substrates suitable for colonisation by *Schoenus* and Charophytes. Deeper turf ponds excavated to between 0.3 and 0.75 m serve to remove enriched substrate and eventually develop open swamp vegetation and ultimately rich-fen vegetation.

Recently excavated turf cutting at Cors Erddreiniog NNR
(Pete Jones).

Revegetation of a turf cutting excavated ten years previously at Cors Erddreiniog NNR
(Pete Jones).

7. Fen Management and Restoration – Water Management

Sufficient supply of water of appropriate quality is of fundamental significance to all fens (see Section 3: Understanding Fen Hydrology and Section 4: Understanding Fen Nutrients). On many fens, intervention in the form of water management – or hydrological remediation - is required to maintain or restore the necessary hydrological conditions to support characteristic fen vegetation and halt natural succession to less desirable habitats. Guidance on deciding whether restoration is necessary, appropriate or feasible is provided in Section 5: Fen Management and Restoration.

This section focuses on the practicalities of water level manipulation, including techniques for raising water levels relative to the land surface, or lowering land levels relative to the water table. Section 8 offers guidance on managing fen nutrient enrichment. Legal and planning considerations are detailed in Appendix V.

Before deciding on any action regarding water management, it is essential to understand how a fen functions hydrologically (see Section 2: Understanding Fen Hydrology), the role of nutrients (see Section 4: Understanding Fen Nutrients) and to agree clear objectives, target hydrological regimes and desired or feasible fen types (see Section 5: Fen Management and Restoration).

> It is generally easier and less expensive to raise water levels than lower land levels. Sometimes restoring a river or stream may be cheaper and more sustainable than trying to lower land levels or raise the water table of a fen.

7.1 A framework to assist decision making in fen water management

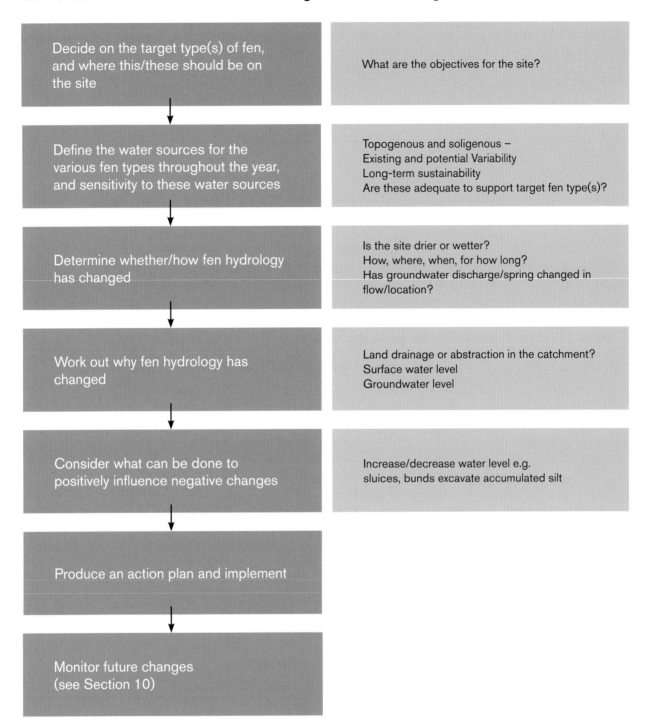

Decide on the target type(s) of fen, and where this/these should be on the site	What are the objectives for the site?
Define the water sources for the various fen types throughout the year, and sensitivity to these water sources	Topogenous and soligenous – Existing and potential Variability Long-term sustainability Are these adequate to support target fen type(s)?
Determine whether/how fen hydrology has changed	Is the site drier or wetter? How, where, when, for how long? Has groundwater discharge/spring changed in flow/location?
Work out why fen hydrology has changed	Land drainage or abstraction in the catchment? Surface water level Groundwater level
Consider what can be done to positively influence negative changes	Increase/decrease water level e.g. sluices, bunds excavate accumulated silt
Produce an action plan and implement	
Monitor future changes (see Section 10)	

Lowering land levels or raising water levels can have significant implications for wildlife and archaeology. Take particular care to consider the impacts on protected species which use the site, such as otter, water vole, great crested newt, certain freshwater mussels or snails, and on irreplaceable archaeological remains.

Trapping and translocation of wildlife, abstraction and impoundment of water, or building structures in or adjacent to watercourses to control water levels, are all controlled by legislation. If fish are present it will be necessary to obtain a licence to move them before any de-silting operations. If electrofishing equipment is going to be used an exemption will be required under The Salmon & Freshwater Fisheries Act (1975).

Appendix V provides a more complete summary of the permits, consents and licences which might be required. Early consultation with relevant EA, SEPA or NIEA staff is recommended.

Consultation with the relevant county or local planning authority archaeologist is recommended before undertaking any work which may affect water or land levels on fens.   University archaeological, geographical or biological science departments may be able to help take and analyse core samples.

7.1.1 Decide on desired or target fen type

Most fens include a range of conditions, and a variety of different types of vegetation. For example a soligenous fen will have drier areas, discrete seepage zones, and areas where water collects, whereas on a floodplain (topogenous) fen, the different types of fen vegetation found will depend on the surface level and proximity to the flood source. Defining what type of fen is aimed for where, taking into consideration topography and available water sources, is crucial before any water management is undertaken. The conservation objectives for a protected site will help to decide or prescribe the desired fen type, but climate and other potential changes in the long term availability, sustainability and variability of the required sources of water will also need to be taken into account.

7.1.2 Define the optimum water sources and regimes for the various fen types over the different seasons through the year

Fluctuation in water levels is entirely natural, particularly on certain types of floodplain where water level may be high in winter but relatively low in summer. Some vegetation, such as that found around water-fringe fens is adapted to these fluctuations – the vegetation mat rises and falls with the water level. Other types of vegetation cannot cope with such fluctuations. For example fen types sustained by groundwater seepage and springs or those in hollows cannot withstand being overtopped by floodwaters, especially when the surrounding land is intensively cultivated or bare soil and intense rainfall increases the risk of higher than normal nutrient loads. Depth of flooding can be as important as frequency. Water quality also needs to be taken into account. An alkaline fen would require continuous discharge from alkaline groundwater in all seasons.

7.1.3 Determine whether/how fen hydrology has changed

Various sources of observational evidence should be used to determine how the hydrology of the fen has changed, including for example:

- observations by an experienced and knowledgeable site manager;

- repeated vegetation sampling (e.g. Common Standards Monitoring);

- assessment of plant community extent from aerial photographs and maps;

- anecdotal evidence;

- research (i.e. results from site specific investigations).

The types of change include water levels, degree/timing of floods, fluctuations and loss of supply.

7.1.4 Work out why fen hydrology has changed

Determining which factors have influenced the fen and been responsible for the identified hydrological changes requires consideration of:

Surface water level change e.g.

− a climatic drier or wetter period (e.g. a few years) that is expected to occur naturally every so often;

− past and recent management or dereliction of water course;

− recent management (or dereliction) of culverts / sluices / outflow valves;

− recent flood management in the catchment (river / lake levels are now different);

− new or changed flood embankment;

− changed variability (frequency and intensity of rainfall events) due to long-term climate change.

Groundwater level change

− a climatic drier or wetter period (e.g. a few years) that might be expected to occur naturally every so often;

− changes in groundwater abstraction quantity or location;

− reduced recharge due to long term climate change and land management changes within the recharge area.

7.1.5 Consider what can be done about the changes

Solutions to redress factors which have negatively influenced hydrology are summarised below. Practical aspects of lowering ground level and raising water tables are described in more detail in the text which follows.

Remedy/options	Considerations
Problem: Ground water drying up **Remedy: Increase soligenous supply**	
Raise the water level in the aquifer by increasing catchment recharge through appropriate land management.	Requires discussions with environmental regulators and external specialist support.
Decrease abstraction from the aquifer at specific times and by amounts that will have a beneficial impact on discharge to the fen.	Normally only realistic where the fen is legally protected (e.g. SSSI / ASSI or Natura 2000), will require specific investigations and could be very costly. This will require discussions with environmental regulators and external specialist support
Artificially increase groundwater level. If possible, and if reduced groundwater supply is due to a local de-watering for example, a re-charge trench can be installed between the fen and the abstraction to raise the groundwater level.	Temporary solution and costly in terms of both finance and energy, but might be the only solution in certain cases. This will require discussions with environmental regulators and external specialist support
Problem: Surface water, fen too dry **Remedy: Increase topogenous supply**	
(a) Increase water retention on the fen by restricting outflow (blocking ditches / changing levels of weirs).	Standing water may result in anoxia especially in peat or soils rich in organic matter. Care should be taken that no standing water remains continually on the surface, or the fen may change to a swamp which will be harder to manage. In 'flow through fens' such as alkaline fens, water should be kept moving through the soil. This kind of management might need consent from environmental regulators and can affect adjoining landowners.

Increase flooding frequency and duration through management of embankments / change in operation of water control structures, or change in flood management of the catchment. Make sure that the flood water does not contain too much silt and/or nutrients that can affect the desired fen type	This kind of management will need consent from environmental regulators and is likely to affect adjoining landowners
Lower the land surface of the fen. In some situations the top layer of the fen can be scraped off; this is particularly beneficial where the surface has become nutrient enriched and when the land level needs to be reduced.	Care must be taken that excavated spoil does not contaminate the new fen surface (see below for further guidance)

Problem: Too much surface water
Remedy: Decrease topogenous supply

Change management of ditches / drains so that water drains out more rapidly. Care should be taken to ensure that the fen will not become too dry; It is good practise that ditch outflows are fitted with water control structures (flood boards, weirs).	This kind of management might need consent from environmental regulators and can affect adjoining landowners
Decrease flooding to the fen by altering flood embankments.	This kind of management is likely to need consent from environmental regulators and affect adjoining landowners

Strategies to restore target hydrological regimes should aim to mimic the natural hydrological functioning of the site in as many ways as possible. For example:

- use the same water source, i.e. groundwater or surface water, to restore appropriate water quality conditions.

- if a site was naturally dependent on continuous groundwater discharge to maintain high soil water levels, remediation through creation of downstream dams or sluices, might give high soil water levels, but could result in undesirable 'stagnant' water with associated low levels of dissolved oxygen.

For sites with relatively uniform land levels, excavations or structures such as bunds (see below) may be required to contain the water and prevent flooding of adjacent land, though care is needed to make sure that any bunds do not isolate the fen from its source of water, such as a stream or river. Past drainage of fen peat may have caused significant shrinkage and the formation of hollows. On sites with varying land level, ensuring sufficient depth of water on the areas of higher ground may result in areas too deep for fen creation where there are hollows or areas of lower ground.

Reversing past management on topogenous fens (i.e. those dependent on ponding up of surface water originating from groundwater, rainfall or surface flow - see **Section 2: Understanding Fen Hydrology**) is more difficult.

Provided the source (aquifer) is not contaminated (for example by nitrate), groundwater is a preferable source for fens, to water from streams and rivers, particularly those with elevated levels of nutrients and suspended solids. Clay and silt particles in the water column hold nutrients such as phosphates and increase the nutrient holding capacity of fen soils through cation exchange capacity (see Section 4: Understanding Fen Nutrients). **Section 8: Managing Fen Nutrient Enrichment** goes into more detail about reedbed filtration and other techniques which can be used to improve water quality.

Past land management may have caused fundamental changes to the soil/peat chemistry. Experience in Holland shows that deep drainage of previously unfertilised fen meadows caused the reduced forms of iron and other minerals to oxidise and the surface to acidify, resulting in the spread of bog mosses (*Sphagnum*) and common cotton-grass (Grootjans & van Diggelen 1995). If this change is undesirable, acidification can be partly reversed by blocking the drains, but strong acidification can only be reversed with calcium- and/or bicarbonate-rich groundwater. This happened by accident at one site in Belgium where wetting a fen with groundwater from a canal reversed acidification (Boeye et al. 1995).

Reversal of adverse hydrological change is not necessarily possible over any timescale, for technical, socio-economic and political reasons. Examples include large-scale flood alleviation schemes protecting extensive areas of rich agricultural land, and reduction of groundwater abstraction where this constitutes a significant proportion of the public water supply. In such cases it may be necessary to consider 'artificial' solutions to achieve favourable hydrological conditions, but take care when considering switching source of supply e.g. ground to surface water. If the cause is short-term natural climatic variability, there is very little that can or should be done.

In some cases, environmental conditions may have changed since the cause(s) of unacceptable hydrological conditions were established. A common example is the increase in surface water and groundwater nutrient concentrations over the last 30-50 years, following large-scale application of artificial fertilisers from the 1950s. This occurred after the extensive drainage of the fens to lower soil water levels and decrease flooding. Simply blocking the drains could now lead to flooding with nutrient-rich waters, which could do as much harm as good to fen vegetation which is highly sensitive to nutrient enrichment.

7.1.6 Produce an action plan and implement

The options for water management should be assessed rigorously against technical and economic feasibility i.e. will it work hydrologically and are the proposed solution affordable. Health and safety implications, operational implications and other risk factors also need to be assessed. Secondary criteria might include benefits to recreation, amenity and sustainability. For example, artificial irrigation of a formerly groundwater-fed fen using pumped groundwater distributed through a system of pipes might approximate the natural hydrological condition most closely, but is unlikely to be the most sustainable option in the long-term.

Bunding and damming techniques (see below) have been developed on a number of cutover peat bogs, and the knowledge is transferable to relatively flat fens with at least one metre of intact peat. The same techniques may also be applicable to flat fens with silt or mineral soil, depending on detailed stratigraphy i.e. which layers hold water, restrict water movement, or act as conduits for flow.

Large valley fens differ from many fens, in that they generally have a central watercourse flanked by seepage areas that may be sloping. Here, the management of the central watercourse becomes important in that the degree to which the river has cut down into its bed determines the hydraulic gradient across the fen, and hence the speed at which water is drawn off and lowered in the soil. While the general techniques of lowering land level, bunding and damming may be appropriate to valley fens, it is also important to consider the larger scale management of the watercourses on which the fens depend. The experience described here has been gained largely in the New Forest, one of the largest complexes of valley mires in the UK.

Direct removal or reversal of the cause(s) will not always restore favourable hydrological conditions in the short-term: it depends in part on the scale of the problem. For example, it may take 10 years or more before the beneficial effects of reducing groundwater abstraction in some aquifers, such as Sherwood sandstone, are realised. In these cases, an 'artificial' interim solution might be needed, and routine monitoring should be continued long-term.

Always consider how any action you take to alter water levels on a fen might impact on surrounding land, for example drainage of adjacent farmland. Similarly think about how changes in the hydrology of the surrounding catchment might have affected a fen in the past, or might affect it in future.

7.1.7 Monitoring

Wherever possible, the hydrological effects of a remediation strategy should be assessed. Monitoring should include characterisation of the baseline (current) hydrological regime, both pre-implementation and post-implementation. The duration of monitoring depends on the likely time for the remediation strategy to take effect. Monitoring of the hydrological effects of installing a sluice to raise water levels might be possible over several hours, or days, but monitoring might be required over a much longer period, possibly years, to determine the success or otherwise of other attempts to restore the desired hydrological regime.

7.2   Lowering the land level

Lowering the land level on fens sometimes happens inadvertently through subsidence as a consequence of adjacent mining activity or shrinkage of the peat following hydrological changes. Most deliberate attempts at lowering land level in relation to the water table are through digging out peat or creating scrapes, generally in small areas. Old turf ponds (rectilinear features with steep sides and relatively even depths) were originally dug to provide peat for fuel, whilst scrapes (with curved, shelving margins and varied topography) have been created to improve habitat conditions for species such as wading birds and dragonflies.

The cutting of peat for fuel (turbary) was widespread throughout Britain and carried on well into the mid 19th century in some areas. Most peat-based fens and bogs have been cut-over, in part at least, including the Cambridgeshire and Lincolnshire Fens and Somerset Levels. A floating raft of species-rich vegetation developed over the former turf ponds, dominated by brown mosses and small sedges, with rarities such as fen orchid (see Section 2: Fen Flora and Fauna). By the late 20th century dense mats of reed and other wetland plants had replaced this more diverse habitat.

A series of three turf ponds dug to different depths at Whitlaw Mosses 10 years ago. The ponds replicate retting pools that were used historically to process flax. The pools were hand dug and the spoil flattened by foot in the surrounding edges to ensure turves were not colonised by tree seedlings (D.Brown).

Smaller excavations are preferable because they produce more edge per unit area than a single large excavation over the same footprint. The length of the edge is important, as it provides a niche for the establishment of species-poor swamp communities dominated by lesser bulrush and common reed. A further consideration is that excavation may impede carbon sequestration through conversion to open water, and produce dry peat which will oxidise and release carbon.

Clear conservation objectives will help decide whether species-poor or species-rich swamp is required. A species-rich swamp will require management of tall species such as reed by mowing or grazing. Smaller excavations are also better because there is less material to be disposed of, and less risk of wave erosion, so allowing emergent vegetation to re-establish more rapidly from the margins, from rhizomes and from the newly-exposed seed bank.

New turf ponds have been dug at Woodbastwick Fen and other localities in the Norfolk Broads using a 360° excavator with wide tracks and mats to avoid damage to the peat. Smaller (<20m wide) shallower (20-30 cm) cuttings have given better results than deeper ($\geq$50 cm) larger (>1 ha) excavations, which have been very slow to establish emergent vegetation.

Removing the accumulated litter and peat to just above the level of the rhizomes of reed or other species (e.g. reedmace and common club-rush) will also allow for more rapid re-establishment without creating large areas of open water. However, Natural England have found in the Norfolk Broads that re-worked cuttings have been slow to develop a submerged or emergent vegetation cover, probably because a significant depth of loose unconsolidated organic silt makes it difficult for aquatic macrophytes to establish. The restoration of diverse fen vegetation has been much more successful where the cuttings have been carried out in 'virgin' fen peat. Cutting peat from intact areas in the Norfolk Broads resulted in relatively rapid re-vegetation with swamp species such as saw sedge, especially where the water depth was less than 30 cm deep. It is important to note that creation of the turf ponds coincided with dry summers in the mid-1990s and there was little inundation with water whilst the vegetation established. Care should be taken in areas of virgin peat as this could destroy a unique archaeological record of that locality.

All turf ponds created in the Norfolk Broads since 1983 have been monitored, and the results of all surveys during that time reviewed. These findings are available in a report held by the Broads Authority "Broadland Turf Pond Surveys 2005 and Analysis of Data 1983-2005".

Creating shallow areas with water depths of 15 - 20 cm (max 30 cm) will favour more rapid re-vegetation with reedswamp or other pioneer vegetation.

Removal of the top layers of degraded peat from Redgrave and Lopham Fen (see case study 5.2) has successfully regenerated the botanical diversity of areas (Exell 2003). Species that have re-appeared include common butterwort, bog mosses, round-leaved sundew, black bog-rush, cross-leaved heath (Erica tetralix) and marsh lousewort. Turf removal has been used successfully at Cors Geirch in Wales, where localised areas of rich-fen vegetation have established in association with seepage areas.

7.2.1 Checking substrate fertility

The upper layers of soil are often the most fertile due to enrichment from surface waters, agricultural activities or defecation by animals. Generally the underlying substrate is more likely to be nutrient-poor, and thus capable of supporting species rich vegetation.

Where aims for site management include reduction of substrate fertility and encouragement of greater species diversity, samples of peat/substrate taken from different depths should be analysed to assess whether surface layers are particularly enriched in major plant nutrients. This can be assessed using a technique called phytometry (see Section 10: Monitoring to Inform Fen Management) in which seedlings of test plant species are grown in soil samples taken from different areas of the site and different depths as appropriate. The tests can be extended with and without additions of nitrogen and phosphorus. Comparisons of the biomass produced in the test and control soils shows whether or not the layer of soil being tested is already enriched with one or both of the major plant nutrients. This is often considered to be a more reliable estimate of what is available to plants than analyses of soil water and soil extracts. While such analyses are useful and informative, they may not show how much is available to the plants, especially when critical concentrations are close to the limits of detection.

An indication of substrate fertility can also be obtained from noting the plants that grow in and around the margins of the proposed area for rejuvenation and comparing them with information provided in, for example, the JNCC's Common Standards Monitoring Guidance

7.2.2 Removal of silt and other sediments

Heavy machinery may sink where the fen has become filled up with silt and other soft sediments. Unconsolidated silts can be removed using a suction dredger, but leaching of chemicals (such as oxidised iron) from the dredged silts can be a pollution risk. It may also be difficult to establish wetland plants in un-consolidated substrates as the plants are uprooted by wave-action.

Some sediment may be rich in heavy metals such as lead, iron and manganese which may leach out. In the case of iron, oxidation may give rise to an obvious ochreous colouration and deposit. Disposal of contaminated sediments to special waste disposal sites is very costly, and requires relevant licences. In addition sediments are often rich in phosphorus which will encourage unwanted plant growth.

> Works adjacent to watercourses should be carefully designed with appropriate controls to prevent silt or other contaminants entering rivers and streams.

A prior desk study of local sources of possible contaminants may suggest whether there is any risk of contamination. As a precaution it is wise to analyse some of the sediment prior to removal for concentrations of heavy metals such as iron, manganese, lead, cadmium, copper and zinc.

Consult your local environmental protection agency (EA, SEPA, NIEA) at the planning stage. They should be able to advise whether material will require analysis.

Morton Lochs, which extend to approximately 8 ha, were originally created in the 19th century as fishing pools within the dune system. The sluggish through-flow of water and the mobile sandy soils meant that by the 1970s, the pools had become infilled. During the dry summer of 1976, the sluices were opened, a diversionary channel was created and the remaining water from the lochs was pumped out.

The silt was then left to dry, before bulldozing and excavating over the whole area through the summer and into the winter before the sluices were closed again.

Silt removal at Morton Loch
(J.Young).

Installation of silt traps on the inflow has been critical to reducing the amount of silt entering the site, but by the 1990s, the lochs were completely full of reed due to the effects on the wetland vegetation of nutrients from adjacent agricultural operations. In the late 1990's a successful programme of herbicide commenced to open the site for the benefit of wintering waterfowl and less invasive wetland vegetation. However without control of waterborne nutrients entering the site, a low level of herbicide control continues.

7.2.3 Disposing of excavated material

Excavated material is best disposed of on site, where it can be used to consolidate existing tracks or bunds, or used as a source material for nearby fen creation projects. It is likely to contain plant materials such as seed and rhizomes, fungi, mosses and bacteria, possibly even invertebrates. Nutrient enriched silt and other scrapings must be removed to a sufficient distance to prevent leachates (nutrients and toxins) seeping back into the fen. Material to be disposed off-site should be tested for contaminants to ensure it is safe to use as topsoil for improving agricultural land or other similar purpose. Finding a suitable use nearby can eliminate or reduce the significant cost of disposing of such waste.

> Disposing of excavated sediment
>
> Piles of excavated sediment and dead plant material can generate nutrients or oxidised leachates which can inhibit some plants or encourage other undesirable ones. This can be a particular problem with sediments rich in reduced forms of iron which will oxidise to oxides and hydroxides of iron as well as dilute sulphuric acid to produce an ochreous leachate.

> At Cors Geirch on the Lleyn Peninsula in Gwynedd, the material removed to create a large turf pond was used as topsoil on a nearby landfill site.
>
> At Minsmere in Suffolk, the rejuvenation of a reedbed was achieved by scraping off the top 30 cm of accumulated litter and surface peat with a 360 degree excavator; the material was placed in windrows and left to rot.

7.2.4 Revegetation

The type of fen that will develop following excavation will depend in part on the seed bank, the living rhizomes of plants left in the substrate and the conditions created. At many sites where the water level has been raised or the surface lowered, vegetation has been allowed to develop without further intervention other than grazing and mowing. Buried seeds often germinate readily when exposed to the air and some may survive many hundreds of years in anaerobic conditions.

> At Dry Rigg Quarry in North Yorkshire, mares-tail (*Hippuris vulgaris*) and bog pondweed (*Potamogeton polygonifolius*) appeared from an area where fen peat had been buried under quarry spoil for many decades. Although it cannot be proved that the seeds were not imported from elsewhere, such as on the feet of waterfowl it is possible that the seeds were present.

To a lesser extent, adjoining fens or sites in close proximity and with hydrological connectivity will contribute viable fragments to assist the re-establishment of fen vegetation. Deliberate introduction of species to excavated areas has had mixed success. Planting out specific fen plants as plugs into turf ponds may be successful where competition from established vegetation is absent or low, but is unlikely to be successful in standing water as the plants are likely to float to the surface and be lost. Planting is best carried out in spring to allow establishment through the summer before wave action from winter flooding can dislodge the plants. **Section 8: Fen Creation** offers more advice on this subject.

Although shallow excavations are preferred because of the ease with which the required plants can become established, depth may be dictated by the degree to which the roots of the existing plants have penetrated. The rhizomes of reed can potentially descend to a metre or more, but most grow 20 - 50 cm below the peat surface. Rhizome depth depends on fluctuations in water levels at a site as well as plant size, with larger species generally having deeper rhizomes. Sedge rhizomes (Carex spp.) are generally much shallower (5 - 10 cm deep) than those of saw-sedge which are usually present at depths of about 20 cm below the surface of the substrate (Conway 1942).

Looking at the rhizomes and seeds at the depth which will form the new surface provides a guide as to what might regenerate. Seeds can be extracted from approximately 300 - 500 ml of substrate by mixing with water and sieving the resulting slurry through 2mm, 500 μm and 125 μm sieves. Material retained on the sieves can be washed off with tap water for examination under a low power dissecting microscope and identification by comparison to reference material and/or published reference works. Leaving the seeds on a damp substrate or in a shallow layer of water in a warm location will reveal which will germinate readily.

7.2.5 Silt traps

The rapid terrestialisation of some fens may be due to the input of large quantities of silt from streams and other watercourses. Installation of an appropriately sized and designed silt trap where the offending watercourse enters the fen can help reduce sediment input, but the long-term goal should be to identify and eliminate the high concentrations of suspended solids in the watercourse.

For silt traps to work effectively, the velocity of water must be reduced sufficiently so that silt will fall out of suspension faster than it will be carried into the fen or body of water downstream. Installation of the silt trap and/or disposal of sediment may require a licence (see Appendix V).

Construction of a silt trap can help intercept water-borne silt to reduce terrestrialisation of fens. The two surface baffles pictured extend 15cm under the surface help reduce the flow (A. McBride).

A small deep pond or a stand of reeds may be a more acceptable solution than an engineered sediment trap if adequate space is available. A reedswamp located where a headwater enters a fen will reduce the velocity and turbulence of water and provide a matrix in which the silt can become lodged.

The accumulation of silt in the reedbeds at Blacktoft Sands RSPB reserve on the Humber Estuary leads to land levels increasing relatively rapidly. Periodic removal of the accumulated sediments is needed to maintain the wetland.

7.3   Maintaining open water

The invasion of open-water by emergent aquatic plants, particularly common reed and bulrush, can occur relatively quickly. Where emergent plants are growing in standing water and are not too dense (water-fringe fen), it is possible to create areas of open water through control of water-levels, if this is required for the conservation of other interests such as invertebrates and birds.

Some brush-cutters and other power tools are suitable for this task, but often the ground is too soft or the water too deep for them to be operated safely. Reciprocating-blade mowers or scythes can work effectively provided reed is not too dense and the area to be cut is relatively limited. Most commercial reed and sedge cutters use pedestrian mowers of various sorts. The Broads Reed & Sedge Cutters Association (BRASCA) have a wealth of practical experience in cutting fen vegetation (see **Section 6: Fen Vegetation Management** and **Broads Reed & Sedge Cutters Association**).

Maintaining open water at Brackagh Bog

At Brackagh Bog in Northern Ireland, which is an extensive area of fen developed from cut-over bog, pools are mechanically excavated on a cyclical basis to simulate abandoned peat cutting practices. The maintenance of open water at Brackagh Bog is essential to maintain the diversity of fen communities and the rich invertebrate fauna for which the area is renowned.

Rectangular pools freshly excavated at Brackagh Bog in Northern Ireland to lower the level of the fen re-establishing the successional process from open water to species rich fen (B. Hamill).

The newly created pools are rapidly colonised by aquatic and fen plants from nearby seed sources and plant rhizomes. (B.Hamill)

Over approximately five years, the pools become completely infilled, creating species-rich fen communities with a diverse fen flora. After a further period of time, the mechanical excavation of open pools in this area will begin again (B. Hamill).

At Leighton Moss in Lancashire, areas of open water are regularly maintained or created by cutting reed below water-level in summer either by hand or with a mower where the ground is firm enough. An alternative is to cut close to the peat surface and raise the water level shortly afterwards. Flooding the cut stems kills the plants as they are unable to get air into the underground rhizomes from the stems and leaves. This approach has also been used for controlling invasive soft rush.

The Broads Authority have used an amphibious machine called a Truxor which has a number of inter-changeable heads, one of which is used for cutting vegetation under water. This machine has been used on flooded fen at Reedham Marshes and at the RSPBs Strumpshaw fen.

7.4   Raising water levels

Fens can be restored or rejuvenated by appropriate adjustment of water supply to re-wet rather than flood the site. This approach was adopted at Shirley Pool in Yorkshire, where water was pumped experimentally onto the site from an adjacent watercourse for a short period (Roworth & Meade 1998). This significantly increased the level of the water table for relatively little expense for the few weeks' duration of the experiment. Alternatively, a wind-driven pump can be used, as for example at the private nature reserve at Rodley.

Water levels can be raised by impeding the natural egress of water entering the site through groundwater seepage, surface flow, and/or from rainfall. This may simply involve raising the water level in drains and other ditches, but in some cases the water will simply overtop the edge of the drain and exit by another route rather than raising soil water levels.

An appreciation of surface contours can be gained from ground survey or by the interpretation of remote data such as LiDAR (Light detection and ranging) which involves the emission, reflection and detection of light radiation using airborne or ground-sited equipment. LiDAR can record vertical differences of a few centimetres (ground-sited) but its accuracy is dependent on there being gaps in vegetation through which the ground is visible. Any programme of ditch-damming or bund creation will benefit from the use of such information.

Pumping water into Ham Wall RSPB reserve to raise the water table (RSPB).

7.4.1 Water-retaining structures - bunds

Bunds are earth banks which can be constructed to impound shallow surface water on a flat fen surface. A series of 'contour' bunds can be used where the fen surface is gently sloping, as in rice paddy fields.

Bunds should be constructed of suitable locally-sourced material that is cohesive, stable, water-retaining material. Clays and other impermeable soils are generally the most suitable. Well compacted peat will retain water to a degree, but is usually prone to seepage, and bunds built of peat may slump over time. Any imported material must be compatible with the target type of fen. For example, while soils derived from sandstones may be suitable for most sites, those from limestone may change the base status and pH of acidic peat fens.

> Materials available from construction projects are particularly likely to have an inappropriately high nutrient status and may contain weed plants such as Himalayan balsam and Japanese knotweed.

Bunds are usually designed with a trapezoidal cross-section to remain stable against subsidence and possible wave erosion. They must be set well back from the edge of drainage channels, and the base of the bund should be keyed into the existing substrate to reduce water seepage. Shallow gradients on the side of the bund will help facilitate access for future vegetation management. Design specification should allow for shrinkage or height reduction after settling, which may be >10% on peat. Potential use of bunds as access routes across fens, particularly for vehicles, should be taken into account in design and specification.

Replace vegetation

second peat fill

maximum water level

0,75m height

first peat fill

key bund into existing peat surface

borrow pit

plastic membrane

PEAT

1m deep trench

2m base width

Cross-section of a typical peat bund with plastic membrane (after: Meade, Mawby & Hammond, 2007).

Excavating spoil within the area to be bunded can create an adjacent 'borrow dyke' or ditch, which will provide additional habitats for aquatic plants and invertebrates and facilitate the control and distribution of water around a site. Construction using a long-reach excavator working on top of the bund allows the machine to make use of its own weight to consolidate the built-up material. The scraping up of material for the bund should not breach aquicludes, or create an unsuitable surface for plant establishment.

Impoundment of large volumes of water above the natural level of the adjoining land is controlled by legislation. Construction of bunds in the floodplain will require licensing. (see Appendix V for further details).

Bund creation at Ham Wall RSPB reserve (RSPB).

Incorporation of a plastic membrane can help make bunds watertight. A facing apron of geotextile or rock armour may be required to protect against wave action or erosion. Overflows or sluices should be incorporated at the right points to allow excess water out, and designed so that the overflow does not erode the bund.

Further details on bund construction can be found in Hawke and Jose (1996) and White and Gilbert (2003).

Bunding or damming drains to raise water levels may be the most effective method of re-establishing earlier stages in the natural succession from open water, but it will not be possible to do this repeatedly. Each time this is done, the water table within the fen will become increasingly elevated above the regional water table, increasing the difficulty with which water can be retained due to the increased hydraulic gradient. The only course of action then would be to lower the fen surface.

7.4.2 Water-retaining structures – dams

Dams are another mechanism for raising water level on fens. The success of a dam is measured by the visible build-up of a head of water on the upstream side. The construction of dams and sluices in reedbeds as described in Hawke and Jose (1996) and for raised bogs in Brooks & Stoneman, 1997 are equally relevant to construction of dams in fens. Specifications for dams and sluices are also provided in the RSPB guide to Water Management Structures.

Dams can be constructed of a range of impervious materials. It is critical that the dam keys into the material beneath and on either side so that water cannot simply bypass the structure, or scour out a passage around the dam. Many ditches have decades of accumulated plant litter which will provide a line of seepage if the dam is simply built on top of it. Scouring around the top corners of a dam can be avoided by installing an overflow, such as a V notch (uncontrollable) or a pipe with an adjustable elbow (where water height can be varied).

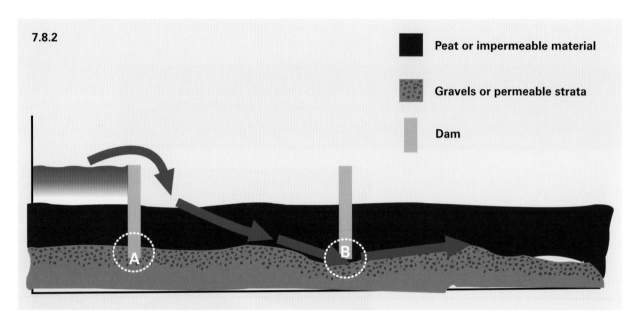

Key dams well into the substrate below (A) otherwise water will by-pass the dam (B).

Dams and bunds must have overflow points capable of taking peak flows so that the soft structure of the bund or the surrounds of the dam do not become eroded. This can be determined by trial and error but the errors can be expensive, and may have implications for neighbouring land. Rainfall in Cumbria that flooded Carlisle in 2005 destroyed kilometres of bunds created on Wedholme Flow as part of the bog restoration programme because the capacity of the overflows was exceeded, as they became increasingly blocked by floating debris.

Corrugated interlocking plastic piling can be driven into peat with a maul (with suitable protection on the top edge of the plastic). This can be used in narrow to moderate sized drains, but a size is reached at which corrugated steel is necessary to withstand the pressure of water without bowing. A wooden beam bolted across the top of the plastic piling reduces bowing, or alternatively a length of steel angle on corrugated steel. Steel piling must be driven in with suitable machinery. Timber planks, particularly elm boards, work well on ditches with relatively high water flow. The theory is that when wet, the timber swells, and so eliminating leaks. However, if the water level falls, the timber shrinks and any debris which becomes lodged in the gaps between the boards prevents re-sealing when the water level rises, allowing seepage through the dam. Further advice on plastic piling is available in Installing Plastic Piling Dams.

7.4.3 Peat plugs

Blocking narrow drains in peat is effectively done by creating a peat plug cut from nearby with an excavator bucket. The weight of the bucket is used to squash the plug into the drain and create a seal. Peat plugs are more cost effective than other dams particularly where the peat thickness reduces to between 50 and 75cm, often with a rock substrate below. In these circumstances rigid dam materials do not provide a watertight seal. However peat dams can only be successfully built on peat with a shallow slope. As the peat dam does not have a spillway, if the gradient is too steep the water flows cause erosion over the top of the dam resulting in failure. Suitable low ground pressure excavators are now more widely available for this work but for small scale operations peat dams are created by hand. Hand built dams can only be formed in ditches no larger than 70cm wide and 60cm deep, whilst with an excavator drain width can extend to a maximum of 150cm with a depth of 120cm depending on the peat composition. Above these dimensions the peat can become unstable. The peat used for damming must be saturated, as once the peat dried it shrinks and looses the ability to retain water and will not form a watertight dam. Therefore, do not use the original ditch spoil and only use the darker peat taken from the bottom and wet sides of the ditch.

7.5   Managing flowing water

In some parts of the UK the management of relatively small watercourses is an integral part of managing fens. The New Forest is a particularly good example, and similarly the Surrey and Dorset heaths. Here, stream beds and associated drains were lowered as part of wider drainage schemes, for forestry for example, which has led to bed levels eroding further upstream into more sensitive areas of fen and mire, thus lowering the water table and drying out the fens. The techniques described below operate on a "landscape level" to arrest and reverse these processes.

7.5.1 Drain filling using heather bales

Heather bales have been used successfully on many sites as a robust and cost effective method of drain filling to halt and prevent erosion cutting back into a fen or mire system. Heather bales can be used to support the leading edge of peat at points of headward erosion, and to halt erosion by conveying water over the bales and on downstream.

The heather is cut locally, for example as part of heathland management, packed into bales approximately 75 cm x 50cm x 50cm, and held in place by chestnut stakes. The bales gradually infill with sediment and become impermeable. To avoid subsidence and degradation, the water table needs to be fairly constant throughout the year so that the bales remain submerged. Impermeable dams of spoil or clay created at intervals along the drainage channel will help support the water level over the bales. Spreading remaining spoil over the surface of the bales once installed can accelerate the establishment of mire and soakway plants and provide some additional support.

In the New Forest, a maximum of 12,000–14,000 bales can be produced in a winter. The limiting factor is their durability during storage; the bales need to be used within a year of being produced to avoid degradation.

Further information is available in the Introduction to the New Forest Wetlands Project

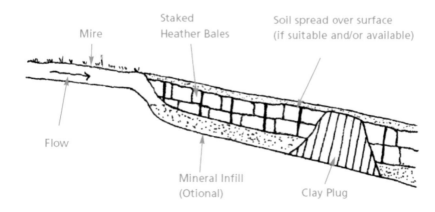

Mire

Staked
Heather Bales

Soil spread over surface
(if suitable and/or available)

Flow

Mineral Infill
(Otional)

Clay Plug

Drain infilling and dam
construction using heather
bales

161

7.5.2 Drain filling using brushwood faggots

Brushwood faggots are another alternative method of blocking up drains, made by bundling birch twigs using twine (either jute or plastic), and staking in place within the drainage channel to prevent movement. Water flowing over and through the packed material will deposit fines and organic matter that aids consolidation and provides a firm substrate safe for livestock to cross, and ripe for colonisation by vegetation. However, at a trial site in Blackensford in 1999, the use of faggots to prevent headward erosion was unsuccessful. Faggots have the best chance of success if used in conjunction with other material such as bank spoil to infill a channel, and where the water table remains above the faggots throughout the year to prevent rapid decay. Faggots can also be used to good effect in conjunction with clay plugs.

Gabion baskets were installed in the New Forest during the early 1990s in an attempt to control erosion. The wire cages were filled with oversize gravel to provide a robust material over and through which the head of water could descend from the level of the mire down into the drainage channel. The success of this technique has varied. The wire of the baskets is vulnerable to the acid waters of the mire, which is thought to remove the protective zinc coating and hasten rusting. Apart from the reduced structural integrity, exposed and broken wire is unsightly and a potential hazard for livestock and people. The water exiting the mire did not always flow over or through the gabion, and in several instances the peat has continued to erode upstream of the gabion. Consequently use of gabions has been discontinued and is not recommended.

7.6   References

Broads Authority "Broadland Turf Pond Surveys 2005 and Analysis of Data 1983-2005

Brooks, S. & Stoneman, R. *Conserving bogs: the management handbook*. The Stationery Office, Edinburgh.

Boeye, D., van Straaten, D. & Verheyen, R.F. 1995. A recent transformation from poor to rich fen caused by artificial groundwater recharge. *Journal of Hydrology* **169**, 111-129.

Conway, V. 1942. Biological Flora of the British Isles. Cladium mariscus. *Journal of Ecology* **30**, 211-216.

Excell, A. 2003. Restoration update – Redgrave and Lopham Fen NNR. *Conservation Land Management* **1** (2), 8-12.

Grootjans, A. & Van Diggelen, R. 1995. Assessing the restoration prospects of degraded fens. In: *Restoration of Temperate Wetlands* (eds. B.D. Wheeler, S.C. Shaw, W.J. Fojt & R.A. Robertson), pp. 73-90. John Wiley & Sons, Chichester.

Hawke, C.J. & José, P.V. 1996. *Reedbed Management for Commercial and Wildlife Interests*. Royal Society for the Protection of Birds, Sandy.

Meade, R., Mawby, F. & Hammond, G. 2007. *Swarth Moor: restoring the fen and raised bog to favourable condition*. Contract FST 19/04/049 Report to Natural England by Roger Meade Associates, Frank Mawby Associates and Penny Anderson Associates.

Meade, R. & Wheeler, B.D. 2007. *Raised bogs from gravel pits? In: Minerals extraction and wetland creation*, Proceedings of a workshop held in Doncaster 26-27 September, 2005 (eds. R. Meade & N. Humphries). pp. 41-49. Natural England.

Roworth, P. & Meade, R. (1998). *Pumping Shirley Pool*. Enact 6 (2), 12-13.

White, G. and Gilbert, J., eds., 2003. *Habitat creation handbook for the minerals industry*. Sandy: RSPB.

Montiaghs Moss (pronounced "Munchies"), which lies a short distance from the eastern shore of Lough Neagh in Northern Ireland (grid reference J092653), was formerly a lowland raised bog. The site has been cut-over to the extent that no remnants of original bog surface remain. The site is linked to Lough Neagh and to nearby Portmore Lough by a man-made watercourse called the Navvies Drain. Successive lowering of Lough Neagh over the past 150 years has probably taken the water table down by about 2.3 m.

Historically many families would have cut peat on the bog and although some of the fen peat could have been cut and dried directly for burning, most of the site demanded a different technique called puddling. The peat was wetted in short trenches, trampled to form a peaty porridge and then spread out in an even layer on adjacent ground to dry. It was then broken into turves that had improved burning characteristics. This technique left a mosaic of pools and 'floors' of different wetness. The practice of hand-cutting turf has now virtually stopped, and natural succession has resulted in many areas which were previously open water becoming choked with vegetation, and Willow/Alder/Birch scrub encroaching on drier areas.

Pools cleared of choking vegetation

The withdrawal of active land management by the local community and subsequent deterioration in site condition led Northern Ireland Environment Agency (NIEA) to begin purchasing plots of land.

Management objectives

The paradox for Montiaghs Moss is that what emerged in the place of the former raised bog was a wonderful mosaic of pools, fen, mire, grassland and scrub, but the human activities responsible for the original loss of habitat, and subsequent creation of such rich biodiversity, are now in decline. The challenge for NIEA is to maintain the current conservation interest and establish the necessary equilibrium to maintain designation features, such as Marsh Fritillary Euphydryas aurinia, other notable invertebrates and fen vegetation in the most cost effective way possible.

Management rationale

It is unknown if the site could ever revert back to lowland raised bog. Left unmanaged it is likely to become dominated by woodland. The moss supports a number of notable plant species and is especially noted for its invertebrate fauna. Water levels on Lough Neagh, and therefore by default on the Montiaghs Moss, are maintained by sluice gates within statutory levels. Rivers Agency maintains many of the existing drains within the site, mainly to reduce the impact of flooding on surrounding farmland. Although Rivers Agency is interested in de-designating many of the watercourses within the site, this can only be progressed where farmland will not be impacted. Ultimately the management of water levels is not within NIEA control. The management approach is therefore to work within the constraints on the site and leave the recovery of lowland raised bog sites to other more viable properties such as at Peatlands Park.

Techniques

In order to replicate the traditions and practices of the area puddling was done by hand digging between 1997 and 1999. Since 2000 a small digger was brought in as a less labour intensive means of creating new pools and deepening existing hollows. In the most extensive area of fen several deeper holes were dug to act as refuges for invertebrates if water levels dropped really low during prolonged dry spells. Many of the new pools were isolated from the other long established ones so nature was given a helping hand by throwing in a few strands of Bog Pondweed *Potamogeton polygonifolius*, which helped accelerate establishment. Irish Damselfly Coenagrion lunulatum has been observed using pondweeds for egg laying by landing on a leaf and then submerging backwards down the underwater stem. Emergent stems of species such as Water Horsetail Equisitum fluviatile are probably used by emerging nymphs and are certainly used for perching by adults. Establishing the correct vegetative infrastructure in the pools is therefore likely to be important for invertebrate species.

Experimental scrapes 2007

Monitoring

The site management team do not usually have time to undertake all of the desired species and habitat monitoring projects, focusing instead on practical work to prevent the demise of many notable species. Monitoring is therefore mainly of a casual nature but some measure of success can quickly be determined by peering into the pools to observe the ongoing development of aquatic vegetation and observing the activities of the abundant invertebrate life. NIEA undertake SAC/ASSI feature condition monitoring of Marsh Fritillary and vegetation. Invertebrate monitoring is contracted out to specialist surveyors. Some ad hoc monitoring is also undertaken by amateurs e.g. counts of Irish Damselfly.

Plans for the future

Future plans include:

- Creation of more fire breaks by excavating existing pools and if necessary opening up new ones.

- Continued land acquisition.

- Drainage investigation to improve hydrological understanding of plots and identify eutrophication risks.

- Continue to work with Rivers Agency to identify drains that can come out of their watercourse maintenance schedule and be managed purely for nature conservation.

Portmore Lough is a 1 m deep, 200 ha circular lough, situated on the south eastern shore of Lough Neagh in Northern Ireland (grid reference J113690), surrounded by a 100 m wide reedbed (the second largest in Northern Ireland), a 100 m fringe of willow/alder carr, and on the western edge, a mosaic of lowland wet grassland and ditches. It is this transition from open water to wet grassland that is one of the site's ASSI designation features.

Water quality and water levels on Portmore Lough are influenced by Lough Neagh through two large interconnecting drainage channels. Water levels were 2.3 m higher and more extreme in the Lough Neagh basin 200 years ago. The last lowering in 1959 allowed the fringe of willow/alder carr to develop at Portmore. This layer of willow fringe was coppiced and in the short dry season lightly grazed.

The RSPB has focused on developing the adjoining lowland wet grassland at Portmore to attract breeding waders, which is central to the south Lough Neagh Lapwing Restoration Project. Lapwing have declined by 65% in 15 years in Northern Ireland. A management regime of 'cut, collect and graze' for 15 years on the meadow has produced a species rich sward enhanced by a bund isolating the meadows from the eutrophic lough allowing only rain water to collect.

Removal of the willow/alder carr and restoration of the water fringe fen was critical in increasing the invertebrate diversity. The carabid beetle *Chlaenius tristis* (RDB1) found here is the first Northern Ireland record. Creating 'openness' and a more diverse transition from open water also favours breeding waders and wildfowl. Restoration of fen at Portmore preserves a once common, but now virtually extinct, habitat around Lough Neagh.

Management objectives
Restoration of 9ha wet willow and alder carr to water fringe fen.

Management rationale
The key to the project is the suppression of reed canary grass (*Phalaris arundinacea*) within the fen and the improvement in water quality of Portmore Lough. Short of isolating Portmore Lough from Lough Neagh, water quality is a regional problem and outside the scope of the RSPB.

The soil within the fen area is weakly consolidated silty clay sediment, with a fragile supportive crust only 80 cm thick. This precluded the use of large machinery and the removal of stumps. Frequent flooding and high winter water levels gave only a short autumn window for mechanical operations.

Techniques
(a) Scrub control by herbicide injection
Willow/alder stems were injected with 10 ml undiluted glyphosate using a petrol driven drill with 10 ml bit and a sheep dosing gun, which produced a 70% kill of stems. The intention was to reduce moisture content in the resultant chip, increasing its value to offset costs. The benefit however extended to reduced stump regrowth and non-regeneration of submerged brash.

(b) Felling and removal

The scrub was cut at surface level using hand-held chainsaws and winched to the boundary using a 3psi SoftTrack vehicle with PTO driven winch. Chipping was carried out using a low ground pressure grab and chipper, blown into tracked dumpers, and removed off site. All vehicles were custom made by/for the contractors. Density of scrub was 100 tonne/ha.

(c) Regrowth of willow and alder

25% of stumps showed signs of regrowth. These were freshly cut with a chainsaw and the surface painted with glyphosate. In some cases, the stumps were also drilled and injected.

Monitoring and review of outcomes

Base line surveys of invertebrates and vegetation in the first year after scrub removal were postponed due to persistent flooding.

Maintaining sward diversity – Disturbance of the sward surface resulted in local soft rush (Juncus effusus) colonisation. The initial diversity of low growing herb flora was threatened by the dominance of reed canary grass. Suppression of this tall herb fen by grazing has proved very effective using Konik ponies. Currently grazing is at 0.75lu/ha but periods of grazing can be short due to flood conditions.

Raising water levels locally – De-designation and damming of the main drain separating the fen from the wet meadows has isolated the adjacent area from the eutrophic effects of the lough. Widening, re-profiling and adding a second bund has created a fresh-water storage body that also raises water levels locally. The influence of this will create conditions suitable for the establishment of fen vegetation at the edge of the wet grassland.

Plans for the future

NIEA's target is to achieve moderate water quality (currently bad) by 2016. Pools and scrapes will be created within the fen area to increase biodiversity. Stump grinding may facilitate mowing in the future. Feasibility of creating a differential age structure within the reedbed has been successfully tested using a Truxor reed cutting boat. A SoftTrack machine has been acquired.

New Forest mires have elements which are typical of both bogs and fens. The variation in vegetation composition is attributable to acidity and water regimes, determined by underlying soils, hydrology, nutrient status, and management particularly grazing and burning pressure. The New Forest supports approximately 2000 hectares of mire habitats, the structural variation is very wide and each mire system is unique (SAC Management Plan).

Since the mid-19th century more than 70% of the New Forest mires have been drained. This was either to further the establishment of trees in enclosures or to reduce the water table and thereby 'improve' grazing on the Open Forest. These activities varied greatly in scale, impacts on the habitats, and in their primary purpose. New Forest peat is thin and rarely in excess of 2 m. This makes them particularly vulnerable to damage from artificial drainage, causing rapid headward erosion and lateral peat slumping.

The botanical diversity is attributed to the alkaline seepage in contact with an underlying clay layer (Headon Beds). By contrast upstream, the acidic influence of plateau gravels gives rise to permanently waterlogged, nutrient poor acidic peat. It supports Sphagnum mosses with other bog species such as bog asphodel (*Narthecium ossifragum*), common cotton grass and white-beak sedge (*Rhynchospora alba*). 'Soakways' exist along natural drainage runnels of valley bogs which are dominated by marsh St John's wort (*Hypericum elodes*) and bog pondweed (*Potamogeton polygonifolius*).

Stony Moors

Stony Moors (23 ha) supports fen and mire habitats well-known for their botanical diversity, largely attributable to the base-rich influence of the underlying clay, which is particularly obvious along the valley spring-line where seepage mires exhibit a rare and characteristic marl flush community. Lime rich marl flushes, (pH around 7.0 or higher) support characteristic species including *Eleocharis quinqueflora*, the brown moss *Palustriella commutata*, and the abundant brown moss *Scorpidium revolvens* (Sanderson 1998).

At Stony Moors there was clear evidence of past drainage activities with incised channels, headward erosion and localised spoil heaps. The drainage was likely to have been 1930's in origin, with some further works associated with the construction of Holmsley Aerodrome in 1941-42. It is likely that soon after drainage the drop in water table caused peat to oxidize releasing nutrients, thereby providing temporary benefits to grazing livestock through increased productivity. However, soon after this initial flush tree species such as willow, birch and pine were able to colonise the degraded mire surface. As a result of this past drainage, secondary woodland has been able to colonise parts of the mire and fen system and associated stream corridor.

Management objectives

In 2005 the Forestry Commission undertook to restore this mire as part of the LIFE 3 Sustainable Wetland Restoration Project. Following significant consultation it was agreed to fell the recent secondary woodland that was encroaching the mire surface and to restore the mire by completely infilling the eroding drainage channel.

Management rationale

The essence of the New Forest mires is that they are open, groundwater-fed fens, a small central watercourse being characteristically flanked by the seepage fen. The valley floor may have developed poor fen and wet woodland on deeper peat in sumps. This component is at risk from headward erosion, and the whole at risk from afforestation.

Techniques

The woodland was felled and the eroding drainage channel was filled in using small clay plugs. Between these plugs heather bales (produced as part of the ongoing management of nearby areas of dry heathland) were staked down in the channel and covered over with remnant bank spoil associated with the original drainage, as outlined in the sketch below.

Outcomes

The immediate result of this work was to bring the water table back up to the surface of the remnant mire. This was soon followed by colonisation of the surface of the infilled drain (the spoil-covered heather bales) with typical soakway mire vegetation.

Plans for the future

Stony Moors is one example of the dozens of mires that have been restored by the Forestry Commission in the New Forest SSSI in the last decade. As part of the ongoing programme of SSSI restoration the Forestry Commission is continuing to develop and apply a range of materials and methods to safeguard previously damaged mire and stream habitats.

Drain and secondary woodland

Felled woodland

Immediately after drain infill showing heather bales and clay plugs (left) and same location in autumn 2008 showing habitat recovery (right)

References

Sanderson, N.A. 1998. Description and evaluation of New Forest grasslands and mires. Contract report for English Nature.

Wright, R.N. & Westerhoff, D.V., 2001. *New Forest SAC Management Plan.* Lyndhurst. English Nature.

Case Study 7.4
Fen Water Management
– The Anglesey Fens

The Anglesey Fens SAC is a complex of six basin and valley-head rich-fen systems located in the Carboniferous Limestone Region of central Anglesey. The component sites range in size from a few ha to over 250 ha and support a range of plant communities referable to the Annex I types alkaline fen and calcareous fen with *Cladium mariscus* and species of the *Caricion davallianae*, as well as areas of base-enriched fen meadow referable to the *Eu-Molinion* (NVC community M24) and other calcareous types (notably M22).

Management objectives
To restore fen features across the site to favourable condition. Hydrology figures as a key factor influencing feature condition.

Management rationale
The Anglesey Fens mainly comprise valley-head and basin wetlands with groundwater inflow confined to the mire margins as a result on low conductivity peat infill (including lacustrine clay, marl and peat). Management of axial and other main drainage features needs to result in maintenance of year round high water-levels and the restoration of shallow hydraulic gradients, whilst avoiding significant overbanking. This is an important issue given that some of the main drainage features arise upstream and outside the sites in intensively farmed catchments. Management of marginal hydrology aims to allow the uninterrupted movement of water from marginal springs and seepages across the mire surface.

Historical Management
Extensive drainage has been a feature of most of the Anglesey Fens. Most was undertaken in an attempt to improve agricultural productivity and included deep arterial main drains as well as numerous smaller 'foot-of-slope' drains to aid drainage off surrounding agricultural land. A key aspect of the latter concerns its role in severing key water supply pathways between groundwater discharge zones and the fen surface.

Hydrological restoration – techniques and outcomes
Hydrological restoration has followed two dominant themes: (i) work to restore high year-round water levels either by installing dams and other control structures in main and other key drains or preventing/minimising further ditch clearance and maintenance, and (ii) restoration of key water pathways between groundwater source areas and the fen surface, either by damming drains or their complete infill. A significant associated benefit of the latter technique has been the creation of shallow open water pools and scrapes suitable for colonisation by Charophytes and other early successional specialists.

Major weir installed by EA in the main drain at Cors Erddreiniog NNR. This structure resulted in a significant (1 m+) rise in water levels in the main drain which runs through the centre of the site, thus rewetting adjacent peats and restoring shallow hydraulic gradients across much of the site. (Pete Jones).

Infilled marginal ditch at Cors Erddreiniog, Anglesey. (Pete Jones).

Chara filled pool on the former alignment of an infilled 'foot-of-slope' drain at Cors Erddreiniog NNR, Anglesey. (Pete Jones).

Plans for the future

Significant further hydrological restoration is planned with the EU LIFE+ funding. Site hydrological regimes will first be conceptualised using the Wetland Framework and limited initial field investigation to assign parts of sites to key WETMECs. Attention will be focussed primarily on restoring groundwater supply pathways interrupted by marginal drainage.

8. Managing Fen Nutrient Enrichment

Section 4: *Understanding Fen Nutrients* explained nutrient enrichment and the role of individual nutrients in relation to fens, and how to assess evidence of enrichment. This section explores the practicalities of different strategies which can be adopted to address nutrient enrichment on fens. These fall into three main categories:

i.   **managing the source or root cause of nutrient enrichment** e.g. catchment management to prevent nutrients from becoming available within the wider landscape through appropriate land use;

ii. **managing the nutrient pathway** i.e. how nutrients get from the source to the fen e.g. through reedbed filtration or creation of buffer zones;

iii. **on-site management/restoration of the fen habitat** to reduce the effects of enrichment by removing nutrients and/ or preventing the release of nutrients already accumulating within the fen

On some fens it may be possible to treat the root cause of the nutrient enrichment, whereas on others where no control can be influenced over the underlying causes or sources, it may only be possible to treat the symptoms. For example, if nutrients are entering a site from a point source such as a stream, then creation of a buffer zone or constructed wetland to help 'mop up' excess nutrients and prevent them entering the fen may be appropriate. However, if the nutrients are entering from a diffuse source such as aerial pollution over which only limited control can be exerted locally, then management of the fen itself to remove nutrients by vegetation cutting and/or grazing may be required. Some practical options for management of nutrient enrichment at each scale are presented below.

8.1 Summary of management options and techniques for addressing enrichment.

Summary of main options for managing fen nutrient enrichment in relation to source and pathway.

Nutrient source/ pathway	Management options		
	Reduce source	Block nutrient pathway	Manage nutrient impact within the fen
Atmospheric - e.g. factory, poultry farm	Beyond scope of individual fen managers – needs regulatory control.	Not generally possible, though marginal tree belts may play a role.	Grazing, cutting, vegetation and litter removal, turf removal, soil stripping
Surface flooding and other point-source impacts, including water affected by sewage plant, road drainage or intensive agriculture	Regulatory control, enforcement and incentives - e.g. Water Level Management Plans, AMP process, Planning System, Capital Works investment.	Prevent water from reaching fen surface if source cannot be tackled and water is not essential in water budget terms. Dredge enriched sediment from rivers and other sources. Install sediment traps Employ constructed wetlands	
Overland flow e.g. fertiliser and eroded soil from farmland in catchment	Targeted / limited fertiliser application. Application of agri-environment and other land management measures. Habitat reversion through application of higher-tier environmental land management prescriptions. Contour ploughing.	Establish buffer zones – consider earth banks/ bunds Remove nutrient enriched sediment from feeder ditches (slubbing) Install sediment trap Employ constructed wetlands for points of focussed runoff.	
Groundwater e.g. intensive agriculture, septic tanks, sewage treatment works	Regulatory control. Land management options include better targeting or limiting of fertiliser application on surrounding farmland; address problems with septic tanks etc.	Probably beyond scope of individual fen managers	
Historical nutrient accumulation within fen soil	Remove enriched soil through turf removal or soil stripping	Soil inversion but very difficult and can create future problems NOT RECOMMENDED	Grazing, cutting, vegetation and litter removal

Summary table of key techniques for preventing or reducing nutrient enrichment

Technique	Rationale for use	Action	Timing	Effectiveness / strengths	Appropriate sites	Limitations / less appropriate sites
Wider catchment management	Reduces nutrient addition to the catchment and its export to the wetland.	Wide range of potential actions, including: Agri-environment and other land management incentive schemes. Habitat reversion schemes (e.g. improved grassland to semi-natural grassland, heathland, woodland etc) through application of high tier agri-environment options. Farm-yard infrastructure improvements such as separating clean (roof drainage) water from foul (farm yards, silage effluent)	Year round	Very effective. Addressing an acute farm-yard problem can effectively shut-off in one go major nutrient sources.	All site types	Can be expensive, requiring capital expenditure. Difficult to enforce.
Buffer zones	Creates a zone of low or zero nutrient addition around the site margins, together with measures to encourage nutrient uptake/retention within buffer.	Definition of low or zero nutrient application over an area of at least 10 m width. Ideally combined with management of rough vegetation in buffer zone to help take-up nutrients and/or trap soil particles, or low earth bunds to 'filter' water.	Any time	Generally regarded as effective, though often used on a precautionary basis without much actually evidence that the technique has worked.	All site types.	
Grazing	Vegetation accumulates nutrients from the soil. Removal of the vegetation thus enables some nutrient off take.	Grazing by animals (preferably cattle, ponies or hardy sheep). Animals need to be moved daily for effective nutrient removal.	Can be year round, but usually April to end October.	Sustainable and potentially cost-neutral or even profitable but labour intensive moving stock. Aids good vegetation structure and composition.	Very wide range	Dry areas for lie-up at night desirable. Fencing usually needed to focus grazing where it is needed. The wettest sites may be ungrazable.

Technique	Rationale for use	Action	Timing	Effectiveness / strengths	Appropriate sites	Limitations / less appropriate sites
Mowing and litter removal		Cut vegetation by hand or machine (flail or swipe mounted on tractor or tracked specialist machine). Removal of cut material strongly recommended - heap as biomass piles at edge of site or remove for composting.	Late summer (July to September)	Usually very effective. Also removes dominant elements of the vegetation, thus aiding growth/recovery of low growing/light demanding species.	Firmer / seasonally drier sites where machinery can be used to aid cost effectiveness – i.e. floodplain fens, fen meadows, some valley and basin fens.	Wet /soft sites may only be possible by hand.
Turf removal and soil stripping	Removes accumulated pool of nutrients in soil/peat. These are typically concentrated in the top 30 cm of the profile.	Hand or more usually machine stripping, the latter ideally with a 12T or lighter 360 degree excavator. Excavated material should be removed off-site or better still re-used on-site for making peat dams and bunds or infilling ditches.	Any-time when ground conditions allow, but preferably avoiding breeding bird season. Undertake on rotation to allow some undisturbed habitat to remain.	Very effective for removing acutely enriched soils which no other technique can easily address. Also can be used to achieve re-wetting by bringing the ground surface closer to the water level.	Most site types	Expensive. Difficult over large areas (e.g. > 0.5 ha) due to volume of resulting material and possible wave action effects reducing recolonisation.
Rewetting/water management	Keeping soils wet prevents enrichment through mineralisation. Hydrological management can also be used to stop enriched water reaching the surface of the fen.	Ditch blocking (dams) or complete infill. Routing enriched water through constructed wetlands. Use of clean water from an alternative source	Usually August to March	Usually effective, though not often in isolation on enriched sites.	All site types	May result in pulse of nutrients, but this is generally short-term. Rewetting will usually be undertaken to rewet soils rather than as a specific nutrient reduction measure.

8.2 Managing the source of nutrient enrichment

The majority of fens receive a proportion of their water supply from the surrounding catchment, either as surface run-off or groundwater recharge. This water can become charged with nutrients from various sources, including point-sources such as leachate from farmyards, septic tanks etc., and more diffuse sources such as fertiliser. Legislation and guidance which seek to limit nutrient-enriching farming techniques are endorsed by financial incentives available through Environmental Stewardship and similar schemes which encourage farmers to reduce nutrient use and pollution. Nutrient enrichment from the surrounding catchment nevertheless remains a problem for many fens, beyond the direct influence of many fen managers.

Catchment management aims to address nutrient enrichment at source, by producing a strategy which addresses all diffuse and point sources of enrichment within a catchment area. Some agri-environment support measures include a premium to encourage a high proportion of farm holdings within a catchment to become involved in this kind of initiative (see **Section 12: Economic Aspects of Fens**).

8.2.1 Crop and soil management

Various projects around the UK, including WWF's Wild Rivers project and West Country Rivers Trust's Tamar 2000 project, have demonstrated the capacity to achieve significant reductions in nutrient enrichment from artificial fertiliser and farmyard manure by providing free nutrient budget service and/or offers of free soil testing which encourage more targeted fertiliser application to optimise plant uptake and avoid leaching of excess nutrients. Other initiatives to target agricultural fertiliser application include computer models such as MANNER for nitrogen management and PLANET for phosphorus, both available on the Defra website.

More general guidance for farmers and land managers which can help with catchment management includes:

- spring is considered the optimal time for application of N;
- cultivation in autumn should be avoided, as it releases greater levels of N;
- fertilisers should not be applied to wet ground or during periods of heavy rain;
- fallow periods and reduced cultivation allow soils to regain good crumb structure;
- contour tillage reduces runoff;
- maintaining over-winter ground cover helps prevent soil loss from erosion.

Basic recommendations for manure application include:

- cultivate soon after slurry applications to encourage uptake of nutrients;
- autumn and spring applications result in higher levels of diffuse pollution;
- N loss is greatest in free-draining soils in the autumn;
- P losses are greatest when soils are wet, typically November and December;
- composting manure before application can inactivate pathogens, increase ammonia release and tends to remove P and N.

8.2.2 Livestock management

Phosphorus is a major component in poultry, pig and milking cattle feed, but is frequently above livestock's requirement. When excreted and eventually spread onto fields, there is a risk of excessive phosphorus enrichment. N and P excretion from pig units can be reduced significantly by changes in feedstuffs, which can also prove cost effective for farmers. A synthetic form of P (phytase) can be added to the diet of poultry and pigs, which decreases the P in manure.

Provision of cattle bridges and fencing to reduce poaching can also be significant in reducing nutrient enrichment (see 6.2.9).

8.2.3 Other land management

A range of other techniques can be used to reduce the release of nutrients and other pollutants within the catchment, for example:

– Installing phosphate-stripping plants on sewage treatment works that discharge into a river that forms part of a fen's water supply.

– Installing or repairing systems which separate clean (mainly rainfall) and dirty water in farm-yards. Replacement of septic tanks with mains sewerage treatment See Defra, UK - Environmental Protection - Water - Diffuse pollution of water

Further specialist advice is recommended to assess appropriateness of these options to specific locations and design detail, particularly for options likely to incur high capital costs (see Appendix V for further advice).

8.3   Managing nutrient pathways

8.3.1 Reedbed filtration

Passing the water which feeds a fen through a reedbed can help trap the majority of the suspended solids and some of the dissolved nutrients before it enters the fen. The reedbed might be a separate area to the fen, specially constructed, or a part of the fen set aside for this purpose. The size of the treatment reedbed needs to be matched to the nutrient loading (i.e. concentration of nutrients multiplied by estimated flow) of the incoming water. Not surprisingly, larger wetlands are required for heavier loadings, but small in-line wetlands can be effective where a fen is fed by seepage, small ditches or streams.

The principles of constructed reedbed treatment systems are well known: water draining vertically down through the rhizomes is used initially to convert any ammonium present to nitrate. Another design, in which water passes laterally through the rhizomes, denitrifies the nitrate to gaseous forms of nitrogen. There will be some uptake of N by the reed, but this is eventually recycled through decomposition of the leaf litter. A high rate of P removal can be achieved by using a highly alkaline or calcareous substrate, such as limestone or crushed brick rubble, so that the phosphate is adsorbed/precipitated to calcium carbonate and other calcareous minerals such as apatite. Constraints on the design of any constructed reedbed may arise from available space, topography and variability in the flows of water in the inflow stream. Natural reedbeds are used for water treatment under certain circumstances, though there may be negative impacts on their conservation value. Hawke and José (1996) and the Constructed Wetlands Association can provide further details.

Drains at the edge of a fen can be used to help intercept nutrients – particularly if vegetated with species which are responsive to nutrients. In addition routing drains into constructed wetlands will improve the effectiveness of nutrient removal.

Marginal interceptor ditch at Cors Erddreiniog (P.Jones).

8.3.2 Buffer zones

Buffer zones are areas established immediately around a fen, or along streams, drains and ditches that bring water to a fen, to intercept nutrients which might otherwise enter the fen as a result of adjacent land management activities. Buffer zones work by increasing the residence time of water in the soil before the water enters the fen, allowing enhanced removal of soluble nutrients by plant and microbial uptake (bacterial denitrification being a key process) and removing sediments by physically trapping the particles.

Oligotrophic Anglesey fen bordered by improved grassland within a dairy farm. The marshy grassland at the edge of this fen acts to some extent as a nutrient buffer, but better site protection would require definition of a formal buffer zone within the field (P. Jones).

Buffer zones can remove over 90% of the N and over 35% of the P from water entering an alluvial floodplain from agricultural land, while losses of N and P from surface water using a riparian forest buffer were measured as 83% and 81%, respectively (Peterjohn & Correll, 1984). Similar high rates of N and P removal have been documented in buffer zones comprising alder wood, poplar wood and grassland vegetation types.

The vegetation type established in the buffer zone does not appear to be critical as long as it is not subject to intensive agricultural management. Trees, shrubs and permanent grassland are all equally suitable. The physical properties of the buffer zone are important, including the structure of the vegetation, size, flow rate of water and gradient. The aim is to reduce the rate of flow of surface water through the buffer zone to enhance potential for nutrient removal before the water reaches the fen. Diverting small streams and runnels across the buffer zone will help increase residency time, as will removal/disruption of any agricultural land drains. Because of the different processes associated with nitrogen and phosphorus uptake, dry buffer zones are better for P removal while wet buffer zones with a high carbon content (such as wet woodland, where leaf fall provides the carbon input) are better for N removal.

The width of the buffer zone is important but optimum width depends on the size of the catchment, the slope adjacent to the fen, soil type and the degree of enrichment. The first 5 to 10 m of the buffer zone is often reported as being the most important for nutrient removal, so the width need not necessarily be great in order to provide benefits. A summary of the complex chemical and biological processes that occur in buffer zones, depending on factors such as carbon/nitrogen ratios, temperature and oxygen availability, together with further information on practical use of buffer zones, is provided in Hawley et al (2004).

Infilling drainage features leading into a fen from adjacent improved grassland offers another means of slowing down the passage of water into fens and thus increases the chances of in-situ nutrient removal by marginal vegetation at the edge of the fen. In addition, breaking field drains and creating Horseshoe wetlands is an option. The impacts of any proposals on drainage or other aspects of neighbouring land should be carefully assessed, and neighbours consulted as required.

Buffer zones can be supplemented with low earth banks (0.2-0.5 m high by 1-2 m wide), sometimes supporting planted hedgerows, to provide an additional physical impediment to surface water flow and thus increased residency time for inflowing water. The use of biomass crops (including elephant grass and willow) as a means of removing nutrients from wetland catchments is in its infancy, but deserves consideration and further research.

8.3.3 Sediment removal from feeder ditches

Nutrient enriched sediments which have accumulated in water supply or feeder ditches which may be negatively influencing fen habitat can be removed by suction dredger, a technique known as 'slubbing'. The sediment is then disposed of away from the fen, usually in small bunds that re-vegetate naturally. This technique has been used to some effect in the Broads, but slubbing is quite invasive. Work should therefore be staggered, cleaning no more than 25% of the fen/ditch in any one year over four years, repeating as necessary on a five to 25 year rotation, depending on sediment accumulation rates. The expense of using the technique, along with the potential for damage to ground and vegetation, makes it appropriate for highly enriched sites only. Further information is provided in the Reedbed Management Handbook (Hawke & José, 1996).

8.3.4 Bund creation

In some cases it is possible to prevent the input of eutrophic water by isolating the fen from the source with a surface bund. Bunds built from clay-rich soils are likely to be relatively impermeable and will also help retain any nutrients which do seep through. This is only possible:

- if there is another cleaner water source available, such as from a second river source or from a borehole. This latter approach was taken at Strumpshaw Fen. Here, the borehole was used for summer water deficit, and river water was allowed to flood onto the fen into holding areas during the winter when nutrient concentrations were diluted by higher flow. This technique is presented as a case study in Hawke and José (1996);

- if the fen is already sufficiently supplied with water from other sources and will not be severely affected by the loss of this water source;

- If the severed pathway does not fundamentally change the hydrological character of the site.

In general, bunding should be seen as a last resort to be considered when the preferable option of improving water quality at source has failed.

8.4 Impact management to reduce the effects of enrichment on fens

Various techniques can be used on the fen itself to reduce the effects of nutrient enrichment. Depending on the degree of enrichment, the accessibility of the site and the management budget available, enriched fens may benefit from a combination of different techniques.

8.4.1 Grazing

Nutrient reduction by grazing relies on transferring nutrients out of the fen system in the form of dung and urine. In order to achieve nutrient removal, stock is moved regularly off the fen (preferably daily) to another dry enclosure or pen. This movement mimics the traditional infield/outfield system, typical of many heathlands. See Section 6: Fen Vegetation Management for further guidance on grazing.

8.4.2 Cutting vegetation and litter removal

Nutrients accumulate in the plant tissue as vegetation grows and at the end of the growing season the above-ground material of herbaceous plants (herbs, grasses, sedges) dies back. The nutrients within this material may be translocated to the roots for over-winter storage and re-used the following spring, released back to the fen system via decomposition or accumulated in fen peat development. On many sites, all three processes occur simultaneously. The principle of cutting and removing vegetation off-site is to remove the nutrients in the live plant material before they are lost/recycled back into the fen habitat.

Cutting should therefore be done at the end of the maximum growth period but before die-back, which for most species is late July or August. Where accessibility allows, machinery such as a brush-cutter can be used, and mechanical rakes are also available. However, on many sites hand cutting or strimming is required along with hand raking to remove cut material. This can therefore be a very labour intensive management technique.

Mowing is usually best undertaken in late summer after the main breeding bird period, and when vegetation biomass is at its peak. Removal of cut vegetation and litter is best delayed for a few weeks to allow material to wilt, reducing the volume of material which needs to be handled.

Cut material should be transported off the fen for composting or burning rather than allowing the material to compost on site, which would result in nutrients feeding back into the system. Locations for burning/composting should ideally be of no (or very limited) conservation interest, and positioned at least 10 m from any watercourse, spring head, flush or seepage zone. Where there is no other option, on-site burning might be required but should be done on a metal sheet to enable ashes to be collected and removed off-site (see section 6.4).

This management is suitable for sites with moderate to high levels of enrichment as the stores of nutrients are depleted over time, and should be completed annually for best effect. Removal of cut litter and vegetation is highly desirable to achieve nutrient off-take and prevent smothering of lower plants. Mowing and removal of vegetation and litter are best undertaken on a rotational basis to allow regular removal of nutrients while disturbing only small areas of the fen habitat at any one time. Grazing is strongly recommended as a follow-on treatment. Cutting is usually combined with attempting to reduce the external inputs of nutrients where possible (see local and catchment scale management).

Litter removal is similar to cutting and removal, but slightly less labour intensive. Again, the aim of this technique is to remove annual litter production before it begins to decompose thereby reducing the nutrients released back into the system. Litter removal in autumn is therefore preferable. It does not reduce those nutrients that are already translocated to the roots, so this technique is better for fens with low to moderate enrichment problems. As for material produced by cutting, the litter should be removed off site for disposal.

An accumulation of litter affects the plant community by altering temperature, nutrient availability and light availability to the soil. In an experiment on a fen in northern Minnesota, litter removal increased peat temperature, increased light availability at soil level, increased the phosphorus content of above-ground plant material, and altered the plant species composition. The phosphorus results may have been due to stimulation of microbial activity following litter removal. Therefore this technique would not be suitable for sites that are P-limited, as an increase in phosphorus availability may enable excess nitrogen to be used, resulting in greater enrichment issues.

Both litter and vegetation removal are best undertaken on a rotational basis to allow regular removal of nutrients while disturbing only small areas of the fen habitat at a time. This also means the technique is likely to be more manageable in terms of labour costs. Research also indicates that on drier sites where water may be a limiting factor or on bare areas where there is no canopy cover, the retention or, in cases of significant bare ground cover, the addition of litter can aid seedling germination and establishment. Therefore, litter removal as a nutrient management tool appears to be best suited to wetter sites with good vegetation cover. Drier sites with good vegetation cover may be better suited to vegetation cutting (but retention of some litter) and sites with significant areas of bare soil are likely to benefit from the addition of litter/cut vegetation to improve re-establishment of vegetation.

8.4.3 Turf removal and soil stripping

Another option for reducing excessive nutrients on fens is to remove the enriched surface layer in which nutrients have accumulated in plant and peat material by turf removal or soil stripping, both of which remove the litter, plant material (including roots) and top layers of peat. Either of these operations can simultaneously make the surface wetter by lowering it relative to the groundwater and create conditions suitable for the development of more diverse nutrient-poor vegetation. A 360 degree tracked excavator is most commonly used, with preference for relatively lightweight (12t) machines, ideally on wide tracks. This approach is being used by the Little Ouse Headwaters Project, http://www.lohp.org.uk.

Area of turf stripping on Anglesey, where a nutrient rich rank vegetation was removed to expose the base rich and relatively nutrient poor strata which can then support a more diverse range of fen species (A. McBride).

Turf stripping is to a shallower depth than soil stripping, with only the moss, litter layer and top few centimetres of peat being removed. Both techniques can also be useful in bringing the surface level of the peat closer to the current water table level, re-creating wetter conditions at the peat surface, along with removing the seed bank of any unwanted plant species. It may, however, also remove any remnant seed bank of fen species and it is often beneficial to combine soil stripping with the addition of cut material from a 'target' habitat type to encourage rapid re-establishment. The latter operation is unlikely to cause further enrichment given that the major nutrient pool is likely to be in the soil, and only a thin covering of cut material is likely to be needed. This combination of techniques has been shown to be particularly useful for fen meadow restoration on former agricultural land, where up to 70% of the target species from the 'donor' fen site established on areas where top soil stripping had occurred before hay spreading, although at small abundances in some cases (Kilmkowska et al, 2007).

To help gauge the depth of top soil strip, some basic information on nutrients should be gathered across the site and down the peat profile. Assessing NPK concentrations at 10cm intervals to a peat depth of 30 to 50cm will help indicate what depth of top soil needs to be removed to recreate nutrient poor conditions. In this case, analysis of soil samples for both bio-available (i.e. extractable) and total N and P, along with pH are useful. These data allow an assessment as to whether a 'flush' of nitrogen or phosphorus might be expected on any associated exposure to air and re-wetting, respectively. Sampling across the site will help identify if there are 'hot spots' of nutrients or areas of lower nutrient status that might be able to be retained intact. Chemical analysis of peatland soils should be undertaken on samples of known volume and the results expressed volumetrically.

The technique is successful even on highly enriched sites such as former arable land. For example, during fen meadow restoration on mineral soils, removal of the top 10 to 20 cm of soil depleted total phosphorus concentration by around 85% and also reduced bio-available phosphorus (Tallowin & Smith, 2001). As the technique actually physically removes nutrients it should only need to be undertaken once, assuming major nutrient inputs are prevented from building up again. There is, however, significant disruption to the fen, including exposure of underlying peat (and possible erosion), loss of the peat pollen/macrofossil archive and damage to any archaeology. This technique should therefore only be undertaken on small areas of fen at a time (generally less than 2 ha, or no more than 10% of the site area) and advice from an archaeologist sought before starting.

Before embarking on costly and potentially controversial work such as turf stripping, it is crucial to remove the original source of nutrient enrichment or take measures to ensure nutrients no longer reach the site. See Case Study 8.1.

8.4.4 Dredging

Mechanical dredging by a machine with a long-reach arm and a bucket can be used to remove nutrient rich sediments which have accumulated over time in ditches, ponds, lakes, reedbeds and other wetlands. However disposal of the spoil is problematic.

8.4.5 The role of re-wetting and water management in nutrient management

Retaining high water levels is important for overall fen management, but in terms of nutrient management keeping peat wet reduces oxidation and mineralisation and subsequent release of nutrients. Therefore, any of the techniques used to retain water on a fen site, or stabilise water-levels (see **Section 7: Fen Water Management**) will benefit nutrient management and, in particular, reduce the likelihood of nitrogen mineralisation and release. However, there is also potential for re-wetting (i.e. raising water levels to re-wet or flood the soil) to result in a 'flush' of phosphorus from enriched soils under anaerobic (waterlogged) conditions.

Re-wetting can result in additional nutrient enrichment problems if eutrophic water is used, or if the natural water inputs to a fen are from a eutrophic source, such as a nutrient enriched river.

8.4.6 Soil inversion

The principal of soil inversion is to bury the top layers of nutrient-enriched soils deeply enough to prevent the nutrients being readily accessed by plant roots. The technique has been used successfully for species-rich grassland restoration, where the top 30cm of soil was buried under around 40cm of sub-soil using a deep plough (Glen et al, 2007). Unlike soil stripping, there is no material to dispose of, but the technique relies on heavy machinery and is therefore only likely to be suitable for drier fens, such as those previously used for agriculture. There is also a risk that phosphorus will be re-mobilized, and careful consideration is required as to whether any phosphorus release is likely to be a short 'flush' or a more long-term release of nutrients which would negate the benefits of soil inversion.

Soil inversion is a relatively new technique which has not yet been tried on fens. Effectively the nutrients are still on site, and could be released by inappropriate future management or utilised by vegetation such as trees which root to sufficient depth to access the buried nutrient store. There is also a risk of ploughing or other soil inversion techniques damaging archaeological remains.

Soil inversion should therefore only be considered as a last resort for nutrient management on fens.

8.5 Monitoring nutrient reduction

Direct measurement of changes in nutrient regime following application of any of the techniques described above is likely to be expensive and is likely to require a fairly sophisticated sampling design over several years. Vegetation will respond to reduced enrichment and hence in general, indirect assessment of changes resulting from nutrient reduction techniques by vegetation and habitat condition monitoring is favoured, which will need to be undertaken for reporting purposes on all statutory sites. Further details of monitoring are provided in Section 10: Monitoring to Inform Fen Management.

8.6 References

Glen, E., Price, E.A.C., Caporn, S.J.M., Carroll, J.A., Jones, M.L.M & Scott, R. 2007. A novel technique for restoring species-rich grassland. In: J.J. Hopkins, ed. *High Value Grassland Providing Biodiversity, a Clean Environment and Premium Products. Proceedings of the BGS/BES/BSAS Conference held at Keele University, Staffordshire, UK, 17-19 April 2007.* Occasional Symposium No. 38, British Grassland Society, pp. 221-224.

Hawke, C.J. & José, P.V. 1996. *Reedbed Management for Commercial and Wildlife Interests.* Sandy: The Royal Society for the Protection of Birds.

Hawley, G., Ross, S, Shaw, S, Taylor, K, Wheeler, B. & Worrall, P. 2004. *Nutrient Enrichment of Basin Fens: Options for Remediation.* English Nature Research Report No. 610.

Klimkowska, A., Van Diggelen, R.., Bakker, J.P. & Grootjans, A.P. 2007. Wet meadow restoration in Western Europe: A quantitative assessment of the effectiveness of several techniques. *Biological Conservation,* 140, 318-328.

Peterjohn, W.T. & Correll, D.L. 1984. Nutrient dynamics in an agricultural watershed: observations on the role of a riparian forest. *Bioscience,* 65, 1466-1475.

Tallowin, J.R.B. & Smith, R.E.N. 2001. Restoration of a *Cirsio-Molinietum* fen meadow on an agriculturally improved pasture. *Restoration Ecology,* 9 (2), 167-178.

Cors Geirch is the largest of the Corsydd Llyn rich-fen SAC and comprises an extensive valley-head fen system fed by groundwater discharge from adjacent calcareous sands and gravels. The site supports a range of plant communities referable to the Annex I types alkaline fen and calcareous fen with *Cladium mariscus* and species of the *Caricion davallianae*. It is surrounded by improved agricultural grassland, with some agricultural improvement spreading onto the relatively shallow fen peats. In 1993 landscaping of a nearby refuse tip created a demand for local top soil and thus an opportunity to strip peat from an enriched rush-dominated pasture on modified fen peat which had been included in a recent habitat restoration potential study (Shaw & Wheeler, 1992).

Peat removal at Cors
Geirch in 1993.
(Les Colley)

Over the course of two weeks, contractors removed the top 30 cm of the agriculturally modified peat profile from an area of 5.5 ha and transported it from the fen basin to the nearest highway using a specially constructed temporary mat and timber road. The substantial volume of peat involved (c. 16,500 m3) would at the time have been very difficult to re-use within the site (for example as part of ditch blocking or bunding operations) and its use for nearby landscaping provided both the means for its disposal and the actual funding for the project. Subsequently, a series of nearby springs and seeps were diverted to flow onto the excavated surface. Vegetation recovery has been monitored and showed the rapid disappearance of residual rye-grass Lolium perenne and the development of a series of initially poor-fen communities with elements of M29 and M9a with Carex lasiocarpa on the wetter soaks, mixed fen–meadow on the drier peats and acid grassland and heath on the driest mineral soils. The appearance of Drosera intermedia on exposed peat was unexpected and may have been unintentionally introduced. Long term management of the scrape has included control of invading willow and grazing. Jones & Colley (2004) provide a detailed description of the project.

Recent photo of stripped
surface showing pony
grazing at edge of M29
runnel. (Les Colley)

This approach can be extremely successful and result in the rapid rejuvenation of enriched and agriculturally modified fen surfaces.

References

Jones, D.V. & Colley, L. (2004). Restoring the fens at Cors Geirch. *Natur Cymru*, No. 11, 17-21.

Shaw, S.C. & Wheeler, B.D. (1992). *Cors Geirch. Potential for the restoration of a wetland reclaimed for agriculture.* Report to the Countryside Council for Wales. Department of Animal and Plant Sciences, University of Sheffield.

9.   Creating Fen Habitat

Concern about the loss of fen habitat and fragmentation of remaining fens has prompted various national and local strategies aimed at creating fens from new, rather than 'simply' restoring extant fen. The UK BAP for wetlands, for example, includes a target to create eight new 'landscape scale' wetlands of which fen might be a major component, as well as a further target to restore 2,800 ha of former fen. Many local BAPs also include strategies for wetland creation, as do some of the regional spatial strategies (formerly Regional Planning Guidance), which provide a broad development 15-20 year strategy for each region in England. In Scotland, wetland creation, including fens, is included in the Rural Development Programme (RDP) and Stewardship schemes (see Section 12: Fens from an Economic Perspective).

This section considers the practicalities of fen creation, including the various steps involved from identifying suitable sites, design of the proposed fen and applying for the necessary consents, to options for vegetation establishment. Each site will vary depending on size, location, hydrology, geology, biology and human aspects, but the techniques and approaches outlined below will provide a basic framework for those considering fen creation, and are equally relevant to many aspects of fen restoration.

Experience of fen creation in the UK is more limited than for some other wetland habitats, but much of the experience gained from reedbeds is relevant to fen creation. The Habitat Creation Handbook for the Minerals Industry (White, G. J. and Gilbert, J. C. (eds) 2003) provides an up to date summary of such techniques.

Anyone involved in fen creation is encouraged to document and monitor their project, and to share their experience to improve our collective knowledge of successful schemes and techniques.

9.1 Scope for fen creation

The Great Fen project is a good example of the kind of wetland creation promoted through the 50-year Wetland Vision project, which will also contribute to UK BAP targets. The aim of the project is to restore, buffer and link two NNRs (Holme Fen and Woodwalton Fen) south of Peterborough that cannot otherwise sustain their interest. Areas within the Great Fen project will also play a role in storing floodwater.

Scope for fen creation is determined by:

- topography
- hydrology
- hydrochemistry
- substratum characteristics
- substratum fertility
- climate
- surrounding land-uses
- legal constraints such as flight safeguarding and planning permissions
- financial resources
- requirements of local community and landowners.

Availability of suitable land is often a limiting factor, which is why the majority of fen creation is part of a mosaic of other wetland habitats within a larger area or scheme. Examples of opportunities for fen creation which may arise include:

- sale of farmland as it comes on to the market, (e.g. parts of Potteric Carr near Doncaster, South Yorkshire, and the Great Fen Project in Cambridgeshire);

- managed re-alignment of coastal defences (e.g. Alkborough Flats, Humberside), especially for brackish fens;

- inland flood risk management schemes (e.g. River Teviot near Hawick in the Scottish Borders, and the River Lossie in Nairn);

- restoration of mineral extraction sites, especially peat extraction (for example Ham Wall in Somerset), sand and gravel workings (e.g. at Hatfield in South Yorkshire and Needingworth Quarry, Cambridgeshire); some quarries (e.g. Dry Rigg Quarry in the Yorkshire Dales National Park) or former colliery workings (e.g. Bleak House, Staffordshire) (see Meade & Wheeler 2007 and Roberts & Elliott 2007).

Obtaining funding for fen creation may have to be combined with other schemes which meet specific criteria, such as the creation of reedbeds for bitterns or swallowtail butterflies and other BAP priority species.

Creating fen from raised bog

In some areas of the UK, removal of raised and blanket bog peat for the horticultural industry has resulted in extensive areas of bare peat or underlying mineral substrate. Where hydrological and hydrochemical conditions (such as acidity of the soil or groundwater, depth of water that can be achieved) are unsuitable for bog re-establishment, or the costs are prohibitive, conversion to fen vegetation may be appropriate (Meade & Wheeler 2007), even if only as a pre-cursor to the development of raised bog habitat in the very long-term. Several highly valued fens developed without any active human intervention on cut-over or otherwise damaged bogs (e.g. Whitlaw Mosses SAC, Crymlyn Bog SAC, parts of Thorne Moors SAC). Given the rarity of raised bog and the lack of opportunities to create new habitat of this type, it is unlikely that the maintenance of fen would be a long-term management objective on such sites.

Middlemuir Moss, Aberdeenshire, a cut over bog showing slow natural colonisation by cotton-grass 15 years after abandonment. Colonisation by fen and bog plants could be enhanced by raising water levels across the whole area. (A. McBride)

9.2   Benefits of fen creation - integration with flood risk management

Capacity of fens to store storm water and help reduce flooding downstream depends on location in the catchment, and the area and depth to which the fen can be flooded. Deliberate flooding with river water may in turn affect the type of fen, depending on the depth and duration of flooding, time of year, nutrient concentrations of any deposited sediment, and land management between floods. Reedbed and associated tall herbaceous fen vegetation may develop on ungrazed fens subject to deep and persistent periods of inundation. If the flooding is not too deep and persistent, with low nutrient/silt loads, and there is light grazing between floods, fen meadow is more likely. However, creation of herb-rich fens in areas subject to seasonal flooding with eutrophic water is likely to be unsuccessful due to high nutrient levels encouraging dominance by reed or reed sweet-grass (*Glyceria maxima*).

Potential opportunities for fen creation may arise as part of sustainable urban drainage schemes (SUDS) such as balancing ponds, set back of river defences and flood storage schemes and washlands (land deliberately flooded to reduce the risk of rivers over-topping). Although often small and of the commoner types of fen vegetation, such schemes are nonetheless valuable. Most new washland creation schemes for flood risk alleviation are unlikely to provide suitable conditions for the creation of fen habitat (Morris et al. 2004), except where persistent groundwater or surface water supplies can maintain permanently wet areas.

9.3 What type of fen?

New fens can be located in lowland situations or at high altitude, and range in size from tens of square metres of flush or spring-head fen, to several hundred hectares of flood-plain fen and reed-beds. The type of fen can vary as much as the size, from a base-rich fen receiving ground-water rich in calcium and other base cations from petrifying springs, to a poor-fen receiving ground-water with low concentrations of base cations, such as the valley mires of the New Forest. The specific hydrological requirements of many fen types (see Section 3: Understanding Fen Hydrology) limit the potential for the creation of some types of fen.

The Wetland Vision launched in 2008 provides a lot of useful information and maps on the types of fen that can potentially be created across England as well as some of the constraints on the creation of wetlands in general.

Reedbeds are a type of fen that may, with appropriate management, develop into more diverse herbaceous fen vegetation as litter, silt and peat build up. The creation of reedbeds on various sites may eventually increase the extent of other types of fen vegetation if natural success is allowed. The length of time over which this may occur is difficult to determine because of the relatively limited experience nationwide of wetland habitat creation.

Leighton Moss in Lancashire was one of the first modern examples of fen creation where arable fields allowed to flood shortly after the First World War rapidly developed into reedswamp. Around the margins greater tussock sedge fen has already developed. Many parts of the reed swamp might have developed into drier herbaceous fen without regular mowing.

9.4   The planning and design process for the creation of new fen habitat

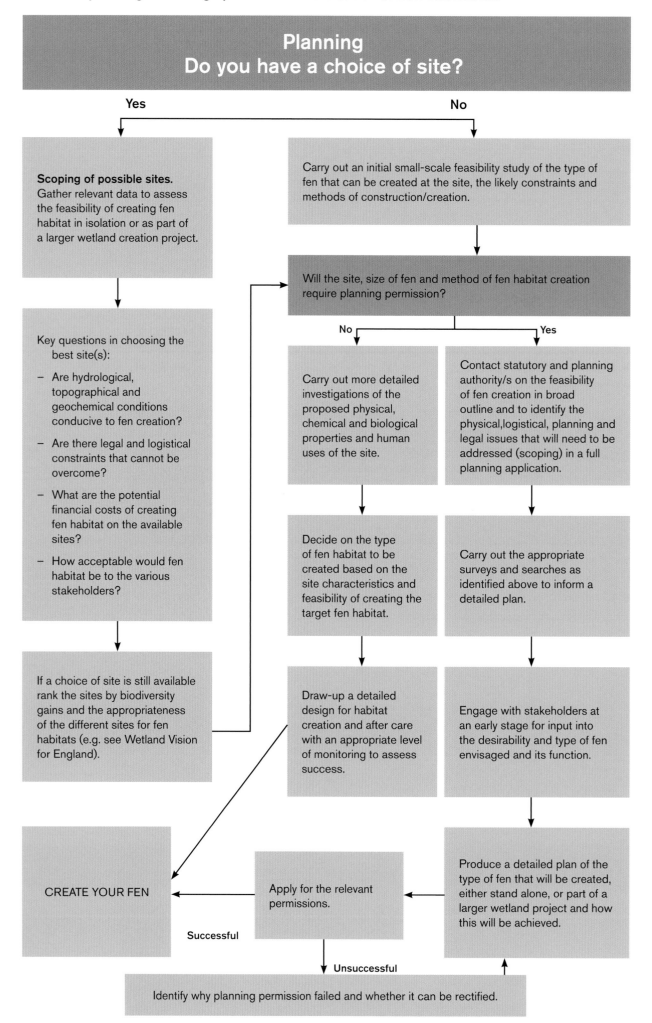

**Planning
Do you have a choice of site?**

Yes

No

Scoping of possible sites. Gather relevant data to assess the feasibility of creating fen habitat in isolation or as part of a larger wetland creation project.

Carry out an initial small-scale feasibility study of the type of fen that can be created at the site, the likely constraints and methods of construction/creation.

Will the site, size of fen and method of fen habitat creation require planning permission?

No

Yes

Key questions in choosing the best site(s):

– Are hydrological, topographical and geochemical conditions conducive to fen creation?

– Are there legal and logistical constraints that cannot be overcome?

– What are the potential financial costs of creating fen habitat on the available sites?

– How acceptable would fen habitat be to the various stakeholders?

Carry out more detailed investigations of the proposed physical, chemical and biological properties and human uses of the site.

Contact statutory and planning authority/s on the feasibility of fen creation in broad outline and to identify the physical, logistical, planning and legal issues that will need to be addressed (scoping) in a full planning application.

Decide on the type of fen habitat to be created based on the site characteristics and feasibility of creating the target fen habitat.

Carry out the appropriate surveys and searches as identified above to inform a detailed plan.

If a choice of site is still available rank the sites by biodiversity gains and the appropriateness of the different sites for fen habitats (e.g. see Wetland Vision for England).

Draw-up a detailed design for habitat creation and after care with an appropriate level of monitoring to assess success.

Engage with stakeholders at an early stage for input into the desirability and type of fen envisaged and its function.

CREATE YOUR FEN

Apply for the relevant permissions.

Produce a detailed plan of the type of fen that will be created, either stand alone, or part of a larger wetland project and how this will be achieved.

Successful

Unsuccessful

Identify why planning permission failed and whether it can be rectified.

9.5 Restraints on fen creation

Planning permission will often be needed for a change of land use which involves 'the carrying out of building, engineering, mining or other operations in, on, over or under land, or the making of any material change in the use of any buildings or other land'. The planning laws and guidance vary between different UK countries, but in England, provided the land is still to be used for grazing, this could be regarded as legitimate agriculture as defined under section 336 of the Town and Country Planning Act 1990. There is no guarantee that permission will be granted, even for habitats such as fens identified as priorities within the local BAP. Proposals will have to be consistent with within other policies and guidance that the authority is obliged to take into consideration.

Planning, consents and licensing

Appendix V summarises legal and regulatory constraints and issues relating to fens, including statutory planning, consents and licensing issues.

The movement of soil, manipulation of hydrological regimes, change in vegetation or land use, creation of bodies of open water and disruption of potential archaeology are just a few examples of the large number of operations that may fall under statutory provisions.

Early consultation is recommended with the relevant planning or regulatory authority:

England	county council
Wales	appropriate unitary authority
Scotland	development control authority – regional/island council, district authority of national park
Northern Ireland	planning service, Department of the Environment

9.5.1 Flood risk

Fen creation is unlikely to be approved if it might:

- increase risk of flooding to other properties or land;

- reduce capacity of the floodplain or flood storage areas to retain water;

- alter floodplain flow characteristics;

- result in adverse water quality, or

- have an adverse effect on other biodiversity interests.

Although fen creation will often have beneficial effects on water quality and water holding capacity, considerable effort and partnership working in the planning stage may be necessary to demonstrate that proposed fen creation will not have an adverse effect on flood storage.

In England, a site specific flood risk assessment prepared by a competent hydrologist is usually required for any wetland creation scheme to determine the change in risk arising from the development and the residual risks. Planning Policy Statement 25 (PPS25) provides information on what this should include.

9.5.2 Access, civil infrastructures and other services

Early consultation with utility and other service providers is essential in planning any habitat creation scheme to determine whether the proposed development may be constrained by gas, electricity, water or telecommunication cables or pipelines, or by transport infrastructure such as railway lines and roads.

Public rights of way crossing the proposed area should be identified and if necessary scope explored for diversion, amendment or improvement. In Scotland or other parts of the UK where there is a right to roam, consideration should be given to how wider access rights will be accommodated or might be affected by the proposals.

The Civil Aviation Authority (CAA) and Royal Air Force (RAF) should be consulted if the site is close to an airport or airfield. The exact location of the proposed site will need to be considered in relation to runways, flightlines/trajectories of aircraft and the location of other wetland or landfill sites in the local area that may create new flightlines used by flocks of birds. Careful design and management of new wetland habitats can successfully reduce the risk of bird strike to acceptable levels.

Larger, heavier species of bird and those which form large flocks tend to cause more problems than others. Although the number of bird strikes with swallows is high, the proportion which result in aircraft damage is relatively small. The advantage of creating fens rather than open water or wet grassland habitats is that the bird species attracted tend to be small passerines rather than large flocks of duck, geese or waders.

"Wetland creation is one of the most problematic development types in terms of bird strike prevention at aerodromes. Wherever possible developers should seek to keep proposals as far from aerodromes as possible and outside the 13 km safeguarded zone of major civil and all military aerodromes. Where this is not possible, careful site selection, design modification and, as a last resort, bird management plans may be sufficient to control any additional risk and avoid an objection from the aerodrome manager or the regulator. Whatever the strategy adopted by a wetland developer, the earliest possible consultation with aviation interests is vital in order to ensure the best chance of achieving a mutually acceptable compromise.'

Extract from 'Taking account of aviation hazards in the development of a wetland vision for England'. Author: Dr John Allan. England Wetland Vision project (www.wetlandvison.org.uk)

9.6 Check list of issues to consider in relation to fen creation

Information required/issues to be considered	Why	Where from
Planning permissions, consents and licensing	Many operations (including water abstraction, landform creation and spoil removal, works on floodplains etc.) require some form of legal or statutory consent. Relevant agencies may be able to advise and assist on most appropriate options, and help to identify or reduce potential issues at an early stage.	Statutory conservation agencies, planning authorities and others. Early discussions and site meetings normally essential.
Soils/geology – type, structure, condition, depth	Soil type and nutrient status influence type(s) of fen that may be created, and function and management thereafter. Soils and geology are also fundamentally linked to hydrological function of fens e.g. water sources, movement, retention, chemistry, which in turn will influence expected vegetation types e.g. reedbed will flourish on nutrient rich sites, where poor fen would fail.	Undertake own survey/investigations to gain general understanding of site. Consult available soil maps e.g. British Geological Survey. Professional advice likely to be required for larger scale projects.
Hydrology	Quantity and quality of water are fundamental to fen function. The underlying solid and superficial geology will largely determine the biochemistry of a site in terms of acidity/alkalinity (pH). The types of rock (chalk, sandstone, shales etc.) and superficial deposits (clays, sands, gravels etc.) will dictate whether water will issue from an aquifer, or whether water will be held on site by an impervious layer and consequently affect the hydrology/hydrological regime of any proposed fen.	Undertake own survey/investigations to gain basic understanding of water sources, quantities, inflow/outflows on site. Consult meterological data. Consult with relevant agencies such as EA (England and Wales), SEPA (Scotland) and NIEA (Northern Ireland) to determine water/abstraction availability. Professional advice and investigations also likely to be required for larger projects.
Topography	Site topography and height relative to surrounding land will largely dictate the way in which water reaches a site and the type of fen habitat that can be created. Topography will also dictate: site/habitat designs long-term function and management whether proposals (particularly those involving manipulation, retention or management of water regimes) may affect other adjacent landowners location, type and scale of water management structures such as sluices, bunds, scrapes etc.	Undertake own survey/investigations or commission professionals
Local biodiversity context	Identifies other similar habitats nearby, from which experience of type, design, function and management can be learned. Will also inform most appropriate type of fen(s) that may be possible or suitable in an area, and may provide local seed sources for vegetation establishment and/or natural colonisation source(s) for new site.	Statutory conservation agencies, local BAP network and environmental organisations, BARS website.

Information required/issues to be considered	Why	Where from
Surrounding landownership/use	Adjacent land (and its ownership) may affect fen function, or be affected by it e.g. is adjacent land being actively drained and/or under conventional agricultural production? Are there other similar wetland habitats nearby that may link biologically or hydrologically with the planned site and form a broader more robust area of semi-natural habitat?	Local farming/landowning groups such as NFU, CLA/SRPBA, local BAP networks, local authority
Climate	Climate data will inform early stages of feasibility scoping in fen creation e.g. will there be enough water? How quickly will it evaporate from open water sources? Climate change predictions suggest that the pattern of rainfall and evapotranspiration is likely to change across the UK in future, and such changes will need to be incorporated into any calculations. Expert advice should be sought at an early stage from a professional hydrologist.	Expert advice should be sought at an early stage from a professional hydrologist.
Finances/resources	Early estimates of cost and resource implication will be essential to determine scope of fen creation projects and subsequent management. External funding or partnership working will be required or desirable	Statutory conservation agencies, voluntary environmental organisations and others who have undertaken similar projects in advance. Local authority funding advisers/co-ordinators.
Knowledge	Gather information upon which to base plans, learn from experience elsewhere to avoid repeating mistakes and ensure best chance of success. Also to share/disseminate your own experience with/to others.	Consult widely with others who have carried out similar projects in the past, including statutory conservation agencies and voluntary environmental organisations
Local community	May have strong views about proposals. In some cases there may be issues or concerns which need to be addressed in order to build support for a project. In other cases input from local community can strengthen or improve planned projects, and help with sourcing and obtaining funding, establishing volunteer networks to assist with management or monitoring and providing opportunities for public enjoyment of the site (see Section 11: People and Fens).	Local community groups, local councils, statutory conservation agencies, conservation organisations
Landowners/graziers/ contractors	Fen creation often involves contracting in manpower and machinery from others e.g. fencing, groundwork, and later grazing. Local contractors will normally have better knowledge of the area, have suitable equipment and in some cases be significantly more cost effective. They may also have invaluable experience of similar work on other sites which can help inform your plans	Local machinery rings, farmer and contractors groups. Other site managers including statutory conservation agencies, environmental organisations, local authorities (e.g. countryside rangers)

9.7 Site assessment

Planning and design of any wetland creation project requires a great deal of site information and data. The following section highlights some of the more important aspects to understand and investigate during the early planning phases, and their relationship with target fen types and creation methods. Section 5: Fen Management and Restoration includes further guidance on site assessment.

9.7.1 Water quantity

Sufficient water of the right quality and quantity is fundamental to any fen. The first essential prerequisite in assessment of the suitability of any potential site for fen creation, or restoration, is therefore to establish the quantity of water supply to the site. Obtaining reliable information on the amount of water entering the proposed fen, and amounts potentially lost via various routes, for each quarter of the year is essential. Ideally records for several years at least should be examined to identify annual as well as seasonal variations.

The water available at a site can be estimated using the following calculation:

Water available = rainfall – evapo transpiration (ET) – seepage losses + seepage inputs

Climate data

The Met Office hold rainfall and evapotranspiration data from which they can produce daily, weekly or monthly estimates for a specific location.

MORECS is a nationwide service giving real time assessments of rainfall, evaporation and soil moisture. (www.metoffice.gov.uk). EA, SEPA and NIEA may also hold relevant information.

MAFF technical bulletin No.34: Climate and drainage (1976), also contains useful information on rainfall and evaporation values.

Information on rainfall and other climatic variables is relatively easy to obtain (see above) but climate change predictions suggest that the pattern of rainfall and evapo-transpiration is likely to change across the UK in the future, and such changes will need to be incorporated into any calculations. The difficulty in accurately calculating water budgets is further complicated by the hydrological complexity of most fens, and the variations in seepage on individual sites depending on soil type, soil structure, and variations in the height of the water table between one location and another (the hydraulic gradient). Expert advice from a professional hydrologist should therefore be sought at an early stage.

9.7.2 Topography

The topography of a site and its height relative to surrounding land will largely dictate the way in which water reaches the site and the type of fen that can be created. Section 3: Understanding Fen Hydrology explains the different types of fen, including those dependent on topography where the water movement is predominantly vertical (topogenous fens) or those fed with the lateral movement of groundwater (soligenous fens) or the often drier fen meadow. A fen may have a combination of soligenous and topogenous characteristics.

Topographical data gathering

Topographical information may be obtained from a number of sources.

- Lidar surveys provide course level data on land levels and topography, which may help in the initial planning phases and scoping of a wetland creation project. Statutory agencies such as EA may charge for supply of data they hold, or this can be purchased or commissioned commercially.

- Professional topographical surveys can be commissioned for a site to provide more detailed data (e.g. up to 5 cm contour resolution). Data will normally be supplied in electronic form for utilisation in computer mapping and design packages and linked to GPS co-ordinates. Costs will vary depending on terrain, survey spec, accessibility etc. Example site, on ATV accessible, dry terrain, in southern England cost approximately £40/ha, using a 20 m grid producing 20, 10 and 5 cm resolution data.

- Simple spot height checks of relative high and low points, heights of sluices/bunds etc. or basic surveys can be undertaken by site staff with rented survey equipment such as auto planes or laser planes at low cost. (e.g. £30-70/week). Some very basic understanding/ experience will be required.

- Winter puddle maps, vegetation maps, fixed point photography and site visits can be the simplest method of obtaining basic information regarding relative land heights, low spots prone to flooding etc.

Undertaking a
topographical survey
(N. Droy)

LIDAR maps can provide a general understanding of the topographical setting of a proposed fen creation site, highlighting the main high and low sports or areas. In this example, the sea bed is shown on the left of the dunes (green) and the low areas behind the dunes (machair) are shown in blue/grey (top right), and may indicate in general ecological terms where wetland habitats are most likely to develop and be maintained. (Courtesy of the Western Isles Data Partnership)

9.7.3 Geology

Underlying bedrock (chalk, sandstones, shales etc.) and superficial geology (clays, sands, gravels etc.) will largely determine the hydrochemistry of a site in terms of water quality and acidity/alkalinity (pH) (see Section 4: Understanding Fen Nutrients). Localised base-rich tills or drift deposits can enable the development of rich-fens in areas with principally siliceous bedrock which will normally give rise to acidic waters. Calcite veins in some metamorphosed rocks, e.g. Silurian gritstones, can also give rise to very small, but floristically diverse base-rich springs and flushes in a generally acidic environment.

The type of bedrock and superficial deposits will also dictate whether water will issue from an aquifer or whether water will be held on site by an impervious layer and consequently affect the hydrology/hydrogeological regime of any proposed fen (see Section 3: Understanding Fen Hydrology). Spring-head mires and seepage fens depend on presence of a suitable aquifer.

Maps of solid and superficial geology are available at a scale of 1:50,000 from the British Geological Survey) either as paper copies or in digital format compatible with MapInfo and ESRI.

Alternatively, LandIS, (www.landis.org.uk) the 'Land Information System', is a substantial environmental information system operated by Cranfield University, UK, designed to contain soil and soil-related information for England and Wales including spatial mapping of soils at a variety of scales as well as corresponding soil property and agro-climatological data.

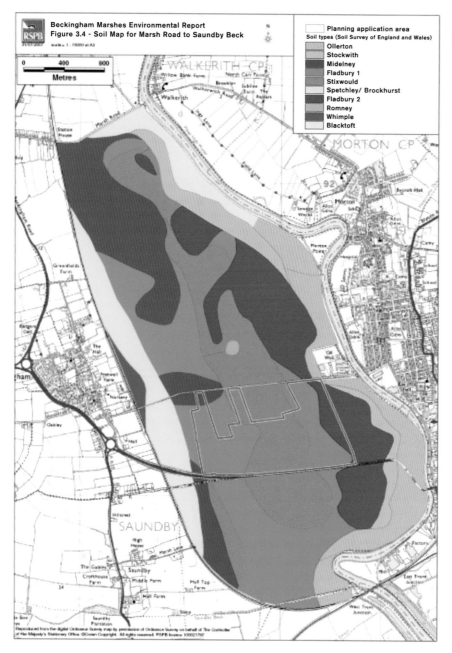

An example of a soil map
for an RSPB site

9.7.4 Water quality

The quality of water entering the proposed site is nearly as important as water quantity, and will to a large extent determine the type of fen that will establish. The pH and concentrations of the major plant nutrients (nitrate, ammonium, phosphate, potassium and calcium) must all be taken into account.

In some areas nitrate concentrations in groundwater have increased significantly and have resulted in the eutrophication of wetlands at the base of slopes or in valley bottoms. River water quality will be affected by upstream land-use and discharges (see Section 4: Understanding Fen Nutrients). Further information and guidelines on how to undertake or commission water quality testing are outlined in Section 10: Monitoring to Inform Fen Management.

9.7.5 Substrate nutrient levels

The texture of the substrate is partly responsible for its fertility, but the quantity of nutrients within the substrate will significantly affect what type of fen vegetation can or will establish. Sands and gravels tend to be relatively nutrient poor and are generally more acidic than silts and clays. Clay soils will always give rise to fertile vegetation types due to their high nutrient holding capacity. If there is a significant quantity of clay it is likely that reed will dominate. There are exceptions to these general principles and the alkalinity of groundwaters reaching the wetland will also significantly affect the type of fen vegetation that will establish. It may be necessary to lower substrate fertility by removing top soil from former agricultural land.

In order to establish moderately species-rich fen vegetation, nutrient levels should ideally be low, especially phosphate concentrations which should be lower than 15 ppm, ideally below 9 ppm. High concentrations of calcium in any groundwater feeding the proposed site will reduce the availability of phosphate through the process of co-precipitation.

Digging a soil test pit, Cayton and Flixton Carrs, Scarborough (N. Droy)

9.7.6 Soil analysis

Soil analysis is used to determine nutrient status and pH of a soil. It usually includes pH, available potassium, phosphorus and magnesium, total nitrogen and sometimes an assessment of soil texture. Analysis is usually undertaken by a specialist laboratory, but the reliability of the analysis depends on sampling accuracy. Further information and advice is provided in Natural England Technical Advice Notes TAN 20 Soil sampling and analysis for habitat restoration and recreation in agri-environment schemes, and TAN 31 Soils and agri-environment schemes: interpreting soil analysis for habitat creation and restoration.

Key points to consider when collecting soil samples:
- Use the correct tool e.g. a cheese corer, screw auger or pot corer
- Sample to the correct depth: 0-20 cm on arable land, 0-7.5 c.m on permanent pasture
- Include the top few centimetres of soil, which may have differing pH or nutrient values
- Take account of variations in soil depth, texture and past management over the sample area
- Take the correct number of sub-samples (at least 25 cores totalling 0.5-1 kg)
- Dispatch samples for analysis as soon as possible

Soil augering and soil samples at Cayton and Flixton Carrs, Scarborough (N. Droy)

Soil texture

Texture is a fundamental soil property influencing key characteristics such as drainage and water storage. Soil texture is determined by the relative proportions of the different sized particles which make up the soil, sand having the largest particles and clay the smallest, with silt somewhere in between. Soils are usually named according to their constituent particles or texture – for example sandy loam or clay. Soils may also be referred to as heavy (clays) and light (coarse textured) to indicate their ease of cultivation.

Clay, sand and silt particles all impart distinctive qualities to the feel of the soil, which enable soil texture to be assessed by hand (hand texturing). In reality, most soils are made up of a combination of different particles, but in general terms:
– sands generally feel coarse and gritty
– silts generally feel smooth and/or soapy
– clays generally feel sticky or plastic

Further advice and information on soil texture can be found in Natural England Technical Advice Note 52: Soil texture

9.8   Site design

Site design should take account of

– soil type

– depth of open water area

– routes for water movement across the site

– risk of erosion during early establishment or successional stages

– planning consents, licenses and permissions

Site visits and careful assessment of every aspect are essential to any fen creation project (RSPB).

If the site is a post industrial or agricultural site with the potential for creating different landforms, it may be possible to create suitable basins, shelves and dykes to facilitate the development of different types of fen and other wetland habitats.

Digger at Ham Wall (RSPB)

9.8.1 Water depth and stability of the water regime

Water depth will influence the type of fen which develops, and is therefore critical in design and ground preparation. Most types of fen vegetation develop where summer water depths vary from up to 10 cm above the substrate to 30 cm or more below the surface at the end of the summer, depending on the type of fen vegetation and water supply mechanism. Winter water levels are significantly higher and can be 30 to 50 cm above the fen surface.

Published eco-hydrological guidelines for some fen plant communities are summarised in the table below. Similar guidelines are being developed for more plant communities, including the *Juncus subnodulosus – Cirsium palustre fen-meadow* (M22).

The mean, maximum and minimum water levels (cm) above (positive numbers) or below (negative numbers) the substratum surface for some fen plant communities.

Explanation of abbreviations: S2 = Cladium mariscus swamp, S4 = reedbed, M13 = Schoenus nigricans – Juncus subnodulosus mire, M24 = Molinia caerulea – Cirsium dissectum fen meadow, S24 = Phragmites australis – Peucedanum palustre tall-herb fen, ‡ = more details for individual sub-communities in the eco-hydrological guidelines (Wheeler et al. 2004).

Plant community	Summer			Winter		
	Mean	Maximum	Minimum	Mean	Maximum	Minimum
M13	-10	5	-30		1	-5
M24	-25	-10	-53			
S2			-15		40	
S24‡	-15	4	-78			
S4	-10	50	-80	50	150	0

Small, shallow areas of open water are preferable to large, deep areas because of the increased risk of erosion around the margins where large waves build up over large areas of exposed water. Aligning the longest length of a scrape perpendicular to the prevailing winds can help reduce wave erosion.

9.8.2 Controlling water level

Water levels on any site are controlled by the rate at which water enters and leaves. Some form of control structure(s) may be needed to control water inflow and outfall, or on larger sites, to control and manipulate water movement between different hydrological blocks. On many sites, simple structures such as pipe dams and drop board sluices will be sufficient.

Water control structures

Flexi pipe sluices: Cheap, easy to install, and an effective method of precise water level control, but only capable of moving low volumes of water. They consist of flexible, ribbed plastic pipe e.g. 300mm single wall aquapipe, incorporated in to an earth bund or dam. Alternatively, rigid pipe may be used, with a right angled 'turner' section installed, which can be rotated to differing positions to allow water to be retained or let out.

Drop board sluices: simple structures comprising a series of boards that drop in to a grooved spillway. Water levels are adjusted by inserting or removing boards. There are many different types of materials that can be used to construct the retaining walls of the sluice including plastic sheet piling, wooden boards and welded metal frames.

See RSPB Water management techniques for conservation – technical case study series (N Droy) for further information. www.rspb.org.uk/sluices

9.8.3 Bunds and borrow dykes

Bunds, or low earth banks, keyed in to an impermeable substrate can be used to retain water above the level of the water table in the surrounding land, and may also help to retain winter floodwater, where this is desirable. Further details of bunds are included in Section 7: Fen Water Management.

9.8.4 Plastic membranes

On sites with very permeable soils, such as peats, it is often difficult to maintain wetter conditions with higher water levels without affecting, or being affected by, neighbouring land. Any functioning land drains or ditches on surrounding land are likely to exert some influence on an intended wetland creation site.

In extreme cases, a plastic membrane can be installed to limit water movement from the wetland to the drier surrounding land, effectively forming an independent hydrological unit. This allows water levels within the fen to be manipulated without affecting the surrounding area, but hydrological isolation is not necessarily a sustainable option for many wetlands. Further information on this technique is available from www.rspb.org.uk/sluices.

9.9 Establishing fen vegetation

The establishment of fen type vegetation on new sites can be challenging. The following information is provided as a summary and reference for those wishing to undertake such action, based upon available best practice knowledge. Whilst there remain as many questions as answers, it is hoped that it will provide readers with the confidence to try new techniques. As with any new undertaking, it is wise to try new methods or techniques in pilot projects or test plots and monitor closely to assess the effectiveness and lessons learnt. Only then should you undertake action across larger areas or projects. Section 9: Monitoring to Inform Fen Management includes guidance on monitoring techniques.

> Getting the hydrological regime right is the key to successful fen creation. Provided the site has been chosen carefully and other fundamentals such as landform have been planned and implemented appropriately, the rest will fall usually into place. Patience (and monitoring) may be all that is required to successfully establish fen vegetation. Good luck!

9.9.1 Choice of species

> The choice of species for establishing fen vegetation should take account of:
> - hydrological regime
> - water quality
> - type of substratum
> - the characteristic plant communities of the region and hydro-morphological type of wetland
> - species characteristic of the area
>
> A topographical survey may be necessary to identify the range of land heights and planting zones. The range of water level tolerance for various species is detailed in Newbold and Mountford (1997).

The hydrological regime and hydrochemistry of a site, including pH, alkalinity and nutrient levels as well as depth and availability of water will determine the plants which can be established. Certain types of fen vegetation are characteristic of peats, whilst others can be found on a wide range of substrates. The New Atlas of the British Flora and visits to local fen sites will provide some indication of suitable species.

The species listed in Appendix IV which characterise a wide range of types of fen vegetation likely to establish in different conditions should be viewed as the minimum species required. *Phragmites australis – Urtica dioica* fen has been left out because of its low value and high cover of the invasive and undesirable nettle. A number of montane/upland fen vegetation types have also been left out, as the opportunities for creating these types of fen habitat will rarely occur. The sub-communities and constancy tables detailed in Rodwell (1995) give further information on characteristic species and requirements.

9.9.2 Options for establishing fen vegetation

Options for establishing plants on a bare substrate include introduction of seed, plug plants and spreading hay as a seed source, but experience from a wide range of different sites has demonstrated that use of pre-grown plugs or vegetative cuttings, tussocks or rhizomes are the most reliable means of establishing many species of fen plant (Amon et al. 2005, Galatowitsch *et al.* 1999). The rhizomatous nature of many fen species helps achieve fairly rapid cover, which is desirable where invasive species are a threat. A high intensity sowing or planting of the target species will not necessarily prevent the establishment of weedy species, but may suppress their growth.

Hydroseeding (i.e. spraying a specially mixed slurry comprising water, seed, mulch, fertiliser and a binder in one operation) over large areas is likely to be prohibitively expensive and have a low degree of success because of the poor germination rate of many wetland species.

9.9.3 Site preparation and timing of vegetation establishment

If the site substrate contains a high proportion of peat or organic matter, especially after peat extraction, the peat may be dry and oxidised. To aid plant establishment, it may be necessary to raise the water level to the surface or above, which will reduce the establishment of rank weedy species and favour more diminutive wetland plants. Design of sluices, bunds and other water control structures should take into account the need to maintain this elevated water level in perpetuity.

9.9.4 Seeds

Some seed merchants supply native wetland plant species of UK provenance, but the range is limited and large quantities are costly. Consult Flora Locale (www. floralocale.org) for further information and guidance. Establishing a few plug plants in suitable areas and allowing these to spread can be more cost effective than broadcasting seeds.

Seeds of some families of wetland plant germinate readily (e.g. *Asteraceae Caryophyllaceae Brassicaceae* and *Poaceae*), whilst others may only germinate after stratification, which involves subjecting the seeds to alternate periods of freezing and warmer temperatures.

Propagating Carex from seed in a nursery is notoriously difficult. In one study the highest rate of germination of bottle sedge seeds was around 20% for fresh seeds whilst several other species required stratification (Budelsky & Galatowitsch 1999). Cold, moist storage of sedge seeds improves germination, but it is easier to propagate sedges from rhizomes or tillers.

Use of seed bombs

'Seed bombs' were used to colonise two newly dug ponds at Whitlaw Mosses NNR in the Scottish Borders in an area with few other wetlands or ponds where leaving nature to take its course through natural colonisation was unlikely to be successful. Material which formed a strand line around the mosses following the retreat of annual winter floods was found to contain a wide range of seeds, mainly sedges and bog bean, as well as large amounts of reed and sedge debris. In 2003 four freezer bags of the damp strandline material were simply thrown into each pond and allowed to disperse naturally. In the first summer few of the plants were evident, but by the second year a wide range of plants that could be attributed to the mix in the seed bombs had started to grow. This included the rare lesser tussock sedge; the main sedge that is growing on the bank edge in the photograph.

Pond inoculated with seed bombs (A.McBride)

9.9.5 Plug plants

Specialist nurseries and some tree nurseries will grow plug plants to order. The plants are grown in a small amount of compost which helps them establish quickly when planted into moist substrate, which can help stabilise substrate to help establishment of other fen plants. Rapid 'greening' of a site is sometimes also important to project funders to demonstrate that work has in fact started.

Planting of plug plants is very labour intensive, and consequently not feasible in large numbers without the assistance of many willing volunteers. It took two men on average a day to plant out approximately 1,500 tillers and tussocks of common cotton-grass and harestail cotton-grass on a cut-over area of Thorne Moors, South Yorkshire using a local source of plants. This is a similar rate to that achieved in the restoration of some Minnesota peatlands where rates of 120 transplants per person per hour were achieved (Johnson & Valppu 2003).

9.9.6 Vegetative propagules

For sedges and some dicotyledonous plants (e.g. bogbean, marsh cinquefoil) the most effective method of establishing plants is to take sections of vegetation/turf from a donor area and transplant to the receptor site. Transplantation should be within a day or two to avoid plants drying out. The receptor site should be wet, but with the water table below the substrate to allow the plants to establish. Water levels can then be gradually raised to their final levels over the next six months.

Vegetative transplantation is best undertaken in spring at the beginning of the growing season which allows plants to develop a strong root and rhizome anchorage before being flooded or upooted by winter wave action.

Planting out reed plugs at Lakenheath Fen (RSPB)

Transplants of cotton grass rhizomes have been used to stabilise loose substrates like peat which would otherwise take many decades to stabilise due to frost heave constantly breaking tender young roots. The tough rhizomes of cotton grass resist the movement and create a stable substrate. In time the dominance of introduced species wanes and other species colonise the stabilised surface. Planting density depends on how quickly the ground needs to be colonised, but in most cases 10 plants/ m2 is sufficient.

On very nutrient poor former raised bog peats in Germany it was recommended that shoots of rhizomatous sedges (e.g. *Carex rostrata* and *Eriophorum angustifolium*) were planted at a density of one shoot per 2 m^2 (Sliva 1999), which resulted in 100% cover of vascular plants within 4 years.

9.9.7 Mosses and liverworts

Mosses and liverworts can be important components of many types of fen and bog vegetation, especially brown mosses in some of the spring-head fens (e.g. M10) and bog mosses in many types of poor fen (e.g. M4, M5, M6, etc. – see Section 2: Fen Flora and Fauna, and Appendix IV, fen NVC classifications). Mosses and liverworts can be difficult to establish where the substrate is dry or has high nutrient levels, but may readily establish naturally from airborne spores where the substrate is maintained in a damp or wet state, or from small stem fragments or individual leaves.

Introducing mosses to fen creation sites

Bog mosses and brown mosses have been established from vegetative sources at a cut-over mire and base-rich fen creation site respectively. Handfuls of mosses were macerated with a modified paint whisk on the end of a variable speed drill to chop the stems into small fragments in a bucket of water, which was then spread by hand across the moist substrate surface.

Experience has shown that the most suitable time to do this is in early spring when the ground is moist and warming. Establishment is then quick and does not suffer from the movements caused by frost heave encountered by attempts to establish vegetation in the autumn. Collection of material is best done locally and requires permission from the landowner, and from the relevant conservation body if the site is designated. Suitable areas for collection should have a similar topography and water source as the area to be seeded.

9.9.8 Hay

Strewing hay is a relatively cheap method of establishing species-rich vegetation. Creating suitable environmental conditions on the receptor site, the viability and correct treatment of the hay seed source are key ingredients for success. It is best to take several crops from the donor site through the season to include species which flower at different times, although many flowers will not set seed if cut back frequently, so two cuts is usually the practical limit. No special machinery is required, but generally the smaller and lighter the better to reduce impact on vegetation.

Getting the best results from hay-strewn seed

Using the hay immediately allows seeds to germinate immediately. If left, the seeds can become dormant, after which it can be hard to stimulate germination. Donor sites for hay should have similar soil and water conditions to the creation site. Take care that the sward does not contain invasive species which may become a nuisance on the created fen.

The proportion of viable seed is usually higher in green hay (i.e. freshly cut and not fully dried), provided the time between harvesting and spreading is less than two hours. The logistics of moving green bales will determine how fresh the bales are: if moved by hand, green hay bales can be very heavy. Dry hay yields fewer seeds, but will not rot so quickly or kill seeds through rising temperatures in decomposing hay.

Small round mini-bales are easy to handle and can easily be rolled back out on the fen creation site. A mini-baler also allows haymaking in wetter areas containing a larger range of wetland species, where larger machinery would get stuck or cause damage. Big round bales are also spread by rolling out. Alternatively unbound bales can be strewn with a muck spreader.

Vegetation establishment at Kingfisher Bridge

At Kingfisher Bridge near Ely in Cambridgeshire, a private scheme attempted to create herbaceous fen vegetation and reedbeds (Beecroft 1998). Several hay crops were taken over a period of a month to collect seed from a wide range of species from nearby Chippenham Fen. The hay was then strewn onto the prepared area. The biggest problems were dominance by weeds from the seed bank in the former agricultural soil, and the high nutrient status allowing these plants to outcompete seedlings from the hay crop. Hand collected seed from Chippenham Fen was also germinated in a poly tunnel before planting out as plugs in the spring of 1997; these seedlings established well. Further information on this case study can be found on www.kfbweb.info.

Hay crops have been successfully used to re-establish a fen in an area that had been drained and used for intensive agriculture for more than 200 years in southern Germany (Patzelt *et al.* 2001). As conditions for restoration were unfavourable, fen meadow hay from nature reserves in the region thought to contain enough viable seeds to assist the development of target communities was spread out on bare peat. Repeated vegetation analysis showed that a combination of topsoil removal to reduce fertility and hay transfer resulted in the establishment of 70% of the species present in the donor material. The dormancy of the seeds was found to be broken by a combination of fluctuating light and temperature cycles and stratification pre-treatment. Germination of the seeds is therefore likely to occur in the spring after an autumn sowing.

A similar process was used in northern Germany (Rasran *et al*, 2006). Between 40% and 70% of the 29 to 41 species per 25 m^2 plot in the above-ground vegetation of the donor hay meadow were present as seeds in the hay. A cluster analysis showed a high similarity between the species composition of the sward and the seeds present in the hay material. The number of seeds ranged from about 2,000 to 12,000 per m^2. The viability of the seeds of both herbs and sedges was high (approximately 80%) whereas the viability of grasses was only about 40%. Due to dormancy the germination percentage was much lower in all groups (20–50%).

9.10 Seedling survival

In the early stages of fen colonisation, self-sown and introduced plants are vulnerable to a number of factors which can result in poor establishment rates. The commonest factors are drought, flooding, frost heave and erosion, grazing by ducks, geese, swans, rabbits and hares. The following mechanisms can help improve seedling survival.

9.10.1 Reduction of wave action

Wave action can be reduced by using temporary breakwaters, such as plastic sheeting or hurdles (Garbisch 2005). More permanent breakwaters such as rock or sandy islands could also be used.

9.10.2 Creation of niches for plant establishment

Bare ground or niches which allow germination and seedling establishment can help in creation and restoration of semi-natural fen communities. Suitable niches can be created by poaching (see Section 6: Fen Vegetation Management). The type of livestock is not important, but timing can be. The best time to create germinating niches using stock is in the autumn when seed is naturally shed. 10- 20% of the sward should be covered by hoof prints. At this level the surface vegetation is open but suppressed enough that it will not overshadow the newly germinated seedlings when growth starts in the spring.

In a study that compared germination and seedling establishment of four fen species (*Carex ovalis, Cirsium dissectum, Molinia caerulea*, and *Succisa pratensis*) in a type of fen-meadow (*Cirsio-Molinietum*) with that of a semi-improved species-poor grass dominated rush-pasture it was found that soil disturbance was the major factor that increased germination (Isselstein *et al.* 2002). Seedling establishment was greater in the fen-meadow than the rush-pasture, which was attributed to the sward being more open. Safe niches for seedling establishment were not present in the rush-pasture. The inability to provide species-specific conditions for seedling recruitment appears to be a major factor limiting establishment of fen-meadow species on creation sites.

9.10.3 Protection from grazing

Grazing of reed seedlings by geese has been a problem at a number of sites. Deer, rabbits and hares readily graze leaves of sedges on more terrestrial sites. The use of protective meshing of fences may be necessary to stop geese walking or swimming into stands of planted out sedge and reed. Wire mesh is only likely to be affordable for small areas, but fences with white tape were found to be very effective at discouraging the entry of Canada geese into an area planted out with Spartina alterniflora (Garbisch 2005). Protection of planted areas is particularly important where there are high concentrations of waterfowl or where people feed ducks and swans. In the UK it was found that limiting open water to very small areas helped prevent geese from flying into areas recently planted out.

Netting of reed seedlings at Needingworth (N. Droy)

9.10.4 Nurse crops

Nurse crops are used to stabilise unstable substrates like silt, and also to create a less hostile environment for seedling growth. Nurse crops therefore need to establish quickly, but over time diminish in vigour allowing weaker fen plants to establish. The use of nurse crops is fraught with problems as plants suited to initial establishment tend to persist as strong components of the vegetation. Examples are reed canary grass and reedmace which will colonise silty nutritious substrates, but continue to dominate for many years if nutrients are available. An alternative is to use non-wetland plants, but this requires ability to control water levels precisely, gradually flooding the area once stabilised.

> On cut-over fen peatlands in Minnesota it was found that a cover crop made up of a mixture of oat (40%), winter wheat (40%) and annual ryegrass (20%) increased the rate of establishment of fen plants significantly on bare peat (Johnson & Valppu 2003).

9.10.5 Weed competition

Where previous land use was agricultural, short-term colonisation by weedy species may have to be accepted as a phase which the fen will go through. Given time, the excess nutrients will usually be mopped up by the vegetation and soil, and a more stable fen community will develop. On newly created fen sites where arable weeds threaten to outcompete desirable fen species, herbicide such as glyphosate may be required. Approval is needed prior to herbicide use in or near water.

Disturbing the soil surface before seeding can stimulate the germination of arable weeds. This can significantly reduce the growth of competing species but there is no guarantee that the same species will not subsequently germinate later if the soil is disturbed.

9.11 Post establishment management

Management is not usually required in the first year after establishment, but thereafter most vegetation will require some management to avoid accumulation of dead leaf litter which will reduce opportunities for colonisation by smaller fen species. Plans should be put in place before the fen is created for the introduction of appropriate grazing and cutting regimes, for scrub control (see Section 6: Fen Vegetation Management) and for control of water levels (see Section 7: Fen Water Management). Replacement of sown or planted target species may be necessary where there has been excessive loss due to intensive grazing by livestock, birds or other wild animals.

9.12 References

Amon, J.P., Jacobson, C.S. & Shelley, M.L. 2005. Construction of fens with and without hydric soils. *Ecological Engineering* **24**, 341-357.

Galatowitsch, S., Budelsky, R.& Yetka, L. 1999. Revegetation strategies for northern temperate glacial marshes and meadows. In: W. Streever (ed.) *An International Perspective on Wetland Rehabilitation*, pp. 225-241. Kluwer Academic Publishers.

Garbisch, E.W. 2005. Hableton Island restoration: Environmental Concern's first wetland creation project. *Ecological Engineering* **24**, 289-307.

Johnson, K.W. & Valppu, S.H. 2003. Fen restoration final project report. Natural Resources Research Institute, University of Minnesota, Duluth.

Meade, R. & Wheeler, B.D. 2007. Raised bogs from gravel pits? In: *Minerals extraction and wetland creation*, Proceedings of a workshop held in Doncaster 26-27 September, 2005 (eds. R. Meade & N. Humphries). pp. 41-49. Natural England.

Rasran, L., Vogt, K. and Jensen, K. 2006. Seed content and conservation evaluation of hay material of fen grasslands. *Journal for Nature Conservation* **14(1)**, 34-45

Roberts, A. & Elliott, G. 2007. The Hanson – RSPB wetland project. In: *Minerals extraction and wetland creation*, Proceedings of a workshop held in Doncaster 26-27 September, 2005 (eds. R. Meade & N. Humphries). pp. 31-34. Natural England.

Rodwell, J.S. (Ed.), 1995. *British Plant Communities. Aquatic Communities, Swamps and Tall-herb Fens*, vol. 4. Cambridge University Press, Cambridge.

Sliva, J. & Pfadenhauer, J. 1999. Restoration of cut-over raised bogs in southern Germany: a comparison of methods. *Applied Vegetation Science* **2**: 137-148.

White, G. & Gilbert, J. 2003. Habitat creation handbook for the minerals industry. RSPB, Sandy.

10. Monitoring to inform fen management

Fens change continuously as a result of external pressures such as drought and groundwater abstraction and due to the natural process of succession. Monitoring is essential to identify changes and their cause, which will inform how management may need to be adapted in future to maintain or restore specific features or species. This section explains the benefits of monitoring, outlines different monitoring techniques which can be used to measure a particular environmental variable or biological feature, and offers advice on design and implementation of a monitoring strategy. It also includes advice on data management, and suggests other sources of useful information about monitoring. Guidance on monitoring visitor numbers is included in Section 11: Fens and People.

10.1 Why monitor?

Monitoring can be used to:

- **Establish baseline data** which describes the existing condition of the ecology, hydrology, climatology and geomorphology of a site, against which changes in condition of the fen or its environment can be gauged. Baseline data is also important in setting targets for future management.

- **Develop an integrated understanding** of the ecological, hydrological and climatological functioning of a site i.e. exactly how individual fens work, including both internal and external influences. This will initially utilise the baseline data and will then be refined with each stage of interpreted monitoring data. Diagrammatic or schematic linking of all the major ecological and environmental processes affecting a fen is fundamental to planning effective management and monitoring, by identifying gaps in understanding and allowing reduction in monitoring frequency where further confidence is not required. For example, a change from MG10 rush pasture to M22 fen meadow may be desirable, but if the fen meadow has only developed after a few years with above average rainfall, progress to fen habitat may require manipulation of drainage systems.

- **Gather information to improve understanding of a fen and help develop objectives for future management**. Necessary information will include the type of habitat and environmental conditions across the site, to support decisions on types of habitat that could be aimed for.

- **Inform the management strategy for a site over time**. For example, in the short-term, water level monitoring data can be used to determine control of a water level management structure, such as a sluice. Over the longer-term, vegetation monitoring data can be used to determine whether habitat management activities are proving effective in maintaining or restoring desirable features, species or condition of the fen, and will also help inform how management might need to be changed in future.

- **Measure the environmental parameters (such as nutrients and water levels) associated with examples of different types of fen** to establish a reference or threshold against which deviations from optimal conditions can be measured or compared, which will help identify what management may be required on individual fens. An example is understanding the contribution of run-off from surrounding fields as part of an assessment of the impact of agricultural discharge on water quality, and subsequent implications for the fen ecology.

- **On-going measurement** of the effect of current or historical management, both to assess success and to refine further management.

Taking a hand-augured soil sample and describing the vegetation on Insh Marshes, Scotland, to establish a baseline for more intensive monitoring of the site hydrology. (J. Schutten)

10.2 Designing a monitoring strategy

Basic principles for designing a monitoring strategy

- The purpose of monitoring is to inform and help focus positive management to achieve the optimum results.
- Identifying what information is required for effective management, and agreeing clear objectives, will help determine what, where, how, when, how often and for how long monitoring should be undertaken.
- In general terms, any good quality monitoring data is useful, and always better than nothing, but identifying what does NOT need monitoring will help focus resources on priority issues.
- Usually the more parameters which are monitored, and the longer the monitoring period, the better.
- Effective monitoring strategies should include details of how data will be recorded, stored, managed and evaluated.
- All monitoring strategies should be reviewed and modified in the light of experience or changes in circumstance.

10.2.1 Setting objectives

The essential foundation for any monitoring strategy is clear objectives which take account of what information is required to help inform management, and how the results of the monitoring programme are likely to be used. For example, monitoring might seek to establish whether there is a causal link between a nutrient source and an area of fen which exhibits signs of nutrient enrichment, or to establish the effects of grazing management.

At least three but ideally 10 replicates of managed and control areas are required to demonstrate an effect so that natural variability between areas is accounted for and any difference between managed and control areas can confidently be attributed to management. Similarly to assess the effect of external environmental pressures, such as lowering of the groundwater table due to abstraction, reduced flooding frequency due to flood management works in the catchment, or an increase of nutrients due to the installation of a sewage treatment works upstream of the fen, monitoring will be required of both the external influence(s), and the way in which these manifest through changes in fen flora and fauna.

10.2.2 What and where to monitor

Monitoring is expensive, and should be focussed to be as cost effective as possible in getting the most informative outcome for the least effort. Deciding **why** monitoring is to be undertaken will to a large extent determine **what** needs monitoring, but **how** monitoring observations or data output will be used will also influence what to monitor, and where.

Observations must be recorded at the right intensity (number of vegetation plots or number of groundwater dipwells) and for the right duration (ideally during the same season for five years) to validate subsequent number crunching. The statistical validity of monitoring data depends on the size or magnitude of the anticipated effect, and the number of samples taken. For example, effective monitoring of a significant and readily observable change in vegetation due to nutrient enrichment might require only five replicated samples in an area subject to enrichment, and the same number in a control area on the same type of fen which is not subject to enrichment. However, many more samples would be required to detect smaller changes of biotic or abiotic parameters, particularly those which are intrinsically variable, such as average stem length or increase in reed due to increased nutrients. A pragmatic approach to this kind of situation is to start with a pilot survey. If the resultant data is insufficient to demonstrate the perceived change, the sample size may need to be increased. More detailed guidance on statistical validity and other aspects of environmental sampling can be found in Ecological Census Techniques (Sutherland, 2006).

The *site environment* can impose constraints on monitoring; some areas might have to be avoided because certain habitats or species are susceptible to trampling for example, or there is public access with the attendant risks of theft or vandalism.

10.2.3 How to monitor

Deciding on how to monitor should be driven by 'why, what and where' and available resources. It is essential to think through the whole monitoring plan so that the correct information with the right level of precision is obtained, and can be carried out throughout the monitoring project. Important to consider are:

- Ensuring the **health and safety** of the people associated with monitoring. A detailed risk assessment should be undertaken to identify risks such as drowning associated with deep water or floating rafts of vegetation, water-borne diseases such as Weil's, poisonous vegetation such as giant hogweed, and animals such as snakes. Given the potentially hazardous and often remote nature of fens, the risks associated with lone working should be taken into consideration.

- **Available resources**: money, time, assets (e.g. hardware, computer, etc).

- The **technical and practical abilities** of the people who will be implementing the monitoring strategy, and those who will be interpreting results or implementing management based on the data obtained. Limited abilities may be a constraint, but there are few methods or techniques which cannot be mastered with appropriate training. Providing clear, concise and 'user friendly' data or monitoring schemes ensures that site management utilises the data to its fullest extent, and does not become overwhelmed by the technical complexities of data or results.

- **Actions and/or contingencies for malfunction or loss of a monitoring point or installation**. Where monitoring data is critical, for example for designated site assessment, it is useful to detail the contingency actions which would be taken to restore or replace a lost monitoring point or installation.

- The required **accuracy and precision** of measurement. Accuracy is the closeness of a measurement to the actual value of the parameter. Precision is the repeatability of a measurement. *An introduction to error analysis* (Taylor, 1997) provides an excellent introduction to the treatment of uncertainties in physical measurements.

10.2.4 When and for how long

Complex statistical techniques can be used to decide optimal monitoring frequencies, but understanding why you want to monitor - for example to prove a link between a nutrient source and enriched vegetation, or evaluating the success of current fen management – generally determines monitoring frequency and duration. For example, increased grazing aiming to micro-diversify vegetation structure, requires monitoring of the vegetation structure before, during and after the management, and the impact of the increased grazing on target species such as invertebrates. Key considerations are:

What is the smallest time unit for the particular interest? In the context of a fen, this varies between one day (for example, short term fluctuations in water recharge) and several years (if the response of the site to longer-term climatic variation was the aspect being scrutinised). A time unit smaller than one day, is of interest for specific testing, e.g. a groundwater pumping test.

Is the parameter to be monitored 'noisy', i.e. does it vary significantly? As a rule of thumb, short term variations, around a tenth or greater than the expected variation during the time of interest will normally cause problems. If the parameter response is noisy, choose a monitoring frequency which is sufficiently high to capture the variations. For example if we monitor water level in the soil and the expected change due to management is a seasonally average increase of 25cm, but daily fluctuations are 5cm due to evapotranspiration, then we need to monitor frequently to separate the management effect from the natural variation.

If the temporal variability of a parameter is unknown, it is appropriate initially to monitor at a high frequency to obtain a scoping level understanding of temporal variability and then reduce the frequency accordingly.

Include both pre-management and post management measurements, for the length of the expected impact. Be prepared as this could be several years! Where the impact is unknown 'pilot' or 'trial' management can provide data to inform the further roll out of larger scale management.

If a protracted monitoring is likely, sturdy monitoring equipment and installations, although initially expensive are a good investment, as the information gathered is the basis for future project spending.

10.2.5 Permission and licences

As good practice contact regulatory bodies such as NE, CCW, SNH, NIEA during development of a monitoring strategy to establish any obligations for permissions and licenses for access and works (including handling of certain protected species of plants and animals) within designated sites. Many of these organisations can provide useful information or data to help inform management decisions (see Section 5: Managing and restoring fens), or offer constructive comments on the design of an effective monitoring strategy.

10.2.6 How to convert observations into management advice

Monitoring observations are only worthwhile if translated into practical management information. For example a change in the area of 'wet soil' during the spring months due to ditch blocking is interesting. However, a fen manager needs to know how this has impacted on the management target. Similarly it is not enough simply to record an increase of species X in the first year after increased grazing has been introduced; what matters is interpretation of whether this is a good or bad development, and if it is a short-term issue or a longer term change.

Statistical analysis is often overlooked or disregarded as too academic but is essential to underpin expensive management proposals and results with hard evidence, and to provide an unbiased, functional understanding of the relation between management effort and observed change.

10.2.7 External help in developing monitoring strategies

An alternative to designing and executing a monitoring programme yourself is to seek help from a third party, for example a consultant. Help might be sought for strategic aspects of a project, such as design of the monitoring strategy, or installation of monitoring equipment and training, leaving the bulk of the routine monitoring to be carried out by in-house staff. Alternatively consultants might be bought in to analyse and interpret monitoring data, or to undertake computer modelling, but this often requires the same (or even more) thought than devising or implementing your own strategy to ensure that you retain 'ownership' of the programme, and are able to understand and utilise the data produced.

Tips on commissioning consultancy input to monitoring

The best and most comprehensive monitoring strategy in the world is of little use if you can't understand it, or if it monitored the wrong thing!

- Think carefully and make absolutely clear what you want to know, and how you want to use the data in the future.

- Make sure that whoever is commissioned to help with monitoring appreciates your own knowledge, experience and levels of technical understanding so that data output is in a form which you can understand and utilise.

- Wherever possible, involve consultants or seek advice from the outset in designing a monitoring strategy to ensure that information gathered is both adequate and appropriate.

- Produce a clear, written specification for the work.

10.3 Biological monitoring techniques – vegetation

Basic botanical survey methods, such as recording species presence and cover in quadrats or transects, are usable in fens, given some adaptation and caution. Suitable methods and some of the practical difficulties are described in the relevant section of the Handbook of Biodiversity Methods (Hill et al, 2005). The plants themselves are effectively sampling the environmental conditions continuously and can provide good indications of the longer term hydrological, climatological and geomorphological conditions.

10.3.1 The role of botanical surveying

Higher plants are the predominant primary producers in fenland habitat, forming the structure and basis of the ecosystem. Habitat quality and diversity is reflected in the plant diversity that supports the overall species diversity of the site. Management to protect and enhance the most natural and diverse plant communities usually forms the basis of the habitat management plan (see Section 5: Fen Management and Restoration). Botanical survey will first define these communities, set the targets for management, and then monitor them to measure the effect of management.

10.3.2 Indicator species

Knowledge of the various plant communities present in an area of fen help the selection as positive indicators of species are strongly indicative of the extent and quality of a community. If the selected species are reliable indicators, monitoring can be based on surveys that plot their location, extent and abundance. A table of suitable indicator species is given in *Common Standards Monitoring (CSM) Guidance for Lowland Wetland Habitats* (JNCC, 2004), against the component NVC communities of fen habitats (see Appendix IV). Negative indicator species (listed in Table 6 of CSM Guidance) such as nettles or bracken are associated with habitat deterioration, such as enrichment or drying out, while others such as Himalayan balsam indicate their own undesirable presence.

Ellenberg indicator values, adapted for the British Isles, are another tool which can be used to interpret the presence or absence of certain indicator species. This system ranks most plant species on five scales for critical habitat factors, including light, moisture, reaction (pH), nitrogen availability and salt tolerance. On the habitat wetness scale, those species adapted to soils that are dry for long periods score 1, while submerged aquatic species score 12. Recording the species present in a consistent area of habitat and calculating averages represents the physical characteristics of the habitat and provides a quantitative index of change. A description of the procedure and lists of values are available in Ellenberg's Indicator Values for British Plants (Hill et al., 1999), with revision and additional species in Plantatt (Hill et al., 2004) and Bryoatt (Hill et al., 2007). All of these can be downloaded from the Centre for Ecology and Hydrology website (www.ceh.ac.uk).

Advantages of the indicator species method include:

– In combination with measurement or assessment of other indicators it can provide a body of negative or positive evidence that is readily understood by a non-specialist audience.

– Results can be recorded in a simple format independent of data handling software which minimises demand on time and resources.

– Spot checks at fixed locations can be combined with whole site 'sweep up' surveys using some of the same species, giving detailed observation of key locations and an overview of the whole site.

- Indicator species tables in the CSM Guidance provide an authoritative basis for assessments.

Disadvantages include:

- The need for a thorough and highly competent NVC survey as a baseline to determine which communities and species are present.

- Community boundaries are not recorded with any geographical precision.

- The indicator species include sedges and bryophytes, so a good level of botanical competence is required.

- Results are not capable of statistical analysis.

Undesirable species for key NVC communities in lowland fens (taken from the JNCC Common Standards Monitoring Guidance http://www.jncc.gov.uk/pdf/CSM_lowland_wetland.pdf)

Negative Indicators (non-woody species)

NVC Community	Phragmites australis	Phalaris arundinacea	Glyceria maxima	Typha latifolia	Epilobium hirsutum	Urtica dioica	Pteridium aquilinum	Rubus fruticosus	Juncus spp	Brachythecium rutabulum	Eurhynchium praelongum	Molinia caerulea	Menyanthes trifoliata	Potentilla palustris	Equisetum fluviatile	Carex rostrata	Glyceria fluitans	Ulex europaeus	Galium aparine	Impatiens glandulifera	Target for species marked as: (some NVC community types have individual targets for different habitat types) — X	Target for species marked as: — O
M4, M5, M6	X	X	X	X	X	X	O	O	X												Not more than one of the 'X' group of species and that <5% cover	Not more than one of the 'O' group of species and that <5% cover
M9	X	X	X		X	X	O	O		X	X	O									No more than rare, <20 shoots in any sample	
M10, M13	X											O										Cover <25%
M14	X	X	X		X	X	X	X	X	X	X	X									Not more than one species and that no more than rare and <5% cover	
M18 + sc*	O	X	X		X	X	X	X	X	X	X										Indicators of enrichment or of drying out: None of these should occur	Acceptable around upwellings or their equivalent on ditched bogs
M21	X	X	X		X	X	O	O		X	X	O									Not more than one of the 'X' group of species and that <5% cover	Not more than one of the 'O' group of species and that <5% cover

Negative Indicators (non-woody species)

Target for species marked as: (some NVC community types have individual targets for different habitat types)

NVC Community	Target (X)	Phragmites australis	Phalaris arundinacea	Glyceria maxima	Typha latifolia	Epilobium hirsutum	Urtica dioica	Pteridium aquilinum	Rubus fruticosus	Juncus spp	Brachythecium rutabulum	Eurhynchium praelongum	Molinia caerulea	Menyanthes trifoliata	Potentilla palustris	Equisetum fluviatile	Carex rostrata	Glyceria fluitans	Ulex europaeus	Galium aparine	Impatiens glandulifera
M22 + sc*, M25 + sc*	Singly or in combination <5% cover	X	X	X		X	X	X	X		X	X									
M27 + sc*	<5% cover							X	X												
M29	Joint cover <5%	X	X		X		X	X			X			X	X	X	X	X	X		
S1	Invasion of inter-tussock space by few large dominant species or >4 or 5 smaller ones																				
S4 + sc*	No more than rare						X													X	X
S9 sc*, S10 sc*, S20 sc*	No more than rare and <25% cover	X	X	X	X																
S12 sc*	No more than rare and <25% cover	X	X	X																	
S24 + sc*, S25 + sc*	<5% cover						X		X												
S27	Not more than one of the 'X' group of species and that <5% cover	X	X	X		X	X	O	O				O								

O column target: Not more than one of the 'O' group of species and that <5% cover

Note. For M6 sub-communities c and d, Juncus acutiflorus and/or J. effusus would not be appropriate negative indicators. Likewise for S27, Phragmites would not be appropriate as a negative indicator for some stands (usually S27b).

10.3.3 Vegetation Mapping

An initial identification of the plant communities present in a fen, with approximate mapping of the community boundaries, is crucial for identification of key species and informing the understanding of physical mechanisms affecting a site. This is usually based on a survey using the NVC methodology (Rodwell J. S. ed. 1991 – 2000).

The NVC methodology is both rigorous (i.e. careful application of the method will yield consistent and reliable results) and robust (i.e. it is not sensitive to minor differences in technique). However, it is a plant community classification method, not a mapping or monitoring method. The recording method is based on selecting locations for quadrats that appear typical of the community that is being observed, well within the boundaries of that apparent community.

A set of NVC quadrats can provide an almost complete species list for a defined area, which can be quickly completed by a check for other species outside the quadrats, using the DAFOR abundance scale. This can provide the basis for the qualitative monitoring of the community in that part of the site.

Basic fen monitoring techniques

Quadrats are square frames (usually 4 square metre (2x2m) on fens) used to sample vegetation. The presence of plant and moss species and their relative density or abundance is recorded within the quadrat. The location of the quadrat is described with a GPS, or marked with a post, so that the vegetation can be re-surveyed and described repeatedly at the same location in future to detect changes. Further information on quadrat methodology can be found in Ecological Census Techniques (Sutherland, 2006).

Transects, or lines, are used to sample vegetation along a gradient or gradual change of the vegetation. The transect can be up to 100 m long or more, the length depending on the changes or gradient to be monitored. Vegetation is normally sampled with a quadrat at fixed intervals, say every 5 m, along the transect, or where tall vegetation (such as reed encroachment) or abiotic changes (such as change in slope, groundwater seepage zone) occur. The environment is also normally measured along the same transect so that changes in vegetation can be correlated to changes in the environment, and vice-versa.

Advantages of vegetation community mapping and survey include:

– The NVC methodology can provide a clear and rigorous description of the plant communities present on the site.

– A set of well recorded NVC quadrats can provide useful species presence and abundance data for a defined location.

– Where well-defined, boundaries between communities can be accurately mapped using appropriate techniques.

– Two sets of data are generated; geographical data for the community extent and qualitative data for the community composition in a particular area of the site.

– The data can be presented graphically, as readily comprehensible maps.

– GIS mapping gives precise measurement of areas, allowing changes to be quantified.

Disadvantages of vegetation community mapping include:

– Skills in botanical surveying and accurate position fixing are needed for all phases of survey and monitoring.

– The distinction between one type of vegetation and another similar community can be subjective and problematic. For example, the transition from moist, seasonally waterlogged soils to permanently wet soils and then to standing water may be the zone of transition from swamp to tall herb fen communities in the NVC classification. This could be a transition from S27 *Potentillo-Caricetum rostratae* tall herb fen to S9 *Caricetum rostratae* swamp, both visually dominated by bottle sedge. Similar transitions occur in other pairs of communities with a common visually dominant species, such as common reed.

– The community definitions derive from a national sampling programme, and are assumed to apply to the survey site; the monitoring programme can thus be hard to defend from adversarial challenges as the site vegetation on the site is not nationally identifiable. This applies particularly to the north of the UK..

– Significant change in the composition of a community can occur, such as the loss of infrequent species, without appearing in the monitoring results.

– At least three, and preferably more, quadrats should be recorded for each apparent community in all compartments or units of the fen, at the baseline stage. For effective monitoring this then needs to be repeated for the key communities, which is time consuming.

– Assumptions about the community type can bias surveying; typically, as fen communities will be expected in fens, change to wet grasslands may be missed.

Accurate mapping of the distinct boundaries between communities is usually beyond the limits of accuracy for hand held GPS units (normally +/- 3 m). This introduces two sources of error, firstly in determining the actual boundary of a community and secondly in determining its location. GPS errors from hand held sets may be systemic and temporal; points along the same line may be recorded with a consistent difference on different days. This problem is not restricted to the GPS system however, since fens are not easy places to use any topographic surveying method. Differential GPS systems, which are more accurate versions of GPS using a fixed base station to provide a corrective signal, usually provide the most accurate practical option. Hiring the necessary equipment may be more practical than purchase because of the capital cost.

A recent development is the availability of a wide area corrective signal, from the European EGNOS satellite system. Hand held sets that are WAAS enabled, and able to receive EGNOS signals, are typically accurate to +/- 3 m. This may be accurate enough for monitoring, depending on the extent of the community and the overall size of the habitat. A 12 figure grid reference (1 m accuracy) for a known point can enable the GPS reading to be checked at the start and finish of work.

A simpler method may be to use anchored fixed points such as dipwells (see below) or deeply driven stakes, with measured distance and direction to the apparent community boundary.

Fixed point photography is very useful for monitoring major vegetation changes such as scrub or typha encroachment. Locations for fixed point photography need to be:

– Representative of the fen area to be monitored;

– Relatively easily accessible without risk of damage getting to the location;

– Marked with a fixed post or reference point in the resulting picture e.g. a certain tree which will always be photographed in the top right hand corner, and a small marker post in the bottom left of the picture.

It is good practise to record with each photo the date, weather and any management carried out in the photographed area, so that this can be used in evaluation of photographs.

Objectivity in NVC Mapping

The NVC methodology provides a very robust and consistent approach to plant community identification. It is however primarily a method of identifying communities, not a mapping and monitoring tool. Quadrat locations are selected by eye as being representative, but this can lead to a subjective approach in visually identifying and mapping communities, which is prone to errors. Visually dominant species that occur in several communities are a common source of error and can lead to misidentification of basic habitat type. For example both greater tussock sedge and common reed are visually dominant in wet woodland, sand dune, open vegetation, swamp and mire NVC communities, but greater tussock sedge occurs in 15 communities and 4 habitats, while common reed occurs in no less than 46 communities and all 5 habitats. Both are constant in several communities, some of which are differentiated by the presence of much smaller and less frequent plants.

To maintain as much objectivity as possible, surveyors should:

- Read and routinely re-read the introductory chapters for the relevant habitat types in British Plant Communities, together with the Users' Handbook (Rodwell J S, 2006).

- Take great care to select quadrat locations that are typical of the actual surrounding community, not of the predicted or assumed NVC community.

- Record an absolute minimum of three quadrats (ideally five quadrats or more) in each community that can provide habitat monitoring evidence.

- Record each quadrat formally, with a habitat description.

- Be alert for linear communities or small isolated communities adjoining the principal communities, and take care to record these separately.

- Whenever a community does not key out easily or there is some feasible doubt over the basic habitat type, use a programme such as MATCH, TABLEFIT, or MAVIS to sort the data.

Rodwell J S, 2006: National Vegetation Classification: Users' Handbook, JNCC 2006

10.3.4 Geo-statistical Vegetation Mapping and similar GIS spatial analysis techniques

These methods combine the accurate mapping of physical attributes, principally topography and hydrology, with random sampling of vegetation. Presence or absence of indicator species is recorded at a large number of very accurately located (i.e. within 1 m) sample points. Statistically based interpolation methods (the most commonly used being 'kriging') are used to predict the occurrence of a species, giving a map layer that models the distribution of that species.

A small quadrat size (e.g. 0.5 m2) can be used, and only important or indicator species need to be recorded if the aim is simply to identify change between years. In order to link back to NVC, a full species list is required. Abundance values can be included, which may help to determine the extent of a community. Common reed at high cover values is characteristic of some fen communities (S24, S25, S26), but also occurs at low cover values in other communities (S17, S27). Ellenberg values for the species included in a survey can also be used to relate the quadrat records to environmental factors, tracking changes in conditions. Repeat surveys do not have to use the same quadrat locations but should achieve the same density of samples.

Whilst vegetation sampling can be done by anyone with good botanical knowledge or survey skills, provided that suitably accurate GPS equipment is used for position fixing, data processing for geo-statistical vegetation mapping demands a high level of training and practise. As a new and evolving technique, there are risks that the particular method used for analysing baseline survey results may be superseded and in-house skills may become outdated, while academic help may no longer be available.

10.3.5 Quadrats and transects linked to hydrological monitoring

This method combines the traditional tools of quantitative botanical surveying with the hydrological model, by using fixed quadrats and transects as described in Wheeler, Shaw and Hodgson (1999). Species presence and cover values in semi-fixed quadrats around locations of ecological and hydrological significance are recorded at fixed intervals of three to five years, providing quantitative data that can be subjected to statistical analysis. Transects along hydrological gradients or other lines of change can tie botanical change to changing physical conditions.

Advantages include:

- Strong linkage of botanical monitoring results to hydrological monitoring.

- Results can be presented graphically.

- Recording can be based on a limited range of species, so that there is no need to identify all species in a quadrat.

- Good position fixing of the survey stations.

- Direct comparison of the survey results from repeat recording of the same locations.

Disadvantages include:

- Bias introduced with the initial selection of survey locations will persist through the monitoring events.

- Large numbers of survey stations are needed for analysis.

- Assumptions about the likely nature and direction of change have to be made, so other processes may then be missed because the survey locations do not relate to them.

- Changes to the survey site locations, to monitor unpredicted processes, effectively set a new baseline and year zero for data analysis.

References for survey methods for vertebrate and invertebrate groups

General texts

Hill, D., Fasham, M., Tucker, G., Shewry, M. & Shaw, P. (eds) 2005. *Handbook of Biodiversity Methods: Survey, Evaluation and Monitoring*. Cambridge University Press, Cambridge

Sutherland, W. (ed.) 1996. *Ecological Census Techniques*. Cambridge University Press.

Mammals

Chanin, P. 2003b. *Monitoring the otter Lutra lutra*. Conserving Natura 2000 Rivers Monitoring Series No 10. English Nature, Peterborough

Strachan, R & Moorhouse, T. 2006. *The Water Vole Conservation Handbook*, Second edition. The Wildlife Conservation Research Unit.

Birds

Bibby, C., Burgess, N., Hill, D., & Mustoe, S. 2007. *Bird Census Techniques: Second edition*. Academic Press.

Gilbert, G., Gibbons, D. & Evans, J. *Bird Monitoring Methods: A Manual of Techniques for Key UK Species*. RSPB, Sandy

Hardey, J., Crick, H., Wernham, C., Riley, H., Etheridge, B. and Thompson, D. 2006. *Raptors: A Field Guide to Survey and Monitoring*. Stationery Office (TSO) Scotland

Amphibians and Reptiles

Gent, A.H & Gibson, S.D., eds. 1998. *Herpetofauna Workers' Manual*. Joint Nature Conservation Committee.

Langton, T., Beckett, C and Foster, J 2000. *Great Crested Newt Conservation Handbook*. Froglife, Halesworth

Invertebrates

Brookes, S.J. 1993. *Review of a method to monitor adult dragonfly populations*. Journal of the British Dragonfly Society, 9: 1-14.

Drake, C.M., Lott, D.A., Alexander, K.N.A. & Webb, J. 2007. *Surveying terrestrial and freshwater invertebrates for conservation evaluation*. Natural England Research Report NERR005. Natural England, Sheffield.

French, G. & Smallshire, D. 2008. *Criteria for determining key Odonata sites in Great Britain*. Journal of the British Dragonfly Society, 24(2), 54-61.

Interest in invertebrates generally focuses on the readily observable groups: moths dragonflies, and spiders. Fens can support the larval stages of specialist butterflies and moths, although the majority of fen specialist insects are small, taxonomically difficult and considered by some to be unappealing. Monitoring is likely to be directed toward those species that are rare or particularly valued.

Information on monitoring techniques for specific species is available from a variety of sources. For example, Thompson *et al* (2003) covers the southern damselfly and

Killeen and Moorkens (2003) covers Desmoulin's whorl snail (available from http://www.english-nature.org.uk/LIFEinUKRivers/species/species.html). Advice and training is also available from specialist societies such as Butterfly Conservation.

Highly competent amateurs with a particular interest in groups such as moths, dragonflies and damselflies may well provide a self-funding, self-managing, long-term monitoring service.

Unlike botanical monitoring, which may need repeating every three to five years, the population of key invertebrate species may need annual monitoring because of the rate of fluctuation, for example because of adverse weather conditions during a brief mating season. Long term monitoring is needed to show a clear trend, and if the trend is downward it may be associated with a change in the plant community. As with plants, the potential loss of a visually striking and uncommon species is more likely to draw in funds for habitat management than 'an evident decline in the diversity and extent of the S27 fen community'. However, the presence of a notable species depends on the right habitat to support that species, and it is the maintenance of that habitat or particular vegetation community that is crucial. This may be related to water quality/quantity, vegetation structure or species composition.

The open water component of a fenland habitat mosaic is not suited to botanical monitoring unless it is mesotrophic or moderately oligotrophic lowland lake. If the water is at all enriched the dominant plants will be algae, either planktonic or filamentous. Work on algal populations is highly specialised, but a simple measurement that can be made is routine turbidity estimation with a Secchi disk. In this habitat, invertebrate community monitoring can provide direct evidence of the habitat quality, but usually requires a boat and laboratory work. A less rigorous technique is to record date, species and intensity of insect hatches as part of daily observation log on sites with full-time staff. Trichoptera (caddis fly) species are sensitive to water quality, whereas some of the large chironomids (biting midges) are highly adapted to low oxygen conditions. Consequently a decline in the sedge hatches and a reduction in the number of chironomid hatches, leading to a few massive hatches of large midge species, is a strong indication of declining diversity due to water quality factors.

10.5 Biological monitoring techniques – vertebrates

Monitoring vertebrate species as indicators of habitat quality on fens is complicated by the fact that most vertebrate species found in fens are either readily observable and highly mobile, or hard to observe generalist feeders or species such as grass snake or water shrew with a high dependence on wetland habitat which are very good at hiding in it, and consequently almost impossible to record.

Birds, bats and otters all forage in wetland areas and some species are wetland specialists, but they will cover a large area and may be foraging elsewhere when a count is made. Their numbers and activity may be a measure of habitat quality at the landscape scale, or relate to distant sites in the case of migratory birds. Fen vertebrate monitoring therefore involves monitoring key species, where they occur, which are dependent on the habitat being in favourable condition.

Some vertebrate species, such as water voles, feed on a wide range of plants and remain in a limited area but the population may be limited by the availability of suitable burrowing sites with adjacent cover above the flood line.

Competent voluntary monitoring is carried out at many fenland sites: the wetland bird survey and the Daubenton bat waterway survey are good examples of well established programmes involving many professional ecologists. The British Trust for Ornithology, the Bat Conservation Trust and similar organisations are good sources of advice. National conservation bodies publish manuals for work with species groups, such as *The herpetofauna workers manual* (Gent & Gibson, 2003).

Breeding success may be the most dependable indicator of habitat quality. For example, bird species that are broad spectrum insectivores with highly visible young are in effect testing the habitat diversity over several weeks and providing quantifiable data, but expertise is required to develop this approach to avoid misinterpretation. For example, a low return of migrants will allow bigger territories and cause less stress on the adults, but if the population is high the marginal territories will be occupied by weaker or less experienced birds, so inner territories should be observed.

10.6 Assembling an overall biological monitoring plan

The principal biological monitoring system for a fen will almost always be a botanical method tied to mapped physical habitat data. Geo-statistical vegetation mapping methods are highly attractive for their objectivity and integration with other GIS based data, but they are resource demanding and dependent on specialised skills. Community mapping is an alternative, if rigorously applied, and uses more widely available skills. Precise questions about changes to the plant community resulting from changes in one identified physical factor can be answered by the use of fixed quadrats and transects and fixed point photography. None of these methods are reliable for particularly rare species, for which the traditional walk-over count may be best.

NVC community mapping is the usual starting point for hydro-ecological studies of a site, and can provide the basis for several techniques. Care over position fixing and boundary mapping at this stage can add a great deal of reliability and simplify future work.

All monitoring methods have advantages and drawbacks; there is a continuum between techniques which are easy to carry out and interpret, and those which are very demanding but more objective. A dual approach is therefore recommended, using one very refined method and one simpler method that allow a sweep-up check over most of the site. Combining an indicator species survey with a standard walking route taking in the perimeter of the fen and an internal circuit can formalise the most traditional but informal of monitoring tools, the manager's walkabout. Long-term standardised practice can provide a very accessible record and a broad interpretation of changes. Formal developments such as Natural England's SSSI woodland monitoring methodology and the River Habitat Survey, offer suggestions for adding value to a walkabout.

The frequency of monitoring surveys has to be chosen with some care, since the most rigorous and objective methods are also the most demanding. Community change may not be apparent over one or two years, so annual full site community mapping would not be a good use of resources. However, a long period between surveys capable of providing strong evidence of change may result in habitat decline becoming well-established before it is detected. Counts of rare herb species should be annual, to allow confidence in series of results that show a long term trend. Community mapping at three to five year intervals will provide useful results.

10.7 Hydrological monitoring of soil water and groundwater levels

Soil water level is an important, and often defining, parameter in relation to ecological distribution within a fen because wetland plants and habitats often have precise requirements in terms of the absolute and seasonally fluctuating elevation of the water level relative to the ground surface. Measurement of soil water levels will therefore normally be an important element of a monitoring programme.

The soil water level in a dipwell will be at the level where the water pressure equals atmospheric pressure in the surrounding soil (also termed the water table). This is not the upper limit of saturated soil conditions, because a capillary fringe will extend upwards from the water table in the soil. The height of the capillary fringe depends on the pore size distribution in the soil and can be approximately calculated if information regarding soil type is available.

The following points should be considered when deciding which of the wide variety of techniques available for monitoring soil water levels is the most appropriate:

Access to the soil water surface for measurement. The simplest (and cheapest) option is a hand-dug open hole or an open hand-augered hole, but the substrate must be sufficiently cohesive for the sides of the hole to remain stable. If necessary, holes should be cleared of any collapsed soil prior to measurement and time allowed for the water level to equalise. Open holes allow direct addition of rainfall to, and evaporation from, the soil water level, which means that the level measured in the hole might not be representative of that in the surrounding soil. This method is not therefore recommended where real accuracy is required, but such cheap, 'quick and dirty' measurements which yield virtually instantaneous results can be an extremely valuable in getting a feel for a habitat and understanding whether more detailed monitoring is required. Open holes are a hazard for small animals and people, so should be filled once any observations on that individual occasion have been made. A better option is installation of a 'dipwell', as described overleaf.

Establishment of a fixed vertical reference point (often termed a *datum*). For measurements of the soil water level to be repeatable, a fixed vertical reference point must be available. Where a dipwell is inserted into a firm substrate, such that it is vertically stable, then its top lip can be used as the datum. Fen substrate is often soft or even fluid (i.e. vertically unstable), but a wooden or metal stake hammered into solid ground at depth will create a separate datum. The datum also enables the measurement of fluctuations in the floating raft.

If the critical parameter is distance above or below the ground surface, a measurement of the distance between the datum and the ground surface at each dipwell is sufficient. If soil water levels across the site need to be related to each other, for example if a water level transect or water level contours across the site is required, the elevation of each dipwell relative to a common ordnance datum needs to be established.

Method of measurement. Manual measurements can be made with a tape measure if the water level will not fall below a level where it is visible, but preferably with an electronic dipmeter. The measurement should be made from, or related to, the datum; this is simple when the datum is the top of the dipwell, but can involve the use of a spirit level and tape measure to check the relative elevations of a dipwell and separate datum. Automated measurements are made using a combined pressure-transducer and data-logger instrument. The pressure-transducer is suspended in the water column, and the measured pressure is proportional to the height of the column of water above it, minus the atmospheric pressure, which must be measured in the locality. A typical pressure-transducer (0-10 m water pressure range) will provide an accuracy of +/- 5 mm, a precision of +/- 1 mm, and the period between downloads of monitoring data is constrained by the need to safeguard data rather than the capacity of the instrument to store the data. It is prudent to download transducers at least every three months to safeguard data.

Box 2: Construction, installation and monitoring of a dipwell

Dipwells can be bought ready-made, or home-made, as described below. DIY construction allows 'bespoke' dipwells to be made, but there are a large number of considerations to be made in deciding the design. For example:

Diameter; dependent on what needs to be inserted into the dipwell, e.g. small pump for cleaning, pressure transducer apparatus.

Length: dependent on the depth of insertion (must cover only the range of fluctuation of the soil water level) and the length of dipwell protrusion above the ground surface. Dipwells can usually be 'cut-down' on insertion to attain the correct height.

Response zone; most commonly holes are drilled throughout the length of the dipwell, allowing water ingress over the whole depth, but it is possible to measure water pressure at specific depths by only drilling holes over a specific interval, e.g. the bottom 30 cm.

Design & construction. A dipwell is a narrow (usually c. 20 – 50 mm diameter), normally plastic tube with drilled holes or slots to allow water ingress. The tube is fitted with an internal basal cap (to prevent ingress of sediment on insertion), and is usually wrapped in a filter sock (kept in place with cable ties) to prevent ingress.

Installation. Dipwells are usually placed in hand-augered holes. The diameter of the hole is determined by whether or not the dipwell is going to be pushed directly into the hole or whether it is to surrounded by a 'gravel pack'. The sediments encountered, and the behaviour of the soil water level, should be recorded during augering. It is recommended that the dipwell cap is secured with a grub screw. If the elevation of the dipwell will be vulnerable to change, for example by cattle tread or expansion/contraction of peat, a solid datum (anchored into the solid mineral substratum), usually a metal pole or a wooden stake, should be installed.

Monitoring. Relocation of dipwells after installation can be very difficult, especially if a dense under-storey of vegetation has developed! Techniques which can be used for re-location include using a GPS or leaving a marker stake in the ground next to the dipwell. Water levels can be measured periodically, using an electronic dipmeter, or a tape measure if soil water levels are close to the surface. Levels will usually be measured downwards from the top of the dipwell (datum), but can also be measured upwards if the dipwell is underwater. Water levels can also be measured at high frequency (effectively continuously) using pressure-transducer and data-logger apparatus; this is a more expensive option but it does generate a higher quality dataset.

The re-location of dipwells for monitoring purposes can be very difficult, especially where 2 m high and dense under-storey of vegetation develops during the spring! Techniques which can be used for re-location include recording the location using a GPS, leaving a marker stake in the ground next to the dipwell, or gluing a metal item (small nut or washer) to the underside of the top-cap to allow re-location using a metal detector.

Similar considerations to the above should be applied to monitoring of groundwater levels in geological formations which underlie, or occur adjacent to, fens using deeper boreholes or piezometers. Borehole installations, which monitor water levels at greater depths and within the superficial or solid geology, are likely to require designing and constructing on site according to the geology encountered. This is a specialist activity requiring drilling equipment and experienced operators.

Field hydrogeology (Brassington, 2006) gives a wealth of practical information and tips on groundwater-related field techniques.

Installing a surface water level point with an automated datalogger (OTT-Mini-Orpheus) in a major ditch feeding Insh Marshes, Scotland. The pipe is 50mm diameter with 1mm slots, covered with geotextile sock to prevent fine particle ingress. (J. Schutten)

Installing a groundwater level observation point (piezometer) at Insh Marches, Scotland. A 50 mm diameter PVC pipe with 1 mm slots, covered in geotextile to prevent ingress of fine soil particles, is inserted into a hand-augured hole (J. Schutten).

10.8   Monitoring surface water flows

Measurement of surface water flow in wetlands can be challenging because channel gradients and flow velocities are often very low. Surface water flows also vary more than soil water levels over the short-term, and it is often difficult to devise a measurement scheme which captures the full range of this variation.

Manual measurements range from straightforward volumetric measurement, using a container of known volume and a stopwatch, through to the use of a current meter. The techniques described in publications such as Shaw (1994) and Brassington (2006), are relatively simple and cheap, and usually within the capabilities of site staff or volunteers.

Automated techniques include a rated channel section (for example a 'flume') or structure (for example a 'v-notch weir'), where the relationship between water level and flow is established and water levels are measured continuously. These techniques are described in publications such as Shaw (1994) and Herschy (2008), but they are more involved and demanding technically and it might therefore be necessary to seek third-party advice on installation and operation.

10.9   Monitoring water quality

The value of regular field measurement of water quality parameters is high: the temporal variation of base-richness (pH), mineralisation (electrical conductivity) and dissolved oxygen, which can all be measured using hand-held meters, can provide valuable information on the seasonal variation of water sources to a site. Regular meter maintenance and calibration is important to ensure precision of measurement.

Concentrations of a wide range of determinants (major and minor anions and cations, trace elements, contaminants) can be found through laboratory analysis of water samples. More comprehensive information on water quality is more powerful in terms of development of the conceptual understanding of the functioning of, and pressures on, a site, but there is a trade-off in terms of cost. A common strategy is regular (e.g. weekly or fortnightly) field measurements, supplemented by much lower frequency (e.g. annual) laboratory analysis of samples.

10.10   Measuring and monitoring enrichment – detailed information gathering

For fen sites with limited enrichment problems or where the source of enrichment is easily identifiable, looking at fen type and catchment land use and broad assessments of water sources and vegetation communities can be sufficient to inform management. However, in some cases greater detail of water and peat chemistry of a site is needed in order to understand what might be causing enrichment and how to tackle it. Detailed assessments are also useful as a monitoring tool, as changes in water and soil chemistry are likely to be identified sooner after management begins than changes in the fen vegetation itself, which might take several seasons to respond.

Changes in nutrient status could be gauged initially by the encroachment of nutrient tolerant species including great willow herb, bulrush, scrub etc. The occurrence of some key undesirable species may be sufficient to warrant a more detailed investigation of nutrient levels in the fen.

More detailed analysis relatively cheaply undertaken by commercial laboratories include chemical nutrients such as total and available (sometimes termed 'extractable') N, P and K along with pH and EC. Most laboratories will supply sterilised water bottles for sample collection. Soil samples can be stored in sealable plastic bags (e.g. freezer bags). Nutrient concentrations can alter rapidly so samples should be sent for analysis as soon as possible, or refrigerated if unavoidable delays arise. The laboratory will indicate how much water or soil sample is required to complete an analysis. Soil samples should be collected using volumetric sampling techniques which are more appropriate to the spongy organic soils often found in fens than techniques which express results by weight.

Sample locations should track the pathway of nutrient input to the fen, and nutrient migration through the fen. Once the sample points have been chosen they should be mapped, using GPS if available, so that sampling can be repeated. The first set of samples will form the baseline for subsequent monitoring and it is a good idea to take as many as practically and financially possible. This may show that there is little variation across the fen and, if so, fewer samples could be taken during the next round of monitoring. The baseline may also detect variations and nutrient 'hotspots' where the number of sampling points needs to be increased.

The timing of sampling should be consistent; frequency will depend on available resources and reason for monitoring. Annual sampling should include both spring and autumn where possible to allow for seasonal variations. Monthly sampling for one year may be sufficient to measure change across a year, but to detect longer-term variations twice yearly sampling over five years is more appropriate. The frequency could temporarily be increased, for example, to examine the affect of a new land management prescription being introduced.

Nutrient monitoring in soils and water – a basic approach

What to test?	Available-phosphorus and available-nitrogen in soil and water
When?	Minimum two times (spring and autumn) per year
Where?	Inlet water source(s)
	Key habitat compartments, e.g. reedbed, wet woodland, open water
Why?	To identify key areas with high nutrients and nutrient sources To monitor changes in nutrients over time
For how long?	Ongoing sampling is highly recommended, or a minimum of three years

Given the potential pitfalls of conventional measurements of nutrient concentration in water and soils, other techniques have been developed to provide more accurate information on the degree to which vegetation has become, or has the potential to become, enriched. These more complex methods of gauging the nutrient status may be necessary where initial assessment has revealed or demonstrated a problem requiring external specialist advice or support from conservation or environmental regulators, or outside organisations such as a university or research programme. Examples of such detailed techniques are:

– **Measuring the N and P content of vegetation**: e.g. mosses. Changes in moss nutrient contents are usually the most sensitive measure, but very little data is available on the values that might be expected of unpolluted systems, and comparison is therefore difficult.

- **Phytometric** tests measure how well a standard plant species grows in a substrate, giving an indication of relative fertility of that substrate, but are of limited use with regard to setting limits to the nutrient pressure on a fen because of the high cost and difficulties in repeating tests. This technique is therefore best suited to one-off comparisons of soil fertility between locations within a site, or between sites.

- **Identifying if the fen is N or P limited**: Small (1-2 m^2) experimental plots of fen vegetation can be chosen in the field and treated monthly with (20 kg P h^{-1} y^{-1} +/- 50 kg N h^{-1} y^{-1}) over two to three years, using dilute solutions. Vegetation monitoring could include species composition, total biomass/unit area, N and P content of vegetation, total N and P in vegetation per unit area. Very clear changes in these parameters have been observed with N and P addition even where the overall changes in plant tissue nutrient concentrations were small. Mosses in particular show a strong response to P under conditions where higher plants are often still N limited.

- **Atmospheric N inputs**: measurements require large data sets to be meaningful, and in general the modelled data provided by www.apis.ac.uk for the 5 km square will provide the most useful data. Exceptions to this would include circumstances where the inputs to the site were likely not to be representative of the area generally, e.g. point sources such as major roads (NO_x) or intensive livestock units (NH_3). In such cases NO_2 or ammonia diffusion tubes could provide useful information.

10.11   Weather

Key weather parameters such as rainfall and temperature can be monitored using commercially available individual pieces of equipment, or multiple parameters can be measured using weather stations. In the UK, the Meteorological Office (www.metoffice.gov.uk) maintains an extensive programme of weather monitoring. Of interest in relation to understanding the inputs and outputs of water to fen sites are rainfall and potential evaporation data. Some monitoring data, usually at a low spatial and temporal resolution, is available from their website, and higher resolution data can be purchased.

10.12   Site Diary

In executing a monitoring strategy, it is important to keep a diary of events which may influence the ecological and physical condition of the site. When read in conjunction with formal monitoring data, information from a site diary can be the key to understanding how a fen functions. Recording methods can include narrative description (with notebook prompts on subjects) or fixed point photography, and might include:

- **Site management activities**: for example, activities to control non-native species, raising or lowering of a water control structure, ditch clearance, mowing, movement of grazing animals, etc.

- **The effects of natural events on the site**: for example, the extent and depth of surface water flooding, the direct effects of an intense rainfall or flooding event, the effects of a prolonged dry period on spring flows and river flows, geomorphological changes, etc.

- **Off-site events**: for example ditch clearance, whether a local groundwater or surface water abstraction has been used or not used for a specific period, etc.

10.13 Surveying

Surveying to establish the exact height of a sample location or other feature can sometimes be used as a monitoring technique, for example to monitor changes in the elevation of a peat surface to determine changes in peat volume through time. More usually surveying is used to establish the relative positions and elevations of monitoring equipment (for example, dipwell datums) and key features within a site (for example, habitat boundaries). This information will invariably increase the aggregate value of site monitoring data as it allows the relationship between various points across the site to be explored.

The spatial position of features can often be established with sufficient accuracy using a hand-held GPS, whilst the relative elevation of features can be established using a simple site levelling kit. These types of equipment can often be borrowed, and can sometimes be affordable on a modest budget.

10.14 Third party monitoring data

Each of the environmental regulatory organisations – the Environment Agency (www.environment-agency.gov.uk) in England and Wales, SEPA in Scotland (www. sepa.org.uk) and NIEA in Northern Ireland (www.ni-environment.gov.uk) – maintains a programme of environmental monitoring which they are usually happy to provide details of. The parameters monitored within these programmes are often those requiring expensive equipment such as solar insulation meters. Other parameters usually include surface water flows and quality, groundwater levels and quality, rainfall, air quality and ecological monitoring (e.g. in-stream invertebrate sampling). The UK regulators also maintain public registers of environment-related licences, for example groundwater and surface water abstractions and discharges, which can be inspected free of charge. A fee may be charged for data supply.

Remote sensing data in the form of satellite imagery or aerial photographs can provide valuable information on temporal changes in the condition of a site.

On a smaller scale, enthusiastic amateurs, for example hobby weather watchers who often post their data on the internet, can be a useful source of data.

Environment Agency, Bristol, UK provides detailed and practical information on the design of groundwater and surface water monitoring networks, and some information on analysis and interpretation of monitoring data.

10.15 Data storage and protection

Monitoring data represents a record of unique historical conditions, and is usually irreplaceable. Effective data management is therefore an integral and essential part of the monitoring process.

Monitoring data should be copied as soon as possible after collection to minimise the risk of loss or damage. Hand-written records should be typed into a computer, and digital data-loggers should be downloaded, both on a regular basis. Explanatory notes on the monitoring data (e.g. doubts about the accuracy or precision of the measurements) should also be entered with the raw data as they are useful when quality-assuring or analysing the data, and hand-written monitoring records should be retained for quality-checking purposes. Data that are suspect or obviously false should be highlighted as such. A record should be made for future reference of any corrections to data which is obviously false.

Storage of data and information on single paper copies is vulnerable to loss or damage. Digital data storage is therefore preferable because it allows easy storage and copying of the data whilst minimising risk of loss or damage. Computerised analysis is also easier if data is stored digitally. Geographical Information System packages can use data from external spreadsheets and databases and provide geo-statistical analysis methods. Quality assurance of collected data is also facilitated by computerised storage. Spreadsheets and databases can be programmed to expect data values within a certain range, and to alert the user if the entered values are unexpected. Visual data plotting on graphs can help identify unexpected values.

The type of software package which is used will depend largely on the volume of data. Spreadsheet storage (e.g. MS Excel) is often adequate for smaller volumes of data (up to 65,000 rows of data in the 2003 version); the data can be seen easily, there are simple options for automated data quality assurance and visualisation, and there are powerful functions for data processing and analysis. Database (e.g. MS Access) storage is more appropriate for larger volumes of data, such as that produced by high-frequency automated recording of water levels using a pressure-transducer and data-logger. The data storage capacity of databases is much higher than that of spreadsheets, but the data visualisation and analysis functions are less accessible to the average user. Daily observation logs and field records from walkover surveys present some data entry problems. As far as possible these should be entered in a standard format that can be coded.

Frequent back-ups of the computer-stored data should be made and preferably on an automated basis. Transferring data to outside organisations can provide an alternative back-up. The Biodiversity Action Reporting System (BARS) has valuable features for recording the broad outcomes of monitoring surveys, and the county or regional Biological Recording Centre can accept species records to date and place. SSSI data should be copied to the relevant national agency (Natural England, CCW, NIEA or SNH).

10.16   Analysis and use of monitoring data

Monitoring seeks to measure a variety of different parameters, or variables, many of which are inter-related. A variety of techniques have been designed to help analyse and interpret these complex inter-relationships.

Graphical techniques used to explore the relationship between variables include:

- Simple time-series graphs of two or more variables. Data with very different absolute values can be plotted together for easy analysis either by the use of a secondary y-axis, or by normalisation.

- Plots of one variable against another; the best-fit line through the data indicates the relationship between the variables, and the degree to which the points cluster around the line indicates the strength of the relationship.

More sophisticated statistical techniques can also be used to quantify the nature and strength of relationships between variables.

Other techniques for analysis and interpretation of data include contour maps, for example soil water levels, and cross-sections through the site.

10.17   Modelling

Modelling involves calculations involving an independent variable (or variables) which attempt to model a dependent variable. It can be used to develop a better (preferably quantitative) understanding of cause−effect relationships between environmental variables, and therefore a refined understanding of the functioning of the site. For example, the independent variables of soil water level or nutrient status might be used in an attempt to explain plant species distribution quantified through geo-statistical analysis. Modelling can also be used to predict the impact of management regimes, and to check for deviations which might represent impacts caused by one or more sources. There are two main types of modelling.

Empirical modelling is a relatively straightforward form of modelling which is used to assess the degree of dependence of one variable on another by experimental transformation of the independent variable(s) through application of mathematical functions in an attempt to synthesise the behaviour of the dependent variable. In simple terms, it can be seen that there is a great deal of similarity between the lines, but there are also some periods where the lines diverge. It can be concluded that the behaviour of the soil water level is strongly dependent on rainfall, but that there are also some other factors which have an influence.

Modelling and output of graphs such as this is also useful in highlighting the periods when the soil water level behaviour is not explained by variations in rainfall.

The illustration below depicts a time-series graph showing hourly soil water level measurements for a dipwell (BD2a) at Cors Bodeilio on Anglesey, and whether there is more or less than average rainfall (cumulative difference from average rainfall (independent variable) over a three month period.

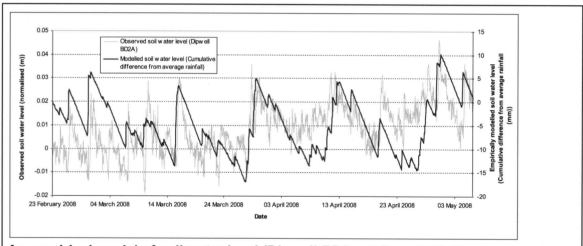

An empirical model of soil water level (Dipwell BD2a at Cors Bodeilio, Anglesey), derived using rainfall data, alongside observed values

Process modelling is a more exacting form of modelling which involves:

  i. development of a detailed understanding of the important physical processes within a system;

 ii. development of mathematical equations to represent these processes directly;

iii. use of these equations with values for the independent values to simulate the dependent variable(s).

Process models can be one-, two- or three-dimensional, and can simulate either average conditions at an instant (termed 'steady-state') or the progression of conditions through time (termed 'time-variant').

A good process model will be more robust than an empirical model in terms of its ability to simulate conditions beyond the range experienced during the monitoring period, simply because it is designed to mimic the functioning of the system being modelled. Examples of process models which might be applied to fen sites include ground and surface water flow models.

Modelling is complex and expensive, and should therefore only be carried out where the site management requires a high burden of proof. An example might be where relocation of a public water supply borehole is being considered, at a cost of millions of pounds, as was necessary to protect Smallburgh Fen which is a designated Natura 2000 site.

10.18 References

Brassington, R. 2006. *Field hydrogeology*, 3rd edition. Wiley-Blackwell, Oxford, UK. ISBN 0470018283.

Entec. 2008. *Guidance on monitoring and investigation at GWDTEs*. Consultant report Entec 19223n066i1 for the Environment Agency.

Environment Agency. 2003. A guide to monitoring water levels and flows at wetland sites.

Hill, D., Fasham, M., Tucker, G., Shewry, M. and Shaw, P. (Eds). *Handbook of biodiversity methods; survey, evaluation and monitoring*. Cambridge University Press, Cambridge, UK. ISBN 0521823684.

Hill. M.O., Preston C.D., Roy D.B. 2004. *Attributes of British and Irish Plants*. Centre for Ecology and Hydrology 2004. ISBN 1870393740

Joint Nature Conservation Committee. 2004. *Common standards monitoring guidance for lowland wetlands habitats*. Available from www.jncc.gov.uk, search under "csm lowland wetlands"

Shaw, E.M. 1994. *Hydrology in practice*. Chapman and Hall, London, UK. 0748744487.

Sutherland, W. (ed) 2006. *Ecological census techniques*. Cambridge University Press.

Wheeler, B.D., Shaw, S.C. and Hodgson, J.G. 1999. *A monitoring methodology for wetlands*. Report to Environment Agency, Peterborough.

Foulden and Gooderstone Commons are a series of groundwater-fed fens overlying the middle, upper and lower chalk aquifers between Downham Market and Thetford in north Norfolk (OSGRTF 762002). The chalk is capped with drift deposits that range from clay to sand and gravel. The fens occur where water can escape from the aquifer through 'windows' in the overlying aquitard, giving rise to springs and seepages, and to areas of more permanent water in pingos. It is important to maintain adequate groundwater pressure, and a groundwater table to sustain fen within the pingoes.

The fens support rich-fen vegetation of the NVC M13 plant community type, and are designated SSSI and SACs within the Norfolk Valley Fens. The shallow-rooting higher plants such as black-bog rush and bryophytes such as *Scorpidium scorpioides* rely on a positive water pressure to maintain their calcium-rich soil water at close to ground level. The degree of water-level variation found in monitored examples of these fens, and its relationship with species diversity, is described by Wheeler & Shaw (2001). Provided such measured values can provide a reliable index of the required *status quo* the soil water level, as sustained by aquifer pressure, should not fall more than about 15 cm below ground level.

Gooderstone Common:
spring and seepage area

North Norfolk is an important area for arable agriculture. Survival of crops and the meeting of quality criteria means irrigation is often necessary. Water is abstracted under licence from boreholes sunk into the chalk aquifers. The Environment Agency has to demonstrate that the licensed abstraction would have no adverse effect on the SAC.

Hydrological modelling techniques
The only basis on which predictions of drawdown can be made is through hydrological modelling. Many models are available, each making a set of assumptions, and each dependent on the quality of the data available to feed into it. Important factors include the slope of the land relative to the positions of boreholes and fens, as this determines the direction of flow within the aquifer. For example applying the THEIS equation to data for Foulden Common predicted a drawdown of 10-20 cm. Compared with the water fluctuation information provided by Wheeler & Shaw for NVC community M13, this could cause significant damage.

Another consideration is the likely cumulative effects on the condition of underlying aquifer, and fens which rely on these aquifers, where more than one abstraction point is involved.

It is also important to take account of the spatial layout of the boreholes, fens, and the topography. A point of stagnation is identified downslope of the borehole, most of the flow towards it comes from the upslope part of the aquifer. While this may be difficult to visualise without a considerable array of complex measurements, it serves to illustrate the range of factors that need to be taken into account in determining adverse effect, and that a simple prediction of drawdown on a plane surface is inadequate.

Although the issue of abstraction close to the Norfolk Valley Fens has been investigated as an effect on the chalk aquifers (which may be fractured into sub-units), it may be made even more complex by the possibility of there being smaller aquifers within the overlying drift. These may also provide important amounts of groundwater for the fens.

Wider relevance

The complex eco-hydrological setting of these sites is repeated in many parts of the UK. For example, the multi-layered deposits underlying the New Forest valley bogs is similarly complex, some strata acting as aquifers, others as aquitards; some are base-rich, others are base-poor. While the abstraction issue is not so evident in the New Forest, the same sort of information about water supply is required for the design of any management measures.

Gooderstone Common:
downstream of springs

Reference

Wheeler, B.D. & Shaw, S.C., 2001. A Wetland Framework for impact assessment at statutory sites in Eastern England. Environment Agency Research & Development Technical Report W6-068/TR1.

11. Fens and People

Human interaction with fens dates back a long way, from early settlement of communities near water and wetlands for practical purposes, to harvesting of reeds for thatching and other economic purposes. As traditional crafts have died out, the links between fens and people have diminished, but the relationship between fens and people remains an important one for many different reasons. Section 5: Fen management and restoration identified the influence on fens of how other people manage land in the surrounding area. As more and more people become interested in wildlife, demand to visit fens increases. The more that people understand and enjoy fens, the more they are likely to support and potentially become involved in fen management initiatives. However, fens are fragile habitats which need careful visitor management to avoid risk of damage. Some types of fen habitat can also present a safety hazard.

This section tracks the relationship between fens and people from a historical perspective, and considers scope to re-engage people with fens, through provision of public access, interpretation and involvement in practical fen management work.

A young visitor to Bodeilio National Nature Reserve, Anglesey, North Wales, learns about the rich wildlife associated with fens (P.Jones)

11.1 An historical perspective

Pollen analysis at Star Carr in Yorkshire has demonstrated that Mesolithic hunter-gatherers camped in the spring and summer next to reed-swamp vegetation as early as 10,700 years ago, taking advantage of the ready supply of food, water and construction materials. Their diet included plants such as bogbean, and animals stopping to drink, provided easy hunting targets. There is evidence that lakeside vegetation was burnt, possibly to encourage new growth and to attract animals. Islands, and the wetlands themselves, offered some protection from predators, both animal and human.

Neolithic and Bronze Age people constructed wooden walkways over the fens to improve agricultural access. Many swords and valuable personal items were deliberately placed around these walkways as offerings. At Flag Fen, near Peterborough, preserved finds include a 1 km long causeway spanning the fen, a large platform and bronze offerings.

The 2 km long Sweet Track across the Somerset Levels dates from approximately 5,800 years ago. It is the world's oldest known engineered roadway, built to allow people to cross the wet fen to dry land for summer grazing (A. Burnham).

Fens also appear to have been ideologically significant. Wetter land and the islands within it were considered important to ancestors, especially in the wintertime. By the Iron Age, agricultural changes, including specialisation, saw widespread expansion of settlement at the expense of forest and marginal land. Summer grazing probably continued and people continued to live near fens, such as at Glastonbury Lake Village. Construction of this settlement on an artificial island in the fen allowed residents to take advantage of fishing, wild fowling, gathering of wood, berries, willow and reeds, using trackways and dug-out canoes. Similar artificial islands or 'crannogs' were developed in Scotland and Ireland, combining access to wetland resources and transport routes with security.

The Romans had a major impact on fens, draining them for peat and salt. Construction of the Car Dyke between Lincoln and Peterborough suggests that the Romans were also making efforts to protect the fenland economy by controlling the water flowing into the area from the higher land to the west. Medieval documentary sources associate seasonal use of wetlands with fishing, wildfowling, rights of turbary (peat-digging), gathering of rushes, coppicing and pollarding.

The 17th century witnessed substantial land reclamation. This was particularly extensive in the Fens of East Anglia where some 142,000 ha of land were drained in the 1600s by Dutch engineers. Subsequent shrinkage of the peat exacerbated drainage problems, which prompted the construction of hundreds of windmills to power the pumps necessary to maintain the lower water table. Between 1660 and 1695 the Scottish Parliament passed a series of acts bringing significant areas of additional land into cultivation. The reclamation of much lowland peat bog, such as the Carse of Stirling, took place at this time.

In more recent times, fens in the United Kingdom have been exploited for peat for horticultural use. Some small industries associated with fen products have survived into the 20th century, such as the willow growing on the Somerset Levels, which has declined due to replacement of baskets with plastic bags and cardboard boxes. However some traditional skills and remedies were revived during the First World War, such as the collection of sphagnum moss from Cleddon Bog in Wales for wound dressings.

Agricultural policies introduced in the 1970s have failed to meet their aim of maintaining rural populations and incomes. An unanticipated but equally serious side-effect has been the loss of biodiversity which has resulted from the landscape degradation directly attributable to these output-based policies. More recently, sensitive agricultural and forestry systems have highlighted the major challenge for land managers in the 21st century of restoring and managing wetlands which for the past few decades have not been considered as an integral part of wider land management.

11.2 Opportunities for involving people with fens

Fens can provide quiet recreation, and offer unlimited opportunities to allow and encourage appreciation of the unique wildlife which they support. On wet fens, defined paths or boardwalks may be necessary to allow public access, but information and interpretation at the edge of the fen can be just as effective as provision of access to the fen itself in promoting enjoyment and understanding. On some sites, visitors may get a better view from adjacent higher land, which can also help set the fen in the context of the wider landscape.

Reserves with very large numbers of visitors, such as Wicken Fen and Ranworth in East Anglia, can afford to make special efforts to allow people to see into the fen from raised hides and visitor centres.

Use of traditional fen products such as reed and sedge thatching ensures that the Norfolk Wildlife Trust's visitor centre and hide at Ranworth Broad (left) and at Tower Hide at Wicken Fen (right) are an integral part of the site's interpretation (B. Madden, Norfolk Wildlife Trust).

Inviting volunteer involvement in fen management, from helping decide priorities to scrub control or other physical work, offers unlimited further opportunities for involving people with fens. Organisations such as the British Trust for Conservation Volunteers (BTCV) can bring in volunteers, or some fens are suitable for hosting teambuilding days for local companies, which can generate extra income at the same time as getting physical work done.

Volunteers helping restore fens along the Ouse as part of the Little Ouse Headwaters Project: hard but rewarding work! (Photo: Little Ouse Headwaters Project)

Key tips on involving people with fens

– Be as inclusive as possible – involve people living adjacent or near to the fen, as well as others who might be interested in using or visiting the fen, and organisations and individuals who might be able to provide resources.

– Think long term to make sure people who might be interested in your fen in future are involved, as well as those who have already expressed interest.

– Find out what people think about the fen, what they value about it, how they use it or would like to use it, and what their concerns might be about proposed management.

– Make the most of every opportunity to engage with visitors and encourage involvement, including during maintenance of paths and boardwalks.

– Bring together all interested parties to ensure that respective needs and concerns are understood, and open up the widest range of resources. Most public funding sources require evidence of how people will be involved as part of funding application. The Little Ouse Headwaters Project is an excellent example of working with numerous different stakeholders (see case study at the end of this section).

– Think carefully about the most effective and inclusive way of establishing constructive dialogue with neighbours and stakeholders. Meetings structured and facilitated to encourage and allow people to discuss their individual ideas and concerns in small groups, and develop creative ideas using props such as maps or photos, often work well whereas traditional 'open' public meetings sometimes result in establishment of opposing factions.

11.3 Who to involve

11.3.1 Visitors

Anyone who goes to a fen – including the site owner(s) and manager(s) – is effectively a visitor. However, the term 'visitors' is usually used to refer to those not directly involved in fen management who are visiting for recreational purposes, which might be a quiet walk or cycle ride, birdwatching or simply to enjoy the sense of refuge which fens provide in more intensively farmed areas. In East Anglia, for example, Wicken Fen is an oasis in the middle of a wide expanse of intensive arable land, a reminder of how the landscape of rural Cambridgeshire may once have looked.

Recreational visitors to fens may include birdwatchers, as part of small or sometimes larger groups (S Street)

Visitor profile can change significantly over time. The arrival of a rare bird may shortly be followed by a large number of bird watchers. Wildlife tour operators and other group organisers may wish to bring people to a fen, and should be borne in mind amongst those to be consulted and involved.

11.3.2 Neighbours

Fens are intimately linked to the catchment in which they are located (see Section 5.3.2 Fens in the context of the wider catchment), and hence the actions of fen managers and their neighbours often affect one another. Such connectivity may not be obvious at ground-level, but even seemingly isolated wetlands may be linked with other wetlands via underground aquifers (see Section 3: Understanding Fen Hydrology). Fens and their surrounding area are also linked in the movement of nutrients and pollutants in surface and ground water (see Section 4: Understanding Fen Nutrients). Larger projects and initiatives may involve many neighbours, including farmers, foresters, landowners, householders, voluntary groups and sometimes local authorities.

Neighbours often have similar land and water management responsibilities to fen managers, though their values and objectives may differ. Raising or lowering water levels to achieve one land management objective may create problems for a neighbour with different objectives. Co-operation between neighbours may allow more effective nutrient management than individual action, and can help secure funding. The RDP currently available throughout the UK (see Section 12: Fens from an Economic Perspective) provide incentives to work with neighbours and offer funding for projects of mutual interest, including those that improve the status of fens and develop visitor management. Angling and wildfowling are common activities around fens, and there are often opportunities to collaborate to reduce conflicts with fen conservation and increase mutual benefits.

11.3.3 Stakeholders

'Stakeholders' are those who have a key stake in a project, or play an integral role in fen management. They may influence, provide funding, already make use of a fen, or be interested in doing so. Neighbours are usually key stakeholders, but stakeholders might also include existing and potential visitors and members of the local community, as well as the owner(s) of the fen, statutory agencies and funders.

11.4 Limitations on involving people with fens

True fen habitat is typically fragile and susceptible to damage. Scrub, reeds and other vegetation may make access difficult, and little may be visible from within the fen. Deep peat and boggy areas can also be dangerous for those unfamiliar with such conditions. Health and safety is therefore a key issue, but not only because of statutory obligations. If we want people to care about fens, we must equally take care of people who visit them.

Health and safety considerations involving people with fens

- Consider and build in health and safety from the start, including a detailed risk assessment, which should be reviewed at regular intervals. The Health and Safety Executive can provide further guidance to help you identify hazards and decide what precautions are required.

- Remember to take account of the health and safety requirements of neighbours and people over than visitors – e.g. adjacent land-owners, contractors, graziers, volunteers etc.

- Attempts to overcompensate will damage both the habitat and the visitor experience.

11.5 Visitor surveys and monitoring

Management for People (Scottish Natural Heritage 2004) suggests five steps critical to sustainable visitor management:

- Involving and communicating with people

- Planning and setting objectives

- Visitor care and welfare

- Monitoring

- Analysis and assessment

Knowing how many visitors a fen attracts, or forecasting how many visitors a fen might attract in future, is important in deciding on the level of effort and resources worth investing, and in designing appropriate paths and interpretation. Varying trends in visitor numbers can help flag up early warnings about potential impacts from visitor pressure and guide longer-term sustainable management. Reliable estimates of visitor numbers, based on surveys, monitoring and other data, are usually essential when applying for external funding for fen management, and can help establish links between fens and local businesses. Automated counters are now relatively cheaply available, designed to withstand moderate or extreme weather and vandalism, ideal for use in visitor centres, or at entry/exit/pinch points on the fen.

Other information about visitors – their interests, expectations, where they have come from and what has prompted them to visit the fen – is also invaluable in planning and effective management of access, interpretation and other physical infrastructure. Management for People (Scottish Natural Heritage, 2004) recommends a range of questions which can help to identify the special attractions of a site. A Sense of Place (Tourism and Environment Initiative, 2001) suggests ways to collect information about visitors' attitudes to interpretation of the site. Combining both types of survey and repeating them at relatively long intervals, perhaps every 5 years, can be a cost effective way of collecting information.

Experience of visitor monitoring on fens

At Ranworth Broad NNR the Norfolk Wildlife Trust visitor centre is only open for seven months, so the 18-20,000 visitors recorded at the centre is an under-estimate of the number of people visiting the reserve: many more people use the boardwalk out of hours and out of season.

11.5 Providing for public access on fens

The provision of access to fens and other wetland habitats allows people to enjoy the wildlife and the landscape but needs to be managed and maintained for the safety of both visitors and the environment. Here a boardwalk invites visitors to explore Hickling Broad National Nature Reserve (Nick Droy)

11.6.1 Legal rights of access

Within the UK there are important variations in peoples' right of access to land and water. The Land Reform (Scotland) Act 2003 confirmed a right of responsible non-vehicular access to most land and inshore waters in Scotland for recreation, and heritage education, including commercial operations based on these activities. People exercising rights of access must do so responsibly, in accordance with the Scottish Outdoor Access Code (SOAC) (http://www.snh.gov.uk/enjoying-the-outdoors/your-access-rights). The SOAC highlights the need for people to avoid damaging property, crops and the environment, stresses the importance of not interfering with land management operations, and also summarises land managers' responsibilities in relation to public access.

Elsewhere in the UK access rights to land are much more restricted to designated rights of way (footpaths, bridleways and byways). Moorland and commons which enjoy open access rights are shown on the Countryside Access websites for England Natural England – Open Access land and Wales http://www.ccw.gov.uk/enjoying-the-country/countryside-access-map.aspx. In Northern Ireland some open access areas have been designated under access agreements with district councils, who maintain relevant information.

11.6.2 Encouraging further access

Providing for public access on fens is not just about respecting and incorporating legal rights of access. Fen management should take account of where people might wish to go, and why, and seek to identify opportunities to involve and engage people with fens, provided access can be accommodated without detriment to sensitive habitats or species.

Visitor management is often planned by defining zones within a site where different activities have priority, for example at the RSPB at Strumpshaw Fen (see case study at the end of this section). Informal ways of influencing what people do and where they go can be just as effective, if not more so, than attempts to physically restrict access. Provision of well maintained paths and boardwalks, good interpretation, hides, and signage will encourage use by visitors and can be used to direct people away from sensitive areas. Developing paths through easier terrain adjacent to a fen offers the chance to show a wider variety of habitat and to set the fen in context.

Planning paths, boardwalks and for public access on fens

- Respect and take account of existing legal rights of public access.

- Consider different modes of access and types of visitor: walkers, horse-riders, cyclists, those with buggies or in wheelchairs.

- Consider how public access may affect sensitive habitats and species, and route.

- Paths or boardwalks to minimise disturbance to breeding birds and mammals

- Link access provision to interpretation.

- Adopt a "least restrictive" access policy to provide for as wide a range of people as possible, including those with restricted mobility or visual impairment. Countryside for All (Fieldfare Trust, 2009) provides further guidance.

- Link access provision to key entry or exit points, visitor centres and hides.

- Explore scope to link the fen with other promoted paths, and/or other habitats.

- Carry out a risk assessment and take heed of visitor safety (see 11.4 above)

Above: A wide range of visitors and modes of transport can be accommodated on fenland sites by provision of suitable access, as seen here at Wicken Fen, Cambridgeshire (photograph courtesy of the National Trust)

11.6.3 Path construction

Paths built on mineral soils, either outside the fen, or on banks within it can be built using any of the standard footpath construction techniques, and are generally cheaper, more durable and less environmentally sensitive than paths on peat.

– Paths should be designed and constructed to allow continued water movement. Where necessary, culverts should be included.

– Hard paths made of mineral soil or dried peat may allow nutrients to be released, and marine peat may create acidity, so it is important to monitor surrounding vegetation to look for adverse impacts. Avoid the use of inappropriate material e.g. limestone on an acid site.

– Paths built on wet peat or peaty soils are more difficult to construct and more susceptible to damage and erosion, but less than perfect conditions underfoot can also be self-limiting on levels of use. The RSPB site at Strumpshaw Fen (see case study at the end of this section) and the Norfolk Wildlife Trust site at Ranworth are good examples.

Experience of path construction on fens

– At **Hickling Broad** the Norfolk Wildlife Trust is moving from boardwalks to paths built on peaty banks made from spoil left over from other management work. The peat is allowed to dry and stabilise, and the path is then built using mineral hoggin (compactable mix of stone and fines) to provide a dry and more robust surface. This type of path should be able to accommodate current visitor numbers of 8-10,000 per year, but might not be able to withstand a sudden increase or influx of visitors.

– **Upton Broad** has an undisturbed peat surface on which paths made of plastic mesh with sown grass were planned. Plant growth within the mesh was poor, so instead a "corduroy" path has been used, composed of 50 mm recycled plastic battens separated by 10-20 mm to allow vegetation growth. The plastic becomes embedded in the peat and vegetation, and at this site water levels are stable so there is no danger of the path floating away in a flood.

– In the valley fens of the **Little Ouse** headwaters the local conservation project (see detailed case study at the end of this section) has used 3 cm plastic Netlon Turfguard mesh to protect the soil surface. Although slippery when first laid the mesh quickly becomes overgrown with vegetation and provides a strong and stable path that can be mown. It is less suitable in shaded areas where sparse plant growth leaves the mesh exposed. Compared with the original peat surface it is particularly resilient to baby-buggies and wheelchairs. Some maintenance is required where the mesh curls at the edges, and mesh-surfaced paths have not proved to be suitable in areas with grazing animals. In fact both horses and cattle have caused problems at these sites as they show an inclination to use paths and bridges, causing damage by deep poaching. Those involved with the site report that sheep seem to be less of a worry, because they are lighter and are often removed earlier in the winter.

11.6.4 Boardwalks

Boardwalks are notoriously expensive to construct and maintain, but are often the only option on fens on deep peat, particularly those overlying lakes or broads that have filled up with organic material which has not yet consolidated. The great advantage of boardwalks is that they allow visitors to see and feel fens as they really are: to enjoy the full 'fen experience'.

A board walk at Bagno Ławki-Szorce, in the buffer zone of Biebrza National Park in north-east Poland, enables visitors to venture into the fen even when the water table is high and to watch the rare aquatic warbler (Acrocephalus paludicola) (M. Street).

The choice of material for boardwalk construction is influenced by specification, anticipated level and type of use, capital and maintenance costs, available resources (manpower as well as financial), environmental impacts, and objectives for site management (see Section 5: Fen Management and Restoration). Traditionally boardwalks were made of wood, which suffers few problems with decomposition in deeper anaerobic peat and water. Recycled plastic is more durable, particularly where exposed above the fen, and has become increasingly popular on many sites. Treated timber should not cause pollution problems provided it has been seasoned after treatment to prevent preservative leaching into water. Any sawdust created during construction should be removed from the site. European larch is more durable than other varieties of larch and can be used untreated.

Further details of boardwalk construction can be found at http:www.snh.org.uk/ publications/ nline/accessguide/downloads/6_2%20Raised%20Boardwalk%20 with%20Edge%20Rails.pdf. It is essential to specify that the boardwalk anchors are firmly embedded in the substrate rather than to try to specify a standard length.

Experiences of using different boardwalk materials

- The National Trust started using hardwood 20 years ago at Wicken Fen but found it deteriorated rapidly and is now replacing it with recycled plastic.

- The Norfolk Wildlife Trust found that tanalised timber boardwalk at Hickling had a life of 12-15 years.

- At Strumpshaw Fen the RSPB found chestnut lasted for about 15 years though the wire netting nailed on it as a non-slip surface lasted for only 5.

- The main problems associated with boardwalks are risk of floating away during flooding, and sinking into peat. At Wicken Fen this has been overcome by anchoring the boardwalk into soil 3 m or so below the peat surface. At Hickling the boardwalk rests on 4 m long 75x75 mm stakes, and at Ranworth the boardwalk sits on jointed, tanalised timber stilts above 6.5 m of quaking mire, incorporating a recycled plastic section for the top 0.5 m for durability.

- Past attempts to float boardwalk on top of peat using sleepers or battens have been abandoned at Wicken Fen, Hickling Broad and Ranworth because of subsidence and rippling as the vegetation died and the peat shrank. However larger 100 mm posts anchored in the peat every 2 m along the path, with cross battens between the posts to provide additional buoyancy, have been successful at some sites.

The 500 m long boardwalk to Ranworth visitor centre is designed for wheelchair access. It is 1.2 m wide, with a kick rail on each side to prevent wheels falling off, with passing places every 100 m or so.

A transboundary boardwalk across fen, built for the first ecotourists to visit the region, crosses from Belarus into Russia (S.Street)

11.6.5 Water borne access

Waterways provide opportunities to manage and transport visitors. Providing good moorings can help limit the impact of people on boats and direct pressure away from sensitive areas. Easily accessible river banks are also welcomed by anglers, who will not normally go through fen habitat unless there is no alternative. Boat trips may allow visitors good views of the fen with minimum disturbance to the wildlife (as at Wicken Fen).

Boat trips are an enjoyable way to visit wetland sites (S.Street)

Dykes, lodes and ditches limit access, and bridges focus it. A lifting bridge at Howe Hill on the River Ant controls access to the fen at different times, helping to prevent disturbance of Schedule I bird species during the nesting season.

11.7 Interpretation

Interpretation is all about increasing enjoyment and understanding. It is an important aspect of reconnecting people with fens, and raising awareness of how special fens are from many different perspectives. Interpretation can be key to attracting visitors, so plays an important part in marketing.

Perhaps the most important word on this panel at Cors Bodeilio National Nature Reserve in Anglesey, Wales is 'Croeso' or 'Welcome' (P.Jones)

Interpretation is all about increasing enjoyment and understanding. It is an important aspect of reconnecting people with fens, and raising awareness of how special fens are from many different perspectives. Interpretation can be key to attracting visitors, so plays an important part in marketing.

The scope for interpretation is limited only by imagination. The rich array of wildlife which fens support is the most obvious focus, but most fens have a fascinating history of many centuries of management and neglect which can provide a strong storyline for interpretation to attract and inspire a wide range of people, some of whom might not necessarily be interested in wildlife. The story of any fen is also inextricably linked with the story of the surrounding area, ecologically and socially. Linking adjacent habitat and reaching out to the wider landscape and nearby settlements offers opportunity can bring in other partners whose contributions can make the story both richer and cheaper to tell. Archaeological finds as well as habitat research results can all add to the interest and appeal of a site for educational and promotional purposes.

 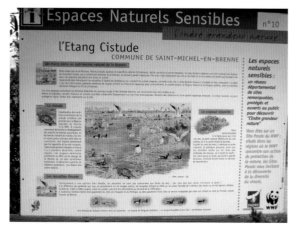

Visual appeal is an important part of design, as demonstrated by these panels in Parc Naturel Regional de la Brenne in central France
(M.Street)

The range of options for interpretive mechanisms is vast, from traditional fixed information panels, leaflets and other printed material to interactive models, guided walks and live exhibits.

Key points to think about in relation to fen interpretation

- **Know your visitors: who** is visiting your site(s), **why** and **what** interests them? What are their expectations?

- **Look at the fen from other peoples' perspective.** What do they see? How can you encourage them to open their eyes and other senses to what else is around them which they may not previously have appreciated?

- **Less can be more.** Over-interpreting a natural site can detract from its intrinsic appeal.

- **Take account of existing and potential interpretation** at other local sites to avoid duplication, but think about establishing a common theme or branding sites clustered in an area.

- **Explore opportunities to stimulate peoples' senses** in different ways to challenge their view of fens.

- **Focus on the unique story** for each site, and how individual sites differ from each other.

- **Set the fen in context** with the surrounding landscape and other habitats.

- **Interpretation should inspire people** and encourage them to contribute to fen conservation, whether through funding, voluntary action, or as advocates.

- **Monitor** response to interpretation.

Hickling Broad interpretation – Norfolk Wildlife Trust

The visitor centre, which is open six months of the year, houses information panels, including some on fens. On the 3 km trail there are two map information boards. Each of the three bird watching hides has an A2 panel offering information on species identification, the grazing regime, the wider landscape, and the bittern project. Visitors to the centre are counted by staff using clicker counters, and there is also a visitor's book.

A panel explaining land use to visitors to Hickling Broad National Nature Reserve (Nick Droy)

Local resources and trades-people can be used to create locally distinctive interpretation and infrastructure. The oak tree sculptures used by the Little Ouse Headwaters project, have 30cm plastic interpretation panels embedded in them. Novel approaches such as this provoke visitors' interest (and sometimes create controversy), helping to establish local identity.

Fens for the future - Wicken Fen Vision, a landscape-scale wetland project that people are encouraged to visit and to realise that it is for them as well as the wildlife (image courtesy of the National Trust)

11.8 References

Health and Safety Executive. 2008. *Risk management*.
http://www.hse.gov.uk/risk/index.htm

Scottish Natural Heritage. 2004. *Management for People*. Battleby.
http://www.snh.org.uk/publications/on-line/heritagemanagement/managementforpeople.asp.

The Fieldfare Trust. 2009. *Countryside for All*.
http://www.fieldfare.org.uk/?page_id=21.

Tourism and Environment Initiative. 2001. *A Sense of Place*. Inverness.
http://www.greentourism.org.uk/SOFP.PDF

Strumpshaw Fen is an RSPB nature reserve on the River Yare in the Norfolk Broads National Park. Every 5 years the management and visitor plan is reviewed. 15-20,000 visitors are expected annually, two-thirds of whom come from within 15 miles; the rest can be described as tourists, including day visitors. The RSPB has begun to ask visitors for information as well as counting numbers.

Location of Visitor Facilities at Strumpshaw Fen RSPB Reserve (Courtesy of the RPSB)

Who is involved?

The site warden maintains informal contact with local parish councils to let them know about events and new developments, and keeps local B&Bs and tourist centres supplied with reserve brochures. 30 local volunteers are key contacts in local communities and act as ambassadors for the reserve. They receive a regular reserve newsletter.

Interpretation

Site interpretation is low key, with panels near other structures such as bridges, and not in the more natural areas. The interpretation has focused on species identification and site management, and is now being developed to tell better stories about the wildlife to be seen and the management that is visible to visitors, such as water management at sluices.

Access provision

Most paths are on raised banks round the edge of the fen, with one cutting through the fen on an old bank. Boardwalk is used in some places, which in future will be of treated timber anchored deep into the peat. The RSPB has mown summer trails over wet meadows at Strumpshaw Fen for 20 years. Soil damage was becoming apparent as accumulated visitor pressure had led to the development of a small sedge sward offering less protection to the peat. A more robust path is now being built around the meadow on mineral soil, from which visitors will be encouraged to venture onto the meadow to look for insects and plants, which will help spread visitor pressure and provide a less regimented experience for visitors.

Across the river, at Wheat Fen, the Ted Ellis Trust provides a route through tall fen habitat to the river. A path is mown with a pedestrian steered mower every June, but always in a new place so as to avoid long term effects on the vegetation and soil.

The RSPB follow the BT disabled access classification (The Fieldfare Trust 2009). Ramps and gates are used wherever possible on the paths rather than steps and stiles to allow ambulant disabled people to enjoy use of the paths, but at present wheelchair access is limited beyond the visitor centre. In the future, RSPB aim to upgrade the outer loop path to allow wheelchair and child buggy use.

Flooding of the River Yare has caused problems with seats and hides floating away. All infrastructure is now securely anchored!

Health and safety

The RSPB has a well established approach to health and safety, focusing on unexpected hazards, particularly at the waterside, for example frequent checks for crumbling banks. Other normal countryside risks, such as tripping over tree roots, are emphasised less. Visitors get to the reserve by crossing a railway line where standard safety measures are applied by Network Rail.

Located on the Somerset levels, Ham Wall is predominantly reedbed and fen on an abandoned peat extraction site. It is a category B RSPB reserve, i.e. managed for quiet enjoyment rather than development as a major visitor centre, but it is an excellent example of provision for all-ability access. Facilities include a boardwalk made from recycled plastic, two viewing platforms (accessible to wheelchairs and buggies), three viewing screens, and tactile interpretation.

Provision of boardwalks at Ham Wall allows users of motorised wheelchairs to enjoy the reserve independently (Nick Droy)

All abilities access and interpretation

Access to viewing platforms has been provided at Ham Wall by car for disabled drivers. The Dog Rose Trust provided specialist advice about working with visual impairment. Tactile signs designed to encourage touch as well as viewing, and incorporating braille, have been made by sandblasting natural wood planks. Disabled anglers have been assisted through provision of all-ability paths and fishing stations.

Local school children wrote poems which have been etched on handrails, and recorded stories on wind-up players that are positioned round the reserve.

Links with local businesses

The reserve keeps a list of recommended B&Bs for visitors. The local hotel benefits from visitors, with some organised walk/meals.

http://www.rspb.org.uk/reserves/guide/h/hamwall/index.asp

Whitlaw Mosses, in the Scottish Borders, comprises four separate fens. Part is designated as an NNR, one of the three purposes of which is to raise national awareness of nature conservation, so there is some pressure to accommodate visitors and ensure minimum standards are met. However, despite promotion on the SNH website, Whitlaw Mosses receives relatively few visitors.

Existing access and target audience

Very narrow boardwalks allow access for monitoring and research. The boards are only 200 mm wide, supported on softwood bearers, and anyone stepping off them would be knee-deep in the fen. Under the Land Reform (Scotland) Act 2003, the general public have a right of access to the site so new safety notices have been erected warning anyone walking on the boardwalks of the associated risks. Otherwise the most frequent visitors are specialist groups. One or two ranger-led walks are held each year. The strategic aim is to focus visitor facilities on Murder Moss (pictured below), where the grassland margin is better suited to visitor access.

At Whitlaw Mosses National Nature Reserve, access is carefully managed for safety reasons and to avoid damaging the fragile environment (A. McBride)

Key stakeholders

Key stakeholders in the site are neighbouring farmers, whose involvement in catchment management is critical to reducing nutrient enrichment of the fen (for further details see Case Study 6.1).

Future plans

There is potential in future to involve some of the 80-100 other basin mires in the area in the interpretative story.

12. Fens from an Economic Perspective

Fens traditionally provided a wide range of products and services of potential economic and social value. Increased mechanisation, changing markets, crafts and traditions have all contributed to changes in the way in which many of these products are valued. The overall economic climate has also changed significantly since fens were at their heyday as a central part of the rural economy.

This section explores the range of products which fens can provide, and considers different approaches to realising the value of these products and services to help fund sustainable fen management. It also explores other economic aspects of fen management, including grants and possible funding sources.

12.1 Direct provision of products

Approaches to marketing and selling fenland products include:

- negotiating a detailed agreement with a third-party commercial enterprise. This should include details of the amount of product (e.g. thatching reed, biofuels) to be harvested, access routes and any other restrictions necessary to protect the conservation interest of the site.

- point-of-sale facilities and workshops for craft products as part of a wetland reserve visitor centre, with a mutual commercial benefit.

12.1.1 Thatching reed

Thatching reed is in demand for maintenance and restoration of thatched roofs, and construction of new thatched property. Revival in the Norfolk reed cutting industry has also been stimulated by increased interest in vernacular traditions and awareness of the sustainability of thatch. Common reed is the principal material used for thatching, particularly since plant breeding regulations have affected growth of specialist long-straw wheat crops. Home-based production of common reed meets about 25% of UK demand, with the remainder met by imports. Common reed is too stiff for bent work, for example on ridge lines, so there is also demand for saw sedge. Reed is cut in winter, sedge is cut in summer.

Reeds cut and stacked ready for sale as thatching material on the Tay Reedbeds, Scotland (M.Milne).

Harvesting and marketing of reed for thatching can provide a valuable source of income to help fund fen management, but the requirement for a 'clean', weed free product and the one or two year cutting cycle is not ideal for biodiversity. Manual cutting and transporting is still used by professional cutters in difficult locations, but the industry revival relies on investment in harvesting machinery, often grant aided. Efficient cutting in well-defined blocks and good facilities for transport of reed bundles, by water or track, are important to the economics of commercial reed cutting. For more information about fen harvesting for thatching, see www.thatch. org.

Reed put to good use for re-thatching of the Wee Bush Inn, Carnwath, Lanarkshire (A. McBride)

Reed is also used on a smaller scale to make screens for bird-watching hides or sale for garden screens.

12.1.2 Basketwork products

Traditional shopping baskets have largely been replaced by plastic bags, but new products such as willow coffins and traditional products such as log baskets sustain a demand for craftwork basketry. Willow withies are still produced on the Somerset Levels, yielding a commercially important crop which is also used for high value artist's charcoal, although the favoured varieties are often non-native cultivars. Economic markets for fen products such as these have protected remnants of the Somerset wetlands from complete drainage. Small-scale willow production is feasible for nature reserve sites, and is promoted by several Scottish sites including local authority owned wetland sites.

Construction of willow hoop and baskets by Les Bates in Wester Ross, Scotland (Les Bates)

12.1.3 Biomass energy and Biofuels

The high productivity of some fen vegetation, combined with winter dieback or leaf loss, makes it potentially useful as feedstock for biomass boilers or anaerobic digestors. The sustainability benefits of these crops should not be ignored, since they require little mechanical work and no fertiliser, making them a near carbon-neutral form of solar energy capture. Willow on short coppice rotation can achieve yields of above-ground dry matter in the order of 12 tonnes/ha, while common reed may be able to produce 15 tonnes/ha. Commercial bulk production of willow, reed and sedge is effectively a short rotation monoculture which is not ideal for biodiversity, but harvesting material as a cash crop can help to fund re-wetting and the progressive extension of wetland, such as that proposed around Wicken Fen. The harvesting of long-rotation willow coppice from wetland sites in west Wales is currently being investigated.

Wood taken from small areas of scrub control, channel clearance and restoration undertaken as part of overall management to maintain or improve fen biodiversity can also generate useful income as a source of biofuel, subject to a local market or processor. Summer-cut material has the added advantage of removing excess nutrients which have entered the site as biomass.

Large-scale commercial agricultural production of elephant grass species is developing, for processing to produce fuel in shredded or pellet form. This sugar cane-like grass can yield up to 20 tonnes/ha with exceptionally efficient metabolism, but monoculture production of an exotic species such as this has little or no direct biodiversity benefit. However, as a perennial crop requiring little or no fertiliser or herbicide input, elephant grass could be of indirect benefit where sensitively incorporated in catchment-sensitive farming schemes, and it could also provide a buffer against intensive agriculture for sensitive wetlands. Giant reed (Arundo donax) is increasingly grown as a biofuel, mainly in developing countries and the United States, but this species could be invasive and harmful in UK wetlands.

Using fen products as biofuel

The feasibility of using locally harvested reeds to heat the Wildlife Trust of South and West Wales' visitor centre was investigated by Metcalfe (2007). Reeds have a similar calorific content (19.6 MJ/kg dry matter) to *Miscanthus*, and ashing properties that are acceptable within modern biomass boilers. It was found that 27 tonnes of air-dry reed would be needed annually to heat the centre and some adjacent buildings. This mass of reed could be obtained from winter harvesting of 2.7 ha of reedbed from the immediate reserve (Teifi Marshes NNR), with possible augmentation from nearby reserves. Initial discussions with the site manager suggested that this rate of harvesting could be sustained whilst maintaining biodiversity. The capital cost of the biomass boiler and associated heating infrastructure was estimated at c. £50,000, and the payback period was between 5 and 10 years, after which the centre would benefit from much cheaper heating than that offered by the current liquid petroleum gas system.

The Wildlife Centre at Kilgerran (www. welshwildlife.org)

12.1.4 Traditional agriculture and associated products

Various fen plants, including Glyceria grasses, are both palatable and highly productive, which has led to a long history of grazing fens and mowing for hay. Grazing plays a dual role in fen management: potential income generation, and a management tool to maintain the diversity of wetland habitats through the eating and trampling of rank vegetation (see Section 6: Vegetation Management). The lifting of slaughter-age restrictions for cattle and increased demand for meat from traditional breeds may increase the demand for rough grazing, but demand for grazing and profitability will always be subject to persistent long term cycles in agricultural economics. The foot and mouth disease outbreak in 2001 and bovine spongiform encephalitis (BSE) restrictions had a significant impact. The costs of infrastructure necessary for grazing, including fencing, handling pens, vehicular access for delivery and removal of livestock all need to be taken into account when assessing the economic viability of grazing fens. Some reserve managers have chosen to keep livestock for conservation benefit alone, rather than letting grazing or selling animals.

'Marsh hay' or 'bog hay' from the East Anglian and Scottish Borders fens was a major commercial product in the days of horse traction and transport. Coarse hay of low fodder value is still favoured for horses and hardy traditional breeds of cattle and sheep for which hay and haylage from intensively managed ryegrass swards can be too rich, provided the hay does not contain ragwort, hemlock water-dropwort or other poisonous plants.

It is worth bearing in mind that grazing or other agricultural use of fens may trigger entitlement (and be essential) to single farm payments and agri-environment schemes.

12.1.5 By-products from habitat management work

Scrub control, long rotation cutting of reeds, restoration cuts and channel clearance all produce bulk materials of potential value as mulch, stock bedding (provided material is free from harmful plant matter) and compost. The economic and environmental disadvantage of these low value bulk products is relatively high transport costs, which often limits sale to local use.

Composted reed and sedge could potentially replace the use of sedge peat as a traditional soil improver, but compost production needs to be on-site or near-site for local sale. Large-scale commercial composting operations supplied by domestic collections and local authority waste usually charge to take away material from other sources. There may also be licence implications for control of leachate from compost, so the appropriate regulator should be contacted for advice (see Appendix V). Cut common clubrush has value for rush work products, and can be marketed as a craft material or made up into saleable items by on-site craft workers.

12.1.6 Pharmaceuticals

Pharmaceutical use in medicines and cosmetics is generating new markets for some wetland plants. Bog myrtle (or sweet gale) has long been used for beer flavouring and insect repellent, but Boots the Chemist have now produced a range of products using the herb for acne treatment and to help delay ageing effects on skin, which is worth several hundred pounds per hectare, compared with less than £20 per hectare for sheep farming. Fens provide a valuable reservoir of gene material with significant potential for further pharmaceutical development in future.

12.2 Environmental regulation

12.2.1 Hydrological regulation

Wetlands have been described as 'the kidneys of the landscape' because of their valuable role in the regulation of water quality and flow. Some fens fill rapidly during floods, and then the floodwater slowly filters back out through the fen plants and soils. This transient water retention function reduces the magnitude of peak flood flows and can help reduce erosion caused by flooding, rather than simply displacing the problem downstream. Fens also provide a resilient source of baseflow for streams and rivers during drought conditions. The value of the hydrological regulation function provided by wetlands is likely to increase as rainfall patterns become more erratic as a result of climate change.

Construction of earth bunds or similar structures to enhance wetland water storage capacity and retard return flow of flood waters to the main river channel is welcome in conservation terms where wetland water levels have previously been reduced, for example by abstraction from an underlying aquifer.

Negative consequences of promoting restoration of the 'natural' function of floodplain wetlands and channels include risk of contamination by surface water runoff from urban and suburban areas (e.g. hydrocarbons and salt) or by sediments, dissolved nutrients and chemicals (e.g. biocides) from agricultural runoff. Careful positioning of Sustainable Urban Drainage Systems can help mitigate such risks.

> Doxey and Tillington Marshes SSSI is a good example of the flood attenuation benefits of wetlands. This 124 ha of floodplain grassland, marsh, swamp and pools reduces peak flood flows through the town of Stafford which lies immediately downstream on the River Sow. Staffordshire Wildlife Trust developed the Staffordshire Washlands Project with the aim of restoring natural fluvial processes to rivers and floodplain wetlands within the county.

In carrying out an Environmental Impact Assessment for a flood alleviation scheme, or a project with flood risk implications, developers have a legal obligation to investigate all reasonable options to fulfill the required function. The responsibility of the wetland manager is therefore primarily to make sure that possible flood alleviation benefits offered by a wetland are included in the cost-benefit analysis.

12.2.2 Attenuation of water-borne contaminants

Wetlands can break down or lock up contaminants, both in surface water and discharging groundwater, thus improving water quality. An example of this is denitrification of discharging groundwater, where microbially-mediated transformation of nitrate to nitrogen gas is supported by the high concentrations of organic carbon and the anaerobic conditions. Over 1200 wetlands in the UK have now been purpose-constructed to attenuate a number of contaminants: to provide a 'final polish' for water which has already undergone treatment, to treat industrial wastewaters, road run-off and landfill leachate, and for domestic sewage treatment from small communities.

Constructed wetlands are designed to mimic the bio-filtration properties of natural wetlands but are engineered according to their location and the concentration, type and volumes of contamination in the water to be treated. Water travels vertically or horizontally through a filtration medium (sand, gravel or soil). The plants most commonly used are common reed and bulrushes (*Typha*). It is important natural wetlands are not used for this function.

Farm effluent run-off has been recognised as a significant diffuse source of pollution for many years. Both UK and European legislation now seeks to protect against such contamination, for example under the EU Nitrates Directive 91/676/EEC and the Water Framework Directive (2000/60/EC). The value of the nitrate treatment potential of wetlands can therefore be promoted for inclusion in, and realisation through, the Programmes of Measures which are developed for achieving good status under the Directive.

A constructed farm wetland at Oldhamstocks Farm, Scottish Borders (A.McBride)

The Coal Authority in the UK describes reedbeds as the 'most ecologically friendly' and visually attractive way of treating mine water, in particular the pollution of watercourses with iron ochre as groundwater levels rebound. The roots of common reed, bulrush and yellow iris filter particles of ferric hydroxide (ochre). Settlement then occurs when these particles collect together and fall to the base of the reedbed. Currently, 10 mg/l ferrous hydroxide entering the Coal Authority's reedbeds will be reduced to less than 1 mg/l. Examples include Kames in Ayrshire, which is a passive wetland system to treat gravitational flow to the River Ayr, and treatment of acid mine drainage from colliery spoils (including iron, aluminium, manganese and zinc) at Quaking Houses, County Durham (a 'CoSTaR' project, based at Newcastle University). Reedbeds for mine water treatment are often combined with public amenity use incorporating picnic areas, paths, benches and viewing points.

Valuation of this service can be through comparison with the cost of an equivalent waste water treatment facility. In the United States it was calculated that the natural Congaree Bottomland Hardwood Swamp in South Carolina avoids the need for a $5 million waste water treatment plant.

12.2.3 Carbon sequestration

Another key role of peat-based wetlands is the regulation of global CO_2 concentrations, and therefore climate change, through storage of a major proportion of fixed carbon in the biosphere. Peatlands cover only an estimated 3-4% of the world's land area, but are estimated to hold 540 Gt of carbon, equivalent to around 74% of the 730 Gt of carbon held in the atmosphere as CO_2. If the world's peatlands lost only 5% of their carbon store through respiration, global CO_2 concentration would rise from its current value of 386 ppm to around 400 ppm.

Carbon is stored in peat by accumulation of dead organic matter under anaerobic conditions, where the soil water level is at or close to the ground surface. Where water levels have been lowered, for example by drainage for agricultural production, the peat carbon store is depleted through aerobic respiration. Restoration of high water levels will halt (and probably reverse) this depletion. Chapter 12 of Rydin and Jeglum (2006) gives an extremely detailed summary of the productivity and carbon balance of peatlands.

Predicting the net carbon sequestration which would result from a planned project is not necessarily straightforward. A high proportion of previous studies have concentrated on ombrogenous bogs, and relatively little information is available for fens. Measurement of carbon cycling is resource intensive, and there are further complications to take into account. Some question the role of wetlands as greenhouse gas regulators, as the release of methane under the anaerobic conditions caused by raised water levels, is approximately 23 times more potent as a greenhouse gas than CO_2. Scientific investigation of the relative effects and amounts of CO_2 and methane release from unsaturated and saturated wetland peats respectively is at an early stage. Interestingly, methane production from saturated peat is known to be higher from sedge-dominated peat than from moss-dominated peat, and also higher from high-pH peat than from low-pH peat, suggesting that there is a higher methane production potential in fenland peat than in bogland peat.

Carbon offset funds are a potential source of finance for fen creation or restoration. These funds have been established to allow consumers to offset their carbon emissions by donating proportional amounts of money. Money is invested in development schemes which reduce greenhouse gases, including projects based on carbon sequestration, but most carbon offset funds currently only invest in schemes in the developing world. Establishment of a local carbon offsetting scheme to support a wetland, or group of wetlands, might be more successful.

There may also be potential to use the UK Government's Shadow Price for Carbon (SPC) as matched funding for a project. Put simply, the SPC is based on an estimate of the damage costs of climate change caused by each additional tonne of greenhouse gas emitted by a proposed project. Annual SPCs have been published by DEFRA for 2007 to 2050. The 2009 SPC is £26.50 per tonne of CO_2, and since each tonne of elemental carbon is equivalent to about 3.5 times its weight in CO_2, the equivalent SPC for elemental carbon is £97.26 per tonne.

An illustration of the concept of carbon sequestration

To illustrate this concept, and to assess the possible magnitude of the sums involved, a simple calculation has been carried out based on the annual carbon balance for wetland meadow habitat within Tealham and Tadham Moor SSSI in the Somerset Levels, published by Lloyd (2006). This study found that the site was loosing a significant amount of soil (peat) carbon (59 gC m^{-2} a^{-1}), which was attributed to soil respiration resulting from inappropriately low soil water levels. The following assumptions were made for the calculation:

A project to raise the water levels to an appropriate level would prevent 59 gC m^{-2} a^{-1} leaving the site; this ignores any potential sequestration if peat growth resumes under higher water levels. Water levels are raised over an area of 100 ha, or about 1/9th of the SSSI.

For the first year of operation, the retained carbon has an SPC value of £5,738, and if the project has a life expectancy of five years, the total SPC value would be £29,860 (using the SPC rates for 2010-2014). These are clearly significant sums, and demonstrate the importance of carbon sequestration through wetlands under the UK government's valuation. Whilst this valuation does not represent 'real' money available for projects, it could account for a healthy proportion of a contribution to a match-funding agreement for many projects. It is also possible that the SPC will change in the future, as appreciation of the effects of climate change improves.

12.3 Support for other environmental services

Although difficult to quantify, fens often provide support for other environmental services, including pollination of crops by wetland species, supply of nectar to bees visiting a wetland, and nutrient cycling. An example of the importance of these services is the Pembrokeshire honey industry, whose yields have been boosted in the poor summers of 2007 and 2008 by the flow of nectar later in the year from nectar-rich Himalayan balsam, a non-native plant which is usually criticised for its invasion of wetlands.

12.4 Provision of cultural resources (or wildlife amenity)

Wetlands provide a wildlife amenity resource in a number of ways, of which recreation is the most commonly recognised, but others include religious, spiritual and aesthetic. Fens are arguably the most accessible wild landscape in the UK. Fen-based nature reserves such as Vane Farm at Loch Leven in Fife, and Leighton Moss in Lancashire, have level paths that are well screened from wildlife. It is possible to park your car, walk a short distance to a hide, then sit and view rare animals in their natural habitat. The level paths provide unrestricted access for people of all ages and abilities, and excellent opportunities for education and interpretation as the main elements of the ecosystem are visible.

The longer-term value of fens as an educational resource in developing society's appreciation of nature conservation, and thus in sustaining the indirect financial resources for site management is extremely important.

12.4.1 Direct income

The simplest way of converting the wildlife amenity value of fens into income is by charging for entry. Charging an entry fee obviously raises expectations in terms of the quality of the amenity and provision of visitor facilities (e.g. boardwalks into deeper areas of fen, comfortable hides, toilets, etc.), but additional income can also be generated by visitor facilities such as cafes and shops. Charging a fee (or asking for a donation) for corporate team-building activities is also a possibility, but any enterprise which charges a fee increases management responsibility and needs to be run properly.

Examples of direct income generated by fens

- Wildfowl and Wetlands Trust (www.wwt.org.uk) charge entry fees for their nine sites around the UK ranging from £5 to £10 for adult day-entry.

- Electric powered boats (including one that is solar powered) provide trips on several of the Norfolk Broads, including reserves closed to other boat traffic such as How Hill and Hickling (see Section 11: Fens and People).

- At Slimbridge, canoe safaris help generate income. Other fens might be able to organise fee-paying boat trips into routinely inaccessible parts.

- RSPB's Loch Insh Marshes is used by Cairngorm Canoeing and Sailing School and Loch Insh Chalets in their provision of local accommodation and canoe hire for trips through the marshes and along the Spey. Further afield in the Netherlands, a company offers holiday accommodation in the form of large rafts moored within wetlands (www.campingraft.com).

- Shooting and fishing are a widespread source of income for wetland sites, for example wildfowl shooting on Caerlaverock Marshes SSSI on the Nith Estuary in Dumfries and Galloway, but careful management is required to safeguard biodiversity, and to avoid conflict with public access.

Another mechanism for funding wetland creation and enhancement is through planning gain agreements. The legal structure for this mechanism varies across the UK, but allows for funds and land to be directed to the provision and management of habitats as mitigation for development losses. The presence of 'wild' but accessible wetland habitat adjacent to a housing development can add considerably to property value, especially those overlooking the wetland (such as the London Wetlands Centre). Further from the site, there are still benefits for general amenity and the local economy.

12.4.2 Indirect income generation

In 'Watched Like Never Before' (Dickie et al, 2006) the RSPB discuss the local economic benefits of spectacular bird species. Together with organisations such as the National Trust and Wildlife Trusts, RSPB have recognised that raising the profile of their charity can also help raise funds, at the same time as helping protect and conserve key species and features.

An example of generating indirect income from a wetland

Between 26th June and 31st August 2004, a watch point was arranged with a neighbouring farmer to RSPB Frampton Marsh nature reserve giving the public the first opportunity to watch Montagu's harriers in the UK. The project received significant media coverage and was visited by 5,660 people. The volunteers worked a total of 1,464 hours, worth over £9,000 to the Society. Car parking charges raised £5,384, a portion of which was paid to the farmer. A sale of harrier artwork made £616 and certificates raised £143 towards installing a bench in Frampton Parish.

Quantifying the benefits of a single action or project on an individual site is often difficult, particularly as part of a long-term process, but utilisation and appreciation of wildlife amenities within the community are critical to raising public awareness of the value of wetlands, and to sustaining and increasing indirect funding for site management.

At the RSPB reserve at Ham Wall, the local hotel's out of season earnings are boosted by parties having a meal after an organised walk round the reserve.

12.5 Preservation services

As a result of agricultural drainage and improvement, particularly over the last few hundred years, fens have become increasingly rare in the UK and Europe. That they have become targets for conservation action is illustrated, for example, by the inclusion of *Calcareous* fens with *Cladium mariscus* and species of the *Caricion davallianae*, and Alkaline fens, in Annex 1 of the EU Habitats Directive. This legislation gives an unprecedented degree of protection to endangered species and habitats within Europe. Although direct income generation may play a critical part in funding fen management, many would argue that it is the preservation of these rare and very special habitats is the most valued of the ecosystem services fens provide. From an anthropocentric perspective, preservation of biodiversity safeguards the future, but currently un-recognised, value of genetic resources for science, medicine and agricultural development. As identified earlier in this handbook, and described more fully by Rydin and Jeglum 2007, (Chapter 6), fens also contain a remarkable resource of well preserved archaeological remains and important palaeo-environmental evidence which can be used to reconstruct various aspects of environmental and cultural history. This is a finite, fragile and non-renewable resource, and one which is becoming more valuable to society with time, because of our developing need to understand historical climatic variations and cultural responses in the context of current climate change. Preservation of this resource is usually entirely compatible with habitat conservation, which normally involves maintenance of high water levels within a site. In turn this promotes anaerobic conditions and preservation of artefacts at greater depths within the substrate. The value of preservation services is realised almost exclusively through indirect funding such as agri-environment grants.

12.6 External funding sources for fen management and restoration

12.6.1 European and UK government funding

The European Union moved away from production subsidies in the latter half of the 20th Century, with the present emphasis being on countryside management for environmental benefits. Participation in the current financial support package aimed at farming businesses, the Single Farm Payment (SFP) scheme, requires compulsory compliance with a basic programme of land management. Subject to compliance with SFP requirements, farmers can choose to apply for further financial support for the creation and management of high value habitat through a menu of options. Owners and managers with demonstrable agricultural use, for example grazed wildlife reserves, are also eligible to apply for these schemes.

RDPs offer financial rewards for good stewardship and management of the land to improve the quality of the environment, but also include options and priorities for economic development and other priorities. RDPs are replacing many of the previous agri-environment schemes such as Environmentally Sensitive Areas (ESAs) and Rural Stewardship. In Scotland, the Scottish Rural Development Programme (SRDP) is the new single umbrella for funding. The Rural Development Programme for England (RDPE) includes Environmental Stewardship (ES). The Welsh parallel is Tir Gofal (to be replaced in 2012 by Glastir). Across the water, RDP takes the form of the Northern Ireland Countryside Management Scheme.

In England, Wales and Northern Ireland, there is an open 'entry-level' scheme that requires the enactment of a general maintenance plan for farmland habitat such as hedgerows, with either a separate higher-level scheme or additional payments for management and creation of semi-natural habitat, including fen. The higher level payments are discretionary, highly targeted, and from a limited budget.

Applications compete on the basis of their potential biodiversity and public amenity benefits. The schemes are complex, offering annual maintenance or creation payments, together with a range of payments for capital items such as sluices, scrapes, fencing, car parking and public access provision. Site-specific advice is provided through the regional offices of the various national bodies such as DEFRA in England, or the SRDP in Scotland. Support and information is also available through the websites of SNH, NE, CCW and Northern Ireland Environment and Heritage Service. In England and Wales, the advisory service offered by the Farming and Wildlife Advisory Group (FWAG) includes survey and production of agri-environment applications.

The area-based rates for management, restoration or creation of habitat are based on a percentage of the notional income that is foregone by not farming intensively, typically ranging from 60% to 98%. At the time of writing, fen management or restoration in England attracted grant of £60/ha/yr for 10 years, potentially with grazing or cutting supplementary payments. Creation of fen from arable or intensively managed grassland could qualify for payments of £380/ha/yr. Similar rates apply to reed-beds and there are optional payments for pond management.

Whitlaw Mosses in Scotland (see detailed case study at the end of Section 6: Vegetation Management) has benefitted from participation of neighbouring farmers in the Environmentally Sensitive Area agri-environment scheme which was established to improve management of the mires, by converting arable land within the catchments to permanent grassland and reducing nutrient inputs. Farmers now have the option to continue receiving payments for this kind of sympathetic management under the SRDP.

Large-scale funding for environmental and nature conservation projects not financed by the EC's standard financial agricultural instruments is also available through the EU LIFE scheme.

In 2008, a 5 million Euro LIFE+ grant was obtained for the restoration of alkaline fens to favorable or recovering condition within the Anglesey and Lleyn Fens in North Wales.

In 2007, the RSPB won a LIFE+ grant in part to protect vital freshwater habitats from destruction relating to climate change.

12.6.2 Commercial sponsorship

Some companies are prepared to fund wetland work in return for good media publicity and on-site acknowledgement, or on the basis of extra business from which they may benefit if extra people come to visit a site. Locally-based companies may be particularly receptive to approaches for funding for small scale initiatives.

Doxey and Tillington Marshes SSSI, an extensive wetland that runs almost into the centre of Stafford, are an excellent example of innovative funding for fen management. Screwfix and Arnold Clark, who recently developed commercial premises in the area, both donated funds for this site.

Regular informal recreational use is very high with around 42,000 visits per year, in addition to those using the cycle path along an old railway track that crosses the site. This enabled the Staffordshire Wildlife Trust to secure Lottery funding for a new pathway system that has improved amenity, further increased visitor numbers, and very effectively reduced disturbance to breeding birds.

12.6.3 Other funding sources

The National Lottery has funded numerous wetland creation and management projects through the Heritage Lottery Fund and Awards for All. Many local authorities have funding co-ordinators who can help advise on Lottery and other sources of funding.

The Cooperative Bank, in association with the RSPB, raised over £2 million between 1999 and 2002 for reed-bed restoration in East Anglia through their charity credit card scheme. The RSPB received £18 for every account opened and 25p for every £100 spent.

12.7 Valuing the true worth of fens

Understanding and appreciation of ecosystem services and the many benefits of fens which cannot be readily quantified in economic terms has developed considerably, but recent research suggests that wetland conservation managers currently have a tendency to stick to familiar ground when identifying and realising the value of fens and other wetlands.

On behalf of the Wetland Vision for England Project, McInnes (2007) reviewed six local Wetland Vision plans in relation to their recognition and use of the ecosystem services concept as a part of their planned resource and management strategy. He found that:

- Reference was made to direct provision of environmental products and services, and environmental regulation services, but there were numerous potential services which were not mentioned.

- More information was given on cultural than other services, and these services were explained more clearly. The language used displayed a much greater empathy with these ecosystem services than with other types, especially for recreational and educational services.

- Biodiversity was not the headline objective for all projects; one project had reduction of urban flood risk at its core. The case studies demonstrated that the philosophical choice of 'either biodiversity or ecosystem services' had been superseded, with all projects accommodating a breadth of benefits without compromising biodiversity objectives.

- There was a clear bias towards the provision of cultural services. Spiritual, inspirational, recreational, aesthetic and educational objectives are considered more important than other ecosystem services.

These summarised conclusions suggest that there is almost certainly scope for identifying and realising the value of a wider range of ecosystem services. The research also raises questions which serve as a useful checklist for all those involved in fen management which if followed through, could provide necessary resources for site management whilst safeguarding the interests of conservation and biodiversity.

Checklist when considering economic aspects of fen management

- Is there more scope for direct provision of fen products compatible with the maintenance of biodiversity?

- Are there alternative avenues of funding to realise the value of the carbon sequestration service offered by fens e.g. local carbon offsetting schemes, or use of the government's SPC concept?

- Can the value of the flood attenuation function of a wetland be promoted, quantified and realised whilst maintaining favourable conditions for biodiversity?

- What scope is there for encouraging neighbour participation in schemes to reduce hydrological or nutrient problems, for example through a linked or joint RDP application which is more likely to attract support than individual proposals?

12.8 References

Dickie, I., Hughes, J. and Esteban, A. (2006) Watched Like Never Before … the local economic benefits of spectacular bird species. RSPB, Bedfordshire. (http://www.rspb.org.uk/Images/watchedlikeneverbefore_tcm9-133081.pdf)

Lloyd, C.R. (2006) Annual carbon balance of a managed wetland meadow in the Somerset Levels, UK. *Agriculture and Forest Meteorology*, 138, 168-179.

Metcalfe, J.P. (2007) Reed boiler project definition for Wildlife Trusts Centre. Consultant report for CCW.

McInnes, R. (2007) *Integrating wetland ecosystem services within a 50 year vision for wetlands*. Consultant report by the Wildfowl and Wetlands Trust for the England Wetland Vision Partnership.

Rydin, H. and Jeglum, J. (2007) *The Biology of Peatlands*. Oxford, Oxford University Press.

Appendix I – Glossary

Adsorption	mechanism by which phosphorus and other chemicals are bound to soil particles and therefore unavailable for plant uptake
Ammonification	conversion of organic nitrogen to ammonia by microorganisms
Anoxia	deprived of oxygen
Aquifer	an underground layer of water-bearing permeable rock or unconsolidated materials like gravel and sand
Aquitard	a bed of low permeability material along an aquifer
Aquiclude	a solid, impermeable area underlying or overlying an aquifer
Bog	acidic mires (pH<5.5) found mainly on peat, but also on some mineral soils
Carr	tree covered fen that has an understorey of fen vegetation
Cultural eutrophication	nutrient enrichment caused by human land management activities
Denitrification	conversion of nitrate to gaseous nitrogen by microorganisms
Eutrophic	high fertility conditions, rich in nutrients
Eutrophication	nutrient enrichment
Fauna	animals associated with a particular habitat
Fen	a wetland that receives water and nutrients from surface and/or groundwater, as well as rainfall. Fens are found on peat and normally wet mineral soils
Flora	plants associated with a habitat
Groundwater	water which has travelled through the soil or underlying rock
High marsh	tidal marsh zone located above the Mean High Water Mark, but term also used for tall rich fen that stands back from the waters edge in freshwater situations
Hydrological regime	the amount of water required to maintain a particular type of fen, and how this varies throughout the year
Marsh	seasonally dry wetlands on mineral soils
Mesotrophic	moderately fertile conditions
Meteoric water	precipitation
Mineralisation	conversion of organic nitrogen to nitrate or organic phosphorus to phosphate, undertaken by microorganisms. Also referred to as decomposition
Minerotrophic	surface fed in part by water which has had some contact with the mineral ground
Mire	intermediate habitat between dry land and open water including fens and bogs, where the water-table is at or just below the substratum surface for most of the year
Nitrification	conversion of ammonia to nitrites and nitrate by microorganisms

Nitrogen fixation	conversion of gaseous nitrogen to ammonia and then to organic nitrogen, requires specialist microorganisms often in a symbiotic relationship with plants (nitrogen-fixing bacteria and legumes)
Nitrogen reduction	conversion of nitrate to ammonium under highly anaerobic conditions
Nutrients	chemical elements or compounds required by plants for growth
Oligotrophic	low fertility conditions, nutrient poor
Ombrogenous	a peat-forming plant community that derives all its water, and dissolved nutrients, from rainfall and other precipitation as opposed to watercourses or below-ground drainage
Ombrotophic	surface fed directly and exclusively by precipitation
Osiers	willows used for basket making
Peatland	all areas with peat, including sites with natural or semi-natural vegetation and areas converted to agriculture or forestry or used for peat extraction
Phytophagous	species which feed on herbaceous and woody plants
Pingo	type of wetland formed in the ice age when a slow melting block of ice was surrounded by outwash materials. When the ice melted it left a water filled depression in the ground
Poor fens	fens fed by acidic water derived from base-poor rock such as sandstones and granites, which tend to support a less diverse flora and fauna than fens fed by more alkaline water
Residency time	length of time water is in contact with soil or rock, which affects the mineral content of the water feeding fens
Rich fens	fens fed by mineral-enriched calcareous waters (pH 5 or higher which therefore tend to support more diverse plant and animal communities than those fed by base-poor water.
Soligenous	wetness induced by lateral water movement i.e. sideways through the soil or rock, as on seepage slopes
Stand	a relatively uniform patch of vegetation of distinctive species composition and appearance, which can vary in size from very small (several square metres) to very large (i.e. many hectares)
Surface water	water standing or flowing at the surface, which may contain rainwater, river water and groundwater
Swamp	wetlands with summer water table typically >25cm above ground level
Topogenous	wetness induced by topography and poor drainage where water movement is predominantly vertical, typically found on open water fringes, in basins or on flood plains.
Wale	single or double wale refers to cutting every year or every 2 years
Water level	the level of water above or below ground
Water table	below ground, free surface water
Wetland	area of land whose soil is saturated with water either permanently or seasonally
Withies	long, bendy willow sticks

Appendix II – List of acronyms used in the text

BAP	Biodiversity Action Plan
BGS	British Geological Society
BTCV	British Trust for Conservation Volunteers
CAA	Civil Aviation Authority
CCW	Countryside Council for Wales
CSM Guidance	Common Standards Monitoring Guidance
DOC	Dissolved oxygen concentration
EA	Environment Agency
EC	Electrical conductivity
FWAG	Farming and Wildlife Advisory Group
GAP	Grazing Animals Project
HAP	Habitat Action Plan
LiDAR	Light detection and ranging
LU	Livestock unit
NE	Natural England
NIEA	Northern Ireland Environment Agency
NNR	National Nature Reserve
NVC	National Vegetation Classification
RAF	Royal Air Force
RDP	Rural Development Programmes
RSPB	The Royal Society for Protection of Birds
SAC	Special Area of Conservation
SAP	Species Action Plan
SEPA	Scottish Environment Protection Agency
SNH	Scottish Natural Heritage
SOAC	Scottish Outdoor Access Code
SPC	Shadow price for carbon
SRDP	Scottish Rural Development Programme
SSSI	Site of Special Scientific Interest
SUDS	Sustainable urban drainage schemes also known as Sustainable drainage schemes as they are also used in rural locations

Appendix III – List of species referred to in the main text and detailed lists of mammals, birds, repitles and amphibians associated with fens

Common name	Latin name
Alder	*Alnus glutinosa*
Angelica	*Angelica sylvestris*
Alder buckthorn	*Frangula alnus*
Bird's eye primrose	*Primula farinosa*
Black bog-rush	*Schoenus nigricans*
Bog asphodel	*Narthecium ossifragum*
Bog bean	*Menyanthes trifoliata*
Bog pimpernel	*Anagallis tenella*
Bog pondweed	*Potamogeton polygonifolius*
Bladder sedge	*Carex vesicaria*
Bottle sedge	*Carex rostrata*
Blunt-flowered rush	*Juncus subnodulosus*
Buckthorn	*Rhamnus catharticus*
Bulrush	*Typha latifolia*
Butterwort	*Pinguicula vulgaris*
Canary reedgrass	*Phalaris arundinacea*
Carnation sedge	*Carex panicea*
Common butterwort	*Pinguicula vulgaris*
Common clubrush	*Schoenoplectus lacustris*
Common cotton grass	*Eriophorum angustifolium*
Common reed	*Phragmites australis*
Common sallow	*Salix cinerea*
Common sedge	*Carex nigra*
Common valerian	*Valeriana officinalis*
Cranberry	*Vaccinium oxycoccos)*
Cross leaved heath	*Erica tetralix*
Devil's bit scabious	*Succisa pratensis*
Dioecious sedge	*Carex dioica*
Downy birch	*Betula pubescens*
Early marsh orchid	*Dactylorhiza incarnata*
Elongated sedge	*Carex elongata*
Fen bedstraw	*Galium uliginosum*
Fen orchid	*Liparis loeselii*
Fen notchwort	*Leiocolea rutheana*
Fen pondweed	*Potamogeton coloratus*
Fen violet	*Viola persicifolia*
Flat sedge	*Blysmus compressus*
Fragrant orchid	*Gymnadenia conopsea ssp. densiflora*
Giant reed	*Arundo donax*

Greater pond sedge	*Carex riparia*
Greater reedmace	*Typha latifolia*
Greater tussock sedge	*Carex paniculata*
Great hairy willow herb	*Epilobium hirsutum*
Grey willow	*Salix cinerea*
Guelder rose	*Viburnum opulus*
Heather	*Calluna vulgaris*
Hemp agrimony	*Eupatorium cannabinum*
Lesser clubmoss	*Selaginella selaginoides*
Lesser pond sedge	*Carex acutiformis*
Lesser reedmace	*Typha angustifolia*
Lesser tussock sedge	*Carex diandra*
Lesser water parsnip	*Berula erecta*
Marestail	*Hippuris vulgaris*
Marsh bedstraw	*Galium palustre*
Marsh cinquefoil	*Potentilla palustris*
Marsh earwort	*Jamesoniella undulifolia*
Marsh fern	*Thelypteris palustris*
Marsh helleborine	*Epipactis palustris*
Marsh lousewort	*Pedicularis palustris*
Marsh pea	*Lathyrus palustris*
Marsh St. John's wort	*Hypericum elodes*
Marsh valerian	*Valeriana dioica*
Meadowsweet	*Filipendula ulmaria*
Milk parsley	*Peucedanum palustre*
Narrow leaved marsh orchid	*Dactylorhiza traunsteineroides*
Oak	*Quercus robur and Q. petraea*
Osier	*Salix viminalis*
Purple loosestrife	*Lythrum salicaria*
Purple moorgrass	*Molinia caerulea*
Ragged robin	*Lychnis flos-cuculi*
Reedmace	*Typha latifolia*
Reed canarygrass	*Phalaris arundinacea*
Reed sweetgrass	*Glyceria maxima*
Round leaved sundew	*Drosera rotundifolia*
Rowan	*Sorbus aucuparia*
Saw sedge	*Cladium mariscus*
Scots pine	*Pinus sylvestris*
Slender sedge	*Carex lasiocarpa*
Soft rush	*Juncus effusus*
Stinging nettles	*Urtica dioica*
Tufted sedge	*Carex elata*
Water horsetail	*Equisetum fluviatile*
Whitebeak sedge	*Rhynchospora alba*
Willow	*Salix spp.*
Yellow iris	*Iris pseudacorus*
Yellow loosestrife	*Lysimachia vulgaris*

Table 1 – Mammal species associated with fens

Name	Scientific name	Protection in law / policy	Preferred habitat
Water Vole	*Arvicola terrestris*	Wildlife & Countryside Act (full protection) UKBAP Priority Species	Prefers sites with wide swathes of riparian vegetation, both growing from the banks and from the water. Banks of earth or silt-shored banks and slow flowing, relatively deep water (over 1m depth) that are not over shaded by trees are also preferred.
Water Shrew	*Neomys fodiens*	Wildlife & Countryside Act (full protection)	Found along the banks of fast and slow-flowing rivers and streams, static water such as canals, ponds, lakes and ditches and in fen, marsh and reed-beds.
Harvest Mouse	*Micromys minuta*	UKBAP Priority Species	Tall, dense grassy vegetation such as reedbeds, rushes and ditches
Otter	*Lutra lutra*	Conservation Regulations Wildlife & Countryside Act (full protection) UKBAP Priority Species	Still (lochs, lakes, ditches, gravel pits) and running (rivers, streams) freshwater systems, coastal saline systems. In addition to rivers and coastlines the following can be important for breeding, feeding and resting: (Environment Agency, 1999) Mature broadleaved woodland Scrub and other tall bankside vegetation Reedbed, sedge beds and willow carr Small streams, ditches and dykes Vegetated mid-channel islands
Bats		Conservation Regulations (all UK species) Wildlife & Countryside Act (all UK species) (full protection) UKBAP Priority Species (Barbastelle, Bechstein's, Noctule, Brown Long-eared, Soprano Pipistrelle Greater Horseshoe and Lesser Horseshoe)	Fens, rivers and open water are often important foraging habitats for bats. Linear features (particularly hedgerows) and edge habitats (e.g. woodland edges) can be important commuting and foraging routes. Roosts may occur in trees and buildings on sites. Daubenton's Bat has particular association with foraging over aquatic habitats

Table 2 – Bird species associated with fen habitats

Name	Scientific name	Period of occurrence in the UK[1]	Protection in law and policy[2]	Preferred habitat features and season of use[1]
Mute Swan	*Cygnus olor*	All year		Vegetated margins of open water bodies The species shows a preference for waterbodies where there are extensive shallows with much floating, bottom, and emergent vegetation.
Garganey	*Anas querquedula*	Mar-Sep	Sch 1; Sch1(NI)	Vegetated margins of open water bodies Favours narrow or well compartmented, sheltered, and shallow standing fresh waters, merging into grassland, floodland, or other wetland, with plenty of floating and emergent vegetation, but not too tall or dense, unbroken, fringing cover.
Dabbling Duck e.g. Mallard Teal Wigeon Pintail	*Anas platyrhynchos Anas crecca Anas penelope Anas acuta*	All year Significantly greater numbers in the non-breeding season Aug-Apr		Vegetated margins of open water bodies Grazed or cut fen in floodplain Most species prefer waterbodies with more or less dense fringing vegetation, with ready access to secure and sheltered resting places. The waterbodies may be small pools or shallow sheltered parts of much larger open waters. Some species, e.g. Wigeon, do prefer much more open landscapes e.g. tracts of flooded grassland across which to forage. When breeding and in the flightless stage of post-breeding moult, birds seek the protection afforded by dense marginal or emergent vegetation and swamps with little open water.
Diving Waterbirds e.g. Tufted Duck Pochard Coot	*Aythya fuligula Aythya ferina Fulica atra*	All year Significantly greater numbers in the non-breeding season Aug-Apr		Vegetated margins of open water bodies In the non-breeding season, favour shallow open waterbodies where they forage upon submerged aquatic resources, plant and animal matter. Most species will tolerate fairly restricted open waters with dense marginal vegetation. Breeds at similar sites where nests are located over shallow water or on ground never far from water; usually in thick cover.
Great Crested Grebe	*Podiceps cristatus*	All year		Vegetated margins of open water bodies Prefers open standing waters usually 0.5–5 m deep. When breeding, prefers ample, but not too dense, emergent aquatic vegetation, especially fringing, with some submerged bottom cover and limited floating growth. On large sheets of water, prefers shallow sheltered bays with islets or fronting reedbeds.
Little Grebe	*Tachybaptus ruficollis*	All year		Vegetated margins of open water bodies A preference is shown for shallow and small waterbodies with muddy bottoms and margins, often with dense growth of submerged aquatic plants. It will tolerate water surfaces covered in extensive floating vegetation so long as diving and swimming is not inhibited. Outside the breeding season, the species preferences extend to more open and exposed waters

Bittern	*Botaurus stellaris*	All year Greater numbers in the non-breeding season Sep - Mar	Ann 1; Sch 1; Sch1(NI); UKBAP	Reedbeds and mixed fen swamp Favours wetland areas or fringes overgrown with tall emergent vegetation, especially reed, giving dense cover close to shallow standing open waters, including small pools and channels. For breeding needs extensive (the majority of birds use reedbeds >20 hectares) undisturbed wet reedbed, with good fish populations.
Grey Heron	*Ardea cinerea*	All year	Sch1(NI)	Vegetated margins of open water bodies Prefers shallow standing or flowing waters, with good fish or amphibian populations. Nests in tall trees.
Little Egret	*Egretta garzetta*	All year	Ann 1	Vegetated margins of open water bodies Prefers shallow standing waters, with good fish or amphibian populations. Nests in trees.
Hen Harrier	*Circus cyaneus*	Oct-Mar	Ann 1; Sch 1; Sch1(NI)	Reedbeds and mixed fen swamp Roosts communally outside the breeding season, in rank ground vegetation in fen, marsh and reedbed areas. Outside the breeding season they forage over fen, marsh and flooded grassland
Marsh Harrier	*Circus aeruginosus*	All year Greater numbers in breeding season Mar-Aug	Ann 1; Sch 1; Sch1(NI)	Reedbeds and mixed fen swamp Roosts communally outside the breeding season, in rank ground vegetation in fen, marsh and reedbed areas. In both summer and winter, the species forages over reedbeds, fen, marsh and flooded grassland. Nests are normally in reedbeds, in other wetlands with tall emergent vegetation and few or no trees. The reedbeds or wetlands can be extensive, or small (less than 1 ha in size).
Water Rail	*Rallus aquaticus*	All year		Reedbeds and mixed fen swamp Favours a composite of fresh water, flat, usually muddy ground, and dense, fairly tall aquatic vegetation. The mosaic of habitat is further enhanced by the close proximity of trees such as willow or other fringing scrub, and of drier patches.
Spotted Crake	*Porzana porzana*	Apr-Oct	Ann 1; Sch 1	Reedbeds and mixed fen swamp Usually found in fairly extensive wetlands, including floodlands, with very shallow fresh water, not oligotrophic, interspersed with ample stands of low plant cover.
Moorhen	*Gallinula chloropus*	All year		Vegetated margins of open water bodies Prefers waters sheltered by woodland or tall emergent plants, and most with small open waterbodies
Common Crane	*Grus grus*	All year	Ann 1	Reedbeds and mixed fen swamp Breeds in open, swamp areas, where the adults have a good all round view, within a reed and fen mosaic. Outside the breeding season also uses floodplain wetlands and agricultural land.

Waders e.g. Lapwing Redshank Curlew Common Snipe Black-tailed Godwit	*Vanellus vanellus* *Tringa totanus* *Numenius arguata* *Gallinago gallinago* *Limosa limosa*	All year Greater numbers in the non-breeding season	UKBAP UKBAP Sch 1; Sch1(NI); UKBAP	Grazed or cut fen in floodplain Outside the breeding season typically frequents open wet ground such as water-meadows, washes, marshy edges of waterbodies. Breed in wet grasslands e.g. flood meadows where grazing and/or hay cutting means the vegetation is relatively short at the beginning of the breeding season. Common Snipe will use taller fen and marsh particularly outside the breeding season.
Short-eared Owl	*Asio flammeus*	All year	Ann 1; Sch1(NI)	Grazed or cut fen in floodplain Occurs in this habitat outside the breeding season hunting for small mammals over unflooded areas where grazing or cutting means that the vegetation is short.
Long-eared Owl	*Asio otus*	All year	Sch1(NI)	High marsh and carr Nests in taller scrub and trees hunting small mammals in the breeding season and switching to roosting birds in the winter.
Kingfisher	*Alcedo atthis*	All year	Ann 1; Sch 1; Sch1(NI)	Vegetated margins of open water bodies Require relatively shallow and slow-moving freshwater, with abundant small fish population on which to feed, and vertical banks of fairly soft material where they can excavate their nesting burrows.
Cetti's Warbler	*Cettia cetti*	All year	Sch 1	High marsh and carr Reedbeds and mixed fen swamp Typically associated with tangled low woody and mixed vegetation such as young willow or alder carr. Habitat often flanks water. The species shows a preference for vegetation that is providing cover over exposed bare mud and suitable for foraging, than that which emerges from water. Where areas of reedbed are inhabited, the species prefers those areas with some scrub.
Savi's Warbler	*Locustella luscinioides*	Apr-Sep	Sch 1; UKBAP	Reedbeds and mixed fen swamp Occurs in larger, wet reedbeds adjoining sedge beds.
Reed Warbler	*Acrocephalus scirpaceus*	Apr-Sep	Sch1(NI)	Reedbeds and mixed fen swamp Favours breeding within stands of reeds that may be small in area. This includes stands of reed fringing waterbodies or in narrow lines along ditches. Breeding and passage birds regularly forage in other vegetation adjacent to reedbeds, such as scrub and carr.
Sedge Warbler	*Acrocephalus choenobaenus*	Apr-Sep		Mixed fen swamp Typically breeds in low dense vegetation, usually avoiding reedbeds in standing water and the presence of trees and tall bushes.
Aquatic Warbler	*Acrocephalus paludicola*	Aug-Sep	Ann 1; UKBAP	Reedbeds and mixed fen swamp Occurs in south and west England on autumn passage and on some sites particularly favours Schoenoplectus dominated areas.

Grasshopper Warbler	*Locustella naevia*	Apr-Aug	UKBAP	Reedbeds and mixed fen swamp High marsh and carr When breeding in wetlands, favours fens, marshy or boggy rough grassland and reedbeds with some bushes
Bearded Tit	*Panurus biarmicus*	All year	Sch 1; Sch1(NI)	Reedbeds and mixed fen swamp Typically found in reed growing by or often in fresh water (including along ditches with a wide reed margin), or immediately adjoining marshes and swamps. Nests where there is a dense litter layer in the reedbed. Outside the breeding season disperses to a larger number of reed dominated sites.
Willow Tit	*Poecile montanus*	All year	UKBAP	High marsh and carr Nests in a hole that it excavates in soft, rotten wood (frequently willow) feeding amongst scrub and wet woodland.
Yellow Wagtail	*Motacilla flava*	Apr-Sep	UKBAP; Sch1(NI)	Grazed or cut fen in floodplain Breeds in open habitats that are grazed or cut for hay, showing a preference for grazed areas as the livestock increase the availability of insect prey. When on autumn passage, it will roost communally in reedbeds.
Reed Bunting	*Emberiza schoeniclus*	All year	UKBAP	Reedbeds and mixed fen swamp High marsh and carr. Favours tall herbage and small shrubs found in marshy and swampy areas bordering water, wet meadows and reedbeds. Outside the breeding season roosts communally in reed and sedge beds.
Passerines Species that roost in fens in the non-breeding season: Swallow Sand Martin Pied Wagtail Starling Corn bunting	*Hirundo rustica* *Riparia riparia* *Motacilla alba* *Sturnus vulgaris* *Emberiza calandra*	Apr-Oct Mar-Sep All year All year All year	UKBAP UKBAP; Sch1(NI)	Reedbeds and mixed fen swamp These species roost communally in reedbeds. Swallow and Sand Martin do so when on autumn passage. The resident species, Pied Wagtail, Starling and Corn Bunting, do so in winter.

[1]The information used is from Cramp (1977-1993), Hardey et al. (2006) and UK BAP species action plans www.ukbap.org.uk

[2]All wild birds are protected by the Wildlife and Countryside Act or its Northern Ireland equivalent, the Wildlife (Northern Ireland) Order 1985

Abbreviations used:

Annex 1 – listed on Annex 1 of the Wild Birds Directive

Sch 1 – listed on Schedule 1 of the W&CAct

Sch 1(NI) – listed on Schedule 1 of the Wildlife (Northern Ireland) Order 1985 as amended by the Wildlife (Amendment) (Northern Ireland) Order 1995

UKBAP – listed as a high priority species in the UK Biodiversity Action Plan

References

Cramp, S. (Ed.) 1977-1993. The Birds of the Western Palaearctic. Oxford University Press, Oxford.

Hardey, J., Crick, H., Wernham, C., Riley, H., Etheridge, B. and Thompson, D. 2006. Raptors: A Field Guide to Survey and Monitoring. Stationery Office (TSO) Scotland.

Table 3 – Amphibians associated with fens

Name	Scientific name	Protection in law / policy	Preferred habitat
Great crested newt	*Triturus cristatus*	Conservation Regulations Wildlife & Countryside Act (full protection) UKBAP Priority Species	Ponds of all sizes, usually devoid of fish and with plenty of weed cover, adjacent to rough grassland, scrub and/or woodland.
Palmate & smooth newt	*Lissotriton helveticus Lissotriton vulgaris*	Wildlife & Countryside Act (protection from sale only)	Full range of water bodies. Fish and occasional drying out of the water body can be tolerated to a certain degree but predation on larvae by fish is still a significant factor. Landscapes dominated by rough grassland contain the highest proportion of breeding sites occupied by Smooth Newts. The distributions of the two species overlap. Palmate Newts have a more western and northern distribution and as a consequence tend to be found more in upland habitats than Smooth Newts. Palmate newts are more tolerant than Smooth Newts of low pH water.
Common toad	*Bufo bufo*	Wildlife & Countryside Act (protection from sale only) UKBAP Priority Species	Preferred habitats include rough grassland, scrub and open woodland. Within these areas large permanent water bodies are generally required. Optimum pond size is around 1000 square metres, with a good cover of emergent and submerged vegetation. Seem to prefer fish ponds as breeding sites which may possibly be attributable to the lack of competition from Common frogs.
Common frog	*Rana temporaria*	Wildlife & Countryside Act (protection from sale only)	Breed in the shallows of a full range of water body sizes. They tend to use small (<100m2) un-shaded ponds with some emergent and submerged vegetation and are also tolerant of fish. Warm spawning sites are more important than the size or shape of the water body. Permanent water bodies are favoured, particularly as frogs hibernate in ponds
Pool frog	*Rana lessonae*	Conservation Regulations UKBAP Priority Species	The last known native population in the UK (which died out in the late 1990s) occurred in Norfolk in a pingo. These pingos form a series of small but usually permanent ponds with little shade and abundant growths of water plants. The surrounding terrestrial habitat is a mixture of open grazed pasture, scrub and open woodland. A population was reintroduced in Norfolk in 2005, and further reintroductions have since taken place. Pool frogs in Sweden form a meta-population with an unpredictable cycle of local extinction and recolonisation. Populations which become isolated (i.e. with no other ponds within 1km) are likely to become extinct.

Table 4 – Fish species associated with fens

Common Name	Scientific Name	Freshwater Habitat	Distribution
European eel	*Anguilla anguilla*	All freshwater habitats	Widespread
Silver bream	*Abramis bjoerkna*	Turbid, slow-flowing, enriched lowland rivers, associated drains and canals	East Midlands and east Yorkshire
Common bream	*Abramis brama*	Characteristic of nutrient rich, lowland lakes and slow-flowing rivers with a clay/mud bottom	Widespread in England generally absent from Scotland, much of Wales and the extreme southwest of England
Bleak	*Alburnus alburnus*	Found in the associated drains and backwaters of larger rivers	Native to the river systems of the Humber and the Wash and Thames but have been introduced to other river systems
Crucian carp	*Carassius carassius*	Small, rich ponds and lakes	Possibly native to south-east England, introduced elsewhere
Gudgeon	*Gobio gobio*	Moderately fast flowing streams to slow-flowing lowland rivers. Also in large lakes, reservoirs and gravel pits	Widespread in England, absent from parts of Scotland and Wales
Roach	*Rutilus rutilus*	Lowland rivers and still waters, particularly tolerant of poor water quality in intensively managed catchments	Widespread
Rudd	*Scardinius erythrophthalmus*	Slow-flowing rivers, lakes and ponds with abundant submerged vegetation	Widespread
Tench	*Tinca tinca*	Slow-flowing, lowland rivers and still waters	Throughout much of Southern Britain, absent from upland areas of Wales and much of Scotland
Spined loach	*Cobitis taenia*	Variety of micro-habitats within shallow rivers and streams, drains, ditches and some shallow lakes. Common factor is presence of fine silt/sand as a substrate.	Occurs naturally in 5 main river catchments in the east of England; The Rivers Trent, Welland, Witham, Nene and Great Ouse.
Pike	*Esox lucius*	Thrives in many different waters, from lakes, canals and slow-flowing rivers and streams	Widespread, absent from northern Scotland.

Three-spined stickleback	*Gasterosteus aculeatus*	All types of water bodies, except rivers with swift currents	Widespread
Nine-spined stickleback	*Pungitius pungitius*	All types of water bodies, except rivers with swift currents	Widespread
Ruffe	*Gymnocephalus cernuus*	Wide range of freshwater habitats but absent from small ponds and fast-flowing rivers	Formerly confined to the catchments of English Lowland rivers draining to the North Sea, but has been introduced westwards and northwards.
Perch	*Perca fluviatilis*	Still-water and fast-flowing water	Widespread

The criteria for selecting species for the table were:
-   Species which require, fast flowing, well oxygenated water were not included.
-   Species present in remote lochs, i.e. vendace were not included.
-   Species which can and/or prefer lowland rivers, drains, slow flowing; turbid, low oxygen concentration and still water bodies were included.
-   Species which can survive in still waters, but need fast-flowing streams to breed, i.e. Barbel were not included.
-   Non-native species, such as zander were not included.

Spined loach is listed on Annex II of the Habitats Directive, but none of the species in Table 4 receive legal protection or are UKBAP Priority Species.

Table 5 – Legally protected invertebrate species possibly occurring in fen habitats

Name	Scientific name	Protection in law	Preferred habitat
Lesser whirlpool ramshorn	*Anisus vorticulus*	Conservation Regulations Wildlife & Countryside Act (full protection) UKBAP Priority Species	Unshaded ditches and drains with a rich flora; a species of drains in grazing levels rather than fens, but may be fen-associated
Narrow-mouthed whorl snail	*Vertigo angustior*	Conservation Regulations (SAC designations only)	Unshaded short vegetation on marshy ground of high, even humidity, subject neither to periodic desiccation nor to deep or prolonged flooding
Desmoulin's whorl snail	*Vertigo moulinsiana*	Conservation Regulations (SAC designations only)	Tall wetland vegetation, chiefly beds of grasses or sedges, growing on wet, but not deeply flooded, ground
Medicinal leech	*Hirudo medicinalis*	Wildlife & Countryside Act (full protection)	Lakes or ponds with dense stands of water plants; remaining British populations are essentially randomly scattered chance survivals
White-clawed crayfish	*Austropotamobius pallipes*	Conservation Regulations (SAC designations only) Wildlife & Countryside Act (taking and sale only)	Streams and rivers; peripheral to fen habitat, but potentially closely associated with fens
Southern damselfly	*Coenagrion mercuriale*	Conservation Regulations (SAC designations only) Wildlife & Countryside Act (full protection)	Shallow, slow-flowing, unshaded, base-rich runnels and streams
Norfolk hawker	*Aeshna isosceles*	Wildlife & Countryside Act (full protection)	Well-vegetated unshaded drainage ditches; a species of grazing marshes rather than fens, but its drains may be fen-associated
Mole cricket	*Gryllotalpa gryllotalpa*	Wildlife & Countryside Act (full protection)	Exact requirements uncertain. No recent records
Lesser silver water beetle	*Hydrochara caraboides*	Wildlife & Countryside Act (full protection)	Well-vegetated unshaded ditches and ponds; recent records are from grazing levels ditches and from field ponds, but older records are from fens and ditches may be fen-associated
Marsh fritillary	*Eurodryas aurinia*	Conservation Regulations (SAC designations only) Wildlife & Countryside Act (full protection)	Grazed grassland with varied structure including large stands of devil's-bit scabious (Succisa pratensis); able to live in a range of grassland types provided these requirements are met, and intolerant of very wet conditions
Swallowtail butterfly	*Papilio machaon britannicus*	Wildlife & Countryside Act (full protection)	Tall herbaceous fen vegetation with abundant Cambridge milk-parsley (Peucedanumm palustre)
Fen raft-spider	*Dolomedes plantarius*	Wildlife & Countryside Act (full protection)	Small pools with overhanging coarse herbaceous vegetation; also known from grazing marsh drains

Appendix IV – NVC fen communities

Approximate range of environmental variables in five descriptive categories

	Very low	Low	Moderate	High	Very high
pH (water)	<5	5-6	6-6.6	6.7-7.1	>7.1
Bicarbonate (mg/l) (water)	<105	106-250	251-369	370-460	>460
Calcium (mg/l/) (peat)	<620	621-1200	1200-2000	2000-3000	>3000
Water depth (cm)	<-25	-25 - -10	-9 - -1	1 – 9	> +9

Source: *Fojt. W.J. (1989), CSD Note No. 45 Quick reference to Fen Vegetation Communities.*

Community	Description Figures in brackets represent mean species per 2 x 2 m quadrat	Habitat conditions and range
Topogenous fens		
S24 Phragmites australis – Peucedanum palustre fen (Peucedanum-Phragmitetum australis p.p. and caricetum paniculatae peucedanetosum)	Composed of tall monocotyledons (e.g. *Phragmites* and *Cladium*) and herbaceous dicotyledons with a lower layer of sedges and rushes and a patchy bryophyte layer. Generally species rich (24)	Associated with flood-plain fens in England, especially in Broadland, where it occupies an intermediate zone between swamp and carr. pH, bicarbonate and calcium all moderate (pH 5-5-6.9). Mean water levels are low, though winter flooding occurs. Fertility is moderate. S24f is particularly low, whilst S24b is higher.
S25 Phragmites australis – Eupatorium cannabinum fen (Angelico-Phragmitetum australis)	Characterised by tall monocotyledons and dicotyledons with variable amounts of small herbs and sedges. Less species-rich than S24 (11)	Found in flood-plain fens, open water transitions and sump areas of valley mires in England and Wales. Generally associated with calcareous, base-rich water and moderately eutrophic (either natural or caused by disturbance). Mean water table levels generally low, though higher than in S24.
S26 Phragmites australis – Urtica dioica fen	Generally dominated by *P. australis* and *U. dioica* but associates are variable. Generally species poor (9).	Associated with eutrophic, neutral to slightly basic water margins throughout the lowlands where winter flooding and summer drying occur. Also found in coastal reed-beds and flood-plains which have been disturbed.
S27 Carex rostrata – Potentilla palustris fen (Potentillo-Caricetum rostratae)	C. rostrata may or may not be dominant but *P. palustris* and *Menyanthes trifoliata* are constant. Species poor (5).	Almost exclusively a topogenous community in basin and flood-plain mires and may occur as a floating mat. Generally water levels are continuously high. pH, bicarbonate and calcium levels are low for rich fen communities. Fertility levels are high.
S28 Phalaris arundinacea fen	*P. arundinacea* is usually dominant, though associates are variable. Species poor (8)	Typical of circumneutral, mesotrophic to eutrophic waters or substrates. Marking the upper limit of water fluctuations in open water transition, flood-plain and basin fens and on stream-sides, especially where enrichment has occurred. Widespread and common throughout the lowlands and upland margins.
M4 Carex rostrata – Sphagnum recurvum mire	See soligenous fens (below)	
M5 Carex rostrata – Sphagnum squarrosum mire	Sedges and scattered poor fen herbs over a carpet of base-tolerant Sphagna. Of medium species-richness (17)	May occur as a floating raft in topogenous and even soligenous fens which are mildly acid or moderately calcareous but oligotrophic. The two main habitats where it is found are in open water transition and flood-plain fens and where a soligenous influx ameliorates an acid environment. Water levels are usually high. Fairly local, mainly in the north-west of Britain.
M8 Carex rostrata – Sphagnum warnstorfii mire	Dominant cover of sedges over an extensive carpet of base-tolerant Sphagna and herbs. Species-rich (36). May be found within montane grassland and below M19 mire.	Strictly confined to waterlogged montane hollows where moderate base-enrichment by drainage from calcareous rocks occurs, mainly in the central Highlands. Water tables are high and stagnant.

Community	Description Figures in brackets represent mean species per 2 x 2 m quadrat	Habitat conditions and range
M9 Carex rostrata – Calliergon cuspidatum mire (Acrocladio – Caricetum diandrae p.p. and Peucadano – Phragmitetum caricetosum p.p.)	Medium to tall fen vegetation, often species-rich, typically dominated by species such as *C. rostrata*, *C. diandra*, *C. lasiocarpa* and *Eriophorum angustifolium*. Sometimes there is patchy *Cladium* and/or *Phragmites*. Bryophytes, particularly *Calliergon* species, are conspicuous. Species-richness very variable (25).	In northern and western Britain mainly associated with basin fens, whilst in the south often hydroseral within flood-plain or even valley fens (but usually associated with topogenous hollows). Calcium and bicarbonate values are usually low and pH moderate. Mean water level is high. Low fertilities are associated with optimal community development.
Swamp communities		
S1 Carex elata swamp	Vegetation dominated by *C. elata* tussocks with some taller herbaceous dicotyledons. Generally species poor (12). Found with S2 and S27.	Associated with open water transitions, mesotrophic to eutrophic, shallow pools and turf cuttings, only in west Norfolk, Cumbria and Anglesey. pH range 5.5 – 7.2 (Norfolk). Water levels up to +40cm.
S2 Cladium mariscus swamp and sedge-beds (Cladietum marisci)	*Cladium* dominated vegetation. Pure stands common and no other species frequent. Species poor (7). Associated with S1and S4 in East Anglia and S27 in NW England.	Found in open water transition, flood-plain and especially basin fens. Usually calcareous and base-rich. Shallow standing water tables. Tolerant of the range -15 to +40cm. Local including Anglesey, Norfolk, Cheshire and Cumbria.
S3 Carex paniculata swamp (Caricetum paniculatae typicum)	Dominated by C. paniculata tussocks. Species poor (8). Associated with S4 and S13.	Found in open water transition, flood-plain and basin fens and in peat-cuttings. Generally base-rich and calcareous (71-74 mg/l). pH range 7.1-8.1, mesotrophic to eutrophic. Able to tolerate a degree of seasonal water table movement. Widespread but local.
S4 Phragmites australis swamp and reed-beds	*P. australis* dominant. Generally species poor (3) though variable e.g. *Galium palustre* sub-community richer.	Widespread in open water transition and flood-plain fens, usually in hydroseral situations. Management extends the community into drier situations but water regimes can be variable. No strict substrate preferences.
S5 Glyceria maxima swamp	Species-poor vegetation (4) dominated by G. maxima with a variable range of associates e.g. *Epilobrium hirsutum*, *Filipendula ulmaria*, *Solanum dulcamara*. In open water transitions it may occur between S14 and S28 and landward of S4.	Mainly found in flood-plain fens (though not confined to fens), often on substrates containing a substantial mineral component e.g. mineral alluvium. May develop as a floating raft. Mean values of pH, bicarbonate and calcium are high, though variable. Water table levels have a low mean value. Associated with eutrophic, fertile conditions particularly with high phosphate levels. Widespread in the lowlands, but of very restricted occurrence in Wales.
S6 Carex riparia swamp	Large tufts of C. *riparia* dominant, hence stands usually species poor.	Characteristic of margins of standing or slow-moving water in mesotrophic to eutrophic conditions in the agricultural lowlands of England and Wales.
S7 Carex acutiformis swamp	Dominated by C. *acutiformis*. No other species constant. May grade into S24 in flood-plain fens.	Eutrophic margins of slow-moving water.

Community	Description Figures in brackets represent mean species per 2 x 2 m quadrat	Habitat conditions and range
S8 Scirpus lacustris ssp lacustris swamp	Typically with a somewhat open cover of *S. lacustris*	Often occupies the deep water limit of swamp vegetation in mesotrophic to eutrophic waters. Sub-communities are related to water depth and trophic status. Notably uncommon in Broadland.
S9 Carex rostrata swamp	*C. rostrata* dominant, with no other species in abundance. Generally species-poor (6). May grade into S27. May occur in mires, grading into M3 pools.	Found in mesotrophic to oligotrophic waters of moderate depth, mainly in the north and west. Pure stands often found in deepest waters.
S10 Equisetum fluvitile swamp	Most abundant species is *E. fluviatile*. Stands generally species poor (6). May grade into S9.	May form a floating raft or occur on mineral substrates. Generally associated with open water transitions in the north and west, mesotrophic to oligotrophic in character, shallow to moderately deep.
S11 Carex vesicaria swamp	S11a *C. vesicaria* sub-community can be almost pure, but a variety of associates occur in the other sub-communities. Associated with slow-moving water landward of S9.	Pure stands are found in deeper water, but mixed stands in slightly drier situations as well as wetter areas. Mainly in Scotland, south of the Great Glen.
S12 Typha latifolia swamp	*T. latifolia* dominant and stands are often species-poor (4). May be associated with S9 and grade landward into S25b.	Widespread through the agricultural lowlands of England but less common in Wales and Scotland. Sub-communities S12b and S12c are found in shallower water with little annual fluctuation, S12a in deeper water with some fluctuation and S12d in deeper water with more stable levels. Waters tend to be mesotrophic to eutrophic.
S13 Typha angustifolia swamp	Dominated by *T. angustifolia*. Species poor (4). May give way to S14 in shallower water.	Found in standing or slow-moving water on silt, neutral to basic. Scattered distribution in England, becoming rare in Wales and to the north.
S14 Spaganium erectum swamp	*S. erectum* generally dominant, but associates can be important.	Very common in shallow mesotrophic to eutrophic water on a mineral substrate and found both in pools and alongside streams and rivers throughout the agricultural lowlands.
S15 Acorus calamus swamp	*A. calamus* may form an open or closed cover. Species poor (6).	Occurs in standing or slow-moving water 20-80 cm deep. Substrate usually silt or clay. pH range 5.7-7.2 Scattered through the English lowlands.
S16 Sagittaria sagittifolia swamp	*S. sagittifolia* dominant and other species usually only occasional.	Most characteristic of moderately deep eutrophic waters and soft silty substrates. Water standing or slow-flowing. Scattered through the southern and central English lowlands.

Community	Description Figures in brackets represent mean species per 2 x 2 m quadrat	Habitat conditions and range
S17 Carex pseudocyperus swamp	Can form almost pure stands or be intermixed with other emergents. May be adjacent to S4 or associated with S24.	Most typical of shallow, mesotrophic to eutrophic, standing or sluggish water. Patchily distributed in the English lowlands and most characteristic of the Midlands.
S18 Carex obstrubae swamp	*C. otrubuae* forms a generally patchy cover and there can be a great variety of associates e.g. Juncus effusus and tall herbs, but most not frequent.	Characteristic of clayey margins of standing or slow-moving, moderately eutrophic waters in the English and Welsh lowlands.
S19 Eleocharis palustris swamp	Dominated by *E. palustris* with few other species frequent. Generally species poor (7).	Found in a wide variety of sites, often over silt, in mesotrophic to eutrophic, standing or running water throughout Britain.
S20 Scirpus lacustris swamp	*S. lacustris ssp tabernaemontani* dominates, with a variety of saltmarsh species and species of disturbed and/or moist soils	Found most frequently in moist, brackish sites with soft gleys of silt or clay.
S22 Glyceria fluitans swamp	*G. fluitans* occurs as a low mat or floating carpet. Generally species poor (5).	Characteristic of shallow, standing or slow-moving water on a mineral substrate in the agricultural lowlands.
M4 Carex rostrata – Sphagnum recurvum mire	Usually cover of sedges (mainly *C. rostrata*) over a carpet of semi-aquatic Sphagna with few other associates. Rather species poor (10). Regarded as poor fen.	Often found along water-tracks within or around raised and blanket mires in the north and west. pH usually around 4. Water levels high and may form semi-floating carpet.
M6 Carex echinata – Sphagnum recurvum/auriculatum mire	Small sedges or rushes dominate over a carpet of more oligotrophic Sphagna with a variable contribution from higher plants. Of medium species richness (17). Regarded as poor fen.	Associated with slopes within M17 and M19 mire systems and overall mineral ground, virtually ubiquitously in the upland fringes. Mainly on peats and peaty gleys irrigated by rather base-poor but not excessively oligotrophic water. Water tables are high. pH 4.5-5.5. Calcium and bicarbonate levels low.
M7 Carex curta – Sphagnum russowii mire	*Cyperaceous* plants dominate over a Sphagnum carpet. Associated herb and grass species limited. Of medium species richness (17). Regarded as poor fen.	Found in hollows and drainage channels in M19 blanket mire and flushes in montane moss heaths at high altitudes (higher than 650m) in the Scottish Highlands. On moist peats irrigated by nutrient-poor water.
M10 Carex diocia – Pinguiculum vulgaris mire (Pinguiculo – Caricetum diociae and Schoenus ferrugineus stands)	In general a low-growing small sedge community. *Schoneus* and *Molinia* may be present. Moderate to high species richness (25). May be associated with a wide variety of peripheral communities.	Mainly occurs in small, often isolated spring fens, though larger stands occur if springs amalgamate to form a flushed slope. Occurs on a wide range of soils, usually not peaty. Bedrock often limestone. pH and calcium levels high (similar to M13) but bicarbonate values are moderate (less than for M13). Water levels moderate, redox high. Fertility levels low. Widespread but local throughout northern England and Scotland, with fragmentary, often rather impoverished stands in Wales and the Midlands.

Community	Description Figures in brackets represent mean species per 2 x 2 m quadrat	Habitat conditions and range
M11 Carex demissa – Saxifraga aizoides mire (Schoenus ferrugineus stands)	This open community containing a rich mixture of small sedges and herbs with many bryophytes occurs among water-scoured runnels. Usually no single vascular plant dominant. Generally species-rich (26). Grades into M37 at spring heads and may also pass into M10	Largely confined to high altitudes in Scotland (though at sea level in far NW Scotland) irrigated with moderately base-rich water on generally steep slopes. Also locally in northern England and North Wales.
M12 Carex saxatilis mire	Short, open sedge sward with sparse herbs and usually low cover of individual bryophytes apart from *Scorpidium cossonii*. Species rich (26).	Confined to margins of high altitude base-rich and calcareous flushes in the Scottish Highlands, with pH 4-6 – 6.3. Probably influenced by long snow-lie.
M13 Schoenus nigricans – Juncus subnodulosus mire	Vegetation usually distinguished by both *S. nigricans* and *J. subnodulosus* and a wide range of low-growing associates. *Phragmites, Molinia* and sometimes *Cladium* may be important. The community has a high mean species-richness (27). When occurring as a hydroseral stage in turf-cuttings it grades into S24 and S25.	Predominantly found in soligenous mires (valley and spring fens) on a wide range of soil types and geological strata in lowland England and Wales. Usually associated with high base-richness, water pH (6.5-8) and calcium concentration, though high base-richness does not seem to be a prerequisite. Summer water levels range from low to high, though moderate to high levels without stagnation appear to be optimal. Sites have a low productivity.
M14 Schoenus nigricans – Narthecium ossifragum mire	*S. nigricans* usually dominant, with *Molinia* generally abundant and bryophytes variable in cover. Regarded as poor fen.	Characteristic of soligenous zones in valleys on peats or mineral soils irrigated by only moderately base-rich and slightly calcareous water. pH 5-6. Calcium levels 5-35 mg/l. So far recorded from SW England and West Norfolk.
M17 Scirpus cespitosus – Eriophorum vaginatum blanket mire	Dominated by mixtures of monocotyledons, ericoid sub-shrubs and Sphagna.	Occupies valley mires as well as forming extensive blanket mire in north-west Britain. Water table levels high, pH usually not much above 4 and often less.
M21 Narthecium ossifragum – Sphagnum papillosum valley mire	Carpets of Sphagna are characteristic with scattered herbs and sub-shrubs. Medium species rich (14). Associated with M29 water-tracks and M14 flushed zones and often grades into M16 wet heath. Regarded as poor fen.	Local community of permanently waterlogged acid, oligotrophic peats in the lowlands of England and Wales, mainly in the south. Waters base-poor and nutrient-poor, with pH 3.4-6.8. Peat depths often quite shallow (20-150cm).
M29 Hypericum elodes – Potamogeton polygonifolius soakway	*H. elodes* and *P. polygonifolius* (single or jointly) may form floating mats on water in runnels and pools. Other higher plants and bryophytes have variable presence. Regarded as poor fen.	Found within M21 valley mires and wet heath/mire transitions. Waters moderately acid to neutral (4-5.5). Calcium concentrations are probably low. Water levels said to be fluctuating, though situations always wet. So far known from west Surrey to Cornwall and through Wales to Galloway.

Community	Description Figures in brackets represent mean species per 2 x 2 m quadrat	Habitat conditions and range
M31 Anthelia julacea – Sphagnum auriculatum spring	*A. julacea* forms mounds, with tufts of *Deschampsia cespitosa* frequent. May grade into snow-bed communities at higher altitudes, but also grades into montane grasslands and grass heaths. May form a mosaic with M32.	An upland community associated with oligotrophic spring-heads on skeletal soils on sloping ground in Scotland, the Lake District and Snowdonia.
M32 Philonotis fontana – Saxifraga stellaris spring	*P. fontana* forms swelling mounds around flushes and seepages, with scattered rosettes of *S. stellaris*	An upland community found on flattish, gently sloping areas around spring-heads and flushes in Scotland, the Lake District, Snowdonia and non-calcareous parts of the Pennines.
M33 Pohlia wahlenbergii var. Glacialis spring	*Pohlia* forms spongy carpets dotted with *S. stellaris* and scattered *Deschampsia cespitosa ssp alpina*. May grade into M32.	Strictly confined to spring-heads associated with late snow-beds in the higher reaches of the Highlands.
M34 Carex demissa – Koenigia islandica flush	Open community consisting of a bryophyte carpet with sparse vascular plants.	On flushed skeletal silty and stony soils on the basalt of the Trotternish ridge, Syke.
M35 Ranunculus omiophyllus – Montia Fontana rill	Usually dominated by M. fontana and *R. omiophyllus* with *Sphagnum auriculatum*. May grade into M29.	Found around spring-heads and rills in upland moors mainly in south-western England and Wales.
M36 Communities of shaded lowland springs and stream banks	*Chrysoplenium oppositifolium* and *Pellia epiphylla* prominent.	Found around lowland springs and stream banks in shady positions.
M37 Cratoneuron commutatum–Festuca rubra spring	*Palustriella commutata* and/or *Cratoneuron. filicinum* dominant, with variable vascular species	Marks base-rich and calcareous springs and seepage lines, mainly in montane sites, though similar stands at lower altitudes are known.
M38 Cratoneuron commutatum – Carex nigra spring	*Palustriella commutata* and/or *Cratoneuron. filicinum* dominant, but there is a rich associated flora of bryophytes and vascular plants.	Confined to base-rich, calcareous and oligotrophic montane springs and flushes around Upper Teesdale and in the central Scottish Highlands, where there is sheep and/ or deer grazing.
Fen meadow		
M22 Juncus subnodulosus – Cirsium palustre fen meadow (Rich fen meadows p.p.)	Variable but usually dominated by a range of grasses, rushes (especially *Juncus subnodulosus*) and sedges (e.g. *Carex acutiformis* and *C. disticha*). Species-richness variable. Regarded as rich-fen meadow.	Found in a wide variety of situations both topogenous and soligenous, on various soil types and geology, though usually on chalk or limestone, in England and Wales. Generally pH, bicarbonate and calcium levels are high. Water level variable. Fertility levels moderate. M22c Carex elata sub-community occurs mostly in East Anglia as local small stands in topogenous mires. M22d Iris pseudocorus sub-community somewhat more widespread but still local in England, stands may be larger.

Community	Description Figures in brackets represent mean species per 2 x 2 m quadrat	Habitat conditions and range
M23 Juncus effusus / acutiflorus / Galium palustre rush-pasture	Characterised by both or just one of the rushes with a range of herbs.	Found in both topogenous and soligenous sites on moist, moderately acid to neutral, peaty and mineral soils, mainly in the west of Britain. Characteristic of relatively unimproved or reverted pasture. Small fluctuations in water table can occur, often giving rise to stagnogley soils with pH 4-6. Usually calcium poor.
M24 Molinia caerulea – Cirsium dissectum fen meadow (Cirsio molinietum p.p.)	Almost always dominated by *Molinia*, typically with *Potentilla erecta, Succisa pratensis, C. dissectum* and smaller Carex species and sometimes with *Gymnadenia conopsea*. Species-richness fairly high. Regarded as rich fen meadow.	Often associated with marginal areas of both topogenous and soligenous fens, though not restricted to these systems. Often quite calcareous and base-rich, with pH levels moderate to high. Mean water levels low. Fertility levels very low to low. Widespread but increasingly local in the southern lowlands.
M25 Molinia caerulea – Potentitlla erect mire (Molinia caerulea – Myrica gale community)	Though the community is variable, *Molinia* is usually abundant. Generally species poor, though rushes and a range of herbs are frequent. *Myrica* gale can form a patchy or dense over-canopy.	Tends to be associated with aerated substrates e.g. seepage zones in topogenous and soligenous mire, but generally moist to very wet. Substrates are peat or peaty soils and even brown earths. pH, bicarbonate and calcium levels are variable, but usually very low fertility. Mainly in the west.
M26 Molinia caerulea – Crepis paludosa mire (Carex nigra – Sanguisorba officinialis community)	*Molinia* and often *Carex nigra* form tussocks. Herbs quite frequent, both tall and short-growing species.	A very local community of moist, moderately base-rich and calcareous peats and peaty mineral soils in both topogenous and soligenous mires in the northern Pennines and Lake District. Prefers a degree of substrate aeration even though it may be flooded in winter.
M27 Filipendula ulmaria – Angelica sylvestris mire (Epilobium hirsutum – Filipendula ulmaria community p.p.)	*F. ulmaria* usually dominant and the associated flora is variable and frequently species poor.	Not confined to fens, but here can occur in both topogenous and soligenous situations. Generally found in moist relatively nutrient rich, circumneutral situations protected from grazing, on mineral and organic soils, with seasonal water table fluctuations. Occurs throughout lowland Britain.
M28 Iris pseudacorus – Filipendula ulmaria mire	*I. pseudacorus* and often *Oenanthe crocata* are frequent to dominant, with scattered *F. ulmaria*. Other tall herbs are found, and rushes and grasses are important in lower tiers.	Confined to moist, nutrient-rich soils along the oceanic seaboard, especially at the upper edges of saltmarshes of sea-lochs of western Scotland.
Fen woodland		
W1 Salix cinerea – Galium palustre woodland	*S. cinerea* dominates the canopy. Ground flora consists of small herbs. May grade into S25 or S26.	Mainly on topogenous sites – flood-plain fens, open water transitions and basin mires, scattered through the lowlands.

Community	Description Figures in brackets represent mean species per 2 x 2 m quadrat	Habitat conditions and range
W2 Salix cinerea – Betula pubescens – Phragmites australis woodland	Canopy of *S. cinerea*, *B. pubescens* and *Alnus glutinosa*. Ground flora related to previous community, from which this has developed.	Found on topogenous sites, particularly flood-plain mires. Most extensive examples in East Anglia and around the Cheshire and Shropshire meres.
W3 Salix pentandra – Carex rostrata woodland	*S. pentandra* and /or *S. cinerea* dominant in the canopy. Field layer quite species-rich, dominated by *Carex rostrata*. May be in a zonation with S27 and M9.	Found on topogenous, base-rich calcareous sites, locally throughout the sub-montane zone of northern Britain but not yet recorded form Wales.
W4 Betula pubescens – Molinia caerulea woodland	*B. pubescens* forms and open canopy. *Molinia* dominates the ground layer and Sphagnum is patchily developed.	Associated with moderately acid peats on a variety of mire types e.g. drying ombrogenous peats and soligenous fens, locally throughout the lowlands and upland fringes.
W5 Alnus glutinosa – Carex paniculata woodland	*A.glutinosa* abundant, with *Salix cinerea*, both often initially rooted in *C. paniculata* tussocks	Found on topogenous usually base-rich mesotrophic to eutrophic sites. W5c is typical of valley-side springs and seepage lines. Local but quite widespread in the English lowlands, with very few localities in Scotland and Wales.
W6 Alnus glutinosa – Urtica dioica woodland	Canopy may be composed of *A. glutinosa*, *Betula pubescens* and/or *Salix* sp. *U. dioica* is constant in the field layer.	Found on topogenous sites – usually flood-plain mires, enriched by silt – widespread but locally in the lowlands

Appendix V – Legal and regulatory considerations for projects involving fens

When planning any project involving fens and other wetland habitats, it is essential to be aware of the legal and planning context and requirements. This needs to be considered very early in the planning stages of any project so that the necessary consents, permits and licences can be secured well in advance. For large and complex schemes a minimum of two years should be allowed for obtaining the necessary permissions.

Initial considerations (as part of the project initiation)

The following questions need to be addressed

- Who owns the land? Is the site freehold or tenanted?

- Are there any existing designations on the site (statutory and non-statutory, for landscape, historic environment, legal rights of way etc)? Are there any other constraints (overhead lines, underground pipes etc)?

- Are there any existing (or potential?) management agreements e.g. agri-environment schemes or planning consents that are already in place?

- Will it be necessary to obtain any consents, licences and permits from relevant statutory agencies and planning authorities for the planned works?

- Are there any flooding or water resource issues, including water supply and discharge consents? Are there any waste management issues e.g. from the need to dispose of excavated material? These are covered by different legislation and different authorities/agencies in England, Wales, Scotland and Northern Ireland and include works in or near a watercourse or floodplain (including the need to undertake a flood risk assessment), water impoundment and abstraction licences/permits and consents to discharge effluent (e.g. from educational facilities).

The following table is intended to provide guidance for those undertaking projects involving fens and other wetland habitats, and summarises who to contact for different issues.

Please note that legislation changes with time. An early approach to the appropriate statutory agencies will save you both time and money. In addition their staff are often able to provide specialised technical advice which will make you project run more smoothly.

Table of Legal and Planning Requirements for Projects involving Fens and Water Resources

Type of Works	Guidance for UK Countries	Organisation to contact
General guidance		
England and Wales	Works to ordinary water courses (including obstructions to flow such as weirs and dams) and works that are in Flood Zones or in, adjacent to, under or over main rivers require Flood Defence Consent from the EA. Maps are held by the EA Works carried out on ordinary water courses in IDB areas require IDB consent. As the best first point of contact, get in touch with your EA Area Biodiversity or Conservation Officer.	EA, IDB
Scotland	The planning process and Controlled Activity Regulations (CAR 2005) controls all works in or near watercourses (ref: Water Environment (**Controlled Activities**) (Scotland) **Regulations 2005**) The Water Environment (Controlled Activities) (Scotland) Regulations 2005	SEPA
Northern Ireland	Works in river channels require consent from the Rivers Agency. Works adjacent to water courses are controlled by the planning process	NIEA
	General Guidance: PPG5 (Pollution Prevention Guidance), published by EA, SEPA and NIEA covers any potential adverse impacts on ground water Environment Agency - Pollution Prevention Guidelines (PPGs)	
River Impoundment		
England and Wales	Impoundment licenses are issued by the EA. See hyperlink http://www.environment-agency.gov.uk/business/topics/water/32020.aspx Flood Defence consent may also be required to build impounding structures such as dams, weirs and sluices.	EA
Scotland	Impoundments require authorisation by SEPA http://www.sepa.org.uk/water/regulations/regimes/impoundment.aspx	SEPA
Northern Ireland	Impoundments require authorisation by NIEA http://www.ni-environment.gov.uk/water-home/water_resources/abstraction.htm	NIEA
Water Abstraction		
England and Wales	Abstraction of >20 cubic metres per day from controlled waters requires an EA licence Environment Agency - Water abstraction	EA
Scotland	Authorisation for all water abstractions under Water Environment (**Controlled Activities**) (Scotland) **Regulations 2005** Authorisation for all water abstractions	SEPA

Type of Works	Guidance for UK Countries	Organisation to contact
Northern Ireland	There is no control of abstraction currently but new legislation is forthcoming and will control abstractions. Common law riparian rights must be respected.	NIEA
Discharge of Effluent		
General Advice	Most clean water fen restoration, re-creation or management schemes will not require a formal consent to discharge. Temporary discharge controls may be required during works being undertaken and advice should be sought from the Regulatory body. EA (England and Wales), SEPA (Scotland), NIEA (Northern Ireland)	
Planning Permission		
Planning Permissions already in place for the site or required for the intended activity.	Existing planning permissions will be registered with the Local Planning Authority. England: County Council, Wales – appropriate Unitary Authority. Scotland - Development Control Authority – the District Authority or Regional or Island Council. Northern Ireland – NIEA	
Waste Management Regulations		
Off-site disposal of soil and waste (for example material generated when lowering land levels)	Off-site disposal of material deemed to be 'waste' needs to be to a licensed site and transported by a registered waste carrier.	EA SEPA NIEA
On-site disposal/ manipulation of waste	On-site disposal or manipulation of waste may require a waste management license. If waste is deposited near a river or on a floodplain, consent from the appropriate agency is required.	EA SEPA NIEA
Changes to land use or landscape		
	Planning permission (from the LPA) may be required if land is taken out of agricultural production, permanent structures are created or erected or the landscape is altered. Special provisions may apply in National Parks – consult the National Park Authority. England: County Council, Wales – appropriate Unitary Authority. Scotland - Development Control Authority – the District Authority or Regional or Island Council. Northern Ireland – NIEA	
Existing Management Agreements		
	This includes agri-environment schemes. Landowners and statutory conservation organisations (NE, SNH, CCW, NIEA, DEFRA) will be able to provide information on land management agreements. Agri-environment schemes differ between UK countries and are reviewed at intervals. Please see statutory conservation organisations websites for up-to date information.	NE CCW SNH NIEA

Type of Works	Guidance for UK Countries	Organisation to contact
Utilities		
	Check site for the presence of gas and water mains, sewerage pipes and electricity cables.	Contact appropriate utilities and companies in your area.
Transport		
	If works are adjacent to a road, the Highways Authority should be contacted and if adjacent to a railway, contact Network Rail If there is an airport in the vicinity, then the issue of bird strike needs to be considered –contact the relevant aviation authority. Wetlands and Bird strike guidance	Network Rail Highways Authority (England) Civil Aviation Authority
Mineral Site Restoration		
England	Guidance is available in the form of Mineral Planning Guidance (MPGs) and Planning Policy Guidance (PPGs)	Mineral Planning Authority (County Council or Unitary Authority)
Wales	Mineral Planning Policy Guidelines (MPPG) provide guidance (National Assembly of Wales)	Mineral Planning Authority (Unitary Authority)
Scotland	National Planning Policy Guidelines (NPPGs) supported by Planning Advice Notes and Circulars	Development Control Authority –Regional or Island Council (one tier areas)
Northern Ireland	Guidance is provided by Planning Policy Statements (PPS) and Development Control Advice Notes (DCANs) but there are none that refer specifically to minerals	NIEA
Protected Species		
Protected wetland species	Some species are protected under European legislation only whilst others are protected under UK legislation. http://www.ccw.gov.uk/landscape--wildlife/habitats--species/species-protection/licensing.aspx http://www.naturalengland.org.uk/ourwork/regulation/wildlife/default.aspx http://www.snh.org.uk/licences/lic-intro.asp	NE CCW SNH NIEA

Useful websites:

Environment Agency
www.environment-agency.gov.uk

Natural England
www.naturalengland.org.uk

Countryside Council for Wales
www.ccw.gov.uk

Scottish Environment Protection Agency
www.sepa.org.uk

Scottish Natural Heritage
www.snh.org.uk

Northern Ireland Environment Agency
www.ni-environment.gov.uk

Key to Abbreviations in Table:

CCW   Countryside Council for Wales
EA   Environment Agency
IDB   Internal Drainage Board
SEPA   Scottish Environment Protection Agency
NE   Natural England
NIEA   Northern Ireland Environment Agency
SNH   Scottish Natural Heritage

Appendix VI – Fen management for bryophytes

In general, favourable management of fens should deliver favourable conditions for fen bryophytes, although there are obvious exceptions when succession has modified the bryophyte flora of a fen and management then impacts on the resulting flora. Ecological change and loss of management appear to be the main causes of the loss of populations of Red Data Book (Church et al, 2001) and UKBAP species from lowland mires in recent years, especially in East Anglia, although whole-scale habitat destruction through drainage is thought to have caused the extinction of three rich-fen mosses including *Paludella squarrosa* in northern England in the late 19th century, and *Meesia triquetra* in Ireland as recently as the 1960s.

Key environmental and management factors for mosses and liverworts

Water chemistry

Bryophytes are highly sensitive to changes in water chemistry. The majority of fen bryophytes require low macro-nutrient (i.e. N, P & K) levels and are intolerant of nutrient enrichment. They vary more in terms of base tolerance, from low base status (poor-fen) species, through neutral water specialists to obligate rich-fen species. It is critical that site managers understand the natural water chemistry of a site and ensure irrigation with nutrient-poor water of suitable base-status.

Kooijman & Bakker (1995) carried out cultivation experiments that showed Sphagnum squarrosum responding to nutrient enrichment more than *S. subnitens*, and *Scorpidium scorpioides* being more tolerant of mineral-rich groundwater than the two sphagna. The common generalist *Calliergonella cuspidata* replaced the fen specialist *S. scorpioides* as nutrient levels rose, and the base-intolerant *Sphagnum squarrosum* replaced *Calliergonella* when inputs of groundwater declined. Such transitions can be observed in situ and may be rapid; sometimes resulting in substantial change in the character of fen features. For example, blocking ditches feeding mineral-rich water into a wetland can lead to the formation of poor-fen (van Wirdum, 1995). Complete competitive exclusions are probably rare (Malson & Rydin, 2009), at least among rich-fen bryophytes, but declines in abundance and vigour can lead to the loss of species to other environmental changes.

Even traditionally managed fens can lose specialist bryophytes because of changes in surrounding land use or atmospheric N deposition (Bergamini et al., 2009): surveys in 1995 and 2006 of 36 traditionally managed fens in Switzerland showed significant losses in fen specialist bryophytes and Red-list plants, and a significant increase in vascular plant biomass. N deposition is implicated in an increase in *Sphagnum fallax* on bogs (Limpens et al., 2003) and clearly has an impact on fens as well. Most of lowland Britain is above the critical threshold for N enrichment of fens (www.apis.ac.uk), making management even more challenging and emphasising the need for restriction of nutrient inputs within the entire catchment of a fen. Grazing or mowing may be needed to remove the competitive vascular plants that develop in response to enrichment. The effects of atmospheric enrichment are often exacerbated by water abstraction (see Case Study 10) and enrichment, as demonstrated by the loss of the UKBAP liverwort *Leiocolea rutheana* from four of its five sites in Norfolk and its decline at the fifth (Church et al., 2001; Swann, 1982).

Hydrology

Changes in hydrological regime can produce unsuitable conditions for key rich-fen mosses. Many experience fluctuating water levels and periodic inundation in the winter, but a rapid or sustained increase in water levels can lead to the loss of species such as *Calliergon giganteum*, which is replaced in deeper, more nutrient-rich water by *C. cordifolium*. Buoyant fen rafts may be more resilient than non-buoyant surfaces, but any rapid change in water levels should be avoided in favour of a gradual rise. Ditch blocking to raise water levels in one part of a fen may divert enriched or chemically unsuitable water on to another part and can have unforeseen consequences on the bryophyte flora.

Management neglect

Hydroseral succession (secondary colonisation), either because of the cessation of management or because of a major environmental change, is often a threat to fen bryophytes, and fen managers need to consider whether natural succession is beneficial to their site or not. For example, the boreal relic rich-fen moss *Tomentypnum nitens* has now been lost to scrub encroachment or vascular plant growth from at least 3 of its 10 Welsh sites (K. Birch, pers. comm.).

On the other hand, localised natural succession may enhance a site, perhaps leading to the reinstatement of ombrotrophic conditions in areas from which they were lost because of past management, but can lead to acidification of areas of rich-fen and consequent loss of specialist bryophytes. Crymlyn Bog in south Wales has experienced multiple successions from fen to raised bog (Hughes & Dumayne-Peaty, 2002), and a vegetation survey in 2009 suggests that part of the east side of this 280 ha complex of fen and swamp is experiencing the start of another succession. Not only is scrub encroaching rapidly, but four species of Sphagnum are locally abundant in communities dominated by *Carex paniculata, Phragmites australis, Typha angustifolia* and *T. latifolia* – combinations not recognised by, for example, Wheeler (1980). The bryophytes being replaced here are either those of neutral fen or rich-fen. This change in species composition can enrich a local flora, for example the arrival of at least six species of *Sphagnum* at Wicken Fen, Cambridgeshire (Preston, 2008) after years of scrub encroachment, reduced winter flooding and, probably, acid rain. A recent focus on maintaining/restoring open fen at Wicken, with consequent scrub clearance, pony grazing and raising of (calcareous) water levels, has caused the loss of several sphagna from their only Cambridgeshire site. Meanwhile, rich-fen mosses such as *Campyliadelphus elodes* were seen in 2008 for the first time since the 1950s.

As always, fen management can have negative impacts as well as positive ones. The alternative would be to allow a complete transition to carr, which might benefit some bryophytes but would undoubtedly cause the loss of other rare species. There is no evidence that the epiphyte flora of British carr is particularly notable, despite its often very high bryophyte biomass, so scrub clearance on fen sites is likely to be of concern only if the ground flora is of note.

Soligenous mires

Soligenous fens are home to the UKBAP liverworts *Barbilophozia kunzeana* and *Jamesoniella undulifolia*, both of which grow in small quantity through base-tolerant sphagna at a handful of sites, for example on the Long Mynd in Shropshire. The scarce temperate form of *Hamatocaulis vernicosus* (Hedenäs & Eldenäs, 2007) is also found primarily in soligenous mires on the upland edge in Wales (Bosanquet et al., 2006) and to a lesser extent in England, Scotland and Ireland. A constant supply of neutral, nutrient-poor water is the main requirement of these species, so management that alters a site's hydrology could have a negative impact on them. The hydrology of sites with *H. vernicosus* is often rather complex: several of its sites in south Wales are in areas where highly calcareous water derived from Carboniferous Limestone over 1 km away spreads on to, or bubbles up through, a peatland, which reduces the pH and provides suitable conditions for *Hamatocaulis*. Quarrying or water abstraction some distance from a flush complex can significantly alter its hydrology. Reduced grazing is currently threatening *Hamatocaulis* on upland-edge commons in Wales, perhaps exacerbated by vigorous vegetation growth because of atmospheric N deposition, and continued light to moderate grazing is necessary to maintain open swards suitable for the notable bryophytes to grow.

Concluding remarks

It needs to be emphasised that our knowledge of the distribution of fen bryophytes remains remarkably patchy. *Paludella squarrosa* was discovered new to Ireland in 1998 (Lockhart, 1999), *Scorpidium turgescens* new to England in 2002 (Porley & Hodgetts, 2005), Leiocolea rutheana new to Scotland in 2001 (Blackstock, 2002), *Sphagnum riparium* new to Wales in 2005 (Jones et al., 2006) and more than five new sites for *Jamesoniella undulifolia* have been found in Cumbria and Shropshire in the last few years. Because of this, it is vital that managers of rich-fens and transition mires get a competent bryologist to survey their site before any dramatic changes in management or hydrology.

Translocation experiments by Malson & Rydin (2007) suggest that it is possible to reintroduce at least some bryophyte species to restored rich-fens using gametophyte fragments as propagules.

However, three of the four species involved (*Campylium stellatum, Scorpidium cossonii* and *S. scorpioides*) are among the commonest rich-fen mosses and continue to thrive in upland flushes, only *Pseudocalliergon trifarium* has shown a significant decline in lowland Britain, and their experiments did not look at more specialised rich-fen plants, such as *Paludella squarrosa, Tomentypnum nitens* or *Leiocolea rutheana*. They recommended surface liming of exposed peat and the use of protective covers over the moss fragments. Maintaining water levels suitable for growth is critical, as Malson & Rydin found significant differences in growth with just 5 cm changes in water depth.

In general, management undertaken for fen habitat or vegetation features is likely to be broadly beneficial for fen bryophytes. The majority require reasonably open conditions maintained by seasonal grazing and/or rotational mowing. Irrigation by water poor in macro-nutrients and of variable base status (depending on the character of the fen feature) is essential, and most species require perennially high water tables, with some benefiting from periodic inundation.

References

Bergamini, A., Peintinger, M., Fakheran, S., Moradi, H., Schmid, B. & Joshi, J. 2009. Loss of habitat specialists despite conservation management in fen remnants 1995-2006. Perspectives in Plant Ecology, Evolution and Systematics **11**: pp. 65-79.

Blackstock T.H. 2002. New Vice-County records and amendments to the Census Catalogue. Bulletin of the British Bryological Society **79**, p. 39.

Bosanquet, S.D.S., Hale, A.D., Motley, G.S. & Woods, R.G. 2006. Recent work on *Hamatocaulis vernicosus* in Mid and South Wales. Field Bryology **90**, pp. 2-8.

Church, J.M., Hodgetts, N.G., Preston, C.D. & Stewart, N.F. 2001. British Red Data Books, mosses and liverworts. JNCC, Peterborough.

Hedenäs, L. & Eldenäs, P. 2007. Cryptic speciation, habitat differentiation, and geography in Hamatocaulis vernicosus (Calliergonaceae, Bryophyta). Pl. Syst. Evol. **268**, pp. 131-145.

Hughes, P.D.M. & Dumayne-Peaty, L. 2002. Testing theories of mire development using multiple successions at Crymlyn Bog, West Glamorgan, South Wales, UK. Journal of Ecology **90**, pp. 456-471.

Jones, P.S., Turner, A.J., Bosanquet, S.D.S. & Blackstock, T.H. 2006. *Sphagnum riparium* discovered in Wales. Field Bryology **89**, pp. 2-3.

Limpens, J., Tomassen, H.B.M. & Berendse, F. 2003. Expansion of *Sphagnum fallax* in bogs: striking the balance between N and P availability. Journal of Bryology **25**, pp. 83-90.

Lockhart, N.D. 1999. *Paludella squarrosa* (Hedw.) Brid., a boreal relic moss new to Ireland. Journal of Bryology **21**, pp. 305-308.

Malson, K. & Rydin, H. 2007. The regeneration capabilities of bryophytes for rich-fen restoration. Biological Conservation **135**, pp. 435-442.

Malson, K. & Rydin, H. 2009. Competitive hierarchy, but no competitive exclusions in experiments with rich-fen bryophytes. Journal of Bryology **31**, pp. 41-45.

Porley, R.D. & Hodgetts, N.G. 2005. New Naturalist: Mosses and Liverworts. Collins.

Preston, C.D. 2008. British Bryological Society Cambridgeshire Group excursions 2007-2008. Unpublished report.

Swann, E.L. 1982. Norfolk bryophytes today. Journal of Bryology **12**, pp. 77-112.

Wheeler, B.D. 1980. Plant communities of rich-fen systems in England and Wales. Journal of Ecology **68**, pp. 365-395.

Van Wirdum, G. 1995. The regeneration of Fens in Abandoned Peat Pits Below Sea Level in the Netherlands. In Wheeler, B.D., Shaw, S.C., Fojt, W.J. & Robertson, R.A. 1995.

Appendix VII – Fen management for vertebrates

Mammals

Water Vole summarised from Strachan & Moorhouse (2006).

Dredge ditches without interfering with the banks; use appropriately sized machinery and do not tip dredgings onto adjacent vegetation.
Work from one bank only and progress upstream, working in short stretches.
For dredging and cutting, leave gaps of 10m-20m in length as untouched refuge areas for Water Voles
At least one third of a ditch should remain undisturbed.
Vegetation removal or cutting should be carried out on a 3-5 year rotation
Where bank reinforcement is required use softer options such coir, willow hurdles etc.
Bank profile should be stepped or with a steeper incline on the upper half of the bank to facilitate burrowing.
Implement management of water levels where infrastructure allows, to prevent flooding or drying out of ditches.

Sensitive periods
Mowing and weed cutting should not take place during April, May and June inclusive
Weed raking shall not commence before the 1st of August
Tree and bush management works shall only take place between October and March
Cutting of reeds is better left until mid-August (the later the better).

Water Shrew

Recommended management
There is a positive association between water shrew presence and presence of reed/grass/sedge tussocks and dense bankside ground cover. Shrews tend to be less associated with streams characterised by dense bankside tree and shrub cover and short grass. Presence of aquatic vegetation is also preferred.

There is also a positive association between water shrew presence and the abundance of aquatic crustaceans, aquatic snails and caddis-fly larvae, and they prefer good water quality (high dissolved oxygen, low Biological Oxygen Demand and low nitrate levels).

Management should therefore aim to keep ditches and watercourses unchoked with vegetation and prevent scrub encroachment along banks. To maintain aquatic plants and invertebrate communities, regular dredgings are required. Sections of ditch should be left undredged as a recolonisation source for aquatic plants and invertebrates. Management of sites should therefore be implemented as for Water Voles above. Maintenance of good water quality should be considered (e.g. through vegetative treatment of water sources to remove nutrients). Regular dredging of ditches also assists in preventing the build-up of nutrients and organic matter in the water.

Sensitive periods
Water shrews breed between April and September, so management actions should be implemented outside these times.

Harvest Mouse

Recommended management
Ensure areas of long grass are maintained by phased rotational cutting. Do not cut entire area of habitat in one operation. Retain mosaic of patches of different ages up to 3-5 years between cutting. Remove arisings to prevent nutrient build-up.

Sensitive periods

Harvest mice breed from May to October, and possibly through to December in mild winters, so time cutting of vegetation appropriately. See Harris & Yalden (2008) for more details.

Otter

Recommended management

Wetlands should be managed in such a way as to retain features of primary importance for otters, notably food supply (fish), high water levels and sufficient vegetation cover. Reedbeds and willow scrub benefit from rotational cutting (Environment Agency, 1999). See Chapter 6 on vegetation management] for further details. Note also that woodland and scrub are favoured habitat for otters, so maintenance of areas of climax and wet woodland should also be considered. Fish are the main prey item for otters, so maintenance of fish stocks is important, and actions such as restocking after pollution incidents may be required. On sites where there is a lack of suitable refuges for otters in a particular watercourse, consider the construction of artificial otter holts (Roper, 2008).

Sensitive periods

Otters reproduce aseasonally, so there are no specific seasonal constraints on works. Work near an otter holt may require a licence (see legislation section below) if disturbance to the otters is likely to occur.

Birds

Birds associated with the margins of open water bodies

Habitat features

The features included here are those areas of tall monocotyledon plants including common reed, sedges, bulrush and rushes that grow as both emergent plants and on waterlogged ground adjacent to an open water body within, or associated with, a fen. Such vegetation frequently occurs as a margin to the water body. It is the open water that attracts the suite of birds listed as associated with this habitat in Table 2. If open water is not present other than as drains or ditches then it is included in the "reedbed and mixed fen swamp" habitat feature below.

Recommended management

Most of the birds identified as associated with this habitat feature favour the margins of waterbodies where they find food, shelter and a place to nest. The few species that feed out in open water e.g. diving duck and grebes, still requiring as minimum, marginal vegetation for securing a nest. Most wildfowl seek open water as a refuge against the risk of predation, with grazers and dabblers remaining in or close by to open water when foraging.

Merritt (1994) describes the creation and management of a 'duck marsh' for wildfowl species. Water management of this habitat requires deliberate intervention and manipulation and the creation of such a habitat is unlikely to be compatible with the other conservation features and objectives of a natural fen. In winter a 'duck marsh' should be managed to have a maximum winter water depth of 0.3-0.4 m, have undulations of +/-100 mm across the majority of the marsh and with a network of deeper channels. Such duck marshes are generally most suitable when greater than 2 ha. Water management of 'duck marsh' continues to remain critical following the departure of most wintering wildfowl. In spring (April – May), water levels should be dropped to and fluctuated around 0-50 mm to provide feeding conditions for passage waders and some wildfowl e.g. garganey. Water levels should then be allowed to continue to drop throughout May and June to expose damp mud. This allows rapid colonisation by annual plant species which set seed throughout the remainder of the summer months. Water levels need then to be raised in September to around 50-100mm, which kills the 'terrestrial' plants whilst liberating the associated seeds and invertebrates. These conditions can result in an abundance of food for passage waders and returning wintering wildfowl. Water levels are then gradually raised to the winter maximum. Where management is directed towards passage waders, a gradual reduction in water levels of a water body throughout the migration periods (April-May and July-September) to continually provide wet mud for foraging is necessary.

Islands above winter water levels within the wider, deep channels of a duck marsh can be allowed to vegetate for use by breeding wildfowl. Where breeding wildfowl are specifically being encouraged, relatively constant water levels during the breeding season are required. This prevents flooding of nests, loss of feeding areas whilst also ensuring the growth of aquatic plants that maintains invertebrates and fish populations for duck species. Preferably wetland habitat being managed for breeding duck should be at least 5 ha in extent, offering well vegetated and sheltered, nest and feeding sites. The structural complexity of a waterbody is important for some breeding wildfowl, with complex shorelines of a long length in relation to the area of water supporting the largest densities of ducks and coot (Fuller 1982). Favoured as suitable nesting sites are well vegetated islands greater than 100 m2 surrounded by deeper water. Extensive areas of sheltered shallow water (up to 0.3 m deep for dabbling duck and 1.0 m for diving duck) close to suitable nesting areas provide the areas necessary for adults and young broods to forage. Merritt (1994) provides further guidance on the design and management of habitat suitable for breeding wildfowl, including the control of the island vegetation. Species such as coot and moorhen will breed in small pools surrounded by emergent vegetation where nest platforms are constructed.

Monitoring and maintenance of good water quality is critical as aquatic vegetation, invertebrate and fish are very susceptible to water pollution e.g. contamination by agricultural run-off. Such a deleterious impact upon these food resources profoundly affects the suitability of waterbodies to waterbirds.

Sensitive periods
Species breed within this habitat largely from March to August, so disturbance should be minimised within this period which includes avoidance of damaging mechanical operations. Disturbance should also be minimised during prolonged periods of cold winter weather when waterbirds energy expenditure increase at a time frozen waters reduces the availability of, and access to, food resources.

Reedbed specialists and birds of mixed fen swamp

Habitat features
The features included here are those areas of tall monocotyledon plants including common reed, sedges, reedmace and rushes that grow as both emergent plants and on waterlogged ground within a fen. If these plants are growing as a margin to open water then their management has been addressed as a separate habitat.

Recommended management
The management of reedbeds for birds, other wildlife and as a crop is detailed in Hawke and José (1996). For the flagship reedbed specialist, the bittern, many breeding sites have been identified as containing over 20 ha of wet reedbed with ditch and pool systems that give access to fish. Such large reedbeds are also used by bearded tit, reed and Savi's warbler but many of the warblers associated with such features in fens can occur in much smaller areas, less than 1 ha if suitable habitat is present. A prerequisite for Cetti's warbler occupying reed beds is adjacent areas of carr or retention of scattered bushes within the swamp, this is also beneficial as foraging areas to reed warbler. Encroachment of scrub must however be controlled to allow no more than 10% of the swamp to develop into woody vegetation (Merritt 1994).

The ability to control water levels in swamp is critical to maintaining conditions optimal to ensure the growth of aquatic water plants, including reed, and to maintain good invertebrates and fish populations. The latter (preferably of rudd, eels and sticklebacks) are important food resources in reed-beds for bittern. During the breeding season constant water levels are also important to prevent flooding of nests and loss of feeding areas. In wet reed, summer water levels should be maintained so as not to vary beyond 0.1m and 0.25m in depth (Merritt 1994). Bitterns amongst other waterbirds prefer wet reed with open water, Merritt (1994) suggesting open water ponds of a 0.25-1 m depth covering a maximum of about 10% of the surface area. The margins of ditches supplying water into the reed-bed should slope gradually (1 in 10) providing foraging areas for species like bittern, and then drop steeply to 2 m to prevent the encroachment of reeds. Hawke and José (1996) and Merritt (1994) provide further details on the creation and design of reed beds in addition to their management. In addition to wet reed, it is important when managing reed for bearded tit to incorporate the preferred nesting site habitat of dry reed with deep reed litter or sedge undergrowth.

Regular cutting of common reed can be valuable in maintaining stands of pure reed and hence the specialised bird community associated with the habitat. Where water levels can be controlled, blocks of reed up to 1-2 ha should be harvested annually between November and February, rotating the cut area so that any one patch is cut every 5-15 years. Careful burning of degenerated reed beds during the winter can induce a large new growth of Phragmites the following summer. Where a reedbed has become too dry through the accumulation of leaf litter, significant bed lowering through the excavation of the accumulated material can be considered where the phasing and rotation of such work is compatible with other significant conservation interest.

Monitoring and maintenance of good water quality is critical as excess nutrient enrichment leads to a loss in the structural qualities of reed, with a lowering of reed density and weak stems. Good water quality is equally as critical in maintaining optimal food resource availability to water-birds of aquatic vegetation, invertebrate and fish.

Sensitive periods
Male bitterns may establish their territories as early as February, the breeding season extending to June. Disturbance within the period February to August should be minimised in respect to bittern and the other breeding species within this habitat.

Birds of grazed or cut fen in an active floodplain

Habitat features
The features included here are those areas of monocotyledonous plants that resemble floodplain grazing marsh and wet grassland through grazing or cutting of the fen. With a low or tussocky vegetation structure outside of late spring and summer and winter flooding, this habitat feature attracts the same suite of birds as does floodplain and costal grazing marsh.

Recommended management
The management of coastal and floodplain grassland is described in Benstead et al (1997), Merritt (1994) and Mountford and Cooke (2003) and the principles detailed there apply to fen habitats when the objective is to manage them to provide a similar vegetation structure, soil conditions and flooding regime for the same suite of birds.

Sward height and structure and the level of the water table strongly influences the community of breeding birds such managed fen habitats can support, especially so waders. Lapwing and Redshank prefer a sward of less than 5cm and 10cm in height respectively, but with a scattering of tussocks across the field up to 15 cm in height (Youngs 2005). Such tussocks are ideal for nesting Redshank and Yellow Wagtail, especially when near to shallow pools or footdrains for the former species. For Snipe and Curlew however, a medium/long sward (15-30cm) interspersed by shorter areas of sward 5 cm long is the optimum prescription. Heterogeneity of sward height is also suggested to be beneficial to Yellow Wagtails (Bradbury & Bradter 2003), providing both nesting and foraging habitat. The sward height of this habitat feature should ideally be maintained from early March through to late June, by grazing lightly with cattle, at a stocking level of around two cows per hectare. A low stocking density helps minimise the risk from trampling of eggs and chicks.

Water level management is critical, which for breeding waders needs to be kept within 30cm of the surface during early March through to late June, so that shallow pools are created in natural hollows in the ground surface. The approach and end result can be greatly facilitated with the use of footdrains with shelving or bermed margins to supply and keep water within wet grassland (Smart

& Coutts 2004). They allow high water levels to be maintained near to the site's surface whilst avoiding extensive flooding. The areas of wet mud and water/mud interface of the resultant habitat are important foraging areas for feeding adults and chicks of both waders and Yellow Wagtail.

In summer, late June onwards, the sward and tussocks should continue to be maintained as in spring where as water levels can be allowed to draw down to allow agricultural operations to take place, e.g. hay cutting. The timing and approach used in taking cuts of hay need to minimise on the risk of destroying flightless wader broods.

In autumn and winter, grazing where possible, should take place to ensure maintenance of optimal sward heights. Field wetness needs to be managed at field surface level so that extensive shallow pools are created. This management regime is also beneficial to wintering wildfowl and waders, the former which graze the vegetation, and this in turn can produce a good sward height for breeding waders. Prolonged winter flooding can be detrimental to soil invertebrate populations that the breeding species are dependent upon (Ausden et al. 2001). Any prolonged winter flooding of areas of wet grassland managed for breeding waders should ideally be controlled so that one area is flooded for 4-5 years and then rotated to a second area. This allows recovery of the invertebrate populations between periods of flooding.

Sensitive periods

Species breed within this habitat from March to August, so disturbance should be minimised within this period which includes avoidance of damaging mechanical operations, eg. silage cutting. Curlew are particularly sensitive to disturbance during the breeding season.

Birds of high marsh and carr

Habitat features

The features included here are the areas in a fen of tall vegetation growing in soils that are not overlain by water throughout the year and may not be waterlogged in the height of summer. The vegetation can consist of Common Reed, sedges and rushes mixed with taller grasses, Common Nettle and willow herb spp. Areas will also contain encroaching and/or managed scrub, most frequently Alder and willow spp. with Hawthorn and Blackthorn on the driest margins. The scrub is a key component of this habitat feature although it may be considered a threat to the integrity of the fen.

Recommended management

The management of scrub of all types is described in Bacon (2003) and this includes guidance on the management of scrub for birds within wetland habitats, including fens.

A mosaic of high marsh and carr vegetation provides the feeding and nesting conditions for a diversity of bird species, particularly passerines including species that have the majority of their population in other habitats. The objective for this suite of birds, where compatible with other significant conservation features, is to maintain a proportion of scrub on site of differing ages through regular, cyclical management. The retention of scattered bushes within swampy and/or high marsh is important for species such as Reed Warbler, where the benefit is in diversifying the feeding opportunities available. Where carr woodland does begin, the interface with swamp or high marsh is of particular importance being a highly productive feeding area for a variety of migrant passerines, especially in autumn. Where the scrub or carr borders wet swamp and whilst providing cover over exposed bare mud, this provides favoured foraging grounds for the resident Cetti's warbler.

Coppicing of marginal scrub or carr woodland on a 5-15 year cycle is beneficial to several bird species such as grasshopper and sedge warblers and reed buntings (Merritt 1994). Such management avoids closure of the canopy which would exclude most passerines typical of open fens whilst attracting a wider range of scrub and woodland generalists to become established (Fuller 1982). The diversity of scrub or carr can be reflected in the species supported. In autumn, the berry laden alder, buckthorn and hawthorn found on East Anglian fens, attracts large numbers of thrushes and starlings. Of the more typical and widespread Salix spp and alder carrs, it's the seed of the alder that attracts in winter the large finch flocks characteristic of fen carr e.g. redpoll and siskin.

Sensitive periods

Species breed within this habitat from February to August, so disturbance should be minimised within this period which includes avoidance of damaging mechanical operations, e.g. coppicing and scrub clearance.

Reptiles

Grass snake

As grass snakes occupy a large home range, maintaining a healthy population may depend on suitable management over a fairly large area of land, which for a population of snakes may cover several square kilometres. General maintenance of fen vegetation and open waters (rotational cutting and / or grazing) to prevent excessive scrub encroachment) will maintain suitable grass snake habitat. Surveys should where possible aim to identify likely hibernation sites so that these can be protected. Possible locations include rabbit warrens in banks or other areas above the flood level. Searching for snakes early in the season after emergence from hibernation may reveal likely hibernation sites. Artificial hibernacula can be provided in the form of part-buried rubble mounds in areas free from risk of flooding.

Egg laying sites, such as compost heaps and manure heaps should be provided. In the case of compost heaps, arisings from management activities can be used. Manure from grazing livestock can also be used if present.

Heaps should be positioned in a sunny position and close to cover, such as hedgerows or long grass. Heaps can be constructed by placing a criss-cross pattern of branches on the ground (which provides ventilation and a means of access to the heap), topped with bark chippings, cut grass, manure etc. Heaps should be replenished annually as the material rots down.

Amphibians are a major prey item for grass snakes and therefore need to be maintained on sites where snakes are present.

Sensitive periods

Mowing of habitat likely to support grass snakes, especially sunny banks adjacent to water, should be avoided between March - October. If mowing during this period is unavoidable, unmown sanctuary areas should be left, and the vegetation should be cut no shorter than 10cm. Undertake mowing on warm days when snakes will be more active, and do not mow early in the morning when the animals will be more sluggish. Heaps should not be disturbed between early May and late September when grass snakes will be using the heap to lay eggs.

Amphibians

Common frog

Frogs occur in a variety of habitats provided that there are suitable breeding ponds nearby, so general vegetation fen management techniques will ensure that suitable terrestrial habitat persists. They are at greater risk of predation in close-mown or close-grazed vegetation, so refuges should be left when cutting large areas of grassland around breeding ponds. Size, shape and depth of breeding ponds is not critical to breeding success; warm breeding areas are more important, so ponds should be located in unshaded locations. Frogs may hibernate in ponds, so prefer permanent waterbodies. Frog tadpoles are eaten by fish, so permanent waterbodies should be located where they are not at risk of being colonised by fish during flood events. Fish should be removed from breeding ponds if colonisation occurs (removal of fish would need to take account of relevant legislation, and a licence from the appropriate authority (e.g. EA, SEPA) would be required to transfer fish into another waterbody).

Encroaching and overhanging vegetation should be cut back periodically around breeding ponds to prevent them from becoming shaded. However, some marginal shading vegetation can be important to provide shelter for emerging froglets, so avoid clearing the entirety of a pond margin in one management operation.

Sensitive periods

Young froglets are at risk of trampling when they emerge from the pond, so management around and of breeding ponds should take place after metamorphosis but before the first frosts.

Common Toad

Common toads have more specific habitat requirements than the common frog. Preferred habitats are rough grassland, scrub and open woodland, and within these areas, large permanent water bodies are generally required. Optimum pond size is around 1000 m2, with a good cover of emergent and submerged vegetation. Common toad tadpoles are not eaten by fish owing to the presence of toxins in the skin. They seem to prefer ponds containing fish as breeding sites, which may be attributable to the lack of competition from frogs.

General management and sensitive periods are as listed above for common frog. Also, toad migration to breeding sites in early spring can exceed distances of 1000m, and there is the possibility of road casualties if site access roads form a barrier along migration routes. Consider installation of amphibian tunnels under access roads in such situations.

Pool Frog

As a general rule pool frogs prefer small to middle sized ponds and avoid lakes. The optimum depth for these ponds is 1-1.5 m with a suitable input/water table whereby water levels are maintained through the spring and summer (to September) for successful breeding. Pool frog tadpoles are distasteful to fish such as sticklebacks, but predation of adults by large fish is thought to affect the pattern of population variation between ponds in Sweden. Ponds should therefore be monitored for fish presence, with fish removed if colonisation occurs. Clusters of ponds should be provided within 200-600 m of each other, linked by suitable terrestrial habitat. Female pool frogs often gather in a separate pond before transferring to the breeding pond. Ponds should have clear access to south-facing banks for sunning.

Pond vegetation structure should be a mosaic of open water, submergent, emergent, and marginal species. Pool frogs lay their eggs in clumps at pond surface near perimeter shallows or more centrally on rafts of vegetation which allow a warmer micro-environment. Regular management of invasive species such as bulrush is recommended to prevent ponds from becoming choked with vegetation.

Trees should not shade the pond area, although pool frogs can often be found in woodland margin ponds. Proximity of woodland offers easy access to suitable terrestrial habitat for foraging, feeding and hibernation. Pool frogs hibernate on land and require suitable frost-free cavities in ground debris, holes, log piles, tree stumps, mossy clumps etc. for hibernation 100-300 m from pond. Hibernation sites can be created relatively quickly and cheaply from part-buried rubble mounds or log piles situated near to ponds in areas free from flood risk. Ideally, terrestrial habitat should include woodland with moist understory with low-growing vegetation, rougher, tussocky sections in grassland areas. Occasional wet ditches are also beneficial.

It is advisable to have as wide a buffer zone as possible between the pond and any agricultural land. If a grazing management regime is used then a low density of cattle is preferred, which should be monitored regularly by the use of static position photographs to avoid overgrazing.

Great Crested Newt

Great crested newts prefer a mosaic of rough grassland, scrub and woodland, so general fen management techniques should ensure that suitable terrestrial habitat is maintained. Grazing livestock, if present, should be excluded from ponds to prevent poaching and overgrazing of emergent and marginal vegetation. Great crested newts are highly negatively correlated with the presence of fish, so ponds should be maintained fish-free and new ponds located in areas not at risk of fish colonisation during flood events.

Overhanging vegetation should be cut back periodically to prevent overshading. Aquatic vegetation should be controlled on a 2-3 year rotation to prevent excessive growth – management should aim to ensure that 50-75% of the pond surface is free of vegetation, especially around the shallow pond edges where adult newts gather for courtship displays. Pond depth should be maintained at between 1-2 m, with periodic dredging to remove accumulated sediments.

Sensitive periods

Works to ponds should be carried out outside of the main breeding season when newts and larvae are most likely to be present. Operations such as vegetation removal, pond desilting and reprofiling should therefore be carried out between October – February. Mowing grass and fen vegetation should be carried out in hot conditions in summer, and vegetation should be cut to no less than 10cm high, with refuges of unmown vegetation left.

Adults hibernate on land between November- February (depending on temperatures), so work involving ground disturbance in areas where great crested newts might be hibernating should be avoided during this time.

Hibernation sites can be created relatively quickly and cheaply from part-buried rubble mounds situated near to ponds in areas free from flood risk.

Smooth Newt and Palmate Newt

These species use a full range of water bodies and are frequent colonisers of new ponds. They will tolerate the presence of fish to a certain degree but predation on larvae by fish is a significant factor, and ponds should be maintained fish-free. Management actions described above for great crested newt will also maintain ponds and habitat for smooth and palmate newts.

Fish

Recommended Management

In most cases fish will be conserved alongside other aquatic organisms by general management measures designed to maintain unpolluted water and to retain essential habitat features that are needed by fish. This includes maintaining natural river and stream profiles that favour invertebrates for food and aquatic plants for food and cover from predators, as well as spawning sites and refuges for fish fry.

Monitoring of fish stocks is recommended if fish are main prey for a priority species. Re-stocking of fish should be considered, especially after pollution incidents, but care should be taken not to introduce fish to ponds used by great crested newts for breeding.

Problems for invertebrates area are created by:

- Carp can stir up mud to produce murky water with few plants or invertebrates: a bad problem in newly dredged ponds where carp have been introduced

- Excessive clearance of water crow-foot etc from chalk rivers

- Removal of woody debris

- Treatment of ponds and lakes against fish-louse. Or 'temporary' drainage to eliminate fish/fish lice, and then restocking with fish

- Fishermen excessively removing aquatic and aquatic marginal vegetation, and further destroying the wetland/water transition by building up the bank

1.1.1 Spined Loach

The following management recommendations for spined loach are taken from English Nature (undated).

- Management which causes a reduction in habitat diversity e.g. channelization of rivers and streams should be avoided.

- Regulate excess stocking of omnivorous course species such as roach and bream

- Prevent introduction of non-native species such as carp to the river system

- Limit any unregulated manipulations, such as the removal of pike, which in turn causes an increase in course fish species such as roach and bream

- Adopt sensitive weed cutting practice. For example cutting down the centre, or perhaps one side of a channel to create a heterogeneous habitat suitable for spined loaches.

- Long term management of macrophytes, through tree planting where appropriate to create shade along one bank

- Dredging should not be undertaken across the whole length of the channel at a given time. Dredging in the centre of the channel, leaving undisturbed refuges may be acceptable

- Dredging should not be more than once every 4 years to enable populations of spined loach to recover and achieve maximum lifespan.

- Frequency of dredging maybe increased to once every 2/3 years where a rotational regime is adopted, always leaving suitable refuge areas.

References and sources of further information

Ausden M., Sutherland W.J. & James R. 2001 The effects of flooding lowland wet grassland on soil macroinvertebrate prey of breeding wading birds. *Journal of Applied Ecology*, 38: 320-338.

Bradbury, R.B. & Bradter, U. 2003. Habitat associations of Yellow Wagtails Motacilla flava flavissima on lowland wet grassland. *Ibis* 146: 241 – 246

Langton, T., Beckett, C and Foster, J. 2001. Great Crested Newt Conservation Handbook. Froglife, Halesworth.

Smart, M. & Coutts. K. 2004. Footdrain management to enhance habitat for breeding waders on lowland wet grassland at Buckenham and Cantley Marshes, Mid-Yare RSPB Reserve, Norfolk, England. *Conservation Evidence* 1: 16-19)

Strachan, R & Moorhouse, T. 2006 The Water Vole Conservation Handbook, Second edition. The Wildlife Conservation Research Unit.

Youngs, T. 2005. Wet grassland practical manual: breeding waders. RSPB, Sandy, UK.

Appendix VIII – Fen management for invertebrates

In general, favourable management of fens should deliver favourable conditions for fen bryophytes, The major invertebrate groups containing species of conservation significance which inhabit fens, in approximate order of importance, are:

Diptera (flies)

This is arguably the most important invertebrate group in fens, with a very large number of species in many families. A wide range of species develop as larvae in saturated peat, mud, or plant litter; others are phytophagous, or parasitic or predatory on wetland invertebrates. The range of families and life-histories is very large, as is the range of habitat requirements. The most important areas tend to be shallowly flooded, seasonally flooded or permanently damp ground with vegetation cover ranging from bare ground though open-structured vegetation and tussocks to continuous tall wetland vegetation, but without a deep build-up of litter. Key families include soldier-flies (Stratiomyidae), crane-flies (Limoniidae, Tipulidae, Cylindrotomidae, Pediciidae), snail-killing flies (Sciomyzidae), long-footed flies (Dolichopodidae), grass-flies (Chloropidae), shore-flies (Ephydridae) and hoverflies (Syrphidae) as well as a number of minor families and small numbers of species from other large families with weaker wetland associations. Where there are associated seepages there may be a different, and potentially important, assemblage. Craneflies and other Diptera often dominate in areas of shaded fen. Where trees and shrubs support a significant amount of dead wood, there may be saproxylic species from several families.

Coleoptera (beetles)

Fens are particularly well-known for their water beetles (in the widest sense, including not only the traditional water beetle families (Dryopidae, Dytiscidae, Helophoridae, Hydraenidae, Hydrochidae, Hydrophilidae, Noteridae, Pelobiidae) but also a number of leaf beetles (Chrysomelidae), weevils (Curculionidae, Erirrhinidae) and marsh beetles (Scirtidae) which have aquatic larvae. Amongst terrestrial wetland groups, rove beetles (Staphylinidae) and ground beetles (Carabidae) are amongst the most important. These predominantly ground-dwelling and near–ground-dwelling groups occupy a wide range of habitat structures, but areas of bare wet ground are important for a number of rare ground beetles, and conditions varying from this to continuous tall cover with litter account for much of the habitat range of Staphylinidae. There is also interest in a wide range of other families, including a wide range of phytophagous leaf beetles and weevils, and members of many other families. Dead wood and wood-decaying fungi on fens can support substantial assemblages of saproxylic beetles. Good assemblages of such beetles are most likely to be found where there is long continuity of mature timber and dead wood, and trees growing in relatively open conditions: such factors may often be met where there is long tradition of pollard willows, for example.

Lepidoptera (moths and butterflies)

This is a species-rich group in fens, where a very wide range of woody and herbaceous plants are utilised as food plants. Many of the scarcest species are associated with tall herbaceous vegetation or beds of reed or other tall monocotyledons: for example, various species of wainscot moth (Noctuidae) feeding on reed and other tall monocotyledons. South-eastern fens, in particular, are well-known for the swallowtail butterfly (Papilio machaon britannicus) feeding on Cambridge milk-parsley Peucedanum palustre, the marsh carpet Perizoma sagittata on meadow-rue Thalictrum flavum, and the dentated pug Anticollix sparsata on yellow loosestrife Lysimachia vulgaris. However, others, such as the marsh pug Eupithecia pygmaeata and silver barred Deltote bankiana, are associated with shorter swards.

Woody vegetation of all types and sizes has value: small chocolate-tip Clostera pigra, for example, feeds on creeping willow Salix repens, other low willow growth, and small regenerating or invasive aspen Populus tremula; the large range of species associated with larger trees and shrubs includes such wood-boring specialists like goat moth Cossus cossus and red-belted clearwing Synanthedon myopaeformis. A specialised group of footman moths is associated with damp scrub and scrub-invaded unmanaged reed-beds: the four-dotted footman Cybosia mesomella, the dotted footman Pelosia muscerda and the small dotted footman Pelosia obtusa.

Araneae (spiders)

Fens are a very important spider habitat, though most of the scarcer species are found in a wider range of wetlands. Almost 14% of Red Data Book spiders are associated to a greater or lesser extent with fens. The rarer species are all associated with open conditions with little or no scrub. The rarer species are generally associated with vegetated wetland, from relatively open wet grassland to tall fen and seasonal swamp with a well-developed litter layer. Several species which are relatively easily captured and identified have been identified as useful key species for monitoring site value and management success.

Hymenoptera (bees, wasps, ants, sawflies, parasitic wasps)

There is a wide range of sawfly larvae that feed on a range of herbaceous and woody plants, including some rare species restricted to fens, or to wetlands including fens. Bees and wasps are not especially diverse in wetlands, but include a number of rare wetland specialists associated in varying degrees with fens: the bee *Macropis europea* requires flowers of yellow loosestrife *Lysimachia vulgaris* for foraging; the wasps *Rhopalum gracile* and *Passaloecus clypealis*, and the bee *Hylaeus pectoralis* nest in stems or galls of common reed *Phragmites australis*; the spider-hunting wasp *Anoplius caviventris* lives in structurally complex vegetation at wetland fringes; and various species require wetland for foraging, or as a source of nesting material.

A wide range of other solitary bees and wasps which nest in dead wood or in dead stems of woody or herbaceous plants may thrive in fens which contain suitable nesting sites in warm, sheltered conditions, and significant assemblages may develop in sites which have a wide structural range and a good set of successional stages. The parasitic families of Hymenoptera are for the most part rather poorly known, and have been given slight attention in site assessment and management for conservation. The number of species is high, however, and the specificity of many species makes it certain that fens are an important habitat for the group.

Hemiptera (bugs)

Members of most British families of Hemiptera may be found in fens. The most important groups and assemblages, in terms of representation of scarce species, are leafhoppers (Cicadellidae) and planthoppers (Delphacidae) associated with moderate to tall monocotyledons, especially where these grow in moderately dense stands or tussocks. There are scarce species also amongst groundbugs (Lygaeidae), plant bugs (Miridae), especially amongst tall herbaceous vegetation. There are few species of great rarity, but the lesser water-measurer *Hydrometra gracilenta*, and the pigmy water-cricket *Microvelia buenoi*, species of water margins and shallows, are worthy of particular note.

Odonata (dragonflies)

The richest assemblages of dragonflies tend to be found in places with a wide range of sizes and characters of permanent and near-permanent waterbody, especially if there is running water nearby. They are thus liable to be found in wetland complexes, of which true fen may form a part. Rich assemblages, however, are not necessarily rich in scarce species. A number of particularly rare dragonflies are associated with fens, or in water-bodies associated with fens or in fenland districts. The variable damselfly *Coenagrion pulchellum* may be a component of ditch systems and ponds in fens; like the Norfolk hawker *Aeshna isosceles*, it also occurs in grazing marsh ditches. The scarce chaser *Libellula fulva* is found in fenland areas, and sometimes found as an adult in large numbers in fens, but breeds in rivers and large drains.

Other rare species have a rather broader ecological range. The small red damselfly *Ceriagrion tenellum* can occur in shallow, well-vegetated water in fens, but rarely: it is more usually a wet heath and bog species. The Irish damselfly *Coenagrion lunulatum* breeds in well-vegetated shallows of mesotrophic lakes and pools in valley bogs as well as pools in valley fen; The southern damselfly *Coenagrion mercuriale* breeds mostly in shallow, base-rich, slow-flowing streams runnels in heathland, and in chalk streams on river flood-plains. The scarce emerald *Lestes* dryas breeds in well-vegetated, often seasonal, ponds and ditches.

Mollusca (snails, slugs and mussels)

The mollusc fauna of fens are at their richest in sites with high calcium levels, and so are better represented in rich-fens. The fauna can be rich, and though the number of uncommon species is small, they include some very rare and greatly declined species. The most important are the narrow-mouthed whorl snail *Vertigo angustior*, Desmouslin's whorl snail *V. moulinsiana* and slender amber snail *Oxyloma sarsi*. Some rare aquatic molluscs are associated with drainage ditches and pools in fenland areas, though they are more strongly associated with grazing marshes: pea mussel *Pisidium pseudosphaerium*, large-mouthed valva snail *Valvata macrostoma*, lesser whirlpool ram's-horn *Anisus vorticulus*, and shiny ram's-horn *Segmentina nitida.*

Trichoptera (caddisflies)

Caddisflies are well-represented in fens. Sites containing a range of water bodies of varying vegetation, size and permanence give the best overall assemblages. There will be additional species if the site adjoins a river or lake, or if it is spring-fed. The number of uncommon species strongly associated with fens is limited, however. The leptocerid *Erotesis baltica* requires shallow, dense, submerged vegetation in clear water; three species without very recent records (*Grammotaulius nitidus, Limnephilus pati* and *L. tauricus*) have so few records that their habitat requirements are scarcely known.

Orthoptera

There are few British Orthoptera, and most of these are of restricted southern distribution. This is therefore not a group of great relevance on most fens. Two species, the mole cricket *Gryllotalpa gryllotalpa* and the large marsh grasshopper *Stethophyma grossum*, had, historically, a strong association with fens and were locally common, but have since declined to possible extinction or to virtual or complete loss from fenland habitats.

Further information on the groups of invertebrates associated with fens is available in Buglife (2006): but not all groups are included, and there is implied variation in the definition of fen in the accounts of different groups in this multi-authored work.

1.1 Identification of invertebrate interest features

Invertebrate species and assemblages which qualify as notified features are identified according to the *Guidelines for selection of biological SSSIs* (NCC, 1989), or according to similar guidelines that have been used to select ASSIs in Northern Ireland, or which appear on the Habitats and Species Directive Annex II.

The two most prescriptive chapters (18 & 19) in the SSSI guidelines are those for butterflies and dragonflies. The guidelines for dragonflies are now superseded by criteria for determining key Odonata sites (French & Smallshire, 2008). The third chapter (17) dealing with all other invertebrates does not list species at all but instead gives a series of principles to identify species worthy of SSSI notification. Using the SSSI guidelines, and working guidance developed since, the invertebrate specialists in each country agency have identified which species are currently known to be notified features.

In simple terms, applying the guidelines results in a site being designated either because it has one or more important invertebrate assemblage or, a strong population of one or more named rare or threatened species. However, qualifying for notification on the criteria does not guarantee a site being designated: other factors, notably threat, are also considered. The SSSI system can be regarded as a selection of sites fulfilling the criteria.

The development of CSM Guidance for Terrestrial and Freshwater Invertebrates (JNCC, 2008) provides further guidance on the identification of interest features, attributes, targets and methods of assessment.

There are few published methods for the assessment of the significance of specific groups and assemblages of invertebrates, and fewer that are relevant to fens. Foster & Eyre, (1992) describe a system of water beetle assemblages which revise a numerical score (WETSCORE) indicative of interest, and define a threshold for a "good" assemblage, but no indication of its actual level of significance. Drake (2004) describes a revised, and simpler, scoring system, devised specifically for grazing marsh ditch systems but of potentially wider value. There are two methods of assessment for saproxylic Coleoptera assemblages (Alexander, 2004; Fowles et al. 1999) which provide values for national significance and, in the former case, for lower levels of significance also, though the selected values are all open to question.

Natural England are developing a system for the assessment and monitoring of invertebrate assemblages which can be used across all habitats. It was primarily designed for Common Standards Monitoring, but is potentially of wider application. Known as ISIS (Invertebrate Species – Habitat Information System) this uses standard sampling protocols to collect invertebrates. Assemblage types are identified from the species list thus obtained, and a numerical estimate derived of the quality of each assemblage. Assemblages are recognised at two levels: the Broad Assemblage Type (BAT) and the Specific Assemblage Type (SAT). Fens fall within the Mire assemblages BAT (W31). Two specific fen assemblages are recognised, Mesotrophic fen (W313) and Rich fen (W314). Fens will, however, often contain additional assemblages in accompanying habitats and contained features.

Invertebrate survey

Features of potential invertebrate interest are relatively easily identified but past changes in management, or fluctuations in water levels, may have resulted in the loss of less mobile invertebrates. Determining whether features are in fact of significant invertebrate interest or value depends on detailed expert survey. Methods for obtaining population estimates and comparative counts for butterflies and dragonflies are outlined in Pollard & Yates, 1993, and Brookes, 1993.

Since the range of invertebrate species likely to occur on a fen is large, the effort needed to obtain a comprehensive picture of the invertebrate fauna is substantial even on a quite small site. In most cases, invertebrate survey will be selective and/or limited by available expertise and resources. For general site assessment, it is preferable to examine a wide taxonomic range and habitat range. Drake et al (2007) provide a range of standard protocols for sampling, lists key groups for the assessment of invertebrate assemblages in fens and other habitats, and provides guidance in the use of the data gained from such surveys in the ISIS application developed by English Nature for monitoring invertebrate assemblages on SSSIs in England, which can provide an assessment of the quality of the fauna as well as providing a basis for long-term monitoring. However, the ISIS application is still under development, the list of methods incomplete, the protocols not uncontentious, and some key groups not readily identified. It is, moreover, a general-purpose system, and it may be preferable to design one for particular sites, based on available expertise, or to divide the site into assemblages other than those identified by the ISIS programme.

A more pragmatic approach is to identify potentially contentious issues and areas at an early stage and target survey at these. Simple questions such as "does the invasive scrub on this site support a significant invertebrate assemblage, and if so how much scrub is needed to support it" or "how important are the invertebrates of this field, and how will they be affected by a change from cutting to grazing" may prove impossible to answer definitively, but survey aimed at answering them will provide better guidance than an attempt to derive an answer to a specific question retrospectively from the results of a general survey. Equally, if the management of a particular feature is not in doubt, and conforms to general principles (for example, the maintenance of marginal willows by rotational pollarding) then survey work may be very valuable for site assessment, but is unlikely to contain useful information for management purposes.

Other than for rare or exceptional individual species, survey for particular species are generally less important than survey for overall interest and assemblages. Target species for detailed examination are likely to be determined by past records from a particular site, by identification of a habitat which appears particularly suitable for a rare species, and/or on the basis of the known fauna of nearby sites.

Less frequent but more detailed survey is more effective for invertebrates than frequent superficial survey (though there may be exceptions if a single species is being monitored). One survey in each management planning period, undertaken in time to feed into the next management plan, is a good default frequency. However, limited survey funding on such occasions might well be better spent in answering specific questions arising from the first period of management rather than in more widespread monitoring or surveillance, provided the habitat response has been satisfactory.

1.2 Evaluation

Evaluation is the process of determining the value of the species assemblages and populations on a site. It enables the identification and prioritisation of the features of ecological interest present on site, and is therefore essential for setting objectives and targets for management and monitoring programmes.

Evaluation should be considered alongside the data search and scoping survey process outlined above, as if funds are unavailable to carry out a comprehensive site audit, it may be necessary to allocate funds to surveys of particular species or groups based on an initial assessment of their likely presence and value (e.g. one would normally prioritise a survey of a UKBAP priority species over a species of less conservation concern).

There are a variety of attributes of a species that may be used as criteria for selection. These can include legal protection status, appearance on conservation priority lists, identification as an interest feature of the site in its designation, population conservation status, commercial value (less likely to be appropriate for vertebrate and invertebrate species), rarity, endangerment (risk of extinction), role as a flagship/umbrella species, importance for ecosystem function (keystone species) and value as an indicator species. In practice, the first three of these attributes are the ones most likely to drive prioritisation for management planning.

The main factors used to determine value are
- conservation priority (i.e. species which are rare or declining)

- abundance (presence of a significant numbers or proportion of a population, regardless of conservation status) [e.g. 1% criteria for birds]

For ecological impact assessment, species are often assigned a value on a scale ranging from international/national (e.g. a nationally significant population of a nationally rare species) through to local (e.g. a population of a species significant at the local level only). An example of this type of scale is provided in the table below, adapted from Hill *et al* (2005).

Examples of evaluation criteria for species

Level of value	Examples of qualifying Vertebrate Evaluation Criteria
International	Populations of regularly occurring globally threatened species (e.g. IUCN red listed species) Internationally important populations of a species (e.g. greater than 1% of a flyway population of birds) Nationally significant populations of an internationally important species Regularly occurring populations of internationally important species that are rare or threatened in the UK or of uncertain conservation status
National	Nationally important populations of a species (e.g. greater than 1% of the national population of a bird species) Significant populations of a nationally important species (e.g. UK Red Data Book species) UKBAP Priority Species requiring protection of all nationally important sites Regularly occurring populations of a nationally important species that is threatened or rare in the region or county
Regional	Regionally important populations of a species Significant populations of a regionally important species Regularly occurring, locally significant populations of species listed as nationally scarce (i.e. which occur in 16-100 10km squares in the UK), or Regional BAP species listed for regional rarity or localisation
County / Metropolitan	Species populations of county importance (e.g. greater than 1% of the county population of a bird species) Significant populations of a county important species (e.g. species listed on a county BAP on account of rarity or localisation)
District / Borough	Species populations of district importance Significant populations of a district / borough important species (e.g. species listed on a local BAP on account of rarity or localisation)

For a site-based evaluation for management planning, the EcIA approach is a useful first step, but may not provide sufficient information on sites with low biodiversity value, or may give insufficient weight to site-specific factors. For example, if a site contains little biodiversity value, the EcIA approach may not offer sufficient distinction between features of low value. It may also undervalue populations of common or widespread species which have local significance for reasons other than rarity.

In these instances, other considerations could be introduced into the evaluation process, such as flagship significance (e.g. a popular species that is valued by recreational users of the site) or historical significance (e.g. a population of a species known to have been present on the site for many years).

The context of the site in the surrounding landscape should also be considered. For example, a site may contain small numbers of a nationally rare species, but larger numbers of a county rarity. It may be more appropriate to prioritise the county rarity over the national rarity if the national rarity is also found widespread on adjacent or nearby sites.

There is usually some degree of subjectivity inherent in the evaluation process. In general, however, the following list should be considered when drawing up a list of features:

- Species with legally protected status (Conservation Regulations, Wildlife & Countryside Act).
- UKBAP Priority Species
- LBAP species
- Rarity criteria (Nationally Notable, Red Lists, BoCC etc.)
- Significant population thresholds (e.g. 1% of population at a range of spatial scales)
- Species scoring systems for assemblages (e.g. SSSI selection criteria for bird assemblages)
- Evaluation criteria for EcIA – National, Regional etc
- 'Flagship' species
- Species of local interest

In general, it will be normal to prioritise species of nature conservation concern i.e. UKBAP species and/or species assemblages of note (see Appendix 1). Note that for invertebrates, statuses need careful interpretation. UKBAP status is of real significance only if the species is habitat restricted and listed because of loss or decline in quality of fen habitat. Many invertebrate groups were assessed for Red Data Book and Nationally Scarce status some time ago, and many species have since changed in status, or become more widely known through increased recording; there is at best an approximate relationship between the formal conservation status of most invertebrates and reality, and an estimate needs to be made of the current actual status of each species with formal status before any assessment or management decisions are based on it. The advice of an invertebrate specialist should be sought to make such a judgement; otherwise one should assume that formal conservation status is deserved and the species should be prioritised accordingly.

Habitat management requirements for invertebrates

Additional considerations for invertebrate habitat management regimes are:
Litter piles from cutting are useful as habitat, especially as hibernation sites; substantial piles rising well above highest water levels are preferable.
Complex small-scale structure may be easier to maintain in a grazed habitat than one managed by cutting/clearing; but more prone to unplanned change.
As a general rule one should aim for constancy, and make change as gradual and small-scale as possible. Avoid sudden changes in density of grazing animals, and never put on a large number of grazers to renovate a site in the early stages of management.
Be tolerant of some scrub representation on 'open' habitat, including carr.
Veteran trees and large timber lying on the ground can support special faunas.

The table below describes broad management requirements for some legally protected invertebrate species. It does not include all the protected species previously identified as potentially associated with fens: there are no currently known fen populations of mole cricket, so it would be premature to suggest its management requirements, and White-clawed crayfish is not considered a fen species, merely a potential associate.

Management of key fen habitat features for invertebrates

Habitat feature	Recommended management	Key considerations
Permanent and near-permanent water, including emergent vegetation	Rotational and small-scale clearance where necessary to maintain conditions; water bodies with grazed margins may need little management, but some water margins should preferably be ungrazed to encourage tall marginals, unless grazing levels are low. Modification of vertical water margins may be necessary to create gentle sloping edges or berms.	Keep fish-free where possible
Seasonally exposed marginal sediments and marginal vegetation	No specific management needed; varied structure should be maintained by management of water bodies and the effects of fluctuating water levels	Maintain natural fluctuations in water levels
Temporary pools and areas of seasonal flooding	Avoid tall or shading growth of vegetation during periods of flooding, preferably by grazing	Maintain natural fluctuations in water levels; ensure constancy of management of surrounding land
Seepages and surface flow	Maintain reasonably constant conditions; grazing preferable in open habitats, but level of grazing critical to maintain open conditions while avoiding damage by trampling	Avoid conversion of flowing to standing water by ponding back in the interest of maintaining or increasing water levels;
Exposed mud/peat (not at water margins)	In grazed sites, trampling should provide sufficient habitat	Important areas are bare, not heavily trampled and poached, and may be small-scale in a mosaic with vegetation
Tall monocotyledon-dominated water margins and swamp	Rotational cutting on a varied but preferably long rotation: with some areas maintained with bare mud beneath; other areas allowed to develop a good litter layer. In small sites, management of small habitat patches may provide sufficient variety	Ensure a range of ages present at any one time; maintain an age range through to very old and scrub-invaded beds if possible
Short and open-structured vegetation over wet ground with little organic litter	Grazing	Avoid changes in management from grazing to cutting; the preferred level of grazing may be determined by the need to maintain overall structural variety rather than a uniformly short sward
Tall continuous herbaceous vegetation on damp soil	Rotational cutting; several lengths of rotation preferable, provided the site is sufficiently large	Avoid changes in management regime from cutting to grazing
Tussocks and tall/short grassland mosaics	Grazing at a level to maintain tussocks standing proud in a shorter sward; assist by cutting selective tussocks if the balance threatens to shift	
Scattered trees and scrub	Determine acceptable/desirable density, thin if necessary, and then selectively remove or coppice scrub/saplings to maintain an approximately steady state; allow local invasion and ensure continuity of young growth. Retain a representative mixture of woody species	Ensure good range of growth stages of all species at all times
Old trees and dead wood	Retain trees into old age; avoid surgery or felling unless absolutely essential. Retain fallen timber on site. Strategy for replacing trees needs planning well in advance.	Associated fauna best developed where trees are fairly scattered and exposed
Continuous and near-continuous scrub/woodland with shaded wet conditions	Little management may be needed, depending on exact circumstances; local thinning of the canopy may be desirable to vary conditions	

Management requirements for protected invertebrate species

Species	Management
Lesser Whirlpool Ramshorn Anisus vorticulus	Found in unshaded ditches and drains with a rich flora. Occupied drains should be cleared frequently enough to prevent domination by tall emergents, but no more frequently than essential; rotational clearance over short stretches is preferable.
Narrow-mouthed Whorl Snail Vertigo angustior	Requires unshaded short vegetation on marshy ground subject neither to desiccation nor to prolonged flooding. Maintaining the very precise hydrological conditions required is critical; management by grazing is the easiest way of maintaining short vegetation, but it is important to avoid excessive grazing and trampling; cutting is preferable to arrest successional change to tall dense vegetation or scrub.
Des Moulin's Whorl Snail Vertigo moulinsiana	Requires tall wetland vegetation over wet but unflooded ground. Maintain a high water table; avoid water pooling and retention; grazing should be light, rotational, or entirely avoided; management by rotational cutting is acceptable, but vegetation should be not less than 70 cm in height in late summer
Medicinal Leech Hirudo medicinalis	Maintain well-structured warm marginal shallows; good amphibian populations are useful in providing tadpoles as food for young leeches; grazing livestock provide food for adults.
Southern Damselfly Coenagrion mercuriale	Requires shallow, slow-flowing, unshaded, base-rich runnels and streams. Maintaining open, unshaded conditions and good water quality is critical. Grazing is the preferred management of surrounding land to maintain open conditions.
Norfolk Hawker Aeshna isosceles	Breeds in well-vegetated unshaded drainage ditches. Rotational management to maintain open conditions and avoid domination by tall emergents, with management only as frequent as essential. Allow for presence of water soldier, an invasive plant. Vulnerable to brackish incursion.
Lesser Silver Water Beetle Hydrochara caraboides	Requires well-vegetated unshaded ditches and ponds. Infrequently managed water bodies in grazed land, with mats of surface vegetation, seem particularly useful; management of any water body should be small-scale and cautious, but open conditions must be maintained.
Marsh Fritillary Eurodryas aurinia	Requires grassland with varied structure including large stands of devil's-bit scabious. Grazing is the only way of maintaining suitable conditions in the long-term, but must be carefully adjusted to avoid loss of structural variation.
Swallowtail Butterfly Papilio machaon britannicus	Requires tall herbaceous fen vegetation with abundant Cambridge milk-parsley. Suitable conditions are maintained by rotational cutting, but the timing of cutting is critically important, avoiding winter.
Fen Raft-spider Dolomedes plantarius	Requires small pools with marginal saw sedge in its single known fen site; suitable conditions can be maintained by clearance as necessary of any water bodies, but if other fen colonies are discovered, it may be that they will occupy a somewhat different habitat.

References and sources of further information

Alexander, K.N.A. 2004. Revision of the Index of Ecological Continuity as used for saproxylic beetles. English Nature Research Reports, no. 574.

Benstead, P., Drake, M., Jose, P.V., Mountford, O., Newbold, C. & Treweek, J. 1997. The Wet Grassland Guide: Managing floodplain and Coastal Wet Grasslands for Wildlife. RSPB, Sandy, UK.

Benstead, P., Jose, P., Joyce, B and Wade, M. 1999. European Wet Grassland. Guidelines for management and restoration. RSPB, Sandy.

Brookes, S.J. 1993. Review of a method to monitor adult dragonfly populations. Journal of the British Dragonfly Society, 9: 1-14.

Buglife (The Invertebrate Conservation Trust). 2006. Managing priority habitats for invertebrates. 2nd edition. CD. Buglife, Peterborough.

Buisson, R., Wade, M., Cathcart, L., Hemmings, M., Manning, J & Mayer, L. 2008. The Drainage Channel Biodiversity Manual: Integrating wildlife and flood risk management. Association of Drainage Authorities and Natural England, Peterborough.

Drake, C.M. 2004. Grazing marsh assemblages and site classification using invertebrates. English Nature Research Reports, no. 579.

Drake, C.M., Lott, D.A., Alexander, K.N.A. & Webb, J. 2007. Surveying terrestrial and freshwater invertebrates for conservation evaluation. Natural England Research Report NERR005. Natural England, Sheffield.

English Nature (undated). The habitat and management requirements of spined loach *Cobitis taenia*. No 244-English Nature Research Reports.

Environment Agency. 1999. Otters and River Habitat Management. Environment Agency

Foster, G.N. & Eyre, M.D. 1992. Classification and ranking of water beetle communities. UK Conservation, no. 1. Nature Conservancy Council, Peterborough.

Fowles, A.P., Alexander, K.N.A. & Key, R.S. 1999. The Saproxylic Quality Index: evaluating wooded habitats for the conservation of dead-wood Coleoptera. The Coleopterist, 8, 121-141.

French, G. & Smallshire, D. 2008. Criteria for determining key Odonata sites in Great Britain. Journal of the British Dragonfly Society, 24(2), 54-61.

Fuller, R.J. 1982. *Bird Habitats in Britain*. T. & A.D. Poyser, Calton, U.K.

Gent, A.H & Gibson, S.D., eds. 1998. Herpetofauna Workers' Manual. Joint Nature Conservation Committee.

Gilbert, O & Anderson, P. 1998. Habitat Creation and Repair. Oxford University Press.

Gilman, K. 1994. Hydrology and Wetland Conservation. John Wiley & Sons

Hardey, J., Crick, H., Wernham, C., Riley, H., Etheridge, B. and Thompson, D.. 2006. Raptors: A Field Guide to Survey and Monitoring. Stationery Office (TSO) Scotland.

Harris, S. and Yalden, D eds. 2008. Mammals of the British Isles: Handbook, 4th Edition. The Mammal Society.

Hawke, C.J. & José, P.V. 1996. Reedbed Management for Commercial and Wildlife Interests. RSPB, Sandy, UK.

Keddy, P. 2000. Wetland Ecology: Principles and Conservation. Cambridge University Press.

Kusler, J & Kentula, M. 1990. Wetland Creation and Restoration: The status of the science. Island Press.

Merritt, A. 1994. *Wetlands, Industry and Wildlife. A manual of principles and practices*. The Wildfowl and Wetlands Trust, Slimbridge, Glos., U.K.

Morris, J., Mills, J., Burton, R., Hall, J., Dunderdale, J., Gowing, D., Gilbert, J & Spoor, G. 1997. Wet Fens for the Future: Feasibility Study Phase 2-A study of the economic, social and soil management implications of creating new wetlands in fenland. Cranfield University

Mountford, J.O. & Cooke, A.I. 2003. Guidelines for the Management and Restoration of Lowland Wet Grassland. Defra, London.

Pollard, E. & Yates, T.Y. 1993. Monitoring butterflies for ecology and conservation. Chapman & Hall, London.

Appendix IX – Further reading

Section 1: Introduction

Hobbs, R. J. & Lindenmayer, D. B., eds. 2007. *Managing and Designing Landscapes for Conservation.* Oxford: Blackwell Publishing.

Rackham, O. 1994. *An Illustrated History of the Countryside.* London: Phoenix Illustrated, Orion Publishing Group.

Section 2: Fen Flora and Fauna

Cramp, S. (Ed.) 1977-1993. *The Birds of the Western Palaearctic.* Oxford University Press, Oxford.

Davies, C., Shelley, J., Harding, P., Mclean, I., Gardiner, R and Peirson, G. eds. 2004. Freshwater fishes in Britain: the species and their distribution.

European Committee for the Conservation of Bryophytes (eds). 1995. Red Data Book of European Bryophytes. ECCB, Trondheim.

Roper, E. 2008. Otters: Atkins Species Guide. Atkins

Section 3: Understanding Fen Hydrology

Acreman M. 2005. *Impact assessment of Wetlands: focus of hydrological and hydrogeological issues. Phase 2 Report.* Environment Agency R&D Project W6-091, Centre for Ecology and Hydrology project C01996.

Boak R and Johnson D (2007). *Hydrogeological impact appraisal for groundwater abstractions.* Science Report Sc040020/SR2, Bristol, Environment Agency.

Environment Agency (2003). *A Guide to Monitoring Water Levels and Flows at Wetland Sites.* National Groundwater and contaminated land centre, Environment Agency, Bristol.

Wildlife Trusts' Water Policy Team. 2005. Wildlife Trusts' Wetland Restoration Manual.

Section 4: Understanding Fen Nutrients

Boeye, D., Van Straaten, D. & Verheyen, R.F. 1995. A recent transformation from poor to rich fen caused by artificial groundwater recharge. *Journal of Hydrology*, 169, 111-129.

Boeye, D., Verhagen, B., Van Haesebroeck, V. & Verheyen, R.F. 1997. Nutrient limitation in species rich lowland fens. *Journal of Vegetation Science*, 8, 415-424.

Bootsma. M.C., Van den Broek, T., Barendregt, A. & Beltman, B. 2002. Rehabilitation of acidified floating fens by addition of buffered surface water. *Restoration Ecology*, 10, 112-121.

Boyer, M.L.H. & Wheeler, B.D. 1989. Vegetation patterns in spring-fed calcareous fens: Calcite precipitation and constraints on fertility. *Journal of Ecology*, 77, 597-609.

Clymo, R.S. 1983. Peat. In: A.J.P. Gore, ed. *Ecosystems of the World Volume 4A. Mires: Swamps, Bogs, Fen and Moor.* Amsterdam: Elsevier, pp 159-224.

D'Arcy, B.J., Dils, R. & Kampas, T. 2000. Diffuse Pollution Impacts: The Environmental and Economic Impacts of Diffuse Pollution in the UK. Colchester: Terence Dalton Publishers.

Davidson, T.E., Trepel, M. & Schrautze, J. 2002. Denitrification in drained and rewetted minerotrophic peat soils in Northern Germany (Pohnsdorfer Stauung). *Journal of Plant Nutrition and Soil Science*, 2, 199-204.

Defra. 2002. The Government's Strategic Review of Diffuse Water Pollution from Agriculture in England. Agriculture and Water: a Diffuse Pollution Review. Unpublished report by Defra.

Dorland, E., Bobbink, R., Messelink, J.H. & Verhoeven, J.T.A. 2003. Soil ammonium accumulation after sod cutting hampers the restoration of degraded wet heathlands. *Journal of Applied Ecology*, 40, 804-814.

Ellis, S. & Mellor, A. 1995. *Soils and Environment.* Oxford: Routledge.

Francez, A.J. & Loiseau, P. 1999. The fate of mineral nitrogen in a fen with Sphagnum fallax and Carex rostrata. *Canadian Journal of Botany*, 77, 1136-1143.

Freeman, C., Liska, G., Ostle, N.J., Lock, M.A., Reynolds, B. & Hudson, J. 1996. Microbial activity and enzymic decomposition processes following peatland water table drawdown. *Plant and Soil*, 180, 121-127.

Gilvear, D.J. & McInnes, R.J. 1994. Wetland hydrological vulnerability and the use of classification procedures: a Scottish case study. *Journal of Environmental Management*, 42, 403-414.

Granberg, G., Sundh, I., Svensson, B.H. & Nilsson, M. 2001. Effects of temperature and nitrogen and sulphur deposition on methane emission from a boreal mire. *Ecology*, 82, 1982-1998.

Grobbelaar, J.H. & House, A.W. 1995. Phosphorus as a limiting resource in inland waters; interactions with nitrogen. In: Tiessen, H., ed. *Phosphorus in the Global Environment.* Chichester: Wiley, pp. 255-273.

Grootjans, A.P., Everts, H., Bruin, K. & Latzi, R. 2001. Restoration of wet dune slacks on the Dutch Wadden Sea Islands: recolonisation after large-scale sod cutting. *Restoration Ecology*, 9 (2), 137-146.

Haycock, N.E. & Burt, T.P. 1993. Role of floodplain sediments in reducing the nitrate concentration of subsurface run-off: a case study in the Cotswolds, UK. *Hydrology Proceedings*, 7, 278-295.

Haycock, N.E. & Pinay, G. 1993. Groundwater nitrate dynamics in grass and poplar vegetated riparian buffer strips during winter. *Journal of Environmental Quality*, 22, 273-278.

Haycock, N. E., Pinay, G. & Walker, C. 1993. Nitrogen retention in river corridors: European perspective. *Ambio*, 22, 340-346.

Heaney, S.I., Foy, R.H., Kennedy, G.J.A., Crozier, W.W. & O'Connor, W.C.K. 2001. Impacts of agriculture on aquatic systems: lessons learnt and new unknowns in Northern Ireland. *Marine and Freshwater Research*, 52, 151-163.

Heathwaite, A.L. 1992. The effect of drainage on fen peat chemistry and drainage ditch water quality. In: O.M Bragg, P.D. Hulme, H.A.P. Ingram & R.A. Robertson, eds. *Peatland Ecosystems and Man: An Impact Assessment.* University of Dundee: Department of Biological Science, pp. 184-190.

Hölzel, N. & Otte, A. 2003. Restoration of a species-rich flood meadow by topsoil removal and diaspore transfer with plant material. *Applied Vegetation Science*, 6, 131-140.

Jordan, T.E., Correll, D.L & Wheller, D.E. 1993. Nutrient interception by a riparian forest receiving inputs from adjacent cropland. *Journal of Environmental Quality*, 22, 467-473.

Koerselman, W. & Verhoevan, J.T.A. 1995. Eutrophication of fen ecosystems: external and internal sources and restoration strategies. *In*: B.D. Wheeler., S,C. Shaw., W,J. Fojt, & R.A. Robertson, eds. *Restoration of Temperate Wetlands.* Chichester: Wiley, pp. 91-112.

Koerselman, W. & Verhoeven, T.T.A. 1992. Nutrient dynamics in mires of various trophic status: nutrient inputs and outputs and the internal nutrient cycle. *In*: J.T.A. Verhoeven, ed. Fens and Bogs in the Netherlands: Vegetation, History, Nutrient Dynamics and Conservation. Dordrecht: Kluwer Academic Publishing, pp. 397-432.

Koerselman, W., Bakker, S.A. & Blom, M. 1990. Nitrogen, phosphorus and potassium budgets for two small fens surrounded by heavily fertilized pastures. *Journal of Ecology*, 78, 428-442.

Koerselman, W., Van Kerkhoven, H. & Verhoeven, J.T.A. 1993. Release of inorganic N, P and K in peat soils; effect of temperature, water chemistry and water level. *Biogeochemistry*, 20 (2), 63-81.

Kurihara, Y & Suzuki, T. 1988. Effects of harvesting on regeneration and biological production of *Phragmites australis* in wetlands. In: Proceedings of the International Symposium on the Hydrology of Wetlands in Temperate and Cold Regions, Joensuu, Finland 6-8 June 1988. Julkaisuja: Academy of Finland Publications, pp. 249-255.

Mainstone, C.P., Parr, W. & Day, M. 2000. *Phosphorus and River Ecology: Tackling Sewage Inputs.* Peterborough: English Nature/Environment Agency.

Marrs, R.H. 2002. Manipulating the chemical environment of the soil. In: M.R. Perrow & A.J. Davy, eds. *Handbook of Ecological Restoration Volume 1: Principals of Restoration.* Cambridge: Cambridge University Press, pp. 155-183.

McCann, M.E.E., McCracken, K.J., Beattie, V.E., Magowan, E., Smyth, S., Bradford, R. & Henry, W. 2005. Investigations into phosphorous requirements of growing/finishing pigs and the use of phytase. In: *Agricultural Research Institute of Northern Ireland. Advances in Pig Research. 24th June 2004. Occasional Publication No 33*, pp. 15-64.

Melack, J.M. 1995. Transport and transformation of P, fluvial and lacustrine ecosystems. In: H. Tiessen, ed. *Phosphorus in the Global Environment.* Chichester: Wiley, pp. 245-254.

Moore, P.D. 1986. Hydrological changes in mires. In: B.E. Burglund, ed. *Handbook of Holocene Palaeoecology and Palaeohydrology.* Chichester: Wiley, pp. 91-107.

Morris J.T. 1991. Effects of nitrogen loading on wetland ecosystems with particular reference to atmospheric deposition. *Annual Review of Ecology and Systematics, 22, 257-279.*

Muscatt, A.D., Harris, G.L., Bailey, S.W. & Davies, D.B. 1993. Buffer zones to improve water quality: a review of their potential use in UK agriculture. *Agriculture, Ecosystems and Environment,* 45, 59-77.

NEGTAP. 2001. *Transboundary Air Pollution: Acidification, Eutrophication and Ground-level Ozone in the UK.* Unpublished report to the National Expert Group on Trans-Boundary Air Pollution.

Newbold, C. & Mountford, O. 1997. Water level requirements of selected plants and animals, *English Nature Freshwater Series No. 5.*

Norris, V. 1993. The use of buffer zones to protect water quality: a review. *Water Resources Management*, 7, 257-272.

Patzelt, A., Wild, U. & Pfadenhauer, J. 2001. Restoration of wet fen meadows by topsoil development and germination biology of fen species. *Restoration Ecology*, 9 (2), 127-136.

Pauli, D., Peintinger, M., Schmid, B. 2002. Nutrient enrichment of calcareous fens: effects on plant species and community structure. *Basic and Applied Ecology*, 3, 255-266.

Paulissen, M., van der Ven, P.J.M., Bobbink, R. 2003. Differential effects of nitrate and ammonium enrichment on base-rich fen vegetation: preliminary results from Scragh Bog, central Ireland. *In: Empirical Critical Loads for Nitrogen – Proceedings.* Berne: SAEFL, pp. 283-288.

Paulissen, M.P.C.P., Van der Ven, P.J.M., Bobbink, R. 2004. Differential effects of nitrate and ammonium on three fen bryophyte species in relation to pollutant nitrogen input. *New Phytologist*, 164, 451-458.

Richardson, C.J., Marshall P.E. 1986. Processes controlling movement, storage and export of phosphorus in a fen peatland. *Ecological Monographs*, 56, 279-302.

Ross, S.M. 1995. Overview of the hydrochemistry and solute processes in British wetlands. In: J. Hughes & L. Heathwaite, eds. *Hydrology and Hydrochemistry of British Wetlands.* Chichester: Wiley, pp. 133-181.

Sharpley, A.N., Foy, R.H. & Withers, P.A. 2000. Practical and innovation measures in the control of agricultural phosphorus losses to water: an overview. *Journal of Environmental Quality*, 29, 1-9.

Shaw, S.C. & Wheeler, B.D. 1991. A review of habitat conditions and management characteristics of herbaceous fen vegetation types in lowland Britain. Unpublished report to the Nature Conservancy Council, Peterborough.

Smith, K.A., Jackson, D.R. & Withers, P.J.A. 2001. Nutrient losses by surface runoff following the application of organic manures to arable land. 2. Phosphorus. *Environmental Pollution*, 122, 53-60.

UK-CHM. 2000. *Reduction of Nutrient Input to Aquatic Systems.* Unpublished report by the University of Georgia.

Van der Hoek, K. & Heijmans, M.M.P.D. 2007. Effectiveness of turf stripping as a measure for restoring species-rich fen meadows in suboptimal hydrological conditions. *Restoration Ecology*, 15 (4), 627-637.

Van Wirdum, G. 1981. Linking up the natec subsystem in models for the water management. *Proceedings and Information/TNO Committee on Hydrological Research*, 27, 108-128.

Verhoeven, J.T.A, Schmitz, M.B. 1991. Control of plant growth by nitrogen and phosphorus in mesotrophic fens. *Biogeochemistry*, 12. 135-148.

Vermeer, J.G. 1986. The effects of nutrients on shoot biomass and species composition of wetlands and hayfield communities. *Acta Oecol./Oecologia Plantarum*, 7, 31-41.

Wassen, M. 1990. *Water Flow as a Major Landscape Ecological Factor in Fen Development.* Unpublished PhD Thesis, University of Utrecht, Netherlands.

Wassen, M.J. Van der Vliet R.E. & Verhoeven J.T.A. 1998. Nutrient limitation in the Biebrza fens and floodplain (Poland). *Acta Botanica Neerlandica*, 47, 241-253.

Weltzin, J.F., Keller, J.K., Bridgham, S.D., Pastor, J, Allen, P.B. & Chen, J. 2005. Litter controls plant community composition in a northern fen. *Oikos*, 110 (3), 537-556.

Wheeler, B.D. & Proctor, M.C.F. (2000). Ecological gradients, subdivisions and terminology of north-west European Mires – Essay Review. *Journal of Ecology*, 88, 187-203.

Wheeler, B.D., Al-Farraj, M.M. & Cook, R.E.D. 1985. Iron toxicity to plants in base-rich wetlands: comparative effects on the distribution and growth of *Epilobium hirsutum* L. and *Juncus subnodulosus Schrank. New Phytologist*, 100, 653-669.

Wheeler, B.D., Gowing, D.J.G., Shaw, S.C., Mountford, J.O. & Money, R.P. 2004. *Ecohydrological Guidelines for Lowland Wetland Plant Communities.* Environment Agency (Anglian Region).

Xiong, S., Johannson, M.E., Hughes, R.M.R., Hayes, A., Richards, K.S. & Nilsson, C. 2003. Interactive effects of soil moisture, vegetation canopy, plant litter and seed addition on plant diversity in a wetland community. *Journal of Ecology*, 91, 976-986.

Yates, P., & Sheridan, J.M. 1983. Estimating the effectiveness of vegetated floodplains/wetlands as nitrate-nitrite and orthophosphorus filters. *Agriculture, Ecosystems and Environment*, 9, 303-314.

Section 5: Fen Management and Restoration

Boyce, D.C., 2004. A review of the invertebrate assemblage of acid mires. English Nature Research Report 592, Natural England, Peterborough. ISBN 0967-876X

Broads Authority, 2004. A supplement to the Fen Management Strategy, Incorporating the Fen Audit. Prepared by Sue Stephenson, edited by Sandie Tolhurst.

Charman, D.J. (2001) Biostratigraphic and palaeoenvironmental applications of testate amoebae. Quaternary Science Reviews, 20, 1753-1764.

Forestry Commission, (undated). New Forest wetland management plan (2006 - 2016). Practitioners' guide. New Forest LIFE project.

Hobbs, R. J. & Lindenmayer, D. B., eds. 2007. *Managing and Designing Landscapes for Conservation.* Oxford: Blackwell Publishing.

Perrow, M & Davy, A eds. 2002. Handbook of Ecological Restoration. Volume 2: Restoration in Practice. Cambridge University Press

Sutherland, J. & Hill, D. eds. 1995. Managing Habitats for Conservation. Cambridge University Press.

Treweek, J & Sheail, J. 1991. Wetland Restoration: Techniques for an Integrated Approach. Institute of Terrestrial Ecology.

Ward, D., Holmes, N & Jose, P., eds. 1994. The New Rivers and Wildlife Handbook. RSPB, Sandy.

Section 6: Fen Vegetation Management

Galatowitsch, S.M. & van der Valk, A.G. 1995. Natural revegetation during restoration of wetlands in the Southern Prairie Pothole Region of North America. In: *Restoration of Temperate Wetlands* (eds. B.D. Wheeler, S.C. Shaw, W.J. Fojt & R.A. Robertson), pp. 129-142. John Wiley & Sons, Chichester.

Grootjans, A. P., Hunneman, H., Verkiel, H., and Van Andel, J., Long-term effects of drainage on species richness of a fen meadow at different spatial scales. *Basic Applied Ecology*, 6, 185-193. 2005.

Scottish Natural Heritage, 1997. *Wetland management for nature conservation.* Information and Advisory Note 82, Scottish Natural Heritage.

Section 7: Fen Water Management

Burgess, N. & Hirons, G. 1990. Management Case Study: Techniques of Hydrological Management at Coastal Lagoons and Lowland wet grasslands on RSPB reserves. RSPB.

Forestry Commission. Undated. *New Forest wetland management plan (2006 - 2016).* Practitioners' guide. New Forest LIFE project.

Horner, R. & Bowell, H. 2003. Will Leighton Moss boom again? *Conservation Land Management* 1 (3), 8-11.

Hume, C. 2008. Wetland Vision Technical Document: overview and reporting of project philosophy and technical approach. The Wetland Vision Partnership.

Koerselman, W. & Verhoeven, J.T.A. 1995. Eutrophication of fen ecosystems: external and internal sources and restoration strategies. In: *Restoration of Temperate Wetlands* (eds. B.D. Wheeler, S.C. Shaw, W.J. Fojt & R.A. Robertson), pp. 91-112. John Wiley & Sons, Chichester.

Newbold, C. & Mountford, O. 1997. Water level requirements of selected plants and animals, *English Nature Freshwater Series No. 5.*

Roworth, P. & Meade, R. 1998. Pumping Shirley Pool. *Enact* **6** (2), 12-13.

Van Andel, J. & Aronson, J. 2006. *Restoration Ecology: The New Frontier.* Blackwell, Oxford.

Walker, D. 1970. Direction and rate in some British post-glacial hydroseres. In: *Studies in the vegetational history of the British Isles* (eds. D. Walker and R.G. West), pp.117-140. Cambridge University Press, Cambridge.

Section 9: Fen Creation

Baines, C & Smart, J. 1984. A Guide to Habitat Creation: Ecology Handbook No.2. Greater London Council.

Beecroft, R. 1998. Kingfishers Bridge. A new wetland in the fens. *Enact* **6** (2), 4-6.

Boeye, D., van Straaten, D. & Verheyen, R. F. 1995. A recent transformation from poor to rich fen caused by artificial groundwater recharge. *Journal of Hydrology* **169**, 111-129.

Bowler, P. & Warwick, S. 2004. Natural wetlands from an artificial site. *Conservation Land Management* **2(2)**, 16-18.

Burgess, G. 1998. Windpumps return to the wetlands. *Enact* **6 (4)**, 19-22.

Cobbaert, D. & Rochefort, L. 2002. Restoration of a natural fen community following peat extraction in eastern Canada. pp. 202-211. In: G. Schmilewski and L. Rochefort (eds.) *Proceedings of the International Peat Symposium Peat in Horticulture: Quality and Environmental Challenges,* Pärnu, Estonia, September 3-6, 2002, pp. 202-211. International Peat Society, Jyväskylä, Finland.

Galatowitsch, S., R. & van der Valk, A. 1996. The vegetation of restored and natural prairie wetlands. *Ecological Applications* 6, 102-112.

Goudie, A.S. & Brunsden, D. 1994. *The Environment of the British Isles – An Atlas.* Clarendon Press, Oxford.

Grootjans, A.P., Bakker, J.P., Jansen, A.J.M. & Kemmers, R.H. 2002. Restoration of brook valley meadows in the Netherlands. *Hydrobiologia* **478 (1-2)**, 149-170.

Horner, R. & Bowell, H. 2003. Will Leighton Moss boom again? *Conservation Land Management* 1(3), 8-11.

Hawke, C.J. & José, P.V. 1996. *Reedbed Management for Commercial and Wildlife Interests.* Royal Society for the Protection of Birds, Sandy.

Headley, A.D. 2004. Substratum enrichment at Crymlyn Bog Csac, South Wales: An analysis of current and future impacts with particular reference to SAC feature fen communities. University of Bradford, Bradford.

Isselstein, J. Tallowin, J. R. B. and Smith, R. E. N. 2002. Factors Affecting Seed Germination and Seedling Establishment of Fen-Meadow Species. *Restoration Ecology* **10(2)**, 173-184

Meissner, R., Rupp, H., Leinweber, P. 2003. Re-wetting of fen soils and changes in water quality - experimental results and further research. *Journal of Water and Land Development*, 7, 75-91.

Morris, J., Hess, T. M., Gowing, D. J., Leeds-Harrison, P. B., Bannister, N., Wade, M. and Vivash, R. M. 2004. Integrated Washland Management for Flood Defence and Biodiversity. Report to Department for Environment, Food and Rural Affairs & English Nature. Cranfield University at Silsoe, Bedfordshire, UK. March 2004

Newbold, C. & Mountford, O. 1997. *Water level requirements of wetland plants and animals.* Freshwater Series Number 5. English Nature, Peterborough.

Parker, D. 1995. Habitat creation-a critical guide. English Nature.

Perrow, M & Davy, A eds. 2002. Handbook of Ecological Restoration. Volume 1: Principles of Restoration. Cambridge University Press.

Patzelt, A, Wild, U. and Jörg Pfadenhauer, J. 2001. Restoration of Wet Fen Meadows by Topsoil Removal: Vegetation Development and Germination Biology of Fen Species. *Restoration Ecology* **9(2)**, 127-136

Sliva, J. 1998. The effect of secondary plant cover on microclimate of post-harvested bogs. In: Sopo, R. (ed.) *Proceedings of the 1998 International Peat Symposium. The spirit of peatlands*, pp. 179-181. International Peat Society, Jyväskylä.

Tallowin, J. R. B. and Smith, R. E. N. 2001 Restoration of a *Cirsio-Molinietum* Fen Meadow on an Agriculturally Improved Pasture. *Restoration Ecology* **9 (2)**, 167-178

Taylor, D. (1997). Avalon's new wetlands. *Enact* **5 (2)**, 16-19.

van der Valk, A., Bremholm, T. & Gordon, E. 1999. The restoration of sedge meadows: seed viability, seed germination requirements, and seedling growth of *Carex* species. *Wetlands* **19**, 756-764.

Wheeler, B.D. & Shaw, S.C. (1995). A focus on fens – controls on the composition of fen vegetation in relation to restoration. In: *Restoration of Temperate Wetlands* (eds. B. D. Wheeler, S.C. Shaw, W.F. Fojt & R.A. Robertson), pp.49-72. John Wiley & Sons, Chichester.

Wheeler, B.D.,Gowing, D.J.G., Shaw, S.C., Mountford, J.O. & Money, R.P. 2004. *Ecohydrological guidelines for lowland wetland plant communities*. Final report Environment Agency – Anglian Region (ed. A.W. Brooks, P.V. José & M.I. Whiteman). Environment Agency, Peterborough.

Wheeler, B.D., Shaw, S.C. & Cook, R.E.D. 1991. Phytometric assessment of the fertility of undrained rich-fen soils. *Journal of Applied Ecology* **29**, 466-475.

Worrall, P. & Peberdy, K. 1994. Wastewater to warblers. *Enact* **2 (2)**, 4-6.

A guide to farmers on the planning system.

http://www.communities.gov.uk/documents/planningandbuilding/pdf/143516.pdf

Section 10: Monitoring to inform fen management

Gavin, H. 2003. Scoping study on guidance for the monitoring of wetlands under the requirements of the Water Framework Directive. Environment Agency WFD Technical Report EMC(02)01/TR. Atkins Consultants.

Gent, T. and Gibson, S. 2003. *The herpetofauna worker's manual*. JNCC. ISBN 1861074506.

Herschy, R.W. 2008. *Streamflow measurement*. Taylor & Francis, Oxford, UK. ISBN 0415413427.

Hill. M.O., Mountford J.O., Roy D.B., Bunce R.G.H. *Ellenberg's Indicator Values for British Plants*. Centre for Ecology and Hydrology 1999. ISBN 1870393481

Hill, D., Fasham, M., Tucker, G., Shewry, M. & Shaw, P. (eds). 2005. *Handbook of Biodiversity Methods: Survey, Evaluation and Monitoring*. Cambridge University Press, Cambridge.

Hill. M.O., Preston C.D., Bosanquet S.D.S., Roy D.B. 2007. *Attributes of British and Irish Mosses*. Centre for Ecology and Hydrology. ISBN 1855312364

Killeen, I.J. and Moorkens, E.A. 2003. *Monitoring Desmoulin's Whorl Snail (Vertigo Moulinsiana)*. Conserving Natura 2000 Rivers Monitoring Series No. 6, English Nature, Peterborough.

Taylor, R. T. 1997. *An introduction to error analysis*. University Science Books, California, USA. ISBN 093570275X.

Thompson, D.J., Purse, B.V. and Rouquette, J.R. 2003. *Monitoring the Southern Damselfly (Coenagrion mercuriale)*. Conserving Natura 2000 Rivers Monitoring Series No. 8, English Nature, Peterborough.

Section 11: Fens and People

Dynamix. (2008). *Outdoor Learning and Play*. Retrieved 5/2/2009, from

http://www.dynamix.ltd.uk/images/stories/downloadable/outdoors.pdf.

Richards, C., K. L. Blackstock, et al. 2004. Practical Approaches to Participation, SERG Policy Brief No. 1. C. E. Carter and C. L. Spash. Aberdeen, Macaulay Institute. http://www.governat.eu/files/files/day_3,_a,_richards_participation_serp2004.pdf.

Staatsbosbeheer. 2009. *Kanoroute De Weerribben*. Retrieved 9/2/2009, from

http://www.staatsbosbeheer.nl/Activiteiten/Weerribben/Kanoroute%20De%20Weerribben.aspx.

The Forestry Commission. 2004. *A toolbox for public involvement in forest and woodland planning*. Retrieved 1/2/2009, from http://www.forestry.gov.uk/forestry/INFD-5XMDS8.

The National Trust. 1992. *Wicken Fen Management - Part A1 Statement of Objectives*. Retrieved 9/2/2009, from http://www.ecoln.com/wicken_fen/m97a1000.html.

The National Trust. 2007. *The Wicken Fen Vision*. Second Consultation Draft. http://www.wicken.org.uk/vision/Wicken%20Fen%20Vision%20Strategy.pdf.

Tourism and Environment Initiative. 2001. *A Sense of Place*. Inverness.

http://passthrough.fw-notify.net/download/695256/http://www.greentourism.org.uk/SOFP.PDF..

Wilcox, D. 2004. *The Guide to Effective Participation*. Retrieved 1/2/2009, from

http://www.partnerships.org.uk/guide/index.htm.

Section 12: Fens from and Economic Perspective

Buss, S.R., Rivett, M.O., Morgan, P. and Bemment, C.D. (2005) *Attenuation of nitrate in the sub-surface environment*. Environment Agency Science Report SC030155/SR2.

Smith, J.W.N. (2005) *Groundwater-surface water interactions in the hyporheic zone*. Environment Agency Science Report SC030155/SR1.

Index